RACE, CITIZENSHIP, AND LAW IN AMERICAN LITERATURE

BY GREGG D. CRANE

CAMBRIDGE
UNIVERSITY PRESS

PUBLISHED BY THE PRESS SYNDICATE OF THE UNIVERSITY OF CAMBRIDGE
The Pitt Building, Trumpington Street, Cambridge, United Kingdom

CAMBRIDGE UNIVERSITY PRESS
The Edinburgh Building, Cambridge CB2 2RU, UK
40 West 20th Street, New York, NY 10011-4211, USA
477 Williamstown Road, Port Melbourne, VIC 3207, Australia
Ruiz de Alarcón 13, 28014 Madrid, Spain
Dock House, The Waterfront, Cape Town 8001, South Africa

http://www.cambridge.org

First published 2002

Printed in the United Kingdom at the University Press, Cambridge

Typeface Baskerville Monotype 11/12.5 pt.   *System* LATEX 2ε [TB]

A catalogue record for this book is available from the British Library

ISBN 0 521 80684 4   hardback
ISBN 0 521 01093 4   paperback

For Leslie and Zoe

Contents

Acknowledgments

Many colleagues and dear friends have generously supported the production of this book. My greatest scholarly debt is to Eric Sundquist and Ross Posnock. But for the instruction each provided and the benchmark each furnished for literary scholarship, I would not have had either the wherewithal or the motive to complete this study. Robert Levine, Samuel Otter, and Brook Thomas gave my book painstaking critical appraisals, which I have endeavored to put to good use. Portions and incarnations of the book also received insightful critique from Frederick Crews, Tim Dean, Jeannine Delombard, Mary Esteve, Dori Hale, Tom Jacobsen, Waldo Martin, Walter Benn Michaels, Roger Smith, Priscilla Wald, and Cindy Weinstein. Thanks are also due to Ray Ryan, Rachel De Wachter, and Audrey Cotterell at Cambridge University Press for their thoughtful shepherding of my typescript into print.

Of course, over the years of reading and writing, I have also incurred obligations of a more personal nature. My parents, Robert and Barbara Crane, nurtured this project with care, counsel, and material support, as did my parents-in-law, the Honorable Donald and Mrs. Janet Ford. Judge Ford provided a set of Supreme Court reports and other legal texts that have greatly facilitated my research, besides making an imposing office prop for an English professor. Ann Ford and Dan Shepherd made my research at the Library of Congress possible by putting me up for extended visits, and their earnest expressions of interest in my research kept me going. Dorothy and Steve Imm gave me much needed encouragement.

Leslie Ford saw this book through the entire process from start to finish, and I have depended on her at every step of the process for astute and honest criticism of my writing and analysis. But my debt to Leslie is even deeper, as I owe to her the greater portion of my knowledge of how conscience and consent mix in a genuine partnership. For giving all this effort both a point and a counterbalance, I owe my daughter, Zoe, something in the neighborhood of ten thousand renditions of "It's a jolly holiday with Mary." And there are not enough dog biscuits in the world to repay Trudy's constant companionship.

Introduction

To merit the near religious veneration it has received, the U. S. Constitution has had to represent something different from and better than a democratic majority's power to enact its will. As Edwin Corwin notes in his landmark essay on the higher law background of the Constitution, most Americans have revered the national charter because they believe it to embody universal principles of justice.[1] And despite the obvious and manifold injustices of American history, this "constitutional faith" in Justice Hugo Black's apt term, has not been wholly misplaced. In its various formulations, the higher law conviction that, in Martin Luther King's words, "an unjust law is no law" has had a marked impact on American constitutionalism, inspiring such milestones as the Declaration of Independence, the Bill of Rights, the Civil War amendments, the Nineteenth Amendment (women's suffrage), *Brown v. Board of Education* (1954), the Civil Rights Act of 1964, the Voting Rights Act of 1965, and *Romer v. Evans* (1996).

To illustrate the ethical basis of the American constitutional system, Chief Justice Earl Warren's 1970 lecture "All Men Are Created Equal" quotes the famous lines from "The New Colossus" by Emma Lazarus, in which the "Mother of Exiles" says to the world, "Give me your tired, your poor, / Your huddled masses yearning to breathe free." Consistent with the heterogeneous American community suggested by Lazarus's poem, Warren imagines culturally heterodox experience as granting one special insight into the nature of justice. Thus, Justice Benjamin Cardozo's experience as a Jewish-American (knowing "first-hand the evils of discrimination") enabled him to separate the egalitarian ideals grounding the Constitution from its racist history.[2] In Warren's allusions to Lazarus and Cardozo, we can infer two key aspects of higher law constitutionalism. First, it tends in a cosmopolitan direction, ascribing the discovery of justice to our ability to cross boundaries of identity, which ability, in turn, enables consensual political and social association among diverse peoples. Second, it is, broadly speaking, cultural in nature. Poems, biographies, sermons, novels, philosophical tracts, photographs, editorials, or plays may express it more fully and more powerfully than any legal precedent and as a result offer insight into the ethical assumptions guiding courts and legislatures.

In distinguishing the ethical terms of public and political association from notions of family, tribe, or blood, Warren's higher law beliefs are part of a venerable tradition in western political theory. Ivan Hannaford traces the distinction between politics (*politikos*) and identity (*ethnos*) back to Aristotle's conception of politics as a distinct human activity expressed in citizenship as a form of civic participation and emerging only when a social order no longer depends "on the observation of hierarchical rules pertaining to the household, family, clan, and tribe . . . The disposition to see people not in terms of where they come from and what they looked like but in terms of membership." In Hannaford's useful formulation, politics refers to the consensual creation of basic standards of coexistence by and for a diverse citizenry: "The *politikos* refers to men of various origins and social standing who leave the household realms of necessity to engage in rational debate and judgment." Those outside the political sphere and excluded from the language of politics, says Hannaford, were called *ethnos*, the root of ethnic, or termed as *barbaros*, embedded in nature, confined to blood relations, and reliant on the habits and folkways of forebears. In Hannaford's account, race and other forms of identitarianism represent the antithesis of politics.[3]

The juxtaposition of identity-neutral norms of political and social coexistence and identitarian practice is a hallmark of American higher law constitutionalism. Warren's address, for example, contrasts the egalitarian theme of the Declaration and the Civil War amendments with the fact of continuing racial discrimination:

Still 102 years after the 14th Amendment was adopted, we find that hundreds of thousands of black children are denied equal opportunities of education; like numbers of adults are denied the privilege of voting; litigants, witnesses and jurors are deliberately humiliated in court rooms; people are denied the right to live wherever they choose; and a myriad other indignities are imposed on millions merely because of their color. Yet we take pride in the Biblical words which are molded into the Liberty Bell which bespoke our independence and freedom – "Proclaim liberty throughout all the land unto all the inhabitants thereof."

In *Regents of the University of California v. Bakke* (1978), Justice Brennan's opinion similarly sets the Fourteenth Amendment's expression "of our abiding belief in human equality" alongside the fact "that the Framers of our Constitution, to forge the 13 Colonies into one Nation, openly compromised this principle of equality with its antithesis: slavery." And Justice Marshall's companion opinion offers an incendiary historical narrative, pressing racist definitions of citizenship up against the purported universalism of the American republic. In the Reconstruction and Civil Rights eras, these sharp contrasts of practice and aspiration were offered to justify experiments, such as the Civil Rights Act of 1875 and affirmative action, aimed at purging the republic of the inequalities created by past identitarian practice. The anti-identitarian aspect of higher law constitutionalism should not be confused with the desire to make all law and governmental action 'color blind.' As Brennan and Marshall argue in *Bakke*, identity-neutral norms of fairness and equity can require that law take into account the historical fact of racial discrimination.[4]

Judicial recognition that higher law constitutionalism draws heavily, if often covertly, on cultural and literary sources can be found in the counter-arguments of its opponents, such as Justice Antonin Scalia's dissent in *Romer v. Evans* (1996) or Chief Justice Taney's majority opinion in *Dred Scott v. Sandford* (1857). In *Romer*, the Supreme Court struck down an amendment to the Colorado state constitution forbidding "special" treatment of gays and lesbians. The Colorado amendment smelled to the Court like hostile class legislation despite the ostensible neutrality of the amendment's language. Unlike the Court's decisions in *Plessy v. Ferguson* (1896) and many other cases, the *Romer* Court looked past the amendment's language to its intent and origin in anti-gay feeling. Writing for the majority, Justice Kennedy observes, "It is not within our constitutional tradition to enact laws of this sort." Of course, in light of the history lesson provided by Marshall's *Bakke* opinion, one would have good reason to counter, as Justice Scalia does in dissent, that it is plainly well within our constitutional tradition to enact laws of this sort. The cultural nature of the Court's reasoning, as Scalia's dissent notes, is signaled by the fact that the majority's opinion is "long on emotive utterances" and "short on relevant legal citation" ("the opinion's heavy reliance upon principles of righteousness rather than judicial holdings"). In Scalia's view, the Court's opinion descends to the level of a *Kulturkampf* over sexual mores. Contending that the constitutionality of antisodomy laws "is unassailable, except by those who think that the Constitution changes to suit current fashions," Scalia's dissent distinctly echoes Chief Justice Roger Taney's argument in *Dred Scott* that the Supreme Court is not the "mere reflex of popular opinion" and hence the constitutionality of slavery had to be judged not by the "fashions" of 1857 but from the perspective of the framers. Taney and Scalia intend the phrases "popular opinion" and "current fashions" to trivialize the import of a continually changing public consensus and to derogate the jurisprudential authority of those artists, authors, orators, activists, philosophers, and journalists centrally involved in shifting that consensus.[5]

On occasion, however, politicians and judges overlook the authority of these cultural shifts to their peril, as Robert Bork discovered when his confirmation as an Associate Justice of the Supreme Court ran afoul of the themes and figures of higher law constitutionalism. Instead of waxing eloquent on individual rights, liberty, and fair play during his confirmation hearing, Bork came across as a cold, intellectual technician, who was more interested in the play of legal concepts than in the lives of Americans affected by those concepts. When Senator Edward Kennedy took Bork to task for criticizing a case invalidating a Virginia poll tax for state elections, Bork replied, among other things, that the poll tax in question was only $1.50. Bork's glib response was a miscalculation inviting Kennedy's self-conscious use of a higher law chestnut. "You and I may not have to worry about where each dollar goes," said Kennedy, "but there are a lot of Americans who do and to suggest that a poll tax, if it is small enough, does not deprive a poor person of a fundamental aspect of citizenship, well, that reminds me of Anatole France's famous remark that 'the law in its majestic equality forbids the rich as well as the poor to sleep under bridges.'" When Senator Simpson, one of Bork's key supporters, set the stage for Bork to display the humane side of his jurisprudence by asking why Bork wanted to sit on the nation's highest court, Bork said not a word about doing justice. Instead, he looked forward to life on the Court as "an intellectual feast." Many who heard or read Bork's response had a strong suspicion as to who would furnish the main course at such a banquet.[6]

Though a more striking failure of higher law dramaturgy would be hard to imagine, Bork's apparent lack of compassion for the weak and downtrodden (most tellingly he seemed to lack sympathy for the plight of discrete minorities in a majoritarian political system) did not violate the norms of code and case. Bork offended not the nation's law but its legal culture: its favored images and narratives of justice. Bork would have had a better chance of confirmation had his performance been informed at least in part by the speeches of Martin Luther King, Jr., the historical scholarship of John Hope Franklin (a witness who testified effectively against Bork's confirmation), Walt Whitman's *Democratic Vistas*, or such fiction as Harriet Beecher Stowe's *Uncle Tom's Cabin* and Richard Wright's *Native Son*.

To the dismay of conservative jurists, such as Taney, Scalia, and Bork, the culture's evolving sense of higher law (the on-going revision of what we deem are the noblest narratives we can tell of ourselves) has periodically exerted considerable pressure on the direction of American law. Curiously, given the dependence of higher law jurisprudence on such non-legal texts as poems, novels, essays, histories, and political treatises, its literary or cultural dimensions have received scant critical or scholarly attention. No book-length study has addressed the reciprocal relation between cultural, political, and legal deployments of higher law reasoning.

Focusing on race and citizenship in the nineteenth century, this study traces and analyzes the efforts of a line of literary and legal intellectuals to articulate the role of conscience in a democratic political system, answering Henry David Thoreau's quintessential higher law question in "Resistance to Civil Government":

Can there not be a government in which majorities do not virtually decide right and wrong, but conscience? – in which majorities decide only those questions to which the rule of expediency is applicable? Must the citizen ever for a moment, or in the least degree, resign his conscience to the legislator? Why has every man a conscience, then?[7]

I begin with the founding fathers' conception of higher law and follow the ebb and flow of its legal and cultural authority: its waning influence on early nineteenth-century politicians and lawyers, its resurgence in the antislavery movement, and its decline in the post-Reconstruction era. The tendency on both sides of the slavery debate to confine the terms of justice to those who resemble the nation's white majority is contrasted with the visionary efforts of Ralph Waldo Emerson, Frederick Douglass, and Charles Sumner to sever the higher law conversation of conscience and consent from identity. The positivist counter-argument that law is the expression of power not morality, a view exemplified by such diverse characters as Roger Taney, Martin Delany, and Oliver Wendell Holmes, Jr., is studied in some detail both to contextualize our understanding of higher law advocacy and to account for the decline of higher law jurisprudence after the Civil War amendments. The final chapter considers the post-Reconstruction resuscitation of higher law in Charles Chesnutt's fiction and Moorfield Storey's legal advocacy, two figures heralding the beginning of another cycle of higher law advocacy that would reach its legal climax in *Brown v. Board of Education* (1954) and the Civil Rights and Voting Rights Acts of 1964 and 1965. This study focuses on race and not such other relevant categories as gender, class, or national origin, in part, out of necessity, yet this focus is warranted by the fact that race provided the most intense and challenging spur to higher law debate in the nineteenth century. The conflict over race has been the seminal higher law issue in U. S. history. From women's equality to gay rights, subsequent deployments of higher law have been indebted to the original higher law arguments made in the nineteenth century on behalf of African Americans.

In distinction to absolutist and more conventionally religious conceptions of higher law as God's will revealed, which were offered both in defense and condemnation of slavery, I am particularly concerned to delineate conceptions of the ethical basis of American law as an interplay of conscience (moral inspiration) and consent (political dialogue), which produces a plausibly universal moral consensus about the terms of justice and citizenship. This consensus becomes *plausibly* universal when it becomes hard to imagine any sentient being not agreeing to such basic values of coexistence. For Sumner, Stowe, Emerson, Douglass, and others, the crisis over slavery, in general, and the Fugitive Slave Law of 1850, in particular, providentially prompted a nearly universal debate about the justness of the nation's law. The social ferment provoked by slavery and racial discrimination represented an important step in the direction of a better, more inclusive moral consensus recognizing black Americans as citizens. The politically engaged form of higher law reasoning deployed by these nineteenth-century figures anticipates Seyla Benhabib's notion of deliberative democracy and Stuart Hampshire's conception of procedural justice, both of which locate the hope for justice in the possibility of public conversation across lines of identity and personal interest.[8]

We get an intimation of the nature of this species of higher law reasoning and the importance of literary and cultural texts to its development by observing Emerson's and Douglass's kindred emphasis on the fluid quality of and the interrelation between aesthetic and ethical judgment. For both men, articulating the nature of either justice or beauty involves the endless play of particular experience and universal concept that is the stock in trade of the judge and the student of art and literature. Because "There is no virtue which is final," in Emerson's view, we err in "ador[ing] the forms of law, instead of making them the vehicles of wisdom and justice." Similarly, for Douglass, "Perfection is an object to be aimed at by all, but it is not an attribute of any form of government. Mutability is the law for all." In "Pictures and Progress" (1861), Douglass contends that the flux of aesthetic experience exemplifies and illuminates the fact that our lives are and should be a continuing process of transformation: "Men talk much of a new birth. The fact is fundamental. But the mistake is in treating it as an incident which can only happen to a man once in a life time; whereas, the whole journey of life is a succession of them." In its emphasis on mutability, this jurisprudence anticipates William James's pragmatist notion that "Truth grafts itself on previous truth, modifying it in the process, just as idiom grafts itself on previous idiom, and law on previous law. Given previous law and a novel case, and the judge will twist them into fresh law."

Higher law constitutionalism's embrace of change is hardly total, however. As Emerson puts it, "this incessant movement and progression which all things partake could never become sensible to us but by contrast to some principle of fixture or stability in the soul."[9] This point of contrast is to be found in the first concepts themselves, the belief in justice or beauty as values properly defining human existence. Hence, though our particular illustrations and applications of such abstract categories as beauty and justice are contingent, tenuous, and fluid, we register and believe in these values as constant. As John Dewey puts it in "Freedom and Culture" (1939), while we experiment with "the forms and mechanisms" of law and society, "the ideal aims and values to be realized" by our political and legal scheme "remain unchanged in substance." These ethical constants paradoxically furnish the necessary basis for ongoing revisions and improvisations. Hannah Arendt's *On Revolution* (1963) cites to similar effect Jefferson's intense opposition to "those who 'look at constitutions with sanctimonious reverence, and deem them like the ark of the covenant, too sacred to be touched.'" Endorsing Jefferson's rejection of "the injustice that only [the framers'] generation should have it in their power 'to begin the world over again,'" Arendt, like Douglass, Emerson, and Dewey, views the confinement of the Constitution, through strict construction, to the framers' particular world view as destroying its creative potential as part of justice's lexicon.[10]

Justice requires both some form of continuity at the level of general principle and some type of ongoing revision at the level of the particular law or practice. Higher law constitutionalism's dedication to the consensual determination of public standards of justice entails certain procedural continuities (the forms of democratic government and the rule of law) as well as a rejection of power as the ultimate justification of legal and social organization. The commitment to consent, of course, can never be simple or singular. A universal moral consensus is not and cannot be required for every exercise of state power. In most cases, majority consent is enough. One may dislike a change in the tax code yet decline to defy the law on the basis that it is not supported by one's consent. From the higher law constitutionalist's perspective, however, radical revisions of fundamental rights must be predicated on, if not a present universal consensus, a sense that the present consensus is so broad that its eventual universality is inevitable. Sometimes such impressions prove to be transitory or illusory (as in the case of prohibition). On other occasions, the emergent consensus proves to be real (as in the instances of the abolition of slavery or women's suffrage).

In attempting to transcend the provincialisms of sect, tribe, and nation, the higher law argument traced in this study anticipates the recent surge of interest in cosmopolitan approaches to justice. Many contemporary intellectuals reared on revisionist accounts of how oppression takes the guise of universalism have come to appreciate consensual forms of social and political relation as the only real alternative to power, recognizing that consent requires, in a heterogeneous political context, a cosmopolitan intercourse capable of bridging differences of identity. As Paul Gilroy puts it, we need to make "a sharp departure from all currently fashionable obligations to celebrate incommensurability and cheerlead for absolute identity," seeking instead the means for "human mutuality and cosmopolitan democracy."[11] Cosmopolitanism adds the figures and themes of transition and movement to higher law argument. A cosmopolitan conception of higher law is concerned less with revealed absolutes and more with the process of translation across divergent experiences and interests.[12]

Scholarly neglect of this cosmopolitan strand of American political theory can be explained in part by a tendency to make a firm distinction between foundationalism and anti-foundationalism. By suggesting the wrong metaphor, this foundational/anti-foundational dichotomy prevents many from fully appreciating the cosmopolitan and pragmatist aspects of nineteenth-century culture and jurisprudence.[13] Foundations pin buildings to a fixed spot and stand thereby for authoritarianism, rigidity, a positivistic certainty about human existence, and the superimposition of a rigid template on experience and people without the possibility of change. The predictable result of this paradigm is that many eschew foundations for no foundation – no starting point, no grounding, no certainty. Yet, if we take justice as the text of our political culture and legal system, then neither the foundationalist nor the anti-foundationalist alternative is adequate. The former is too rigid and the latter excludes the ethical starting point for the project of justice. We might better represent the quest for justice as an infinite number of lines beginning from the same starting point, or we might invert this figure and think of justice as the center of an infinite number of different lines of inquiry. Either metaphor allows us to account for the divergent conceptions of justice in different societies and eras while simultaneously being honest about the leap of faith that constitutes the *primum mobile* of all such conceptions.

Another factor explaining the neglect of the cosmopolitan higher law argument lies in the identitarianism that has gripped the academy for some time. Privileging race and all things particular, local, and "authentic," cultural and literary critics turning to American political and legal history have sought to claim that it reveals a homology between racism and the universal values of the higher law tradition. Discovering an evil equivalence between constitutional reform and repression, Saidiya Hartman's *Scenes of Subjection*, for instance, finds that abolitionist sympathy "acted to tether, bind, and oppress" and that the advocacy of black citizenship in the Civil War amendments facilitated "new forms of bondage." In lieu of the higher law universals of abolitionism and reconstruction, Hartman offers the "[e]veryday practices" of group identity. But, as Douglass would have readily understood, Hartman's claim that these local practices of identity are also "utopian expressions of freedom" is incoherent.[14] To claim that the local and particular practice of another era, milieu, or people has value for others is to instantiate a universal perspective capable of bridging such differences. Hartman's very attempt to recover these "everyday practices" evidences the cosmopolitan perspective she would seem to deny. While Hartman's study alerts us to how the paradigms of oppression influence even fervent arguments on behalf of the oppressed, her argument is weakened by its hyperbolic conflation of sympathy and coercion.

Merely observing and analyzing the obdurate presence of racism in the practice and theory of American law and society, for such scholars, lamely ducks the harsh reality that democracy boils down to racism. Matthew Frye Jacobson, for instance, orients his tremendously informative study on the function of race in American history with the observation that racism is "not anomalous to the working of American democracy, but fundamental to it."[15] While an historically apt and provocative assessment of much of the practice of American democracy, this comment is misleading to the extent that it implies an inherent or necessary connection between democracy and racism. The higher law argument of Charles Sumner, Frederick Douglass, Ralph Waldo Emerson, and others offers American political and cultural theory an alternative to the merger of race and democracy. This vein of American jurisprudence gives us a vantage from which to observe both how the racist's version of American political theory disguises power as divinely inscribed social hierarchy and how the critic responding that democracy is fundamentally predicated on racism disguises the seizure of power that he or she desires as "racial justice." Neither side recognizes that it shares with its putative opponent the same reduction of justice to the possession of power.

Of necessity, I have ranged broadly across disciplinary lines. Nineteenth-century higher law jurisprudence is developed in a wide variety of texts, such as Francis Lieber's political theory, Harriet Beecher Stowe's antislavery novels, Ralph Waldo Emerson's antislavery addresses, Frederick Douglass's oratory and autobiographical writing, the legal arguments of Salmon Chase and Moorfield Storey, and the political speeches of William Seward and Charles Sumner. The interdisciplinary nature of this book's subject hopefully illuminates the limitations of law and literature studies that substitute speculation about whether the discourses can or should speak to each other for an examination of historical evidence that in fact they have had interaction. Martha Nussbaum (*Poetic Justice* [1995]), for example, wonders – in hypothetical and didactic terms only – whether literature might give law a moral lesson or two. And Richard Posner (*Law and Literature* [1988] and *Overcoming Law* [1995]) and Wai Chee Dimock (*Residues of Justice* [1996]) postulate essential differences between law and literature, curtailing substantial conversation between the fields. By contrast, studies by Brook Thomas, Robert Ferguson, Eric Sundquist, and others have undertaken the analytic exploration of the intricate and multivalent historical interactions between law and literature and offered thereby a model for this project.

While the chief aim of my book is to furnish an historically accurate and engaging account of a type of higher law jurisprudence, I have also sought to give this portrait a polemic edge, lending support to recent interest in a chastened version of Enlightenment universalism and the growing dissatisfaction with identity-centered notions of society and justice. In the hands of its best nineteenth-century advocates, Emerson, Douglass, and Sumner, higher law offers a cosmopolitan discourse of justice and citizenship enabling people of diverse backgrounds, experiences, and allegiances to set and revise the basic terms of their coexistence through an inclusive process of conscience and consent. Such higher law arguments best represent the alternative of consent-based notions of political and social association to such power-based conceptions as slavery and Jim Crow, which attribute the possession of power to a natural or divinely inscribed racial inherence.

CHAPTER I

Higher law in the 1850s

On March 11, 1850, William H. Seward, former Governor of New York and future Secretary of State under Abraham Lincoln, gave his first speech before the Senate. Seward's topic was Henry Clay's proposed omnibus compromise bill, which included admission of California as a free state and a new, more potent Fugitive Slave Law. As oratory, Seward's speech was something of an anticlimax after Daniel Webster's performance in favor of the compromise four days earlier. As the scholarly, bespectacled Seward carefully and undramatically read his speech, the galleries rapidly emptied. Indeed in substance as well as performance, much of Seward's speech was not particularly provocative. Seward complained that, by lumping together very different pieces of legislation, such as the admission of California and the Fugitive Slave Act, Clay's compromise bill prevented separate consideration of each measure on its own merits. Echoing a theme in Webster's March 7 speech, Seward dismissed John Calhoun's anti-compromise argument that California's admission as a free state unfairly disrupted the sectional equilibrium essential to the South's partnership in the Union. The Union was not, Seward contended, a joint venture between independent sections. Given the unexceptional nature of his opening contentions and his colorless performance, many of those leaving the galleries early must have been surprised to learn of the firestorm of criticism ignited by Seward's comments on slavery and the Constitution.[1]

Halfway through the speech, instead of joining Clay and Webster in the fraternal venture of saving the Union, Seward threw down a gauntlet on the issue most sharply dividing the country. He flatly denied "that the Constitution recognizes property in man" and asserted, in a phrase that became infamous, that the nation's charter must heed "a higher law." The sectional conflict necessitating Clay's compromise was, in Seward's words, "a convulsion resulting from . . . compromises of natural justice and of human liberty." The turmoil created by the South's aggressive proslavery agenda and Northern capitulation had to be checked, not nurtured by further compromise. Seward predicted that the Fugitive Slave Law's manifest iniquity would inspire an expanding "public conscience," "transcending" party politics and sectional interests, to reassert (and more clearly define) the ethical basis of the American legal and political system.[2]

The higher law tradition invoked by Seward to read slavery out of the Constitution is complex and includes a wide range of formulations, but the core idea is constant and may be expressed (if not implemented) simply: to be legitimate, law must be just. Of course, slavery was defended as well as attacked on such terms. For example, George Fitzhugh argued that benevolently authoritarian institutions, such as slavery and marriage, represented the only moral way of addressing pervasive and apparently natural human inequalities. Sounding a similar note in defense of his compromise bill, Henry Clay characterized attempts to induce slaves to escape as a baffling and cruel disruption of an intimate and familial relation between servant and master. John Calhoun's compromise speech described the Constitution's recognition of slavery as a matter of trust; the North, in Calhoun's view, was attempting the morally contradictory feat of breaching its promises and simultaneously claiming superior moral authority for its duplicity.[3]

In contrast to his Southern opponents' attempt to fix higher law in divinely created hierarchies or timeless constitutional bargains, Seward cannily recognized both that a society's moral consensus delimits the scope and effect of its laws and that that consensus is mutable. Offending the basic moral norms of the Northerners among whom it was to be enforced, Seward argued, the Fugitive Slave Law was doomed before it was enacted – "Has any Government ever succeeded in changing the moral convictions of its subjects by force?" While Seward's conception that law derives its legitimacy from the dominant moral consensus did not necessitate the end of slavery (that such a consensus could well endorse slavery was all too plain in the nation's history), his sense that the culture's ethos was shifting in an antislavery direction would prove apt. And his version of higher law implied the important role literary and cultural figures could play in shaping the nation's jurisprudence by revising its public morality.[4] This implication was picked up by his critics. Seward was lambasted for opening constitutional jurisprudence to "the casuistry of theologians, the dicta of modern philosophers, and the suggestions of metaphysical theorizers." Higher law, *The Republic* charged, "gives [Seward] a scope as wide as the winds."[5]

"No portion of Gov. Seward's late speech ... met with a wider or more unsparing condemnation," observed the New York *Tribune*, than the notion that constitutional doctrine could be governed by the nation's changing moral notions. Many Northerners and Southerners saw Seward as seeking to replace the rule of law with anarchy. Individuals following Seward's lead could, it seemed, simply pick and choose which laws they would obey, claiming that inconvenient laws were immoral. As the Richmond *Enquirer* put it, "The prominent idea set forth is, that the persons who fancy themselves aggrieved by the operation of a law they have sworn to respect and obey, can at any moment relieve themselves from the duty of obedience, and the responsibility of rebellion, by announcing that their conscience ... forbids the compliance which the law demands." The *Democratic Review*, a conservative Northern journal, similarly exclaimed, "The principle announced by Mr. Seward, from his place in the Senate, and avowed by other leading abolitionists, recognizing a law superior to the Constitution, in interpreting that instrument, at once converts it into a dead-letter. The Constitution becomes obsolete. It is in fact abolished. It is a fanatical dogma; it is Mr. Seward's conscience." Such hyperbolic reactions substituted the straw man of anarchic and self-serving assertions of individual conscience (whether honest or fraudulent) for Seward's realistic acknowledgment that a democratic society's shifting mores undeniably affect the course and scope of its law. Seward was, after all, talking about the "public conscience," a weighty if amorphous entity not easily or quickly moved.[6]

The more germane fear aroused by Seward's higher law argument emanated from its universalist potential. Seward described the country not as a self-contained sovereign that could do as it pleased within its own borders but as "a part of the common heritage of mankind" "bestowed" and regulated "by the Creator of the Universe." Seward's speech implied an American government regulated by such universally acceptable "axioms in political science" as equality, knowledge, virtue, freedom, and government by consent – principles that on their face admit no distinctions of race, ethnicity, class, or gender.[7] In these facets of Seward's speech, many perceived the frightening vision of a cosmopolitan, heterogeneous American citizenry consensually arriving at norms of justice through a political discourse unbounded by such supposedly natural limits as race or gender. Thus, even though Seward was hardly the radical his political enemies made him out to be (he urged a Republican alliance with Stephen A. Douglas in 1858 and supported President Andrew Johnson's lenient version of Reconstruction) and despite the fact that his speech framed its challenge to slavery with such conservative pieties as manifest destiny and white supremacy, many of his harshest critics quite presciently sensed that the consensual aspect of Seward's version of higher law would open the door to the scariest kinds of social and political innovation. Seward's higher law argument was associated with "European" reformers and socialists "flocking hither by thousands" and a parade of such horribles as racial amalgamation, socialism, and women's rights. Such cosmopolitan freethinking could be potentially fatal both to an identification of the nation with the Anglo-Saxon tribe and to a definition of the nation's governing ethos as the born-in-the-blood traditions of that tribe.[8]

What frightened some appealed to others. Like Seward, Frederick Douglass conceived of the higher law crisis facing the American republic in cosmopolitan terms. The glaring contradiction between the Constitution's foundation in higher law and the continued existence of slavery was not just an American problem but an impediment to global progress: "American Slavery blocks the wheels of the car of Freedom." Douglass saluted the influence of the foreign reformers, such as George Thompson, on American law and culture, and suggested a parallel between the internal stranger, the African American, and the external stranger, the foreign reformer. Both can bring an outsider's perspective to correct the provincial biases limiting American justice.[9] The cosmopolitan cast of Douglass's thoughts is not particularly surprising given the considerable relief from racial proscription he had experienced in Britain, the important support he received from British friends, and his cosmopolitan literary tastes, but it was also consistent with black abolitionism.[10] In 1835, for example, the Fifth Annual Convention for the Improvement of the Free People of Color unanimously resolved that the words "colored" or "African" as identifying terms were not appropriate given the universalist nature of their higher law argument. William Whipper's address at this convention is worth quoting at length for its anticipation of many of the themes of higher law arguments made by Seward and others for an antislavery reading of the Constitution:

Having placed our institution on the high and indisputable ground of natural laws and human rights, and being guided and actuated by the law of universal love to our fellow men, we have buried in the bosom of Christian benevolence all those national distinctions, complexional variations, geographical lines, and sectional bounds that have hitherto marked the history, character and operations of men; and now boldly plead for the Christian and moral elevation of the human race . . . We shall aim to procure the abolition of those hateful and unnecessary distinctions by which the human family has hitherto been recognized, and only desire that they may be distinguished by their virtues and vices . . . We plead for the extension of those principles on which our government was formed, that it in turn may become purified from those iniquitous inconsistencies into which she has fallen by her aberration from first principles.[11]

A few months after Seward's speech, a committee of black Philadelphians adopted antislavery resolutions, echoing Seward's insistence that the Constitution be read as coherent with universal moral norms, his allusion to the image of "the panting fugitive," and his certainty that aiding fugitives from cruel bondage cannot be legitimately proscribed by law. And, in 1855, the Colored National Convention in Philadelphia expressly cited Seward's "higher law speech" as authority for its antislavery reading of the Constitution.[12]

Thus, while the prevalent reaction to Seward's higher law argument was one of outrage, it did find a sympathetic audience. The Anti-Slavery Society published ten thousand pamphlet copies of Seward's speech, and the New York *Tribune* lauded "Gov. Seward" for speaking

the word that Ages will embalm and Eternity approve. He has given the clearest and fullest utterance yet heard to the earnest, abiding convictions of the most generous, enlightened, humane and progressive portion of the American People – not yet a majority of the whole mass, but rapidly increasing in numbers and in strength – he has bodied forth in eloquent and impressive words the thought of that gathering.[13]

Seward's speech satisfied the increasing number of Northern Whigs who wanted someone in Washington to take a bold ethical stand against the perceived proslavery tilt of the national government. Many were particularly happy to see Webster admonished for his complicity in the Fugitive Slave Law. Such Whigs felt, as Merrill Peterson notes, that Seward had given the speech that Daniel Webster ought to have given.[14] In the wake of Seward's speech and the uproar it caused, a diverse collection of lawyers, poets, novelists, philosophers, preachers, and journalists were inspired to take up the higher law theme. When he heard higher law reckoned a kind of joke by lawyers and politicians, Emerson began taking notes on what he thought would become a treatise in defense of higher law jurisprudence. Ainsworth Rand Spofford, future Librarian of Congress, wrote a pamphlet laying out the rationale and authorities for a higher law approach to the Constitution, and William Hosmer wrote a book defending higher law jurisprudence. As was often noted, echoing Seward, the Fugitive Slave Law did good work in forcing Americans to articulate with greater clarity what they held to be the moral basis of their political and legal system.[15]

Many sympathizers found Seward's speech irrefutable on the point that the public conscience, at least in the North, would not tolerate the Fugitive Slave Law. By transforming "hospitality to the refugees from the most degrading oppression on earth into a crime" while "all mankind [except slaveholders] esteem that hospitality a virtue," in Seward's words, the law created a searing moral crisis for Northerners imagining the moment when the shivering fugitive might appear at their door seeking comfort and aid. Even for those deeming abolitionists fanatical, the image conjured by Seward's speech seemed to pose an insuperable moral and psychological barrier to obedience. The law in the abstract might require such callous behavior, but actually getting good people to comply would be another matter. As the *Tribune* put it, "If Mr. Webster supposes that any mere legal morality can overrule that which God puts into the heart of every genuine freeman, he is much mistaken." No law, the *Tribune* asserted, could "make it the duty of Mr. Webster nor any other human being, when a panting fugitive presents himself at his door begging for shelter and the means of escape, to arrest and bind him and hand him over to the pursuers who are hot upon his trail . . . When public sentiment gets ahead of a law, that law loses all efficiency."[16] Henry David Thoreau found the Fugitive Slave Law's requirement that one "be the agent of injustice to another" to be such a profound violation of the moral foundation of law as to warrant breaking the law and stopping the machinery of government. Though he would "suffer much, sooner than violate a statute that was merely inexpedient," Theodore Parker declared, "when the rulers have . . . enacted wickedness into a law which treads down the inalienable rights of man to such a degree as this, then I know no ruler but God, no law but natural justice."[17]

That the barest sketch of the decent citizen forbidden by law from aiding the shivering fugitive could so powerfully reveal the moral nullity of the Fugitive Slave Law, in effect, created a special role for literary renderings of this jurisprudential crisis. A detailed narrative could, it seemed, definitively visualize the law's moral impracticability. Soon after Seward's speech, Harriet Beecher Stowe sought to fill this need with a short parable, "The Freeman's Dream" (August 1850), which proved to be a trial run for the fugitive slave scenes in *Uncle Tom's Cabin* (1852). In "The Freeman's Dream," Stowe imagines the Northern farmer who, faced with fugitive slaves seeking his aid, conforms to the law. Subsequently, he dies, meeting his fate in the form of an adverse divine judgment: "Depart from me ye accursed! for I was an hungered, and ye gave me no meat." The farmer is condemned for choosing the lower law of men instead of the higher law of God. Explicitly weighing in on Seward's side of the argument, Stowe's story censures those "who seem to think that there is no standard of right and wrong higher than an act of Congress, or an interpretation of the United States Constitution."[18] Even if the Fugitive Slave Law were not reversed by the top-down processes of legislative or judicial action, it could, it seemed, from the higher law perspective, be upended by the contrary moral consensus mobilized in part by such cultural interventions as Stowe's antislavery fiction. Once fully aroused by a cultural/political partnership of literary figures, abolitionists, journalists, philosophers, preachers, politicians, and lawyers, this consensus hopefully would bring the nation's law in line with its higher law ethos.

The measure of success that such higher law advocacy had is suggested in an 1864 *North American Review* article, "The Constitution and its Defects." The article notes that during the first decades of the nineteenth century "the work of testing the morality of national legislation by the application of fundamental principles was abandoned by the leading minds of the country." But looking back from 1864, one felt ashamed by "the general contempt and ridicule excited . . . by appeals to the 'higher law'" which only betokened the simple truth that

government is after all a conventional arrangement, entitled, no doubt, to the utmost respect, and not to be disturbed unless it plainly fails to answer the purpose for which it was instituted; but that cases may arise, not calling for revolution, in which justice and truth are so outraged, under color of law, that it becomes the duty of good citizens to be guided rather by the principles of morality, on which the law ultimately rests all its claims to obedience, than by the law itself.

Given the "general contempt and ridicule" meeting Seward's appeal to higher law in 1850, we should pause to ask why he thought (correctly as it turned out) that his argument would fly. A brief examination of Seward's precedents answers this question and illuminates the concepts central to higher law's resurrection in the 1850s.[19]

HIGHER LAW PRECEDENTS

For Seward's generation, the touchstone for higher law reasoning was the American Revolution. At the risk of oversimplification, one could assert in 1850 (or now for that matter) that, because the founding fathers justified their defiance of English law on moral grounds, higher law constitutes the ultimate critique and authorization of the American legal system. Higher law appears throughout early American political theory, which, following Rogers Smith's magisterial study *Civic Ideals*, can be usefully separated into three general categories: the republican tradition emphasizing civic virtue or the renunciation of individual interests for the good of the community; the liberal tradition stressing the protection of individuals' rights against government incursion; and an inegalitarian ascriptive tradition, as Smith terms it, defining the American political ethos of both the republican and liberal natural rights varieties as the natural inheritance of a mythic Anglo-Saxon or American race.[20] Higher law conceptions run through all three of these theoretical perspectives, and higher law is central to three additional themes in early American political culture. The first of these is the religious vision of America as a "redeemer nation" illuminating for the world the ideal of righteous government. The second is the related belief in human progress. And the third is an incipient cosmopolitanism appearing in certain discussions of the American Revolution and the Constitution.

Overlaying and connecting the first five of these six aspects of early American political thought is a triangular relation between *conscience* (the repository of ethical concepts, such as the republican notion of public virtue or the liberal tradition of inalienable rights, that legitimate or limit law), *consent* (the democratically formed consensus about the ethical basis of law), and *resemblance* (an insistence on racial and cultural similitude circumscribing the application of the first two principles). Focusing on one aspect of American political thought to the neglect of the others (e.g., the liberal tradition's emphasis on individual rights) occludes the triangular pattern linking these different points of emphasis. And without having this interrelation of conscience, consent, and resemblance in focus, one tends to miss or devalue the cosmopolitan dimensions of American political thought. The loss is considerable, as cosmopolitanism has the potential to sever conscience and consent from resemblance, making it both the most threatening and most vulnerable of political conceptions. Its presence is fleeting and its moments of great political and cultural influence are rare, yet, for many, it defines the nation's promise. In their cosmopolitan moments, the framers conceived of American political discourse as a medium through which the evolving moral consensus of a heterogeneous people could take constitutional form. In "The Origin of Government and Laws in Connecticut" (1798), Jesse Root found the validity of the common law to be based on "unwritten customs and regulations" that have the "sanction of universal consent."[21] The requirement of universal consent, far from being a hopelessly utopian ideal, is basic to the project of building an inclusive political discourse. Lincoln would proclaim the requirement of universal political consent as the "sheet-anchor of American republicanism," and his statement, "No man is good enough to govern another without that other's consent," became a kind of higher law motto for the first president of the NAACP, Moorfield Storey, who, like his predecessors, Ralph Waldo Emerson, Frederick Douglass, and Charles Sumner, found in the framers' occasional cosmopolitanism the antithesis of identity as politics.[22]

THE REPUBLICAN TRADITION

For the generation authoring the Civil War amendments, the Revolution showed how higher law inspiration can become consensus and how consensus can compel a revision of the polity's fundamental law. The suggestion by Seward and others that Americans bear a collective responsibility to ensure that their legal system comports with higher law derives from the early republicans' conception of civic virtue. Severing ties with England did more than get rid of a king and serve the self-interests of the colonists; it advanced the establishment of a just form of government.[23] And this new republic depended on the reciprocal influence of the citizenry's moral character and their government's ethical nature. As John Adams put it, republican government

introduces knowledge among the people, and inspires them with a conscious dignity becoming free men; a general emulation takes place, which causes good humor, sociability, good manners, and good morals to be general. That elevation of sentiment inspired by such a government, makes the common people brave and enterprising. That ambition which is inspired by it makes them sober, industrious, and frugal.[24]

And a virtuous citizenry, educated by their participation in a republican form of government, would, in turn, assure the virtue of the government. In *The Rights of the British Colonies Asserted and Proved* (1764), James Otis declared that, when confronted by immoral laws, a citizen's inaction and silence is shameful. Republicans predicted that the political deliberations of citizens duty-bound to maintain the ethical quality of their government and the reciprocal and salutary influence of that form of government on their deliberations would reveal new paths of political virtue obscured by past errors and, paradoxically, recover the lost democratic innocence of an Anglo-Saxon past.[25]

Instead of inherited station and power, early republicans offered a mix of ethics and democratic consensus as the basis for and mechanism of virtuous government. As James Otis put it, a just form of government is not founded on mere "*compact* or *human will.*" It is grounded ultimately on the "*unchangeable will of* God, the author of nature, whose laws never vary." This divine law directs human government to serve "the *good* of mankind," but, as Otis notes, God leaves the implementation of this edict to us: "The form of government is by *nature* and by *right*...left to the *individuals* of each society." The upshot of this human discretion is that government, though not founded on any mere contract, turns out in practice to be founded on a particular kind of consensus as to the form of government and law that comes closest to securing "the *good* of mankind." Otis's comments capture the way in politics (if not in religion) higher law reasoning begins with an idea of bright-line moral absolutes but, because God or Nature leaves the practical details to human beings, takes its form and effect in the mutable realm of consent. Tories responded to the republican substitution of conscience and consent for an inherited hierarchical arrangement of status, property, and power much as proslavery advocates would later respond to the higher law arguments of antislavery advocates. They claimed that such an approach would unleash social anarchy – "the bands of society would be dissolved, the harmony of the world confounded, and the order of nature subverted."[26] What gave the republicans confidence that the sky would not fall upon their new consensual world order?

Two social ingredients made the republican mix of conscience and consent seem practicable to the revolutionary generation (and many of their antebellum heirs). The first was the notion that the commonwealth was an organic community whose interests and outlook were generally homogenous. As Garry Wills describes, Thomas Jefferson suspected that "a certain homogeneity was necessary in any society of men contracting with each other on the basis of mutual affection." The Declaration's figure of "one people" implicitly drew on a myth of Anglo-Saxon liberty deeming the Americans' capacity for self-rule as a shared racial heritage. In asserting their constitutional liberties, British colonists, in James Otis's view, recovered a family tradition: "liberty was better understood and more fully enjoyed by our ancestors before the coming in of the first Norman tyrants than ever after."[27] It followed from the assumption of a shared heritage and organic unity that what was good for the whole was good for the part, and, reflecting the egalitarianism of this political theory as well as the fiction of homogeneity, any part could represent the whole in a kind of elemental civic fungibility.

The second factor favoring the republican politics of conscience and consent was humankind's innate moral sense. The theory developed by such eighteenth-century philosophers as the Earl of Shaftesbury, Joseph Butler, Frances Hutcheson, David Hume, and Adam Smith that humanity is universally endowed with a benevolent form of moral intuition decisively influenced revolutionary era republicanism and antebellum higher law arguments against slavery. These philosophers felt that Locke had overemphasized rationality in describing the mind's processes. Locke's concept of right reason – an empirical calculus of sense impressions and inductive extrapolations – was incomplete. It left out the emotional and aesthetic aspects of human nature. Human beings were inherently capable of deriving exquisite happiness and pleasure from the self-sacrifice that for republicans constituted public virtue.[28] For Jefferson and other republicans, the possession of a sympathetic moral sense defined humankind. Following Hutcheson, Hume, and Smith, Jefferson found that "nature hath implanted in our breasts a love of others, a sense of duty to them, a moral instinct, in short, which prompts us irresistibly to feel and to succor their distresses." The moral instinct, in the words of an anonymous Boston pamphlet writer, made "[t]he happiness of every individual" depend "on the happiness of society." As Richard Sennett puts it, "what people shared was a natural compassion, a natural sensitivity to the needs of others, no matter what the differences in their social circumstances."[29] That such a benevolent moral faculty was innate to the entire populace, from the ploughman to the professor, in Jefferson's famous phrase, supported the founders' confidence in the citizenry's ability to create and sustain an ethical form of government. Dedicated amateurs, these early republicans wanted no professional army to fight their battles and no professional legal or political class to make their laws.[30] Republican moral sense theory empowered the average citizen to judge fundamental questions of political legitimacy and recognized the relevance of literary, religious, and philosophical works, illuminating the dictates of fellow feeling. As Robert Ferguson has shown, the lack of sharp disciplinary boundaries between various kinds of legal and cultural discourse corresponded with the framers' conception that the attempt "to form a more perfect union" was a hybrid act of imagination.[31]

Of course, given the divergence of different individuals' affective responses, one might well wonder at the founders' belief in the possibility of ethical consensus. In addressing this issue, early republicans and their antislavery descendants could draw on the relation moral sense psychology charted between the affect provoked by an immediate experience and that produced by contemplation of the common good. David Hume's influential account of this relation begins by acknowledging that our moral sense responds most ardently to the people and events nearest to us both in terms of human relation and in terms of physical experience. Of particular import to this agency of moral affect are the "lively idea[s]" we have "of everything related to us": in particular, the "human creatures . . . related to us by resemblance." (As one might anticipate, the idea that moral affect originates in resemblance complicates certain abolitionist invocations of moral sense theory, such as *Uncle Tom's Cabin*.)[32] However, notwithstanding their power, our affective preferences for the proximate coexist, in Hume's view, with a rational acceptance of those rules enabling a society of individuals with diverse interests and relations to coexist peacefully and productively. For Hume, the "three fundamental laws of nature" on which "peace and security of human society entirely depend" are the right to own and sell property and the binding nature of our voluntary commitments.[33] Unlike the innate affective responses of the moral sense, these basic norms of social coexistence are matters of consensus and natural only in the sense that people inevitably invent them when they "observe, that tis impossible to live in society without restraining themselves by certain rules." Once recognized by rational self-interest, however, such conventions have an affective dimension of their own, affording pleasure because they "tend to the peace of society." Through a process of political education about and participation in creating the legal conventions and rules requisite for society's peaceful existence and progress, we are led from the more intense and immediate affective response one feels at the sight of a friend or relative in dire straights to a shared pleasure in discovering that certain rules are good for society.[34]

RIGHTS

Gordon Wood has argued that republicanism expired with the framers' focus protecting divergent individual interests. Finding republican themes and tropes continuing into the nineteenth and twentieth century, J. G. A. Pocock counters, rightly I think, that Wood overstates the end of republicanism.[35] Indeed, such a terminus would be hard to locate given the permeability of the division between republicanism and the liberal natural rights tradition. Because both theories attempt to articulate the ethical consensus legitimating American government and law, there are many points of overlap and intersection between them.[36] The difference is chiefly a matter of emphasis. Where republican theory stresses the coherence between the republic's official jurisprudence and the shared ethos of the citizenry, liberal theory imagines an opposition, focusing on those most basic rights all agree should protect the individual from the government.

The idiom of rights was, as Jack Rakove has pointed out, as natural to the colonists as the republican language of public virtue. First and foremost, the colonists conceived of rights as an essential bulwark against the predations of power. Power was aggressive; it has "an encroaching nature"; "if at first it meets with no control [it] creeps by degrees and quick subdues the whole." Foreshadowing Simon Legree, who tells Uncle Tom to feel his hand made "hard as iron from *knocking down niggers*," colonists figured tyranny as "the hand of power," "grasping" and "tenacious," "what it seizes it will retain."[37] Rights, by contrast, are not something graspable but are, in John Dickinson's words, "born with us; exist with us; and cannot be taken from us by any human power without taking our lives. In short, they are founded on the immutable maxims of reason and justice."[38] Significantly, *rights* denotes a protected sphere of personal autonomy and liberty whose precise shape and dimensions are unspecified. To amplify the term by referring to life, liberty, and the pursuit of happiness does not really resolve the ambiguity (the familiar triad does not, for instance, tell us how to adjudicate conflicts between different people exercising their "rights"). This ambiguity is both the product of and predicate for the continuing cultural and political dialogue through which American society frames and revises its notions of basic individual freedoms.

Perhaps more than any other philosopher, John Locke taught the revolutionary generation how applying "right reason" to sense experience reveals the original equality of people and their rights to life, liberty, and property.[39] And Locke offered a compelling philosophical conception of human beings in a state of nature consensually forming the basis and nature of their government.[40] Thomas Paine's *Common Sense* (1776) begins with a Lockean narrative of "a small number of persons settled in some sequestered part of the earth" who, like the first people on earth, find that in "a state of natural liberty . . . society" is, as a matter of necessity, "their first thought." As the creation of their consent, the very existence of this primitive society attests to the members' inherent and equal authority. The fact that, in creating civil society, each citizen ceded some authority to the government required a distinction between the rights of self-governance that could be alienated (initially by means of the social compact and subsequently by means of the governmental charter) and the individual rights that could not be alienated (rights of life, liberty, and property). The latter signify the continuing authority of the individual to endorse and later revise the governmental charter. For the framers, the Revolution had left the American people in a state of nature, and the proper goal of drafting and ratifying a constitution was a social compact not between ruler and ruled but among citizens who had banded together to promote the welfare of the whole. To this end, the delegates to the constitutional conventions were not drawn from standing state legislatures but directly elected by the people.[41]

The Lockean account of natural rights, as Richard Tuck notes, differed from most rights theories, which "have been explicitly authoritarian rather than liberal."[42] In Locke's view, such conservative political theory boiled down to the assertions that "*all Government is absolute Monarchy*" and "*no Man is Born free.*" Locke's American heirs similarly rejected conservative conceptions of law as merely the expression of the sovereign's power. In response to the emergent positivism of British jurisprudence, which classed the British constitution not as an expression of higher law, but as just another, though more basic, form of positive law, American Whigs reaffirmed the higher law notion that certain basic and universal values, including the protection of individual rights, either legitimated government or invalidated it.[43] The doctrine of judicial review exemplified the practical force the earliest citizens were willing to give to their conceptions of higher law. In contrast to the British system, in which, as Blackstone described it, "no power could control" even the unreasonable enactments of Parliament, judicial review gave American judges the authority to curb the excesses of majority power by voiding legislation contrary to the principles of justice expressed in the Constitution.[44] The dichotomy colonial republicans perceived between the nobility of the unwritten British constitution and such unjust and arbitrary acts of Parliament as the Stamp Act and the Townshend Acts came to correspond in American jurisprudence with the distinction between what was constitutional and what was merely legal. *Constitutional* meant something better than and anterior to mere law. The Bill of Rights and the Preamble's stated goals of establishing justice, promoting the general welfare, and securing the blessings of liberty embodied the ethical basis of the new republic in contrast to the edicts of shifting legislative majorities, which often expressed merely the self-interest of a particular political coalition. This sentiment animates Chief Justice John Marshall's famous distinction between the Constitution and a code.[45]

RESEMBLANCE: IDENTITY AS POLITICS

As Rogers Smith has pointed out, following Edmund Morgan and Reginald Horsman and others, the republican and rights traditions were alloyed with and limited by a prerequisite that the members of the body politic must resemble each other in language, culture, religion, and appearance. The ascriptive side of early American conceptions of higher law is well captured by Jefferson's proposal for the Great Seal of the United States. John Adams told his wife that Jefferson's seal had on one side "the children of Israel in the wilderness, led by a cloud by day and pillar of fire by night; and on the other side, Hengist and Horsa, the Saxon chiefs from whom we claim the honor of being descended, and whose political principles and form of government we have assumed." Adopting the Exodus story, the seal's first side would seem to embody the moral universal of freedom and the millennialist mission of the American republic in a symbol that superficially, at least, cuts across race lines, but the seal's flip side reverses the thrust of the symbolism to represent the ethos animating the new American government as the racial legacy of a certain tribe.[46]

This ascriptive tendency can be felt in a subtler fashion in Thomas Paine's touting of the imminent "birthday" of a new, more diverse "race of men." Not limited to British descendants, Paine's new "race" included immigrants from different parts of Europe but excluded blacks and Indians. Similarly, J. Hector St. John de Crèvecoeur's famous letter, "What is an American," lauds America as an "asylum" for "the poor of Europe" yet recasts a limited assortment of northern European immigrants as a new homogenous society closely tied to the soil.[47] In Paine and Crèvecoeur, one can feel the outward push of an incipient cosmopolitanism being contained by what each man senses is the outer limit of an indispensable form of social resemblance. Even such open-minded figures as James Otis and James Wilson were influenced by ascriptive thinking. Otis insisted that "righteousness must be the basis of law" but identified the colonists "not as the common people of *England* foolishly imagine . . . a compound mixture of *English, Indian,* and *Negro,* but [as] freeborn *British white* subjects." In his "Lectures on Law" (1790), James Wilson, one of the Constitution's more cosmopolitan framers (a Scottish immigrant himself), followed Jefferson in describing the basic structure of Anglo-American constitutionalism as a Saxon legacy.[48] Of course, the ascription of democratic principles to a British lineage does not necessarily indicate an acceptance of slavery or disfranchisement of black Americans. Otis identified liberty as the heritage of an Anglo-Saxon people but also accepted that all "colonists, black and white, born here, are free born British subjects," and Wilson was a staunch opponent of slavery.[49]

RELIGION

The higher law doctrine that, in the words of Martin Luther King, Jr., "an unjust law is no law" has a long lineage in religious thought, including St. Augustine, Aquinas, John Calvin, Thomas Hooker, Jonathan Edwards, and many others. Aquinas's conception is paradigmatic: higher law is the body of eternal principles of justice promulgated by God; natural law represents that part of God's eternal law ascertainable by human beings through the use of their reason; human law which conflicts with higher law is void *ab initio* (from the beginning).[50] The early republicans' notion of higher law was deeply influenced by the Puritan insistence on a present God, appearing in nature, historical events, and the "actual pattern of reality to which revelation had given the key and which reason, following upon revelation, could discern." The failure to conform the rules and processes of human government to God's law betokened earthly disorder and rebellion. Preachers in the revolutionary era drew upon this intersection of religion and politics to derive the right of revolution from the conflict between the higher law of God and the lower law of humankind.[51]

Contrary to the tenor of its title, Charles Chauncy's sermon, "Civil Magistrates Must Be Just, Ruling In The Fear Of God" (1747), demonstrates that an ethical or religious view of law need not speak from an absolutist clarity to announce a static legal order. Foreshadowing Ronald Dworkin's distinction between concepts and conceptions (concepts are large principles never fully or finally defined, such as fair play, and conceptions are our specific attempts to achieve and illustrate those abstractions, such as a legal prohibition on a specific kind of discrimination), Chauncy contends that

a distinction ought always to be made between government in its general notion, and particular form and manner of administration. As to the later, it cannot be affirmed, that this or that particular form of government is made necessary by the will of God and reason of things. The mode of civil rule may in consistency with the public good, admit of variety: And it has, in fact, been various in different nations: Nor has it always continued the same, in the same nation.[52]

The movement in Chauncy's sermon between divine principle (universal and certain) and human implementation (diverse and experimental) corresponds to the merger of religious inspiration and Enlightenment rationalism one often finds in the founders' political rhetoric. For instance, in "A Dissertation on the Canon and Feudal Law" (1765), John Adams finds that tyranny and injustice abate where "knowledge and sensibility have prevail'd among the *people*." But, as Ernest Tuveson points out, Adams's tone oscillates between rationalism and the religious language of the apocalypse, which Tuveson aptly terms "apocalyptic Whiggism." In Adams's apocalyptic Whiggism, the establishment of a republican form of government in America heralded the millenial advance for humankind and the end of the dominant corruption and oppression fostered by the Roman church.[53]

While the founders' coupling of inspiration and reason would prove to be an important prototype for politically oriented higher law arguments against the constitutionality of slavery, millenialist aspirations and Enlightenment rationalism were not always blended in the fashion of Adams's "Dissertation." Religious higher law arguments against slavery sometimes spurned law and politics altogether. Adopting a Christian anarchism, Garrisonians believed that human government should not be substituted for a government by God. In 1836, Henry C. Wright, a Congregational pastor from West Newbury, Massachusetts and the most anarchistic of antislavery radicals, wrote in his journal that "God has a Government & Man has a government. These two are at perpetual *War* . . . Man is not content to rule over the animal creation. He would get dominion over man. He tries all arts to obtain this end. *I regard all Human Government as usurpations of God's power over Man.*" Arguing for God-directed self-control as the true source of public order and dispensing with the messy and uncertain processes of political argument and compromise, William Lloyd Garrison's conception of government stressed conscience and moral absolutes, not consent and human experiment.[54] Predictably, the pattern of Garrison's influence did not follow the script of his argument. As Eric Foner notes, Garrisonian argument had considerable influence on the politics of antislavery and eventually on the formation of the Republican party. Many politicians, such as Salmon Chase, Charles Sumner, Thaddeus Stevens, and Joshua Giddings, drew on Garrisonian representations of moral inspiration and the millennialist destiny of the American nation as the starting point for cultural and political debate about the just direction of constitutional jurisprudence.[55]

PROGRESS

The nineteenth century was, as many have observed, dominated by the idea of progress. George Bancroft made progress a central theme of his massive *History of the United States*, and Francis Lieber described American jurisprudence as a slow but steady process of upward evolution.[56] Foreshadowing the proto-pragmatist intuition shared by Charles Sumner, Frederick Douglass, Ralph Waldo Emerson, and others that the Constitution was capable of *becoming* antislavery, Jefferson expressly coupled the concept of progress and the Constitution. In his famous letter to John Adams on the "natural aristocracy," Jefferson contends that our awareness of the progress we have already made (e.g., by eliminating the legal preservation of inherited status through such doctrines as primogeniture and entails) should direct our approach to law:

Some men look at constitutions with sanctimonious reverence, and deem them like the ark of the covenant, too sacred to be touched. They ascribe to the men of the preceding age a wisdom more than human, and suppose what they did to be beyond amendment . . . I am certainly not an advocate for frequent and untried changes in laws and constitution. I think moderate imperfections had better be borne with; because, when once known, we accommodate ourselves to them, and find practical means of correcting their ill effects. But I know also, that laws and institutions must go hand in hand with the progress of the human mind. As that becomes more developed, more enlightened, as new discoveries are made, new truths disclosed, and manners and opinions change with the circumstances, institutions must advance also, and keep pace with the times. We might as well require a man to wear still the coat which fitted him when a boy, as civilized society to remain ever under the regimen of their barbarous ancestors.[57]

As anticipated by Charles Chauncy, Jefferson allows for intellectual and moral progress to continue to shape and reshape the Constitution, creating, in effect, a notion of constitutional progress. The revolutionary generation's concept of progress provided a template for antislavery arguments seeking to combine moral inspiration and rational debate in a flexible constitutional jurisprudence capable of opening up the terms of citizenship and basic justice to black Americans.

COSMOPOLITANISM

Looking back at the two chief prerequisites for republican confidence
in conscience and consent – a homogeneous community and an innate
moral sense – the contradiction between the identitarianism of the former and the universalism of the latter would seem readily apparent.
While certainly not invisible to the founders, this contradiction was neither as plain nor as central as it would seem to later generations.[58]
Because the founders argued for universal values, such as liberty and
equality, on behalf of a people they imagined as generally similar in
origin and culture, they did not have to cross the Rubicon of racial difference. Higher law arguments on behalf of black Americans could not
avoid the issue. Sumner, Douglass, Emerson, Thaddeus Stevens, and
certain other farsighted individuals found the answer to this conflict in
American jurisprudence by severing the higher law universals of conscience and consent from the notion of racial and cultural resemblance.
Ironically, the antecedent for this radical turn of antebellum higher law
argument resides in the reverse side of the framers' identitarianism: their
nascent cosmopolitanism.

This paradox can be traced back, at least in part, to moral sense psychology. While, according to Hume, we feel first and most strongly for
those who seem like us, we are led from the immediate circle of proximate events and close relations outward to a more inclusive and abstract
appreciation of the social good. Like Hume, Adam Smith accepted that
humankind is endowed with a benevolent moral sense that feels "for others." Sympathy, for Smith, revealed the "natural jurisprudence" or moral
direction of government to which "[e]very system of positive law" should
aspire. Following his Stoic precursors, Smith's conception of sympathy
had an expressly cosmopolitan aspect:

Man, according to the Stoics, ought to regard himself . . . as a citizen of the world,
a member of the vast commonwealth of nature. To the interest of this great
community, he ought at all times to be willing that his own little interest should
be sacrificed. Whatever concerns himself, ought to affect him no more than
whatever concerns any other equally important part of this immense system.
We should view ourselves, not in the light in which our own selfish passions are
apt to place us, but in the light in which any other citizen of the world would
view us.

The innate and natural concern for others, in Smith's view, expanded
outward from family and tribe to the nation and the globe. We can hear
an echo of this cosmopolitan ethical perspective in the Declaration of

Independence, which "declar[es] the causes" for the Revolution out of "a decent respect to the opinions of mankind."[59]

Thomas Paine's *Common Sense* offers a similarly concentric pattern of enlargement of moral outlook to explain how colonials of diverse backgrounds can band together and form a new people:

A man born in any town in England divided into parishes, will naturally associate most with his fellow-parishioners (because their interests in many cases will be common) and distinguish him by the name of *neighbour*; if he meet him but a few miles from home, he drops the narrow idea of a street, and salutes him by the name of *townsman*; if he travel out of the country, and meet him in any other, he forgets the minor divisions of street and town, and calls him *countryman*, i.e. *countryman*; but if in their foreign excursions they should associate in France or any other part of *Europe*, their local remembrance would be enlarged into that of *Englishmen*. And by a just parity of reasoning, all Europeans meeting in America, or any other quarter of the globe, are *countrymen*; for England, Holland, Germany, or Sweden, when compared with the whole, stand in the same places on the larger scale, which the divisions of street, town, and country do on the smaller ones; distinctions too limited for continental minds. Not one third of the inhabitants, even of this province, are of English descent. Wherefore I reprobate the phrase of parent or mother country applied to England only, as being false, selfish, narrow, and ungenerous.

Though limited by the principle of difference central to resemblance and identity as politics (English identity dissolves into European identity and European identity dissolves into American identity but the distinction of "us" versus "them" remains pivotal), the telescopic movement toward a global prospect is, in Paine's view, helpful for the task of forging an American identity in terms of political faith, not national origin. The colonists' varied ancestry will, Paine hopes, help to prevent kinship ties from obscuring their common cause against British tyranny, but, he adds, even if all were of British descent, the blood bond would mean nothing in the face of the political differences separating the colonies from Britain. In keeping with its cosmopolitan mixture, Paine suggests that international exchange and commerce be America's "plan." The antithesis of a stagnant filial devotion to Britain, such commerce, through nurturing multiple international connections, would appropriately foster the growth and development of an already diverse people.[60]

The cosmopolitan tendency of the founders' political outlook enters constitutional jurisprudence in the Federalists' countermajoritarianism. In *The Federalist*, Number 10, James Madison famously targets the problem of malign majorities – "factions" – enacting laws that serve their self-interests without regard for the common good or the inalienable rights of political minorities. The particular concern for Madison and many Federalists was the passage of redistributive legislation threatening the vested economic interests and private rights of a propertied minority (e.g., debtor relief laws). But Madison's comments are not limited on their face to such economic matters; his condemnation of tyrannical majorities is broadly phrased in the higher law terms of the republican and rights traditions: "the public good is disregarded . . . and . . . measure[s] are too often decided, not according to the rules of justice and the rights of the minor party, but by the superior force of an interested and overbearing majority." Majorities, Madison fears, may come to view the democratic process as the supple tool of their power, and his aim is to conceive of devices within a consensual form of government retaining the government's moral direction by checking majority will.[61]

In Madison's analysis of this problem, factions are more likely to form and to enact their will at the local level where there is greater homogeneity. Madison's solution of embracing heterogeneity moves in a distinctly cosmopolitan direction: "Extend the sphere" of society "and you take in a greater variety of parties and interests," and, consequently, "you make it less probable that a majority of the whole will have a common motive to invade the rights of other citizens; or if such a common motive exists, it will be more difficult for all who feel it to discover their own strength and to act in unison with each other." While the express goal of Madison's practical suggestion is to diffuse the political power of local prejudices and interests, his proposal implies a diffusion of local identities in a broader, more ecumenical national identity.[62] Of course, the diversity Madison had in mind was limited to differences of region, religion, and class within the American nation. Early in *The Federalist*, John Jay, the first Chief Justice of the Supreme Court, sounds a distinctly uncosmopolitan note, describing Americans as "one united people – a people descended from the same ancestors, speaking the same language, professing the same religion."[63] Yet, even with such qualifications, the important link Madison and other founders made between diversity and justice anticipates the more thoroughgoing cosmopolitan path that such antislavery constitutionalists as Douglass and Sumner would take.[64]

THE EBB OF HIGHER LAW

After a glance at the founders' political theory, we may wonder not that Seward made a higher law argument against the Fugitive Slave Law but that it was met with such widespread scorn. The hostile reaction meeting Seward's invocation of higher law marks the ebb of higher law in the first half of the nineteenth century. Of course, higher law never completely faded from American law. It survived, as we will see, in the freedom of contract doctrine, protecting private contracts from legislative interference, and it had some prominent apologists in the decades following the Constitution's ratification. In the 1830s, Francis Wayland, President of Brown University, Lydia Maria Child, and William Ellery Channing published books deeply immersed in the higher law reasoning of the founders. The antislavery arguments of Child and Channing influenced many New England intellectuals, such as Charles Sumner, Ralph Waldo Emerson, and Wendell Phillips.[65] But thinkers like Wayland, Child, and Channing were part of a distinct minority. Larry Tise has shown how a conservative counterrevolution that began in 1795 and accelerated in the ensuing decades displaced higher law conceptions of the Constitution and the Declaration of Independence:

Nearly every development in the conservative experience contributed in some fundamental way to the creation of an America that could almost instinctively reject abolition and abolitionists. In terms of social values the conservative counterrevolutionaries replaced Revolutionary equalitarianism with a decidedly strong preference for a deferential social structure. Any social movement that had as its aim the equalization of condition for all men fell on deaf ears in the case of conservative Federalists once their counterrevolution was under way.

This conservative counterrevolution sought to halt the reformation of society and government begun in the Revolution and reconceived the universal value of liberty as synonymous with freedom within an established social order.[66]

It is not particularly surprising that the South proved a fertile ground for this counterrevolution. Many factors, such as the utility of slavery for cotton production and the threat of slave violence, tended to disconcert Southern belief in more liberal formulations of higher law and led Southerners to retreat from the abolitionism such beliefs inspired.[67] The conservative drift of Southern thought is reflected in the editorial reversal of *The Southern Literary Messenger*, the South's premier literary journal. In the first years of its publication in the mid 1830s, the *Messenger* published moderate condemnations of slavery, such as the statement of a prominent Southern jurist that "We regard [slavery] . . . as a great evil, which society sooner or later will find it not only to its interest to remove or mitigate, but will seek its gradual abolition, or amelioration, under the influence of those high obligations imposed by an enlightened Christian morality." By the 1850s, however, the *Messenger* had moved to the unqualified proslavery position represented by James P. Holcombe's argument that slavery was consistent with natural law.[68] The cast of such proslavery thought was anticipated in 1832 by Thomas Dew's argument that higher law consisted not in the fictions of equality and social compact but in a conservative and religious respect for natural hierarchies of power, such as gender inequality and paternal authority.[69] Dew contended that man is by divine design born into different circumstances, with unequal capacities, and this form of difference always has and always will lead to slavery. And it was clear "from the fact that slavery was the necessary result of the laws of mind and matter, that it marked some benevolent design, and was intended by our Creator for some useful purpose." That purpose, according to Dew, was the human progress made possible because superior men gained leisure and opportunity by subjugating their inferiors. Slavery was the price of civilization.[70]

The decline of the founders' higher law ethos was part of a major shift in American jurisprudence. As Morton Horwitz points out,

By 1820 the legal landscape in America bore only the faintest resemblance to what existed forty years earlier. While the words were often the same, the structure of thought had dramatically changed and with it the theory of law. Law was no longer conceived of as an eternal set of principles expressed in custom and derived from natural law.[71]

Increasingly, nineteenth-century politicians and lawyers inclined toward the positivist conception of law rejected by the revolutionary generation. The Declaration of Independence and the Revolution came to be seen as merely reconfiguring political power from a monarchical to a democratic form. In the Virginia constitutional convention of 1829, a representative named Campbell described the majority's right to govern as flowing from their "natural" power "either to compel . . . or to expel the disaffected" (an idea that Thomas Dixon would later put in the mouth of Abraham Lincoln as "We must either assimilate or expel").[72] This positivist trend went hand-in-glove with the increasing professionalization of law. In contrast to the founders' vision of republican law and government as protected from corruption by the participation of disinterested amateurs, law and politics became the province of a specialized class of professionals. In *The Life of the Mind in America*, Perry Miller notes the passing of the republican amateur in the person of James Fenimore

Cooper's atavistic hero, Natty Bumbo, whose sense of justice, unlike that of Judge Templeton, is a matter of common sense and instinct. Where the early republicans had conceived of heart (moral sense) and head (rationality) as operating together, each beneficially tempering the other, professional attention to consistency of result and deference to legislative sovereignty mandated that the head should control the heart, creating, in Robert Cover's term, a moral-formal dilemma for judges who did not cease to have moral feelings when they put on judicial robes.[73]

Supreme Court cases addressing slavery offer a revealing view of the positivist direction of American law. In deciding to return slaves taken from a foreign ship to their Spanish claimants, Chief Justice Marshall's opinion in *The Antelope* (1825) begins by making clear his own antislavery sentiments. He praises the "humane and enlightened individuals of Great Britain" who roused "the feelings of justice and humanity" and inspired legislation outlawing the slave trade. However, unlike "moralists," Marshall notes, a jurist must resolve controversies on the basis of the relevant law, which in this case was foreign law permitting the slave trade. Though the result in *Amistad* (1841) is happier than that of *The Antelope*, the Court's reasoning carefully avoids giving higher law argument any apparent force in the outcome. In deciding not to turn over the alleged slaves to their purported owners, Justice Joseph Story's decision studiously avoids giving weight to the higher law arguments made by Roger Sherman Baldwin and John Quincy Adams. "If these negroes were . . . lawfully held as slaves" under the applicable foreign law, the Court according to Story would have no alternative but to return them to their foreign owners. Fortunately for the *Amistad* rebels, Story states, "it is plain beyond controversy" that they were "kidnapped" in Africa and "unlawfully transported to Cuba." A year later, Story revisited the conflict between higher and lower law posed by slavery in *Prigg v. Pennsylvania* (1842). The conflict involved Pennsylvania's personal liberty law, which was designed to protect free Negroes from being wrongly seized as fugitive slaves but which in practice also impeded the recapture of slaves. Brushing aside the suggestion of Pennsylvania's Attorney General that the Court "read the Constitution in the benign spirit of the golden rule, to do 'unto others as we would have them do unto us,'" Story found the state's personal liberty law void as it poached on the exclusive federal authority over the recapture of fugitive slaves.[74] In *Jones v. Van Zandt* (1847), the Court rejected the higher law argument of William

Seward and Salmon Chase on behalf of a man who had aided fugitive slaves, seeking to erase any lingering suspicion that the justices would allow personal feelings to interfere with their professional duty. Justice Woodbury's opinion bluntly limits the Court's role to the exposition of the majority's political will.[75]

By returning men and women who had risked all for freedom to lifelong bondage, the nation's judges and politicians had, for many antebellum citizens, abandoned their duty to square American law with the fundamental norms of justice. Abandoned by the men of law, the higher law tradition was taken up with historic results by activists, poets, novelists, philosophers, and preachers, urging an antislavery construction of the nation's charter. Part of the literary effort to rekindle the nation's higher law faith consisted in upbraiding the elected officials and judges for forgetting their ethical responsibilities. In this vein, James Russell Lowell's homespun spokesman, Hosea Biglow, mocks John Calhoun's efforts to prevent congressional discussion of slavery: "Human rights haint no more / Right to come on this floor, / No more'n the man in the moon . . . Freedom's Keystone is Slavery." And John Greenleaf Whittier's "Ichabod" bitterly memorializes Daniel Webster's complicity in the Fugitive Slave Law's enactment:

> Of all we loved and honored, naught
>   Save power remains;
> A fallen angel's pride of thought,
>   Still strong in chains.
> All else's gone; from those great eyes
>   The soul has fled:
> When faith is lost, when honor dies,
>   The man is dead!

Emerson similarly condemned "Mr. Webster's treachery," urging that Webster should avoid using the word "liberty": "The word *liberty* in the mouth of Mr. Webster sounds like the word *love* in the mouth of a courtezan." In *The Key to Uncle Tom's Cabin*, Harriet Beecher Stowe attacks the elevation of political power over the dictates of conscience, lamenting that even the best American jurists were content to be mere expositors and not reformers of law. Anticipating and influencing many of the themes of later antislavery literature, Lydia Maria Child contended in her *An Appeal in Favor of That Class of Americans called Africans* (1833) that "earthly considerations should never stifle the voice of conscience." Taking a cosmopolitan view of slavery akin to Seward's, Child compares American slavery with its antecedents in history and with the practices of other nations. Child demonstrates with considerable lucidity how slavery violates the nation's republican and natural rights traditions:

All ideas of property are founded upon the mutual agreement of the human race, and are regulated by such laws as are deemed most conducive to the general good. In slavery there is no *mutual* agreement; for in that case it would not be slavery. The negro has no voice in the matter – no alternative is presented to him – no bargain is made.

The beginning of bondage is the triumph of power over consent in Child's apt formulation.[76]

These literary invocations of higher law were anticipated and paralleled in a largely unobserved fashion by judicial efforts to protect private contracts from legislative interference. Freedom of contract doctrine (later termed substantive due process) preserved higher law as an effective legal concept. Our understanding of higher law's ebb in law and rise in literature should be framed by an awareness of its continued influence on judicial nullifications of state legislation interfering with the contractual freedom of private individuals. Foreshadowing many of the formal as well as thematic elements of literary arguments against slavery, freedom of contract cases, such as *Dartmouth College* (1819), create a higher law connection between legal and literary imaginings of justice in the antebellum period, and the freedom of contract doctrine itself offered an important substantive precedent for the literary and legal arguments against Jim Crow law made at the end of the century by such figures as Charles Chesnutt and Moorfield Storey.

The exchange between Justices Chase and Iredell in *Calder v. Bull* (1798) represents the seminal debate on the judiciary's higher law authority to strike down legislative interferences with private contracts. Justice Chase argued that judicial review empowered the Court to protect private contracts from legislation violating the higher law principles founding American law and society:

I cannot subscribe to the omnipotence of a state Legislature, or that it is absolute and without control . . . There are certain vital principles in our free Republican governments, which will determine and overrule an apparent and flagrant abuse of legislative power; as to authorize manifest injustice by positive law; or to take away that security for personal liberty, or private property, for the protection whereof the government was established. An act of the Legislature (for I cannot call it a law), contrary to the great first principles of the social compact, cannot be considered a rightful exercise of legislative authority . . . It is against all reason and justice, for a people to entrust a Legislature with such powers . . . The genius, the nature, and the spirit of our state governments, amount to a prohibition of such acts of legislation.

Sharply differing with Chase's opinion, Justice Iredell responded with what would become the typical positivistic rejoinder to such higher law reasoning:

If... [a] legislature... shall pass a law, within the general scope of [its] constitutional power, the court cannot pronounce it to be void, merely because it is, in their judgment, contrary to the principles of natural justice. The ideas of natural justice are regulated by no fixed standard; the ablest and the purest men have differed upon the subject; and all that the court could properly say, in such an event, would be, that the legislature (possessed of an equal right of opinion) had passed an act which, in the opinion of the judges, was inconsistent with the abstract principles of natural justice.

Too subjective to accomplish the consistency required of judicial decision, higher law reasoning also had the anti-democratic result of judges substituting their morality for the will of the people.[77] Iredell's position triumphed in the style of the Supreme Court's opinions. Henceforward, the justices made a point of writing their opinions as though they were deferring to legislative sovereignty. But, in substance, the Court often followed Chase's example, expanding its authority to overturn legislation that seemed contrary to traditional notions of justice, especially when contract or property were at stake.[78]

Dartmouth College (1819) offers a particularly revealing example both of the Court's willingness to "do justice" in certain circumstances and the Iredell-like gloss the Court would give its higher law rulings. The case considered whether a state legislature could take control of a private college established by grant of the British Crown. Finding Dartmouth College's founding charter to be a contract, the Court held that New Hampshire's bid to turn Dartmouth from a small, private liberal arts college into a public university violated the Constitution's freedom of contract clause ("no state shall pass... any law impairing the obligation of contracts"). Admitting that the framers did not have college charters in mind when they drafted the freedom of contract clause, Chief Justice Marshall's opinion is careful to describe the Court's expansive construction of the clause as guided by "law" as well as "justice." Justice Story's concurrence similarly tries to spin the Court's higher law extension of the freedom of contract clause as positivism, stating that "It is not for judges to listen to the voice of persuasive eloquence or popular appeal. We have nothing to do but to pronounce the law as we find it." Not entirely disingenuous about the Court's ethical concerns, Story's opinion also admits that the decision "is equally consonant with the common sense of mankind, and the maxims of eternal justice."[79]

The Court's ostensible deference to law camouflaged any emotion the brethren felt regarding the threat to Dartmouth. While certain sympathies may be inferred from Marshall's emphasis that Dartmouth was an eleemosynary and educational institution (i.e., an alma mater not unlike those attended by the justices), to gain a more direct view of the emotional drama behind the Court's Iredellean language, one has to turn to reports of Daniel Webster's famous oral argument on behalf of Dartmouth. Citing Samuel Chase's opinion in *Calder* as well as David Hume, Webster expressly invoked higher law, urging that laws impairing private contracts "are contrary to the first principles of the social compact."[80] But, perhaps more telling than the higher law substance of Webster's argument for our examination of later literary invocations of higher law was the overt pathos of his oratorical performance. In his peroration, Webster pulled out all the stops:

This, Sir, is my case. It is the case, not merely of that humble institution, it is the case of every college in our Land! It is more. It is the case of every eleemosynary institution throughout our country – of all those great charities founded by the piety of our ancestors, to alleviate human misery, and scatter blessings along the pathway of life! It is more! It is, in some sense, the case of every man among us who has property of which he may be stripped, for the question is simply this: Shall our State Legislatures be allowed to take that which is not their own, to turn it from its original use, and apply it to such ends or purposes as they in their discretion shall see fit?

At this point Webster paused. Looking directly at Chief Justice Marshall, he concluded:

Sir, you may destroy this little institution; it is weak, it is in your hands! I know it is one of the lesser lights in the literary horizon of our country. You may put it out! But, if you do so, you must carry through your work! You must extinguish, one after another, all those greater lights of science which, for more than a century, have thrown their radiance over our land! It is, sir, as I have said, a small college. And yet *there are those who love it*!

At this point, Webster broke down – "His lips quivered; his firm cheeks trembled with emotion; his eyes were filled with tears." He shook himself and continued: "Sir, I know not how others may feel but, for myself, when I see my Alma Mater surrounded, like Caesar in the senate-house, by those who are reiterating stab after stab, I would not, for this right hand, have her turn to me, and say, *Et tu quoque, mi fili! And thou too, my son!*"[81]

Webster's triumph was manifest in his audience's tears – the entire court, gallery as well as judges, was awash in tears. They had been "wrought up to the highest excitement," as Justice Story recalled years later. Even the usually cool Chief Justice's eyes were "suffused with tears." Story's retrospective description stresses the dramatic perfection of Webster's combination of higher law sentence and moral sense drama:

[There was] in his whole air & manner, in the fiery flashings of his eye, the darkness of his contracted brow, the sudden & flying flushes of his cheeks, the quivering & scarcely manageable movements of his lips, in the deep guttural tones of his voice, in the struggle to suppress his own emotions, in the almost convulsive clenchings of his hands without a seeming consciousness of the act, there was in these things what gave to his oratory an almost superhuman influence. There was solemn grandeur in every thought, mixed up with such pathetic tenderness & refinement, such beautiful allusion to the past, the present & future, such a scorn of artifice & rancor, such an appeal to all the moral & religious feelings of man, to the love of learning & literature, to the persuasive precepts of the law, to the reverence for justice, to all that can exalt the understanding & purify the heart, that it was impossible to listen without increasing astonishment at the profound reaches of the human intellect.[82]

Fiery, flashing eyes, clenched fists – these would become the telltale signs of higher law feeling in Stowe's *Uncle Tom's Cabin* and in approving descriptions of Frederick Douglass's antislavery oratory, the success of which was often measured in his auditors' tears. By inculcating in his audience the sympathetic feelings of the moral sense, Webster's performance certified its higher law argument.[83] Although belied by the Court's tone, putting Webster's performance together with the Court's favorable ruling suggests how stirring representations of higher law could, in certain circumstances, still move the judiciary to strike down legislation despite the Court's disclaimers in the slavery cases. Webster's ability as a politician and lawyer to oratorically incarnate what Story terms "the maxims of eternal justice" became legend. For many, Webster's dramatic performances embodied a continuation of the founders' highest aspirations, an appreciation making his fall in supporting the Fugitive Slave Law all the more precipitous.[84]

HIGHER LAW AND CONSENT

The version of higher law animating freedom of contract doctrine and literary arguments against slavery emphasizes the theme of consensual human relations. The significance of this accent on mutual assent as fundamental to a just society can be seen by comparing the views of Ainsworth Rand Spofford and George Fitzhugh. This stark contrast reveals with considerable theoretical lucidity how higher law constitutionalism was supposed to work and what it might produce. Spofford is usually remembered for his transformation of the Library of Congress into an institution of national significance. Librarian of Congress from 1864 to 1897, Spofford reconceived the Library on a grand scale as both the legislative library for Congress and the national library for the American people. His efforts made the Library the largest in the nation and resulted in the construction of what was then the largest library building in the world. In 1850, Spofford was a Cincinnati book-seller who had established contacts with intellectuals such as Emerson by arranging their lecture stops in the river city. Negative response to Seward's higher law speech led Spofford to write an anonymous pam-phlet, *The Higher Law Tried by Reason and Authority*, defending higher law jurisprudence with unusual lucidity and force. Spofford's argument de-cisively influenced Emerson and, through Emerson, reached many, in-cluding Charles Sumner, one of the leading lights of Reconstruction, and Moorfield Storey, the future President of the NAACP. As recognized by Emerson in a letter confessing his debt to Spofford, *The Higher Law Tried by Reason and Authority* offers an excellent analysis and summation of authority for consensual higher law jurisprudence. Clearly echoing the early republicans' higher law faith, Spofford's analysis clarifies certain elements of higher law and illuminates its more radical implications.

Spofford opens with an account of how the Fugitive Slave Law reani-mated the nation's ethical scrutiny of its legal system. Given the dramatic questions this law raised about the ethical character of the American peo-ple and their laws, "It is no wonder that you hear of it at every corner, that you read of it in every book and newspaper." It is "agitated in clubs and coffee-rooms, in the cars and on the steamboats, in the street, the store and the market-place." In Spofford's formulation, "Men are drawn to this subject by a triple cord of duty, of passion, and of interest," one hears the continuing influence of the founders' conceptions of public virtue, moral sense, and the interests of the individual. The Fugitive Slave Law, in Spofford's view, compels a reconsideration of the principles legitimat-ing American law. Working backward from legal edict, Spofford finds that "*foundation of all law is public opinion*," and that "ITS SOLE SANCTION IS ITS REASON AND JUSTICE." Our duty to obey the law derives neither from moral absolutes we divine in moments of private meditation nor from the political power of public opinion but from the conversation between the two – conscience and consent.[85]

For Spofford, higher lawmaking starts with inspirational concepts: "There is such a thing as Natural Right; there is a distinction between right and wrong anterior to Human Law"; and "some sentiment of justice is natural to man." We proceed from these beliefs to engage public opinion, attempting through debate and political action to sway the nation's ethical consensus. Success in shifting this higher law consensus will as a consequence shift the lower law of courts and legislatures. Civil disobedience, Spofford argues, often plays a key role in the process of higher lawmaking. Indeed, civil disobedience can be a necessary first step in a fundamental revision of the legal system. To urge obedience while a law is legislatively reversed is "common sense upside down." The political majority favoring the law is unlikely to undo its work, until compelled by "the irresistible voice of the people." Instead, "The natural method, that which history points out, and reason approves, and justice sanctions, is just precisely the opposite of this." First, the injustice of the law in question becomes "apparent to some." In reflection, these individuals try "the law by reason and conscience." Finding the law unethical, they resolve "not to obey it," and their disobedience excites "public opinion." All that can be offered to uphold the law is brought forth and "discussed and agitated." If the law begins to lose the hearts and minds of the public, "the friends of justice" begin "to outnumber its foes," then a "revolution" ensues ("something which never goes backward" and cannot be stopped). The law is disobeyed "again, and again, and still again," until it comes "to pass that the law [can] not be executed; – the law which cannot be executed, must . . . be repealed." Passive obedience while seeking repeal is merely a recipe for preserving the *status quo*. More must be done to rouse the public conscience and generate a new consensus. Tyranny, says Spofford, afflicts democracies in the form of unchecked majoritarianism; higher law reasoning and advocacy is a means of checking the otherwise unbridled injustices wrought by majorities.[86] Spofford's portrait of higher law as a politically engaged dialogue between conscience and consent should shatter the common caricatures reducing both higher law reasoning and transcendentalism to a kind of individual, private inspiration alien to the messy world of politics and leading to retreat and political quietism. Higher law inspiration does not cohere theoretically with retreat (any more than Emerson's notion of poetic inspiration coheres with silence); it mandates dialogue, debate, discussion, and political action in order to shift the operative consensus, giving legal concepts, such as individual rights, new content and new life.

In response to the argument that higher law reasoning unleashes an anarchic nightmare of subjective (and self-serving) determinations of the morality of laws, Spofford asserts that, because a consensus emerges out of the public trial of private inspiration, he and others can be confident that, in appraising a law unjust, it is heaven they hear and not the devil or their own self-interests. The process of higher law revision may begin with an individual pitted against society, but through the collective exercise of the community's moral sense, eventually the view of one becomes that of the few, and then the many. And it is the trajectory toward a new consensus about justice that validates the opinion of the one against the charge of delusion or relativism. For instance, as Spofford notes, the injustice of the Fugitive Slave Law is hardly the idle fancy of one or even a few: "In a wide intercourse with men of all modes of thinking at the north, we have yet to find one willing to say he would aid in executing the Fugitive Slave Law."[87]

Spofford's refusal to "deify the law" implies an incipient pragmatist jurisprudence: "Either a people must be governed by their own present sense of truth and justice, or they must not." "When will men learn that infallibility," Spofford asks, "is forever impossible to man; that there is, and can be, no stereotyped rule of action prescribed beforehand for all cases; that each day brings with it quite new and original relations, and must be judged on its own merits, or it will be misjudged?" In sum, Spofford's approach begins with moral imperatives but honestly confronts the facts that there are no bright-line, once-and-for-all answers to the question of what justice demands and that unjust laws are corrected and justice achieved only in the here-and-now of experiment, debate, and consensus formation. Putting principle, the initial impulse of one's present sense of right and wrong, into practice inevitably leads to an acceptance of mutability. By rejecting the idea that we are bound by the Constitution to act in ways we deem immoral, Spofford does not mean to suggest that the framers were immoral. That what offends now was tolerable to them, Spofford suggests, is irrelevant to the present moral consensus that decides the legitimacy of law. Spofford's argument, in effect, liberates each generation to create its own Constitution.[88]

Perhaps the most prescient of slavery's defenders, George Fitzhugh, articulated with considerable logical force how the higher law emphasis on consent renders nature irrelevant to the structure of society, consequently enabling such monstrous innovations as interracial marriage or polygamy. Born in 1806 to a prominent Virginia family, Fitzhugh was an autodidact, reading law and political philosophy in an eclectic and idiosyncratic fashion. Making his mark not as a lawyer but as a political writer, Fitzhugh contributed hundreds of articles to the *Richmond Enquirer*, *De Bow's Review*, the *Southern Literary Messenger*, *Lippincott's Magazine*, and the *Southern Magazine* of Baltimore. He is chiefly remembered today for his two proslavery books, *Sociology for the South, or The Failure of Free Society* (1854) and *Cannibals All! or, Slaves Without Masters* (1857).[89] Fitzhugh's proslavery polemic appalled abolitionists. Garrison termed it the "gospel according to Beelzebub."[90] Though somewhat nonplussed by his extravagant defense of slavery as the basis of all forms of social organization, Southerners predictably applauded Fitzhugh's writings. More recently his work has been recuperated primarily by historians, like Eugene Genovese, who value Fitzhugh's critical analysis of capitalism. A determined contrarian, Fitzhugh, as C. Vann Woodward puts it, "saw retrogression in what others hailed as progress, embraced moral pessimism in place of optimism, trusted intuition in preference to reason, always preferred inequality to equality, aristocracy to democracy, and almost anything – including slavery and socialism – to laissez faire capitalism."[91]

Fitzhugh penetrated the slavery debate's rhetorical muddle of race, rights, public virtue, and constitutional compacts to find an inexorable conflict between two models of society and government. The proslavery model was based on the *extrinsic* authority of God (or Nature) who (or which) had ordained inherent inequalities among humankind, and the antislavery model was based on the *intrinsic* authority of the consent of the polity's members. Any attempt to make the consensual version of higher law seem natural by figuring self-government, rights, and equality as the birthright of a mythic Anglo-Saxon people was, in Fitzhugh's analysis, a delusion. Natural equality was a contradiction in terms, and the logical thrust of republican social compact theory was to negate the relevance of race and other innate differences to the structure of law and society.[92] Conversely, endorsing slavery on the basis of natural inequalities between the races logically entailed an acceptance of authoritarian and hierarchical legal and social structures wherever one found inequality. For Fitzhugh, the choice was clear. One either saw the existing inequalities of power (e.g., that men are physically stronger than women) as the edicts of a higher power (God or Nature) predetermining one's political and social structures, or one decided that, despite these apparent inequalities, humankind could arrange itself and order its relations as it saw fit by the contractual mechanisms of consent-based political theory.[93]

In keeping with its distinguished lineage ("Jefferson's 'fundamental principles' and Mr. Seward's 'higher law' mean the same thing"), Fitzhugh characterized the antebellum rebirth of higher law as "the great moral and intellectual movement of the day."[94] The thrust of this consensual version of higher law was not merely to "remedy and remove" slavery but to eradicate all hierarchical forms of social and political authority. Such higher law reasoning works, according to Fitzhugh, by a process of sentimental or moral sense analogy. A sympathetic "feeling" for the slave (induced more by Northern fiction than by real acquaintance with the generally benevolent circumstances of slave existence) leads to questions about the institution of slavery. Feelings for the slave metamorphose into sympathy for "wives, children, apprentices, wards, sailors, soldiers, and hirelings." Higher law advocates "begin to discover that the principle and practice of slavery is found interwoven with all human relations and human institutions," and, "with unflinching philanthropy," they resolve "to 'cut sheer asunder' all those relations," thereby threatening all forms of social and political stability with ongoing or recurrent "social revolution."[95] Because "Men change the fashion of their thoughts, as women change the color and the form of their bonnets," consensual higher law reasoning was as frightening for Fitzhugh as it was for Chief Justice Roger Taney and as it apparently continues to be for jurists like Antonin Scalia (hence, Taney's and Scalia's shared hope that the Supreme Court not be made the handmaiden of fashionable shifts of public opinion).[96]

The alternative to the anarchic unraveling of American society, for Fitzhugh, consisted in forms of human association based on and reflecting the naturally unequal distribution of power, such as slavery, marriage, property, parental authority, and the family. The family's innately hierarchical structure, with the husband and father at the head, formed the model for all natural and just forms of government in which the weak were protected by the strong. The naturalness of the family's hierarchical arrangement disproved the social compact theory of Locke and his heirs: "Fathers do not derive their authority, as heads of families, from the consent of wife and children." Social contracts, equality, natural rights, and the consent of the governed, as well as the right of revolution to sweep away corrupt human institutions, were the destructive fantasies of abstract or visionary thinkers, such as Jefferson and Seward, who knew only how to tear down, not how to construct, a society. Real prophets, like Moses, built a just social order based upon the natural fact of inequality and the understanding that justice only comes in the paternalistic form of the strong protecting the weak.[97]

Fitzhugh called for conservatives to push back against the rising tide of higher law advocacy: "We must imitate their zeal and activity." Sensing that higher law was most potently advanced in literature and in the

press, he insisted that Southern courts "put down such presses as the
Tribune and the Liberator, to gag Parker and Beecher, negro Redmond,
and the wise women" and called for an "honest, unbiased account"
of slavery and the slave trade to counteract "Dred or the Log Cabin"
and "the incendiary disunion tendencies of those popular works." In
Fitzhugh's view, the racial resemblance felt between the white reader
and such slave characters as George and Eliza Harris in *Uncle Tom's
Cabin* was particularly likely to inflame higher law objections to slavery.
Counteracting such affecting literary representations was so manifestly
important as to convince Southerners, Fitzhugh hoped, to abandon race
in their defense of slavery.[98]

A POLITICAL BENCHMARK FOR HIGHER LAW IN THE 1850S

Comparing Spofford and Fitzhugh usefully clarifies the theoretical stakes
of higher law, but we also need to observe the messier, more mongrel manifestations of higher law in antebellum politics, such as the mix of morality
and race in the speeches of Clay, Calhoun, Webster, and Seward on the
Compromise of 1850. A brief comparison of these speeches will help
us to measure the degree to which Stowe, Sumner, Emerson, Douglass
and others moved in the higher law direction Spofford outlined and
Fitzhugh feared: toward an anti-identitarian discourse of conscience and
consent.[99]

The first of these famous addresses, Henry Clay's speech of February 5
and 6, 1850 in support of his compromise bill seeks common ground between the sections in a conflation of morality and kinship. For Clay, the
slavery conflict is a family matter in two senses. First, it is a point of
dispute between members of the same national family. Northern interference with slavery is a breach of "fraternal connection" ("it is a mark
of no good brotherhood, of no kindness . . . that a man from a slave State
cannot now, in a degree of safety, travel in a free State with his servant").
Second, slavery is itself, in Clay's view, a familial relation under attack by
Northern fanatics luring "family servants from the service of their owners." Clay recalls "an instance in my own family" in which "the seduced
slave" implored her former mistress "to furnish her the means of getting
back from the state of freedom into which she had been seduced, into
the state of slavery, in which she was much more happy." Figuring this
interference as a seduction drama, with the slave cast as a rustic virgin
tempted by worldly Northerners to her demise in the free states, Clay
turns the trope of seduction against antislavery advocates, who invoked

it to condemn the sexual predations of slaveholders, and implies that the abolitionist and the Lovelace-like seducer are connected by a cosmopolitan perspective inimical to family stability. At the emotional climax of his speech, Clay pleads for the preservation of the Constitution and the Union as a kind of sacred marriage: "Like another of the great relations of private life, it was a marriage that no human authority can dissolve or divorce the parties from." Marriage relations are, of course, contractual, but marriage is a contract with a difference: once this contract is sealed, it becomes like a blood relation, permanent, non-consensual, hierarchic. Consent becomes nature in Clay's figuration of the national charter as a marriage, and Clay's trope suggests a happy national family, with a common ancestry and a shared destiny, beset by zealots who would deform this unity with abstract conceptions of consensual relations not bounded by blood.[100]

Rejecting both Clay's compromise and sentimental allusions to kinship and familial duty, Calhoun's address on March 4, 1850 takes a cool, positivistic approach to the sectional crisis. For Calhoun, the Constitution is a contract between sovereign powers. One party to the bargain, the North, simply wants to breach this agreement, and the motive for this breach lies in the North's will to power. Already the stronger of the two sections, the North wants to reduce the South to permanent subjection, and agitates the slave question in order to add free states (e.g., California), shifting the balance of federal power permanently in its favor. Thus, while important as the mechanism of this conflict, slavery turns out not to be the primary issue. In the best case, the Constitution functions as a permanent bargain adjusting and protecting the self-interests of these sovereign powers from the ravages of open and continuing political competition. Absent such protection, in Calhoun's view, the South has no reason to continue in the Union.[101]

Daniel Webster's March 7 rejoinder, "The Constitution and the Union," condemns the threat of secession as a betrayal of family ties. Speaking "not as a Massachusetts man, nor as a Northern man, but as an American," Webster asks, "What am I to be? An American no longer? . . . Why, Sir, our ancestors, our fathers and our grandfathers would cry out shame upon us." For Webster as for Clay, our "attachment to the Constitution" cannot be separated from feelings of "brotherly love."[102] This sentiment runs through much of Webster's oratory, which often features the figure of the nation as family. Rejecting Hayne's (and Calhoun's) description of the Union as a confederation of "sovereign states" and the Constitution as their contract, Webster's celebrated

"Second Reply to Hayne" contends that a single people, not states, forged the Revolution, declared independence in 1776, and formed a "perpetual union" in the Constitution. Thus, Webster is entitled to claim kinship not only with Northern patriots but also with those of the South: "I claim them for countrymen, one and all, the Laurenses, the Rutledges, the Pinckneys, the Sumpters, the Marions, *Americans* all, whose fame is no more to be hemmed in by State lines, than their talents and patriotism were capable of being circumscribed within the same narrow limits."[103] In his 1812 "Address before the Washington Benevolent Society," Webster describes how we become better, nobler, and more deserving of emulation by our children, by emulating our ancestors: "It is in the power of every generation to make themselves, in some degree partakers in the deeds, and in the fame of their ancestors, by adopting their principles, and studying their examples." While there are many illustrious examples of heroism in world history, our hearts guide us to an imitation of those moral exemplars we most resemble, those of our fathers. Wielding the myth of a shared Anglo-Saxon identity to reunite the founders' fractious heirs, in "The Completion of the Bunker Hill Monument" (1843), Webster styles the differences between Northern and Southern colonies as "only enough to create a pleasing variety in the midst of a general family resemblance."[104]

Webster's rhetorical investment in the figure of the national family helps to account for the contradiction between his unequivocal assertion in the March 7 speech that the duty to return fugitive slaves is indisputable "as a question of morals and a question of conscience" and his private condemnation of slavery as an evil "founded only in the power of the strong over the weak." Slavery may be a moral blot ultimately unworthy of the American people, but the moral and affective basis of the Constitution and the Union is national kinship. The feelings and fact of shared kinship symbolized by the Constitution, in Webster's view, countermand abstract or "fanatical idea[s]" of granting civil recognition to blacks who do not, by definition, bear any resemblance to the national family. While hoping that the "mild influence" of Christianity would eventually lead the Anglo-American tribe to eliminate slavery, Webster conceives of direct intervention on behalf of slaves, such as disobeying the Fugitive Slave Law, as an unthinkable preference of the moral claims of strangers to those of one's own family.[105]

In reply, Seward brusquely dismisses Webster's characterization of the unquestionable moral propriety of the Fugitive Slave Law, yet he also describes the national crisis occasioned by slavery in terms every bit as tribal, organic, and familial as those used by Clay and Webster:

The population of the United States consists of native Caucasian origin, and Exotics [immigrants] of the same derivation. The Native mass rapidly assimilates to itself and absorbs the Exotic, and these therefore constitute one homogenous people. The African race, bond and free, and the Aborigines, savage and civilized, being incapable of such assimilation and absorption, remain distinct, and owing to their peculiar condition constitute inferior masses, and may be regarded as accidental, if not disturbing political forces. The ruling Homogenous family was planted at first on the Atlantic Shore, and following an obvious law is seen continually and rapidly spreading itself westward year by year, subduing the Wilderness and the Prairie, and thus extending this great political community, which as fast as it advances, breaks into distinct States for municipal purposes only, while the whole constitutes one entire contiguous and compact nation . . . The question now arises, Shall this one great People, having a common origin, a common language, a common religion, common sentiments, interests, sympathies and hope remain one political State, one Nation, one Republic? or shall it be broken into two conflicting and probably hostile Nations or Republics?"[106]

What sets Seward's invocation of national identity apart from those of Clay and Webster is his refusal to fuse morality and kinship. Unlike Clay and Webster, Seward keeps his familial and ascriptive treatment of national identity discrete from his account of the immorality of the Fugitive Slave Law, leaving ambiguous what he sees as the relation between the two. While for Clay and Webster the emotional power of a family resemblance within the Union mandates a public morality tending to the interests of the tribe first and last, Seward seems to derive from this family resemblance a kind of confidence that extending justice to the enslaved is not only right but does not threaten to dissolve the national identity or the continuities of tradition that seem to make self-rule and moral consensus possible. Whatever comfort he derives from images of national unity and a shared heritage, Seward's belief that the Constitution must be construed in deference to "public conscience" locates the higher law norms of justice in the fluidities of consensus not in the mythic fixities of blood.

These four speeches can be arranged on a scale with power at one end and consent at the other. Calhoun's vision of the Constitution as a contract between sovereign powers belongs at the first extreme. By focusing on power, Calhoun achieves a logical consistency missing in the other speeches. Sacrificing coherence for emotional appeal, Clay and Webster conflate ethics and identity, obscuring thereby the importance of either power or consent to the course and content of American law. Morality, however, cannot both be a matter of choice and a matter about which one has no choice. By conceiving that one's moral obligations begin at home and then open outward, Webster would avoid this contradiction, but his prioritization does not answer when one can or should choose the moral claims of the stranger to those of the family or when the perspective of the stranger reveals that the supposed moral claims of the family are false. Webster's March 7 address implicitly answers "never" to such questions, reducing morality to blood and erasing the possibility of consensual change. Seward merits the place of honor at the other extreme from Calhoun. In describing the constitutionally relevant moral consensus as cosmopolitan in perspective and scope, Seward glimpses a jurisprudence not bound by identity. Though he does not dispense with the opposition of "us and them," Seward goes so far as to indicate that American justice must be measured by its universalist approach to the claims of the outsider.

The rhetorical prominence of the national family in the Fugitive Slave Law debate reflects the era's propensity to explain political and social relations by reference to race. One of the precursors for nineteenth-century American racialism was Johann Gottfried von Herder's romantic conception that each race has its own genius, its own particular perspective on the universal truths of existence, and that no one of these vantages or races is better than the others. Samuel Fleischacker aptly describes Herder's view as a modified cultural relativism in which universal truths are known only through dialogue between and among the various peoples' diverse perpectives.[107] While faithfully registered in W. E. B. DuBois's notions of racial genius in *The Souls of Black Folk* (1903) and "The Conservation of Races" (1897), misprisions of Herder's pluralist notions of identity fed the triumphal Anglo-Saxonism marking the slavery debate.[108] As Reginald Horsman points out, by 1850 the mythic identity of American Anglo-Saxons as a separate, innately superior people had become a fundamental part of American political rhetoric.[109]

White supremacy received scientific validation from such ethnological texts as Samuel George Morton's *Crania Americana* (1839). Morton contended that the discrepancies he observed in his examination of the world's largest scientific collection of human skulls did not comport with theories of the unity of human kind.[110] Josiah Nott and George Gliddon, two of Morton's best-known followers, contended that "History and observation both teach that . . . the Mongol, the Malay, the Indian, and the Negro, are now and have been in all ages and places inferior to the

Caucasian." According to Nott, "[n]one but the fair-skinned types of mankind have been able hitherto, to realize, in peaceful practice, the old Germanic system [of self-rule] described by Tacitus." By contrast, unable to "reason," the "*Dark*-skinned races" "are only fit for military governments."[111] John Van Evrie, a Northern physician, similarly contended that the Caucasian's mental superiority equipped him for both popular government and the domination of inferior peoples. Van Evrie devotes a chapter of his popular *Negroes and Negro "Slavery"* (1853) to arguing that the Negro's incapacity to speak the white man's language proves his God-given political disability, an assertion highlighting the scientific as well as political relevance of black literacy exemplified by Frederick Douglass and others. Language is so deeply rooted in racial identity that the Africans of Haiti, Van Evrie predicts, will inevitably and spontaneously relapse "into their native African tongue." Unlike Fitzhugh, who rejected the liberal higher law notions of the Declaration of Independence altogether, advocates of a *herrenvolk* democracy, such as Van Evrie, Nott, Gliddon, and Chief Justice Roger Taney, infer the word "white" in the phrase "All men are created equal."[112] Because the darker races lack the rationality essential to consensual political and social relations, all non-hierarchical, consensual relations must be limited to those within the white racial family, consigning non-whites to authoritarian forms of government and society.

The antislavery rhetoric of Seward and other Republicans did not escape the era's ubiquitous racism. For example, Francis P. Blair, one of the proponents of the Republican colonization plan (which gained the support of such early black nationalists as Martin Delany, Henry Highland Garnet, and H. Ford Douglas), wrote in 1858 that "It is certainly the wish of every patriot that all within the limits of our Union should be homogeneous in race and of our own blood." Yet, while Republicans often made political "appeals which smacked of racism," it would be a mistake, as Eric Foner notes, to collapse their gestures toward conscience and consent into a hypocritical cover for racism simply because we find the tropes and themes of racial identity in the same text. The Republicans did recognize "the essential humanity of the Negro, and demanded protection for certain basic rights which the Democrats denied him," and, flawed though their policy was, "the Republican stand on race" was in advance of "the prevailing opinion of the 1850's."[113]

The influential political theory of Francis Lieber furnishes a revealing instance of the way higher law reasoning could coexist with and exceed racialist notions. Like many in his generation, Lieber's views on slavery and the Constitution shifted during the 1850s. Initially repelled by the cavalier disregard of the rule of law evinced by some abolitionists, as the conflict over slavery intensified in the 1850s, Lieber increasingly moved toward the position of such radical republicans as Charles Sumner and Frederick Douglass. Lieber castigated Taney's *Dred Scott* opinion as "illegal, unjurisdictional, immoral and disgraceful," and, when the Virginia Supreme Court drew support from the *Dred Scott* decision by saying that a slave had no civil rights, Lieber raged that the decision "crie[d] to the high heavens for signal punishment." In July, 1860, he suggested in moral terms that would have appealed to Flannery O'Connor, "What we Americans stand in need of is a daily whipping"; in the past, when other nations had defied "right, morality, and justice, God in his mercy has sometimes condescended to smite them." Rejecting the notion that law could be explained simply in terms of power, Lieber insisted that liberty exists only "where the minority is protected, although the majority rule." Protecting the fundamental rights of minority members from the majority's democratic power was, for Lieber, one of those norms of fair play and justice so basic as to be plausibly deemed a matter of universal consensus.[114]

Lieber's argument for free trade offers insight into the fluid and contractual nature of his higher law conceptions:

There is no such thing as inherent value. Value requires a thing desired, and a person desiring. Value is a relation. Gold has no inherent value for the starving man on a wreck: a crumb of bread would be preferred by him ... Free trade is nothing more than protection against obstruction. The true name for the protectionist would be obstructionist ... Rapid circulation promotes civilization; and as civilization advances, it requires circulation increased in extent and in rapidity. Man removes natural obstacles by roads, canals, navigation, and he creates greater ones by protective tariffs ... Exchange is an exclusive characteristic of man, and a basis of his highest interests and aspirations.[115]

Lieber's political economy replaces notions of inherent value created by external authority (God, Nature, or Tradition) with the more mutable values created through circulation and trade. Communication, travel, commercial agreement, and civilization are connected in an expanding matrix of human interrelations through which definitions of value are constantly created and modified. Commercial exchange, in other words, serves as a synecdoche for a broader system of defining rights, social and civil recognition, and reciprocal obligations through a process of increasingly cosmopolitan intercourse and agreement.

Given the emphasis on consent and exchange in his conception of value, we may well pause at some of Lieber's descriptions of Anglo-American justice:

We belong to the Anglican race, which carries Anglican principles and liberty over the globe ... We belong to that race whose obvious task it is, among other proud and sacred tasks, to rear and spread civil liberty over vast regions in every part of the earth, on continent and isle. We belong to that tribe which alone has the word Self-Government ...

The myth of "Anglican" identity threatens here to dissolve Lieber's consensual vision of higher law and the protection of the minority in a wash of blood and racial heritage, but, as in the case of Seward's higher law speech, the substance of Lieber's jurisprudence does not collapse into his racial figures. Though he accepts that the tradition of self-government belonged at least initially to a particular people and paints that historical narrative in the warm hues of Herderean racialism, Lieber's belief in the virtue of that jurisprudence does not depend upon the "Anglican" race's inherent superiority.[116] Like Herder, Lieber rejects the notion of racial superiority: "We have nowadays always the Caucasian race in our mouths. If that *race* is so preeminently superior, how did it happen that civilization flourished on the Ganges thousands of years before the Caucasian race began to work itself out of the mire of barbarism?"[117] There is a revealing kinship between Lieber's views and those of Albert Gallatin. Gallatin's 1847 pamphlet *Peace with Mexico* distinguished between superior institutions and racial superiority. He recognized the former but not the latter. In Gallatin's vision of the United States as redeemer nation, its mission

is to improve the state of the world, to be the "model republic," to show that men are capable of governing themselves, and that this simple and natural form of government is that also which confers most happiness on all, is productive of the greatest development of the intellectual faculties, above all, that which is attended with the highest standard of private and political virtue and morality.[118]

As immigrants, Lieber and Gallatin tended to take a comparative view of the contributions of a particular people. Thus, the excellence they attribute to Anglo-American jurisprudence, if it is to be meaningfully deemed an excellence, has to transcend the parochialisms of race and nation, offering a better form of justice to global culture.

The degree to which the substance of Lieber's notions of justice surpasses the hereditary figures he uses to describe their evolution is indicated by his objection to Taney's *Dred Scott* opinion. In contrast to Taney, who claims his opinion is driven by history (the proslavery consensus of the founding generation), Lieber celebrates the fact that Americans "conceive of the rights of the citizen more in the abstract" than the English, who slavishly follow historical practice. The *Dred Scott* holding that "people of color . . . are not citizens" reflects the fact that "the first basis of all justice, sympathy, is wanting between the two races." In Lieber's view, we properly "conceive of the rights of the citizen in the abstract . . . as attributes of his humanity" not as the property of race or tribe. Race impedes justice, which is a matter of "abstract" (i.e., anti-identitarian) human relations founded upon mutual sympathy.[119]

It was not a coincidence that, as higher law constitutionalism crested in the 1850s and 1860s, race thinking reached new levels of intensity. The intensity of each reflected the pressure of the other. Both can be felt in the higher law tableaux of Harriet Beecher Stowe's antislavery fiction, where figurations of conscience and consent contend with notions of resemblance. For many antebellum Americans on both sides of the slavery question, Stowe's antislavery fiction was most impressive for its definitive representation of the issues and the people involved in the great moral/political contest over slavery and the Constitution. Anticipating Elizabeth Fox-Genovese's comment that certain "texts have the power to crystallize the pervasive discourses of any society and thus to shape their development," Mary Chesnut, the Southern diarist, considered Stowe's novel as epitomizing and mobilizing an irrepressible antislavery trend in the spirit of the times. Southerners might have seen that slavery was doomed, Chesnut observed, if they had "read less of Mr. Calhoun's works" and read such "signs of the times" as *Uncle Tom's Cabin*.[120] Writing from South Carolina, Francis Lieber commented to a friend that "'Uncle Tom's Cabin'" sells here rapidly . . . Our papers have coined a word – *Uncle-Tomitude* – to sneer at the sympathy with the African. The fact is not a bad proof of the hold which the book takes." George Fitzhugh, as we have seen, worried that the South had not produced any imaginative literature sufficiently gripping to counteract *Uncle Tom's Cabin* and *Dred*. Salmon Chase, future Chief Justice of the Supreme Court, noted in his diary the effect *Uncle Tom's Cabin* had on him: "Uncle Tom's Cabin – What a character & the book what a sermon! I cannot read it without tears. Surely it is 'tuba, mirum spargens sonum.' [Bugle, spread the wonderful sound]." Chase found in the novel an accurate typology of national character, such as the type of the cruel plantation mistress whose cultured manners hide her moral degeneracy. Eliza Harris's hair-raising flight across the Ohio river, leaping desperately from ice floe to ice floe with the slave hunters at her back and baby at her breast, provided an unforgettably exciting and romantic picture of heroic fugitive, and the dramatic versions of Stowe's novel featured it as one of their show-stopping spectacles.[121]

Eliza's plight offered a kind of narrative proof that American law, as William Seward had argued, had gone off its proper foundation. Eliza's escape, the revolutionary fervor of her husband, George Harris, and Uncle Tom's apotheosis as a Christ figure became icons of higher law constitutionalism, presenting conceptions of citizenship and justice suffused with feelings of compassion and empathy. The next chapter examines Stowe's contribution to higher law constitutionalism, considering in particular how and to what degree Stowe's figurations of higher law are constricted by their fixity and typicality.[122] By comparing the firm outlines of Stowe's higher law images to the more abstract and protean presentations of higher law reasoning in Emerson, Douglass, and Sumner, one can glimpse the struggle to divest the processes of conscience and consent from the prerequisite of resemblance, a struggle within the intertwined literary and legal imaginations of citizenship and justice in nineteenth-century America.

CHAPTER 2

The look of higher law: Harriet Beecher Stowe's antislavery fiction

Appalled by the kidnappings of African Americans in the wake of the Fugitive Slave Law and with few alternatives as a woman for voicing her opposition, Harriet Beecher Stowe turned to fiction as a way to change the direction of the nation's law by prodding its conscience.[1] Stowe's sense of the political power of literature is expressed in a letter she wrote to Lord Denman (formerly the Lord Chief Justice of England), urging the English to take up literary cudgels against American slavery: "In your reviews[,] in your literature, you can notice & hold up before the world, those awful facts, which but for you, they would scornfully go on denying as they have done." Modestly admitting that law was "not her work" or her "field," Stowe, nonetheless, was sure that amateur or literary jurisprudential efforts could lead to institutional revision: "It seems to me, that this tremendous story cannot be told in the civilised world, without forcing attention."[2]

Stowe's belief in the power of women's literary efforts, in particular, to mold public opinion and shape public policy was not without precedent. Lydia Maria Child's *An Appeal in Favor of that Class of Americans Called Africans* (1833) helped to convince future senators Charles Sumner and Henry Wilson, as well as Wendell Phillips, William Ellery Channing, and Thomas Wentworth Higginson of the injustice of slavery and racial discrimination. Child described slavery as an "ugly edifice" "built of rotten timbers," "stand[ing] on slippery sands," which, "if the loud voice of public opinion could be made to reverberate through its dreary chambers," would "fall, never to rise again." Slavery was immoral, in Child's view, because it defied the contractual principle legitimating property. While "[a]ll ideas of property are properly founded upon the mutual agreement of the human race," "[i]n slavery there is no *mutual* agreement. The negro has no voice in the matter – no alternative is presented to him – no bargain is made." Child's depiction of the conflict between slavery and the American republic's consensual basis helped to lay the groundwork for the following decades of antislavery advocacy, including *Uncle Tom's Cabin* and *Dred*.[3]

Given Stowe's aims, the political orientation of most evaluations of her antislavery novels is hardly surprising. Frederick Douglass appreciated *Uncle Tom's Cabin*, despite its colonization theme, for the way its searing images galvanized antislavery feeling in the North. Martin Delany attacked the novel's racialism as fueling the worst tendencies in American politics. As Robert Levine has shown, Douglass and Delany articulated their emerging political rift in terms of their divergent reactions to *Uncle Tom's Cabin*. In response to those charging Stowe with polluting art with politics, a review of *Dred* praised the novelist for showing the novel to be "so potent an instrument for doing good . . . we cannot afford to give it up." A Richmond *Enquirer* review of George Fitzhugh's *Cannibals All!* rued the fact that, though "In every mode of argument the champions of the South excel," "they have produced no romance quite equal to 'Uncle Tom's Cabin.'" Denouncing the attempt to put the South on trial by "'higher law' men . . . in their Uncle Tom's Cabins, pulpits, schools and rostrums," George Frederick Holmes feared the success Stowe's images were having in framing the national debate and providing the symbols and vocabulary of the constitutional struggle over slavery.[4]

More recent assessments of Stowe's antislavery fiction have similarly centered on its political value. Ann Douglas, for instance, attributes to Stowe a regressive sentimentalism that "flatters [its] audience," "does not quicken their aspirations," and produces such comforting camp icons of mass consumerism as the "Teen Angel" and Miss America. At best, Stowe's sentiment, in Douglas's view, "provides a way to protest a power to which one has already in part capitulated." Jane Tompkins, by contrast, characterizes Stowe's fiction as "a monumental effort to reorganize culture from the woman's point of view." Domestic fiction, such as *Uncle Tom's Cabin*, offers "a critique of American society far more devastating that any delivered by better-known critics such as Hawthorne and Melville." At the conclusion of *The Plight of Feeling*, Julia Stern extols Stowe's fiction for its "enormous social force . . . and its (symbolic) connection to the drafting of the Emancipation Proclamation (1862) and to the Thirteenth Amendment to the Constitution, which abolished slavery (1865)."[5]

One tendency in such contemporary criticism is to praise Stowe's fiction to the extent that it privileges the particular not the universal, the embodied not the abstract, the feminine not the masculine, emotion not reason, sympathy not law, and so forth. For instance, in "The Ecstasies of Sentimental Wounding in *Uncle Tom's Cabin*," Marianne Noble characterizes Stowe's deployment of "the sentimental wound," a bodily experience of anguish caused by identification with the pain of another, as "a critique of abstract, disembodied notions of personhood." The terms of Noble's approval would have been strange to the author herself and her antebellum admirers, who would also have been baffled by Noble's assertion that "It is fundamentally impossible to bridge the gap separating one person's experience from another's."[6] Regardless of whether or in what particular circumstances this contention may be true, our notions of justice, for Stowe, Douglass, Sumner, and others in the political antislavery movement, impel us to attempt such bridging. Even if the experiences of different individuals remain in some sense or for some purposes particular and discrete, we must be capable of translating perspectives, interests, beliefs, and inclinations if our political and legal order is to attain to anything better than the rule of the strong.[7]

Harriet Beecher Stowe's images of good-hearted and law-abiding Northerners confronted by weary and shivering fugitives in *Uncle Tom's Cabin* were intended to and did bring home for many of her readers the momentous contest between conscience and law created by the Fugitive Slave Law. Northern whites prepared to tolerate this evil so long as it was kept at a distance – the wickedness of a distant province – were appalled at the idea of being legally coerced into participating in it. Critical characterizations of Stowe's antislavery fiction as dividing sentiment and law, heart and head, a slave's particular suffering and general ethical norms tend to obscure her contribution to higher law jurisprudence.[8] Putting Stowe's notion of sympathy back into its constitutional context makes it difficult to read her as privileging the particular over the universal and the heart to the exclusion of the head. Her emotionally charged tableaux are designed to enlist our sympathies (e.g., Eliza Harris's escape across the Ohio river or Uncle Tom's martyrdom) in a general recognition of the legal claims of black Americans to simple justice and citizenship by reason of their moral agency.[9]

Reconnected with the antislavery constitutionalism shaping and being shaped by her writing, a tension emerges not between sentiment and law but between identity and conscience in Stowe's higher law images. For Stowe as for the founding fathers, the feeling of resemblance plays a key role in our emotional intuition of justice.[10] Stowe's higher law tableaux work to inculcate in the reader a feeling that he or she resembles the fugitive slave as well as the sympathetic Northerner aiding the fugitive.

Such resemblance requires either careful modulation of description so that the black American's features and lineaments can produce a sense of partial recognition (e.g., Eliza Harris's polished manners, proper speech, and light complexion) or the presence of some emotional feature deemed inherent in human nature (e.g., Eliza's maternal devotion). Of course, by accepting the necessity of resemblance, Stowe's abolitionist images echo the proslavery contention that blacks do not sufficiently resemble white Americans for civic inclusion. In addition, Stowe's images of the fugitive slave and the good Northerner risk framing slavery not as a matter of consensual ethics but of paternalistic ethics – the obligation of the powerful to care for the weak – calling to mind the famous antislavery image of the shackled slave on his knees in a posture of supplication, asking "Am I not a brother?" While his query claims a kind of elemental civic membership, his posture suggests that what he needs is protection not partnership.[11] What bothers many of Stowe's contemporary readers may well have less to do with her use of sentiment than the anti-consensual aspects of her depictions of justice.

The promise, limitations, and influence of Stowe's visualizations of higher law form the subject of this chapter. Though circumscribed by the typicality of her heroes and undermined by her lack of confidence in consensual models of law and society, Stowe's fiction portrays black Americans as moral agents, and her recognition of moral agency and heroism in such different characters as Uncle Tom, George Harris, and Harry Gordon opens the door to an interracial polity. Examining the tensions in Stowe's higher law images between identity and conscience and between paternalist and consensual ethics also provides, by contrast, a clearer view of the ephemeral but important cosmopolitan thread in the higher law approaches of such figures as Emerson and Douglass, where consent replaces identity and the universal terms of ethics and self-government seem to be severed from supposed inherencies of race.

STOWE'S HIGHER LAW PICTURES

The crux of the higher law crisis created by the Fugitive Slave Law flashed on Stowe in an argument with a friend, Professor Thomas Upham. Stowe challenged Upham whether "he would obey the law supposing a fugitive came to him." Upham "hemed & hawed," and, when a fugitive appeared at his backdoor the next day, he gave the fugitive money and provisions. This biographical detail illuminates two of Stowe's primary aims in writing *Uncle Tom's Cabin*: first, to convince Northerners that the

Fugitive Slave Law had made the conflict between the law of slavery and higher law their problem, and second, to force this realization home by means of vivid images that would in effect place a fugitive at the door of every reader, challenging the reader to choose between lower and higher law. She compared her method to "that of a painter" and described her goal as presenting slavery "in the most lifelike and graphic manner possible." Stowe found that the visual potential of literature gave it an edge over political argument: "There is no arguing with pictures, and everybody is impressed by them, whether they mean to be or not."[12]

As she intuited would be the case, the broad cultural and political appeal of her antislavery fiction derives largely from the iconic power of her higher law images. Her characters, their appearances, actions, and words, are types of justice and injustice, whose clear and firm outlines and details are quickly and unmistakably interpreted for higher law significance. The moral pattern of compassion and Christian forbearance embodied in Uncle Tom is set against the positivist type of unregulated power represented by Simon Legree. The dramatic interactions Stowe stages between such typical characters are designed to trigger in the reader an intuition of slavery's moral and legal invalidity. This intuition will seem conclusive and unimpeachable to the reader not because it is based on superior argument and evidence but because it springs unbidden from the well of sympathy innate to human nature.

Stowe's notion of sympathy derived from the moral sense philosophy central to the founders' republicanism. Sympathy was an important part of the emotional responsiveness, shared by the ploughman and the professor, as Jefferson put it, which authoritatively discerned the ethical norms upon which law must be based to be legitimate, but which, in any event, must be obeyed if one is to live morally. Stowe famously posits the authority of this form of moral intuition in the "Afterword" to *Uncle Tom's Cabin*: "[W]hat can any individual do? . . . They can see to it that they feel right. An atmosphere of sympathetic influence encircles every human being; and the man or woman who feels strongly, healthily, and justly on the great interest of humanity, is a constant benefactor to the human race. See then to your sympathies in this matter!" Stowe became acquainted with moral sense theory through her avid reading of British sentimental fiction, such as Samuel Richardson's *Pamela* and *Clarissa*, novels dramatizing how the psychology of feeling directs ethical behavior. Under the guidance of her sister, Catherine, Stowe studied such moral sense philosophers as Joseph Butler. Stowe carefully read Butler's *The Analogy of Religion, Natural and Revealed, to the Constitution and Course of*

Nature (1736), abstracting each chapter before teaching it to her pupils at Catherine's school in Hartford, Connecticut.[13]

In *The Analogy*, Butler distinguishes between the religious commands we obey because they are perceived to be right in themselves and those we obey because a superior power, God, requires it: "Moral precepts are precepts, the reasons of which we see; positive precepts are precepts, the reasons of which we do not see. Moral duties arise out of the nature of the case itself, prior to external command. Positive duties do not arise out of the nature of the case, but from external command." Normally, we obey both types of religious injunction, but situations can arise where moral and positive commands conflict so that "it is impossible to obey both." In such cases, the moral command trumps the positive injunction. Like other moral sense philosophers, Butler considered the very existence of a moral sense discerning right from wrong to be the best evidence of its preeminent authority: "the moral law is . . . written upon our hearts; interwoven into our very nature. And this is a plain intimation of the Author of it, which is to be preferred, when they interfere." In "Of the Nature of Virtue," an essay appended to *The Analogy*, Butler describes the moral sense as the highest principle of human nature, uniting head and heart, reason and intuition, and governing such less noble aspects as hunger and fear. The truths comprehended by this faculty of moral cognition, "whether called conscience, moral reason, moral sense, or divine reason; whether considered as a sentiment of the understanding, or as a perception of the heart," comprise the fundamental moral authority for "all civil constitutions."[14]

The spontaneous eruption of sympathy in a reader confronting a telling image of the clash between the Fugitive Slave Law and the higher law of Christian charity, for Stowe, was a sure signal of the statute's invalidity and the entitlement of the enslaved to certain fundamental human rights. This sympathetic response should lead to dialogue, moral consensus, and a revision of the lower law so as to accord with the higher. In her depiction of the debate between Senator and Mrs. Bird in *Uncle Tom's Cabin*, Stowe illustrates how this process works. The scene begins with a description of the Birds' home: "The light of the cheerful fire shone on the rug and carpet of a cosey parlor, and glittered on the sides of the tea-cups and well-brightened teapot, as Senator Bird was drawing off his boots, preparatory to inserting his feet in a pair of new handsome slippers." This moment of domestic felicity resonates with an earlier scene in the novel: the description of Uncle Tom's cabin. Both dwellings have a home's defining qualities of warmth, comfort, and order.

But the description of Uncle Tom's home, like a travelogue, notes such exotica as rough log walls, curiously bright scriptural prints and dishes, "a portrait of General Washington, drawn and colored in a manner which would certainly have astonished that hero," and a grown man, Uncle Tom, learning to write from a boy of thirteen. By contrast, the familiar traits of the Birds' bourgeois home tell us that we are in the presence of the National Family writ small. The Birds in their typicality represent an elemental version of the familial themes sounded by Clay and Webster in defense of the Fugitive Slave Law. Such domestic scenes are the source of all fellow feeling, the *point d'appui* of sympathetic relations and duties. By invoking the trope of seduction in which Northern fanatics (like Richardson's Lovelace) break up happy Southern homes, Clay drew upon the affective power of the domestic scene to cultivate respect for slavery as part of Southern home life. In Stowe's version, however, this sentimental nexus directs a different conclusion on the morality of the Fugitive Slave Law.[15]

Worn out by the "tiresome business" of legislating, the Senator has returned home to Ohio for some "good, home living," registering a distinction between his public career and private, domestic life. Mrs. Bird queries him regarding the Fugitive Slave Law,

"[I]s it true that they have been passing a law forbidding people to give meat and drink to those poor colored folks that come along? I heard they were talking of some such law, but I didn't think any Christian legislature would pass it!"

"Why, Mary, you are getting to be a politician, all at once."

"No, nonsense! I wouldn't give a fig for all your politics generally, but I think this is something downright cruel and unchristian. I hope, my dear, no such law has been passed."[16]

In their dialogue, each assumes his or her conventional role and area of expertise: the lawmaker-politician and the moralist-homemaker. However, to accept these conventional roles as delineating two utterly distinct forms of discourse and understanding, law and morality, is to ignore the legal significance of Mrs. Bird's attack on the putative authority of the Fugitive Slave Law and the symbolic value of their legal–moral intercourse. Feelings generated within the moral sense's stronghold of home and family definitively indicate to Mrs. Bird that the Fugitive Slave Law is ethically void. The deference normally given to positive law out of expedience, if not an assumption of the law's inherent moral basis, no longer applies.

When asked by Mrs. Bird whether the law forbids offering basic humanitarian aid to fugitives, Senator Bird replies with the taxonomy of the

law itself, "that would be aiding and abetting," as though the superstruc-
ture of the law accounts for the source of its authority. Mr. Bird refers to
the political expedience of maintaining a union with slaveholding states
to counter Mrs. Bird's moral outrage at a law that forbids the charitable
provision of food and shelter to runaway slaves:

Mary, just listen to me. Your feelings are all quite right, dear, and interesting,
and I love you for them; but, then, dear, we mustn't suffer our feelings to run
away with our judgment; you must consider it's not a matter of private feeling, –
there are great public interests involved, – there is such a state of public agitation
rising, that we must put aside our private feelings.

Mr. Bird invokes the public–private distinction to suggest that the amateur's moral feelings have no role in setting public policy, but such pro-
fessionalism is as alien to Mrs. Bird as it was to the founding fathers.[17]

Mrs. Bird's disclaimers, such as "I don't know anything about politics,
but I can read my Bible; and there I see that I must feed the hungry,
clothe the naked and comfort the desolate," are disingenuous to the
extent that they seem intended to separate the legal and moral areas of
expertise. And her belief in the moral sense of sympathy as disclosing
the moral foundation of all proper public policy ("Obeying God never
brings on public evils") has more to do with law than the conventions
of her wifely role permit her to admit. Mrs. Bird, as Stowe's homespun
higher law spokesperson, expresses the founders' interdependent beliefs
in a legal system grounded in virtue and sanctioned by the citizenry's
moral sense.[18]

The Birds' decision to defy the law is decisively pushed forward by
Eliza Harris's appearance:

A young and slender woman, with garments torn and frozen, with one shoe
gone, and the stocking torn away from the cut and bleeding foot, was laid back
in a deadly swoon upon two chairs. There was the impress of the despised race
on her face, yet none could help feeling its mournful and pathetic beauty, while
its stony sharpness, its cold, fixed, deathly aspect, struck a solemn chill over him.

As Seward and other antislavery advocates had before her, Stowe finds
the fulfillment of Mrs. Bird's argument for conscience in the image of "the
real presence of distress": the image of the shivering fugitive appealing
for aid. Through "the imploring human eye, the frail, trembling human
hand, the despairing appeal of helpless agony," and the fundamental
resemblance between black and white families, such pictures work a kind
of "magic" on their audience's sympathy. Though the fatal impress of
race is faintly visible in Eliza's face, that difference is muted by her ladylike

and white appearance and overcome by the common ground of parental feeling. The Birds, like Eliza, have lost a child. Mr. Bird "had never thought that a fugitive might be a hapless mother, a defenceless child, – like that one which was now wearing his lost boy's little well-known cap." Not unlike Webster's passionate invocation of the maternal image in his argument on behalf of Dartmouth College, Stowe's affecting depiction of the plight of mother and child conjures her audience's most elemental notions of justice.[19]

In lauding Mr. Bird's decision to aid Eliza's escape, "Your heart is better than your head, in this case, John," Mrs. Bird concludes the higher law process they have just dramatized. The process begins with Mrs. Bird's moral inspiration, which leads to rational dialogue and debate between husband and wife, forcing the opposition of higher and lower law into clear relief and planting the seed of conversion in Mr. Bird. Once the moral–legal conflict has been brought to a crisis by Eliza's appearance (the "real presence of distress"), the instrumentality of Mr. Bird's reason, like the instrumentality of law itself, turns back to the higher law principles ultimately validating the legal system. Wrenched from the abstractions of his legal and political rhetoric in favor of the Fugitive Slave Law by Eliza's presence and her family's resemblance to his own, Mr. Bird presents "a sad case for his [Webster-like] patriotism," but a fine case for Stowe's higher law jurisprudence.[20]

Far from representing an opposition of law and morality, the Birds' dialogue embodies the process of inspiration and conversation through which the public conscience is animated and revised. The Birds' joint efforts to aid Eliza and her son manifest their new consensus as to the Fugitive Slave Law's invalidity. In the end, Mr. Bird, the lawmaker, acts upon the higher law impetus of sympathy ably if disingenuously urged by his wife as the foundation for all law. Mrs. Bird represents the higher law authorization for the acts of Congress personified by her husband. The one without the other is monologic and incomplete, a legal instrumentality without the moral and emotional reason for its existence.

Depicting higher lawmaking as a family matter, Stowe tends to closet the terms and process of moral consensus within the bounds of kinship, a limitation coming into sharp relief when her domestic images of higher law are compared with Abraham Lincoln's political attack on slavery which carefully avoids mixing the public language of justice with the private language of familial relations. Condemning Justice Taney's *Dred Scott* decision, Lincoln asserted that the universals of the Declaration of Independence include "ALL men, black as well as white," but he also (notoriously) protested "against the counterfeit logic which concludes that, because I do not want a black woman for a slave I must necessarily want her for a wife . . . In some respects she certainly is not my equal; but in her natural right to eat the bread she earns with her own hands without asking leave of any one else, she is my equal, and the equal of all others." This passage does more than merely express Lincoln's racial biases. In terms of moral sense affect, Lincoln's image of "the bread she earns with her own hands" is shorthand for an elaborate narrative image not unlike that of Uncle Tom's rustic but homey cabin. Though his humble image is designed to move us, Lincoln stops well short of imagining the black woman as on her knees asking for help and claiming civic recognition in the figure of family relations ("Am I not a sister?"). Instead, as the creator of property through labor, she embodies the principle that ownership of one's labor transcends distinctions of family, class, gender, and race and affirmatively instantiates civic, if not social, equality. Ironically, Lincoln's image is the more universal for its racist avoidance of the idea of resemblance.[21] Attempting to merge private, familial relations with broader public conceptions of justice, Stowe's image of the Birds' higher lawmaking confuses the primary site of identity, the family, with the means to create just relations between people of different families, different identities. To change the governing political ethos so as to include a diversity of civil membership requires a discourse capable of transcending home and identity. Stowe would present the discourse of sympathy as a bridge between the races, but her figural emphasis on resemblance gets in the way.

The degree to which her characters seem confined by their types limits our ability to see them as moral agents capable of consensual change or new forms of social and political association. For instance, the typicality of Mr. and Mrs. Bird makes it hard to envision them expanding their discussion to include women's suffrage, or for that matter including Eliza in their debate on the Fugitive Slave Law. And as the archetype of the shivering fugitive, Eliza's very appearance – a frail and desperate mother needing protection – obviates the necessity of seeking her approval for the next leg of her escape, which the Birds indeed plan without her counsel or consent. As a woman and supplicant, she must take what they give. The ethical thrust of the passage is thus contradictory, pushing simultaneously toward the higher law mix of conscience and consent (within the white National Family) *and* the paternalistic ethics requiring the strong (white Americans) to care for the weak (black Americans): the ethical basis of slavery.

Stowe's ambivalence in imagining higher lawmaking as a consensual process potentially including black Americans comes to the surface most powerfully where she comes closest to envisioning such a possibility – in the dialogue between Eliza's husband, George Harris, and his white friend, Mr. Wilson. En route to Ohio, George has stopped at a Kentucky inn. Despite George's disguise as a Southern gentleman "with a dark, Spanish complexion," Mr. Wilson recognizes him and attempts to dissuade George from violating the law of slavery. An extended dialogue ensues in which George and Wilson rehearse various arguments for and against obeying the law of slavery. Harris caps his victorious argument with a description of the litany of horrors he and his family have been subjected to by the law of slavery – the sale of his mother, the whipping of his sister, the theft of his labor, and the obstruction of his marriage. The violation of such universal norms as the sanctity of marriage and family, as well as the total abridgement of George's right to his own labor, fill Wilson with tearful sympathy and righteous indignation and lead him to defy the very law he had just been urging George to obey. Guided by compassion to aid George's escape, Wilson recognizes George's higher law claims to the status and rights of a human being.[22] Unlike Eliza's encounter with the Birds, George addresses Wilson as an equal, seeking not Wilson's charity but his agreement that George's flight from bondage is right and proper. George's speech is a model of higher law polemic, as he effectively moves from the logical argument that a government based on the consent of the governed cannot rightly impose legal obligations on a class excluded from the democratic process to a recitation of images designed to stir Wilson's sympathies and galvanize his will.

The chain reaction of logic, sympathy, and outrage leading Wilson (and the reader) to recognize and join with George's cause is mediated by the way in which George's person and manner fit the antebellum era's romantic type of the revolutionary leader. This resemblance is made plausible for Stowe's white readers by George's "fine European features, and a high, indomitable spirit," inherited from his white father (who is "from one of the proudest families in Kentucky"). George's features lend his invocation of the higher law requirement "that governments derive their just power from the consent of the governed" a kind of visual authority. The higher law principles thought to be the special heritage of the Anglo-Saxon people sound right coming out of George's mouth, and the combination of appearance and passion validate George's humanity and entitlement to government by consent. Lest we miss the point, Stowe has

Mr. Wilson note, "George, something has brought you out wonderfully. You hold up your head, and speak and move like another man," overtly signaling the symbolic coherence between George's demeanor and his revolutionary decision to resist the tyranny of slavery. "[D]elivered with tears, and flashing eyes, and despairing gestures," George's very physiognomy symbolizes and authenticates his republican ardor: "I'll fight for my liberty to the last breath I breathe."[23]

A considerable part of the romantic appeal of George's "declaration of independence" derives from physical attributes embodying higher law sentiment, such as his "dark eye" which burns with "the fire" of his moral "indignation." From descriptions of Lord Byron or the protagonists of Sir Walter Scott's and James Fenimore Cooper's historical romances to portraits of Webster and other orators of the day, Stowe's audience had a large stock of such conventional images of the romantic hero. In contrast to the serene balance of rationality and feeling in Gilbert Stuart's portraits of Thomas Jefferson and George Washington, in which the sitter's astute but sensitive gaze assures us of his sincerity and thoughtfulness, the romantic version of heroic leadership stresses flashing eyes, tears, and gestures signaling a barely contained emotional intensity that threatens at any moment to burst forth in a fury of decisive action. Observers of Webster's March 7 speech said that when the issue of secession arose his "eyes appeared like two balls of fire, and his gesticulation indicated the strength of his patriotic impulses." Throughout his address, his "burning eyes" were fixed on Calhoun. Describing Webster's oratory before the Supreme Court, Justice Story recounted

the fiery flashings of his eye, the darkness of his contracted brow, the sudden & flying flushes of his cheeks, the quivering & scarcely manageable movements of his lips, in the deep guttural tones of his voice, in the struggle to suppress his own emotions, in the almost convulsive clenchings of his hands without a seeming consciousness of the act.

Webster himself conceived of eloquence as the "God-like" power to incarnate physically the emotional force animating an argument which otherwise would have the limited appeal of mere logic.[24]

As the modernists have taught us, the image of "burning eyes" works by convention, not by imagistic concreteness or specificity. But what concern us here are not solely the formal assumptions of Stowe's descriptive technique but the political dimension of her conventional forms of affective identification. Stowe boldly makes the mulatto Harris a kind of black Daniel Webster (a neat irony given Webster's moniker "Black Dan" for his dark complexion) or a black George Washington (like the famously curious print of the first President Uncle Tom has on his mantle). But George Harris's eloquent embodiment of higher law jurisprudence – the correspondence of inner moral insight and convincing outer expression – is plainly dependent in Stowe's formulation upon his racial resemblance: he looks like "us." Thus, though to some extent she envisions George Harris as breaking out of the racial chrysalis imposed by slavery (Mr. Wilson's observation of the great change in George) and participating in the formation of a better moral consensus about the nature of justice (the agreement reached between George and Mr. Wilson), her image of George as a romantic type of noble mulatto molds him once and for all in a particular identity with a particular destiny, which in his case is to leave the country. His fate – expulsion – coheres with his type – the articulate, revolutionary hero qualified for membership in the American body politic but for the sable tinge he inherits from his mother.

Stowe is far from comfortable with picturing a higher law ethos that entitles African Americans to enact a revolution or to join in forming an interracial polity, and her discomfort is registered in her attribution of George Harris's revolutionary ire to his white patrilineage and her containment of Uncle Tom's great physical strength in a feminized and maternal vision of black character. Uncle Tom's "truly African features" look nothing like "us," and consequently he does not get to speak the republican language of revolution. Tom's strength stands as a romantic racialist type for his patience and endurance (essential qualities for a martyr), and similarly his "child-like earnestness" indicates a kind of moral purity and lack of self-consciousness.[25] To note Tom's symbolic disqualifications for the role of the republican hero is not to deny the provocative nature of Stowe's creation in Tom of a black Christ or the emotional power of Tom's compassion. But it is in Tom that Stowe's higher law argument veers most sharply away from a jurisprudence of consent toward one of divine authority. Tom is not a political martyr but a Christian martyr; he dies to save souls from God's harsh judgment (Legree's fate), not as an agent of a new moral consensus.

So far we have been dealing with individuals not communities. The misjudgment of visualizing higher lawmaking in terms of resemblance within a polity can be seen in Stowe's depiction of the Quaker community of Rachel and Simeon Halliday. This benevolent society constitutes a kind of icon of the higher law community – a society united in and governed by its collective moral sense. Rachel Halliday leads this benevolent and peaceful polis not by virtue of some power that she possesses but by reason of the moral authority manifest in her "loving words, gentle moralities, and motherly loving kindness," which solve "spiritual and temporal" problems. Her gentle commands, "Thee had better" and "Hadn't thee better?" do not refer to the threat of punishment or the promise of reward but to the auditor's sense of morality. "The danger of friction or collision" within her busy but harmonious community is abated through the joint exercise of the community's moral sense. Rachel's rule represents a kind of higher law ideal where the rule of law is always respected because it is identical with the dictates of conscience.[26]

Revealingly, two outsiders, George Harris and Phineas Fletcher, a convert to Quakerism, interrupt the Quaker community's consensus of pacifism, sympathy, and self-sacrifice with expressions of rebellious indignation and revolutionary intent. When cautioned by Simeon Halliday against acting violently out of the heat of his "young blood," George responds that he would "attack no man" but would fight to the death to prevent the recapture of his wife and son. And, while Phineas agrees with Simeon that the "temptation" of armed resistance is best avoided, he adds, "if we are tempted too much, – why, let them look out, that's all." The combination of George's and Phineas's unapologetic willingness to use force to oppose oppression and their status as outsiders suggests that identity and higher law jurisprudence are interdependent, the one defining the other.[27] And, by associating the right of revolution and racial or cultural heterogeneity, Stowe intimates her own fear that the good-hearted rule of higher law sympathy may be impracticable in the face of social diversity and factional competition for power and dominance.

In effect, Stowe's image of the frictionless moral unity and homogeneity of the Quaker community erases consent from the higher law mix of conscience and consent. Stowe's Quakers do not have to argue or negotiate the terms of justice. They just obey the same inner voice.[28] The sameness of her Quaker exemplars reflects Stowe's apprehension that the prospect of racial heterogeneity raised by the abolitionist campaign would fracture the homogeneity that makes the higher law moral consensus condemning slavery possible in the first place. The fear that racial heterogeneity nullifies the possibility of moral consensus in effect removes consent from consensus. If consent were determinative (the shared moral agency of all human beings qualifying them for participation) then the partnership agreement would be whatever the partners agreed to. The moral justification of the agreement would lie in the fact that it was truly consensual. Stowe's vision of the Quaker community suggests the degree to which antebellum white Americans were uncomfortable with such open-ended notions of moral consensus, bringing racial and other "natural" differences in the back door as a barrier to certain forms of heterogeneous innovation. In short, the insistence of Stowe's images on various forms of resemblance as the prerequisite for moral consensus checks her democratic faith in consent.

The stark alternative to consent is power, and in Stowe's antislavery fiction one can find ample evidence of Stowe's attraction to power as a replacement for moral suasion and consensual models of association. In instances such as Eliza Harris's harrowing escape, for instance, readers are carried, as Stowe herself is, from sympathy to an intense indignation that makes them yearn for the power to challenge the legal tyranny of slavery with violent means.[29] We are relieved when Eliza is aided by the reformed slaveholder, John Van Trompe, because his "honest, just heart" animates a huge, powerful frame that is capable of violently resisting Tom Loker and his slave-catching henchmen. Regardless of Quaker qualms, the resolve of George Harris and Phineas Fletcher is plainly heroic, and their battle with Tom Loker on a rocky promontory recalls similar scenes of romantic heroics in Cooper's *The Last of the Mohicans*. Harris is Stowe's mulatto Duncan Heyward and Fletcher, the able woodsman, is her Hawkeye. They protect the vulnerable Eliza and Harry from Loker as Heyward and Hawkeye protect Alice and Cora Munro in Cooper's romantic adventure. In narrative expiation for her indulgence in the satisfying violence of the action/adventure tale, Stowe does not kill Loker but merely wounds him so that in convalescing in a Christian home he can be converted. Yet, even in the climax of her novel, Uncle Tom's martyrdom, an apotheosis of Christian compassion and self-sacrifice, Stowe cannot wholly resist the attraction of power, and she has George Shelby strike Tom's murderer Legree to the ground. It simply is not enough to know that Legree will suffer in perdition; we must see his malign force answered here and now.[30]

Stowe's second antislavery novel, *Dred*, explores in greater jurisprudential detail the relation of consent and power. In *Dred*, Stowe comes closer to imagining a black revolution enacting the republican and liberal principles of the Declaration of Independence, a shift brought about in Stowe's outlook by the outbreak of violence in Lawrence, Kansas and Preston Brooks's savage beating of Charles Sumner on the floor of the Senate, which Stowe portrays twice in *Dred*.[31]

In *Dred*, Stowe describes the cultural crisis created by slavery as a kind of moral–emotional dissonance:

Documents containing sentiments most dangerous for slaves to hear have been publicly read and applauded among them. The slave has heard, amid shouts, on the Fourth of July, that his masters held the truth to be self-evident that all men were born equal, and had an inalienable right to life, liberty, and the pursuit of happiness; and that all governments derive their just power from the consent of the governed. Even the mottoes of newspapers have embodied sentiments of the most insurrectionary character.

Such inscriptions as "Resistance to tyrants is obedience to God" stand, to this day, in large letters, at the head of southern newspapers; while speeches of senators and public men, in which the principles of universal democracy are asserted, are constant matters of discussion. Under such circumstances, it is difficult to induce the servant, who feels that he is a man, to draw those lines, which seem so obvious to masters, by whom this fact has been forgotten.[32]

The revolutionary rhetoric of the higher law tradition creates a cacophony with the tutelage of slavery – they cannot be harmonized. Universals clash with the language of race, and the terms of consent conflict with those of power. In contrast to Chief Justice Roger Taney's attempt to weld the language of self-governance to race in *Dred Scott*, Stowe has a keen sense of the fluid and uncontainable nature of higher law utterance in the public sphere of newspapers, political speeches, and national holidays. After hearing or seeing the ubiquitous words of inalienable human rights, the slave, in Stowe's words, cannot be induced "to draw [the] lines" Taney would, a few months after the publication of Stowe's novel, describe as the "deep and enduring marks of inferiority" impressed by white Americans on African Americans in order to exclude the latter from "the [American] political family." Anticipating Taney's "marks of inferiority," Stowe's reference to "those lines" correlates visual signs and language, raising a question as to whether lines and words will provide the means for fluid human relations or will represent the fixed boundaries separating categories of human being. Stowe seems to answer this question both ways.[33]

By characterizing the higher law principles of the American Revolution as "sentiments most dangerous" or "sentiments of the most insurrectionary character," Stowe indicates the emotional nature of any recognition of the "principles of universal democracy" and the potential for revolutionary action those feelings inspire. Feeling "that he is a man," the slave becomes aware of his entitlement to "life, liberty, and the pursuit of happiness" and his right to revolt against the "absolute despotism" of slavery. While higher law universals, in Stowe's view, are capable of inspiring a radical transformation in black Americans, this alteration turns out to be a kind of racial imitation. Black Americans moved by the rhetoric of the founding fathers do not merely become more independent, assertive, and less slave-like; they become white. Thus, Denmark Vesey attempts "the hopeless project of imitating the example set by the American race, and achieving independence for the blacks."[34] Aside from the unpleasant ambiguity regarding this project's "hopeless" nature, Stowe's reference to the "example set by the American race" courts the inference that, like Clay and Webster, she views higher law theory as the heritage of the white race, not a set of universal truths.

Consider the effect of Judge Clayton's plainly unjust state high court decision on the face of a slave, Harry Gordon, the half-brother of the novel's villain, Tom Gordon: "Harry's face became pale, his brow clouded, and . . . a fierce and peculiar expression flashed from his dark blue eye."[35] Harry's reaction illustrates the actual, flesh and blood, consequences of Judge Clayton's legal abstraction. As in the case of George Harris, Harry's flashing blue eye and pale face make him a romantic image of the white revolutionary hero. While infuriated by the tyranny of slave law, Harry becomes white, or, as Stowe describes Denmark Vesey, he becomes an "imitation" of "the American race." Unlike George Harris, however, Harry is mute at the moment of greatest higher law outrage, a detail indicating Stowe's movement away from suasion and consent in *Dred* (when Harry does speak later in the novel, his sympathetic white auditor, Edward Clayton, is not converted, as Mr. Wilson is by George Harris). At the level of abstraction, Stowe is comfortable casting the "dangerous sentiments" of higher law in universal terms, but when she puts them into play within the concrete and specific circumstances of her narrative, she gives them the coloring of race.

In *The Key to Uncle Tom's Cabin*, Stowe cites the 1829 North Carolina case of *State v. Mann*, as authority for her fictional study of slave law. *Mann* so provocatively demonstrated the ethical breakdown of the American legal system that Stowe made her fictional version of the case the pivotal crisis of *Dred*. *Mann* involved a female slave, Lydia, who had been "hired" for a year to John Mann. Mann shot and wounded Lydia when she attempted to flee a beating. The trial court found Mann guilty of assault and battery. Judge Thomas Ruffin of the North Carolina Supreme Court reversed the conviction on the basis that, in the system of slavery, "the power of the master must be absolute, to render the submission of the slave perfect."[36] Ruffin was not blind to the force of a Stowe-like higher law argument: "I must freely confess my sense of the harshness of this proposition . . . And as a principle of moral right, every person in his retirement must repudiate it," but Ruffin contended "the actual condition[s]" of slavery require that the slaveholder possess absolute power. Cruelty, such as Mann's, is usually effectively mitigated by a correspondence of "the private interest of the owner," "the benevolences . . . seated in the hearts of those who have been born and bred together," and the "deep execrations of the community upon the barbarian, who is guilty of excessive cruelty to his unprotected slave." Retiring the moral sense from judicial process and consigning higher law critique of the law of slavery to the private feelings of citizens, Ruffin's rendering of the benevolent and familial feelings of the slave and slaveholder for each other turns the relations of property and power into the self-regulating relation of moral sentiment and conforms the practice of slavery, if not the law of slavery, to the principles of higher law.[37] Having distinguished moral critique as an important aspect of proper acculturation, Ruffin can frankly admit the law of slavery is about power and identity. The "disparity in numbers between the whites and blacks" is "dangerous" to the whites, and, as a consequence, the white race uses its legal institutions to ensure its survival and its dominance. Ruffin's positivist approach to the law of slavery is more than a mere matter of professional duty. It is necessitated by the specter of heterogeneity.[38]

Ruffin's opinion intrigued Stowe. She wondered "that such a man, with such a mind should have been merely an *expositor*, and not a *reformer* of law."[39] The decent man's professional deference to power puzzled Stowe, causing her to reconsider in greater detail the relation of morality and power in law. In *Dred*, Stowe uses a debate among three slaveholders as to the proper way to raise slaves to flesh out the ubiquity of power in what seem to be different theories of law. Each of these men is a lawgiver, adjudicating disputes and legislating rules for his slave population. Edward Clayton, a sympathetic Southerner and a lawyer, conceives of the law as grounded in the sympathetic feelings of the moral sense. His vision of legal authority takes the form of a paternalistic benevolence not unlike that espoused by George Fitzhugh:

"It is a debt which we owe," he said, "to the character of our state, and to the purity of our institutions, to prove the efficiency of the law in behalf of that class of our population whose helplessness places them more particularly under our protection. They are to us in the condition of children under age; and any violation of their rights should be more particularly attended to."

Mr. Jekyl, another slaveholder and lawyer, argues that law is properly based on majority tradition. The law of slavery is justified not by power but on the theory that "the white race had the largest amount of being" and therefore "had a right to take precedence." Jekyl's incorporeal notion of "being" in its metaphoric emphasis of size simultaneously registers and evades the importance of actual physical might to the legitimating principles of majority tradition.[40]

Like Simon Legree, Tom Gordon bluntly accepts the positivistic reality of slavery regretfully served by Ruffin's opinion: "The best way of educating is, to show folks that they can't help themselves . . . Just let them know that there are no two ways about it, and you'll have all still enough." For Gordon, all human interaction boils down to the question of power, and the undeniable reality of the unequal distribution of power is the sole justification necessary for its exercise. The possession and exercise of power figure more or less overtly in all three arguments (the higher law argument of Clayton that his "helpless" slaves should obey him because "what I command is right in the sight of God," the pragmatic view of Mr. Jekyl that the metaphysical largeness of the white race's being authorizes white domination, and the frank and brutal positivism of Gordon that the white race has "the power" and need only teach slaves the "weight" of its "fist").[41] The appearance of power in all three versions of temporal authority and the marked absence of consent conveys Stowe's own growing positivistic realism. Stowe's position is not as different from Ruffin's as she would imagine.

Stowe's juxtaposition of Tom Gordon's rhetoric of tyranny with Dred's biblical polemic of revolution frames the moral contest over slavery as a dynamic of power. As he brings extreme force to bear on those who might foment revolution, Gordon summons the insurrectionary menace, which he, like his precursor Alfred St. Clare, would deny is even possible. Proportioned to meet and overcome Gordon's malevolent strength, Dred's "magnificent stature" and "herculean strength" incarnate a fearful and attractive revolutionary power: "the energy of that avenging justice which all nature shudderingly declares." Both Gordon's oppression and Dred's rebellion are born of the recognition that people living under tyranny possess the right of revolution. Ruffin's *Mann* opinion is part of this recognition, an attempt to contain a nascent revolutionary force, as is Stowe's novel, which tenders the threat of revolution as support for her antislavery argument. Historical precedent for this overlap in abolitionist and proslavery arguments can be found in Nat Turner's rebellion, which prompted not only the creation of the American Anti-Slavery Society in Philadelphia but also the enactment of a Virginia code section providing for the fining and imprisonment of anyone who maintained that slave owners have no right of property in their slaves and an Alabama code section that mandated the execution of any person who "advise[s] or conspire[s] with a slave to . . . make insurrection . . . whether such insurrection be made or not."[42]

Sympathy's disheartening legal impotence is epitomized by Judge Clayton's decision of Milly's case (Stowe's dramatization of *Mann*). Recognizing the evil involved in the case, Judge Clayton speaks "of what is" and does not "pretend to justify it." But Judge Clayton's fear that "[u]nder the influence" of his son's "eloquence the case may go the other way, and humanity triumph at the expense of law," presents in inverted form Stowe's fear that "eloquence" and "humanity" have been severed from the machinery of law, leaving only violence and martial power as the means of recognizing and protecting basic human rights.[43] Judge Clayton attacks his son's Fitzhugh-like analogy of the slave's situation to that of the child: "There is no likeness between the cases." The basis for interpreting the law of slavery, Judge Clayton avers, lies not in moral responsibilities supposedly created by the fact of unequal power but in majority custom: "The established habits and uniform practice of the country, in this respect, is the best evidence of the portion of power deemed by the whole community requisite to the preservation of the master's dominion." As in Mr. Jekyl's comments, the jurisprudential weight of custom is figured as a matter of size, the inevitable legal effect of the practice of "the country" and "the whole community." The degree of power legally allocated to the slaveholder is commensurate with the gravity of the community's opinions, not the pennyweight of any particular individual's determination of morality.[44]

If the slaveholders' political and economic power constitutes the energy animating and directing Southern society, customs – the habits and practices of that society – contain that energy in the habiliments of acceptability, and these norms of respectability constitute important signals to outsiders (i.e., the North) that the practices in question are more than the aberration of a few individuals. The metaphoric quality of the figure of majoritarian size when applied to slavery's customs and practices becomes apparent when one notes that, as Kenneth M. Stampp has pointed out, "nearly three-fourths of all free Southerners had no connection with slavery through either family ties or direct ownership." Indeed, in some regions, slaves and free blacks outnumbered the entire white population.[45] The trope of majoritarian size in Judge Clayton's opinion, as in Mr. Jekyl's conception of the largeness of the white race's being, is a symbol of slaveholding power rather than a demographic facsimile of

Southern society. Because it suggests a congruity of law and the feelings and expectations of an entire society, the figure of majoritarian custom proffers to Judge Clayton, as it would to Justice Taney in *Dred Scott*, a particularly seductive trope in which power is disguised as a vast, inert presence, a culture's state of mind.

Francis Lieber's political theory, as we have seen, reveals the fraud involved in presenting mere majority rule as higher law. The alternative is a legal system in which the will of political majorities is constrained by basic principles of justice plausibly deemed to constitute a universal moral consensus. Although she raises this problem in confronting Ruffin's judicial positivism, Stowe avoids answering what is meant by consent in the higher law mix of conscience and consent. The absence of consent is particularly manifest in the failure of Edward Clayton, the most sympathetic of the novel's white characters, to enter into meaningful dialogue with the blacks he defends. Unlike Mr. Wilson, who is converted by George Harris's eloquent declaration of independence, Clayton is not transformed by Dred's revolutionary jeremiad. Clayton trivializes Dred as a "curious psychological study" and a subject of "quaint and poetic interest" and reduces his revolutionary declaration to a "wild jargon of hebraistic phrases, names, and allusions." Consensus between Dred and Clayton is impossible, despite the connection between their views, because the latter sees the former as a type. Clayton's alternative to Dred's visionary revolution is a project of black education and uplift, which, due to the intransigence of racism among whites, necessitates emigration. Accepting both the practical necessity of emigration and majority power as the only means of securing one's rights, Stowe's second novel clearly foreshadows the black nationalism of Martin Delany's *Blake*.

Even with its limitations, in its outward trajectory and the expansiveness of its embrace, Stowe's notion of sympathy challenged her era's constitutional jurisprudence. Though hampered by the rigidity of her types and weakened by her faltering confidence in consensual models of legal order, Stowe's antislavery fiction clearly recognizes black Americans as moral agents, people capable of moral choices and behavior of the highest sort, and her recognition of moral agency and heroism in such characters as Uncle Tom, George Harris, Harry Gordon, and Dred opens the door to interracial political partnership even as other aspects of her fiction seek to close it. The growth and transformation of such characters, though true to type, represents the possibility of national change. As moral agents, black Americans are capable of creating a new social contract or reforming an old one. In short, they are capable of citizenship. Attempting to put higher law into practice, *fiat justitia ruat coelum* ("let justice be done though the heavens fall"), Edward Clayton undertakes the project of educating and preparing his slaves for citizenship – in effect, for assuming a role in expunging racialist readings of both the Constitution and the Declaration. The racialist trap of Stowe's pictorial method restricts this potential movement toward a politics of conscience and consent but does not erase it. Charles Sumner's higher law constitutionalism illustrates how the cultural authority of Stowe's images could be pushed further in the direction of consent.

STOWE AND SUMNER

Any inquiry into the political influence of *Uncle Tom's Cabin* must begin with the novel's phenomenal success. When published in book form (March 1852), it sold 10,000 copies within a few days. In the first year of publication, 300,000 copies of the novel were sold in the United States. Lending libraries could not keep enough copies to satisfy their patrons. Many saw *Uncle Tom's Cabin* as a turning point in the mobilization of antislavery feeling in the North. Though Garrison censured the colonization theme of the novel as well as the novel's suggestion that the duty of non-violent resistance was solely incumbent on black Americans, he praised the novel and its descriptive power. Longfellow and Lowell liked it. Even the acerbic George Templeton Strong came to admire the book and its author (though he would also dismiss it as sentimental romance most appreciated by weeping women). Strong termed Stowe's second antislavery novel, *Dred*, "a strong and telling book."[46] Predictably, Southern response to *Uncle Tom's Cabin* was generally hostile. George Frederick Holmes, the South's most prominent reviewer, saw Stowe's higher law arguments as the "very evangel of insubordination, sedition, and anarchy." The thesis of the novel, according to Holmes, is that "any organization of society . . . which can by possibility result in such instances of individual misery . . . must be criminal in itself, a violation of all the laws of Nature and of God." Such an approach "strikes at the very essence and existence of all community among men, it lays bare and roots up all the foundations of law, order and government."[47]

The success of Stowe's antislavery fiction and the intense reactions its searing portraits of slavery provoked would seem to make it inevitable that her novels had a important role in shaping the political debate of the 1850s and the higher law revision of the Constitution in Reconstruction.

Yet, there is a striking absence in Stowe scholarship of any detailed exploration of the political and legal influence of her work. Perhaps out of a sense of disciplinary boundaries, many literary scholars are chary of crediting Stowe's fiction with any tangible political or legal effects. In their reluctance to explore the jurisprudential aims and results of Stowe's writing, such scholars unwittingly side with George Frederick Holmes who mocked Stowe's entry "into the tangled labyrinths of that lady-like study, the criminal law in regard to slaves," and her translation of "the technical language of jurisprudence" into "female tattle."[48]

Some contemporary scholars, such as Jane Tompkins and Thomas Gossett, sense the novel had a tangible political impact but hesitate to look for the traces of *Uncle Tom's Cabin* in the political and legal record of the era. Thomas Gossett's very useful book suggests that "it is probable that the novel had a profound effect on opinion with regard to slavery in the North in the 1850s" yet hesitates to pursue this hypothesis into the precincts of politics and law:

From 1852 to the beginning of the Civil War in 1861, political leaders rarely commented on *Uncle Tom's Cabin*, publicly or privately. It was not usual for political leaders or commentators to discuss the ideas of the time in terms of novels, and the fact that this novel had been written by a woman made it even less likely that it would be discussed by them.

While the *Congressional Globe*, state and federal case law, the correspondence of prominent politicians and jurists addressing race, slavery, and citizenship generally support Gossett's characterization that contemporary literature, such as *Uncle Tom's Cabin*, was not at the forefront of mid-nineteenth-century political and legal debate, this generalization misses many important exceptions. And these exceptions indicate a shift in the nation's political discourse toward a higher law approach to citizenship imbued with the language of sympathy and sentiment, a shift that Stowe's very popular antislavery fiction helped to underwrite.[49]

Literature was hardly absent from mid-century political debate. The Bible, Shakespeare, Pope, Cervantes, Cicero, Rousseau and many others find their way into political debate with considerable frequency. *The Merchant of Venice*, for example, was frequently used as the Ur-image of equity in the Reconstruction debates. And there is considerable evidence that politicians and jurists, like many Americans, were deeply affected by Stowe's antislavery fiction, finding it either persuasive or a hostile cultural force with which they had to contend. A telling example can be found in the Library of Congress's collection of Chief Justice Roger

B. Taney's papers, which contains the beginnings of an essay on slavery and antebellum sectional hostility. Apparently written on the eve of the Civil War, the author deplores the election of Abraham Lincoln and condemns abolitionist challenges to a proslavery constitutional order that has successfully protected slave states from "free state aggression." The essayist blames the constitutional crisis on the "political hate" that the North has "diffused" through its schoolrooms, pulpits, and "a novel of a character well calculated to raise the morbid thought of fanatics, which portrayed in pictures of exaggeration the evils of slavery."[50] This reference to *Uncle Tom's Cabin* is striking. It is as though the professional curtain of legal doctrine and procedure shrouding judicial reasoning has been momentarily pulled back, revealing a jurist's angry recognition that official jurisprudence is susceptible to unwelcome cultural revision. Even if not written by Taney, this fragment is significant evidence that at least one of his contemporaries (probably a lawyer, given the writer's detailed familiarity with specialized legal concepts and precedents) viewed the Constitution as subject to reinvention by literary artists who worked in concert with religious leaders, philosophers, educators, and politicians.

As the fragment in Taney's papers recognizes, Stowe's literary labors gave her a cultural platform of enormous scope from which to denounce slavery and to advance antislavery readings of the Constitution and the Declaration of Independence. This potential was recognized in Lord Carlisle's preface to the English edition of *Uncle Tom's Cabin*, which rightly found that Stowe's novel inspired Senator Charles Sumner's famous "Freedom National, Slavery Sectional" speech, calling for the repeal of the Fugitive Slave Law. Indeed, legislative debates on the issues of slavery, race, and citizenship bear many signs of the political authority of Stowe's higher law images. Ohio Representative John Bingham (the prosecutor in Andrew Jackson's impeachment trial and primary drafter of the Fourteenth Amendment) clearly alluded to one of the most dramatic moments in *Uncle Tom's Cabin* in objecting to an amendment of the Fugitive Slave Law proposed in 1860 as a part of an eleventh hour union-saving compromise. Noting that his comments would provoke sneers of "higher law," Bingham argued

that the amendment proposed . . . does not relieve the American people from the unjust obligations imposed upon them by the act of 1850, by which, at the beck of the marshal, they are compelled to join in the hunt – to make hue and cry on the track of a fugitive slave woman who is fleeing, with her babe lashed upon her breast, from the house of bondage. I will not perform that service, and I ask any man on that side whether he will?

Given the fact that in 1860 the Fugitive Slave Law was still the law of the land with no legal precedent qualifying or terminating its obligations, Bingham's comments derive jurisprudential authority solely from the higher law tradition that unjust laws do not merit obedience. The compelling emotional force of his higher law position is furnished by the image of the fugitive mother and her babe made famous by Stowe's vivid rendering of Eliza Harris's escape. Bingham and other Republicans repeatedly pointed to this scene as the key test of the illegitimacy of the Fugitive Slave Law.[51]

The extended influence of Stowe's antislavery writing can be felt throughout the congressional debates on black citizenship and Reconstruction. In 1866, Senator Lyman Trumbull of Illinois used the comic figure of Stowe's Topsy to mock democratic fears of Chinese and Gypsy citizenship. *State v. Mann*, the 1829 North Carolina case made famous by Stowe's *The Key To Uncle Tom's Cabin* and fictionalized in *Dred*, is cited by the congressional Committee on Slavery and the Treatment of Freedmen as a quintessential example of the injustice of slave law: "It seems to have been settled with great deliberation that a master may shoot his slave, male or female, by way of correction, and that he is not liable therefor to indictment." Asserting that equality before the law means "that the poor man's cabin, though it may be the cabin of a poor freedman in the depths of the Carolinas, is entitled to the protection of the same law that protects the palace of a Stewart or an Astor," Senator Henry Wilson's comments on the Freedmen's Bureau Bill indicate the degree to which Uncle Tom's humble cabin permeated the era's lexicon of fundamental justice. Representative Jehu Baker's praise of the Fourteenth Amendment's equal protection clause in 1868 as conforming to the higher law dictates divined by kindheartedness similarly evinces the influence of Stowe's fictional paean to sympathy. Equal protection of the laws, says Baker, "is so obviously right, that one would imagine nobody could be found so hard-hearted and cruel as not to recognize its simple justice." One can modestly observe, I think, that, when in 1868 the dominant political party tests the appropriateness of their Constitutional amendment by reference to kindhearted justice, we have come a considerable distance from the scorn heaped upon William Seward's invocation of higher law in March of 1850.[52]

Though a full discussion is beyond the scope of this study, a brief examination of popular images of Abraham Lincoln highlights the nation's shift in the 1860s toward Stowe-like figures of compassion. A higher law reading of Lincoln's image might, at first glance, seem inappropriate given the care he took in distancing himself from higher law arguments for civil disobedience. Insisting that his aim was to conserve not overthrow the Constitution, Lincoln's First Inaugural Address urged citizens to obey the Fugitive Slave Law. In addition, unlike more radical higher law advocates such as Frederick Douglass, Charles Sumner, and Thaddeus Stevens, Lincoln quite plainly announced his aversion to racial mixing and his support for segregation and colonization. Yet, Lincoln's politics also reveal a belief that the law of the land must comport with elemental justice derived by the moral sense, and this belief classes him with the higher law advocates seeking the moral basis for a just society, albeit a less radical one. Attacking Stephen Douglas's indifference to the morality of slavery, for example, Lincoln contended that on matters of right and wrong there was no middle ground. Lincoln's political oratory played a critical role in advancing a higher law conception of the Constitution. Lincoln's Gettysburg Address, as Garry Wills has argued, remade the Constitution

not, as William Lloyd Garrison had, by burning an instrument that countenanced slavery. He altered the document from within, by appeal from its letter to the spirit, subtly changing the recalcitrant stuff of that legal compromise, bringing it to its own indictment . . . The crowd departed with a new thing in its ideological luggage, that new constitution Lincoln had substituted for the one they brought there with them.

Paralleling the higher law constitutionalism of Frederick Douglass, Charles Sumner, Thaddeus Stevens, and other more radical Republicans, for the old proslavery compromise Lincoln substituted a Constitution read through the lens of the Declaration of Independence's universals. His Second Inaugural address's characterization of the Civil War as an atonement in blood for the offense of slavery would put what for many would be the definitive higher law gloss on a conflict destined to reconstruct American constitutional law in accord with the fundamental norms of justice.[53]

　　Photographic and painted portraits of Lincoln came to stand for the type of leader who is guided "by the better angels of our nature," whose very visage expresses the combination of compassion and wisdom requisite for higher law justice. Unlike portraits of earlier leaders, such as Webster and Calhoun, which often emphasized other kinds of qualities (paintings of Webster emphasized his massive head and glowering look, while those of Calhoun, the Iron Man, emphasized his cold piercing gaze and stern unflinching demeanor), Honest Abe's portraits, by contrast, capture a homely-handsome face etched with lines of care and sad eyes full of compassion. Such images include a charming portrait of Lincoln and his son Thomas (Tad) taken by the Brady studio, Washington, D.C. (February 9, 1864). Wearing spectacles and reading from a large book on his lap, Lincoln is seated, with his son standing at his side, looking down on the same text. There is a visual echo between the watch chains of son and father – the touching imitation of the parent by the child. Lincoln and his son are in close physical proximity, Tad's right arm apparently resting on either the back of Lincoln's chair or Lincoln's left arm. A sweet image which might have been merely commonplace had Lincoln lived became emotionally supercharged after assassination severed the parent and child caught so close here in the photographer's simulacrum of candid home life, father and son preoccupied and unaware of the photographer's or our gaze. A series of very popular family prints was derived from this photograph and another like it. Even though the political utility of these widely popular prints was not fully appreciated at the time, their popularity signified a new figural emphasis on compassion and fellow feeling in American notions of justice.[54]

Stowe's antislavery fiction created an important precedent for such affecting images of national leadership. Her portrait of Senator Bird achieves a comparable affect through the inclusion of similar details. The presence of children, the domestic setting, the signs of physical and emotional intimacy in both Stowe's portrait of Senator Bird and in the portrait of Lincoln with his son refigure political leadership as not merely strong, but as emotionally capable. Writing about the best-known portrait of Lincoln in its day, a painting done by William Edgar Marshall (a New York-born painter and engraver), Lincoln's law partner, William H. Herndon, said that it captured Lincoln "in kindness, tenderness and reflection combined." Charles Sumner thought the picture captured Lincoln "in his most interesting expression, where gentleness and sympathy unite in strength." The Marshall image presents Lincoln at his most handsome. His prominent features – the high forehead, over-hanging heavy brow, deep sockets, mole, slightly aslant mouth, and lined face – are all here but softened, as seen through the mist of sentiment. The eyes have the clear yet meditative quality that characterizes all of the best portraits of Lincoln. And in those eyes people have always wanted to find kindness, honesty, fairness, and moral courage – traits transforming the politician and lawmaker from a mere tool of power into a great leader and a universal symbol of justice.[55]

Perhaps the best evidence of the reciprocity between Stowe's anti-slavery fiction and political arguments for an antislavery construction of the nation's charter, which would eventually culminate in the Civil War amendments, can be found in the literary/political partnership of Stowe and Charles Sumner. We get an apt illustration of this partnership from a series of events unfolding around the Kansas/Nebraska Act (which re-pealed the Missouri Compromise's prohibition of slavery above the lati-tude of 36 degrees, 30 minutes, allowing Kansas and Nebraska to choose whether they would enter the Union as either slave or free states). Tak-ing a hint from the "Appeal of the Independent Democrats," drafted by Sumner, Salmon Chase, and Joshua Giddings, which protested Stephen Douglas's first version of the Nebraska bill, Stowe devoted some of her royalties from *Uncle Tom's Cabin* to the collection of a "united clerical protest of New England" against the Nebraska Act. After the petition was presented, Stephen Douglas responded in a vitriolic denunciation of the meddlesome extra-legal intervention. Douglas's rant offered Sumner an important opportunity to attack slavery on the floor of the Senate – an opening that was particularly significant because a preponderance of the Senate's members had, through procedural means, largely blocked the agitation of the slavery issue by Sumner and allies. The back and forth tandem of Stowe's and Sumner's efforts exemplifies an alliance recog-nized by contemporaries who associated the legal labors of the politician with the literary labors of the novelist.[56]

But more pertinent to this study is the fact that the sentimental images and tropes so charismatically adduced against slavery in *Uncle Tom's Cabin* form a prominent rhetorical aspect of Sumner's antislavery advocacy, in particular the sentimental cast of his higher law argument. In "Freedom National, Slavery Sectional," his first great address as a Senator, Sumner introduces himself not as a politician but as a disinterested friend of hu-man rights and democracy who speaks "from the heart" and who attacks an evil institution "which . . . palpitates in every heart and burns on ev-ery tongue." Like Stowe, Sumner uses the image of the "shivering fugi-tive" seeking aid to force his audience to confront the immorality of the Fugitive Slave Law:

The good citizen, who sees before him the shivering fugitive, guilty of no crime, pursued, hunted down like a beast, while praying for Christian help and deliv-erance, and then reads the requirements of this Act, is filled with horror . . . Not rashly would I set myself against any requirement of law . . . But here the path of duty is clear. By the Supreme Law, which commands me to do no injustice, by the comprehensive Christian Law of Brotherhood, by the Constitution, which I have sworn to support, I AM BOUND TO DISOBEY THIS ACT.

Sumner's arguments against slavery and race proscription also often emphasize the disruption of the domestic scene as the quintessential moment of moral outrage. An antislavery address Sumner gave in 1855 climaxed its condemnation of the law of slavery with the observation that this law gave slaveholders the power "to separate families, to unclasp the infant from a mother's breast, and the wife from a husband's arms."[57]

Stowe's influence on "Freedom National, Slavery Sectional" can be felt in Sumner's trope of tears as the outward manifestation of the moral sense: "Not a case occurs [under the Fugitive Slave Act] which does not harrow the souls of good men, bringing tears of sympathy to the eyes, and those other noble tears which 'patriots shed o'er dying laws.'" Sympathy, for Sumner as for Stowe, properly governs human behavior and reveals the course of justice. He counts on its arousal in the public on behalf of the fugitive: "But the great heart of the people recoils from this enactment. It palpitates for the fugitive, and rejoices in his escape." In contrast to proslavery criticism of literary intrusions on the nation's constitutional jurisprudence, Sumner singles literature out as an apt tutor of the moral sense, praising Stowe in particular:

Sir, I am telling you facts. The literature of the age is all on [the slave's] side. Songs, more potent than laws, are for him. Poets, with voices of melody, sing for Freedom. Who could tune for Slavery? They who make the permanent opinion of the country, who mould our youth, whose words, dropped into the soul, are the germs of character, supplicate for the Slave. And now, Sir, behold a new and heavenly ally. A woman, inspired by Christian genius, enters the lists, like another Joan of Arc, and with marvellous power sweeps the popular heart. Now melting to tears, and now inspiring to rage, her work everywhere touches the conscience, and makes the Slave-Hunter more hateful. In a brief period, nearly one hundred thousand copies of "Uncle Tom's Cabin" have been already circulated. But this extraordinary and sudden success, surpassing all other instances in the records of literature, cannot be regarded as but the triumph of genius. Better far, it is the testimony of the people, by an unprecedented act, against the Fugitive Slave Bill.

Sumner's praise reflects the romantic notion that, in Shelley's famous phrase, "poets are the unacknowledged legislators of the world."[58]

Whether we might find such a claim considerably exaggerated (or implausible because it assumes literature is somehow not molded by precisely the same cultural context producing the politics of the moment), the fact that Charles Sumner, a politician who as much as anybody moved the nation toward a revision of its fundamental charter and basic notions of citizenship, found it plausible is concrete evidence of the political influence of Stowe's emotionally redolent images. In claiming the political authority of the tears and rage provoked by Stowe's novel, Sumner creates an identity between their projects. This identity is established in his introduction of himself at the beginning of his speech not as the current model of ambitious, self-interested politician (the professional politician so castigated by the republicans of the revolutionary era) but as a disinterested friend of humanity who speaks from the heart. Sumner reanimates the republican notion of civic virtue, coloring it with the tears of Stowe's sentimental fiction as the moral health of the body politic.

Though Sumner's oratory is for modern readers hampered by its rhetorical ornaments and overabundant allusions (a style already dated by the 1850s, having been displaced by the plain speaking style of the Jacksonian era), his denunciation of racism and slavery and his prophetic vision of history's verdict still have considerable power:

Rude and ignorant they [the fugitive slaves] may be; but in their very efforts for Freedom they claim kindred with all that is noble in the Past. Romance has no stories of more thrilling interest. Classical antiquity has preserved no examples of adventure and trial more worthy of renown. They are among the heroes of our age. Among them are those whose names will be treasured in the annals of their race. By eloquent voice they have done much to make their wrongs known, and to secure the respect of the world. History will soon lend her avenging pen. Proscribed by you during life, they will proscribe you through all time. Sir, already judgment is beginning. A righteous public sentiment palsies your enactment.[59]

The justice of the fugitives' claims to freedom is linked in this passage (as it is in Stowe's novels) to the affective power of their exciting, adventurous, compelling romantic narratives of personal heroism. The force of the reader's recognition of the fugitive slaves' humanity and moral strength is proportional to the affective success of their narratives. The fusion of a certain kind of narrative and fundamental ideas of justice reflects the moral sense psychology's parallel of rhetorical affect and ethical awareness – both are animated by the same mechanisms of human emotion and sympathy.

But Sumner's prophecy significantly adds the dimension of historical change to the affective connection between the consensus of what is moral and the consensus of what constitutes a compelling narrative. Behind Sumner's appreciation of Stowe's fiction as opening the public's mind by stirring its heart is an implicit appreciation of literary innovation.

Literature, such as Stowe's novels, offers persuasive new conceptions of old truths ("all that is noble in the Past"). While higher law inspiration is absolute, inherent, and traditional, in history this inspiration takes effect in the shifting social construction of a moral/political consensus. Creating a new heroic icon, the black patriot struggling for freedom, the fugitive slave narrative breaks the higher law ethos of the American Revolution out of its racial chrysalis. Reflecting an intuition that tastes in narrative and the stories we tell of fundamental justice are inseparable, Sumner's prophecy suggests that shifts in culturally authoritative narratives of justice move in tandem with shifts in political theory and jurisprudence. Sumner rightly, I think, senses the decisive import of favored narratives of justice which constitute the concrete illustrations of the abstract political verities we proclaim at national holidays – the heroes of the one are the heroes of the other. Sumner's comments signal a new and powerful role for the black advocate, like Douglass, who escapes slavery and who authors his story – he is both hero and author of romance and higher law jurisprudence; he incarnates romantic adventure and is the living exemplar of a theory of government and law his experience eminently qualifies him to explicate. Sumner pushes Stowe's inspiration beyond itself toward a more fulsome model of African American citizenship and a mutable conception of higher law constitutionalism – a conception that found its best advocates in Ralph Waldo Emerson and Frederick Douglass.

CHAPTER 3

Cosmopolitan constitutionalism: Emerson and Douglass

Ralph Waldo Emerson and Frederick Douglass both appreciated *Uncle Tom's Cabin's* success in reaching "the universal heart."[1] Yet, while sharing Stowe's higher law conviction that American law must be founded on universal ethical norms, Emerson and Douglass differed from Stowe in two important and related aspects.[2] First, they rejected the emphasis on racial type characterizing Stowe's appeal to the nation's conscience, and, second, they resisted the absolutism of Stowe's higher law vision. Both wanted to distinguish higher law from images and conceptions limiting the possibilities of human transformation and reducing moral agency to merely obeying the certainties of divine ordinance. Higher law, for Emerson and Douglass, was a mutable human creation, an ongoing attempt to put moral inspiration into political dialogue and legal practice.

Both sought to sever the Constitution's foundational principles of conscience and consent from the prerequisite of racial and cultural resemblance. Emerson's antislavery addresses use irony to dissolve the connection between race and justice and abstraction to draw the Constitution into the process of cultural revision he describes in "Circles" and "The Poet." Emerson's irony and abstraction, in effect, clear a constitutional space for black citizenship and moral agency – a space that, in avoiding the fixities of his own racial views, Emerson leaves empty. In his oratory and autobiographical writing, Douglass presents his own protean self-transformations as an analogue for a fluid Constitution continually being rewritten by new participants and a cosmopolitan perspective appropriate to an era when "Intelligence . . . penetrat[es] the darkest corners of the globe . . . Oceans no longer divide, but link nations together. From Boston to London is now a holiday excursion. Space is comparatively annihilated. Thoughts expressed on one side of the Atlantic are distinctly heard on the other."[3] More than anyone else in his era, Douglass embodied and argued for the world citizen as the model republican, fulfilling

Emerson's call for a "great imaginative soul" and "broad, cosmopolitan mind" to reinvent the nation's basic lexicon of justice and citizenship.[4]

An examination of the cosmopolitan constitutionalism adopted by Emerson and Douglass should begin by addressing a couple of objections. First, given the era's dominant nationalism (present in even the most radical of reformers) and the centrality of the Constitution as a nationalist symbol, cosmopolitan constitutionalism might seem to be a contradiction in terms. Sacvan Bercovitch, for example, has alerted us to the way that the national myth of "the American Way" subsumes virtue and consent in the exceptionalist identity and mission of "the American people." In this myth, "nation" means "Americans," and "Americans" means "the people," and "the people" means those who enjoy "the simple sunny rewards of American middle-class life" – an equation occluding racial, class, and gender divisions and defusing political dissent. While apt (capturing, for instance, the substantial tension introduced in this American myth by such advocates as Douglass and Emerson), Bercovitch's account addresses neither cosmopolitan challenges to the enclosure of conscience and consent in the chrysalis of national identity nor the question of whether nationalism and cosmopolitanism are necessarily incompatible.[5] Clearly, the elevation of one nation's interests and its particular myth of identity to the exclusion of other considerations is the antithesis of the cosmopolitan perspective. Yet, in a republic devoted to making its laws and political behavior conform with universal ethical norms, where those norms are determined by a dialogue among the varying ethical perspectives of a diverse citizenry and consider the views of other nations and other times, nationalism is compatible with cosmopolitanism. Such an ideal animates Emerson's and Douglass's attacks on the nationalist veneration of a shared racial ancestry *and* their express devotion to the American nation to the extent that it aspires to and achieves justice.[6] Their cosmopolitan approaches to the American nation and its charter anticipate what Kwame Anthony Appiah calls "cosmopolitan patriotism"–"a form of patriotism" allowing "us to love our country as the embodiment of principles, as a means to the attainment of moral ends."[7]

Alternatively, one might wonder whether it is anachronistic to term Emerson's and Douglass's views as cosmopolitan given nineteenth-century America's association of cosmopolitanism with "superficiality and even shiftlessness."[8] While this generalization accurately indicates the era's fear of unrooted strangers, confidence men, and painted women, it leaves out Emerson's and Douglass's conceptions of justice and citizenship. If we equate cosmopolitanism with the perspective of a well-traveled individual lacking in moral fiber, how do we account for Emerson's declaration that "the legislation of this country should become more catholic and cosmopolitan than that of any other"?[9] To locate Emerson's and Douglass's views of the Constitution, we need to abstract their cosmopolitanism from the fictional and historical narratives conjured by the term. Typically, the cosmopolitan novel centers on a figure who, learning social conventions, is able to move from one class to another (one thinks of "the Cosmopolitan" in Melville's *Confidence Man*, Lucien Chardon in Balzac's *Illusions Perdue*, Ralph Touchett in James's *Portrait of a Lady*, or the eponymous hero of Cahan's *The Rise of David Levinsky*). Such fictional narratives of bourgeois mobility intersect with the Habermasian historical narrative of the public sphere. The coffee houses, cafés, coaching inns, theaters, public squares, and opera houses of the public sphere furnished the arena for cosmopolitan mobility. The possibility for such social movement was, in the larger historical narrative, created by the emergence of a capitalist economy and an urban middle class, a material and epistemic transformation redirecting social organization away from status toward contract, from *gemeinschaft* toward *gesellschaft*.[10]

Certain aspects of this cosmopolitan narrative may well provoke disgust. Appalled by the elitism motivating bourgeois assimilation of upperclass social practices, one sickens at the snob who, in gross imitation of a decadent aristocracy, looks down his nose at the unrefined honesty and rough goodness of the rustic. The flip side of such revulsion is often nostalgia for the closely knit organic community of family and village in which ennui and alienation are unknown and virtue feels as certain and permanent as the soil the community works. Though such reactions are understandable, confining the term "cosmopolitan" to this particular narrative outline obscures the idea's broader import for Emerson and Douglass. Taken abstractly, it denotes something at once far grander and more fundamental than any mere narrative of social climbing. Cosmopolitanism indicates the central importance of diverse experience to the faculty of judgment, which, in Hannah Arendt's words, "adopts the position of Kant's world citizen."[11] Through judgment, according to sections 40 and 41 of Kant's *Critique of Judgment*, we assimilate new events to the categories we use to structure and organize our experience.[12] One result of the interplay between particular experience and category is that our categories change, as, for instance, when a different kind of fiction recalibrates our definition of the novel or when a new technology, such as the Internet, forces us to rethink our basic concepts of intellectual property. Judgment is cosmopolitan in at least two distinct ways. First, it begins with an experience that does not conform to our habitual ways of looking at the world. In its most elemental form (e.g., the childhood processes of reflection, argument, and modification jarred into action by the disturbing discovery that another family does not do as one's family does), judgment depends on a new or heterodox experience. Second, this novel experience comes entangled with a need to compare our judgment of the experience's meaning and significance with the judgments of others (a common example might be the compulsion to read reviews and talk with others *after* seeing a provocative film). The cosmopolitan "enlargement of mind" gained by taking other points of view into account is central to Kant's conception of judgment.

While sections 40 and 41 of the *Third Critique* focus on aesthetics, as section 60 states, this form of judgment "is at bottom a faculty for judging of the sensible illustration of moral ideas."[13] Kant's conception of judgment, as Samuel Fleischacker notes, is "at home most familiarly in law and literary and other aesthetic criticism." Aesthetic judgment "provides the foundation of the kind of conversation relevant to morality: conversation about particulars that must be placed in some valuative category but are, often, too distinctive to fit easily into any single such category." Aesthetic and ethical judgment share an "unnerving endlessness of moving between universals and particulars" and an "uncertainty that permeates moral thinking at its best."[14] Under pressure from diverse experiences and cosmopolitan conversations provoked by those experiences, our conceptions of beauty or justice shift, creating an uncertainty not in the concept itself but in the finality of any attempt to define the concept, any attempt, in Emerson's words, "to nail the stars to the sky."[15]

A Kantian kinship between Emerson and Douglass can be felt in the prominence each gives to the fluid quality of and the interrelation between aesthetic and ethical judgment. For example, Emerson declares in "Circles" that "There is no virtue which is final" and in a later antislavery address criticizes Americans for "ador[ing] the forms of law, instead of making them the vehicles of wisdom and justice." Douglass similarly avows that "Perfection is an object to be aimed at by all, but it is not an attribute of any form of government. Mutability is the law for all." Both men laud literary or aesthetic experience for illuminating the ceaseless process of revision involved in valuative judgments. "Literature" furnishes "a point outside of our hodiernal circle through which a new one may be described," says Emerson in "Circles":

In my daily work I incline to repeat my old steps, and do not believe in remedial force, in the power of change and reform. But some Petrarch or Ariosto, filled with the new wine of his imagination, writes me an ode or a brisk romance, full of daring thought and action. He smites and arouses me with his shrill tones, breaks up my whole chain of habits, and I open my eye to my own possibilities.

By intruding on our habitual ways of thinking about and experiencing the world, literature opens new perspectives on fundamental concepts such as beauty and justice. Douglass describes aesthetic experience as an appreciation of nature's or art's ceaseless "Creating, unfolding, expanding, renewing, changing, perpetually, putting on new forms, new colours, issuing new sounds, filling the world with new perfumes, and spreading out to the eye and heart, unending scenes of freshness and beauty [and] all pervading and never resting life." The flux of aesthetic experience, in Douglass's view, exemplifies and illuminates the fact that our lives are and should be a continuing process of transformation:

Men talk much of a new birth. The fact is fundamental. But the mistake is in treating it as an incident which can only happen to a man once in a life time; whereas, the whole journey of life is a succession of them. A new life springs up in the soul, with the discovery of every new agency by which the soul is raised to a higher level of wisdom, goodness and joy. The poor savage, accustomed only to the stunning war whoop of his tribe, and to the wild and startling sounds in nature, of winds, waterfalls, and thunder, meets with a change of heart the first time he hears the Divine harmonies, of scientific[?] music: and the child experiences one with every new object, by means of which it is brought into a nearer and fuller acquaintance with its own subjective nature. With every step he attains a larger, fuller and freer range of vision.[16]

Because the cosmopolitanism of Emerson and Douglass connects the shifting perspective of diverse experience and intercourse to the process of judgment, it should be seen as a specific type of universalism. Unlike the absolutist who claims to know the ordering principles of the universe, their cosmopolitan has not arrived at any such conclusions, is still in transit, informing his/her judgment about the just society with the experience of different languages, beliefs, and perspectives.[17] From the vantage of this form of universalism, both the snob's scorn for the rustic and the provincial's xenophobic rejection of "foreign" or strange experiences represent a refusal to exercise the cosmopolitan faculty of judgment. As justice is a universal value ("Justice satisfies every body"), the nation's fundamental

legal principles must be approached, in Emerson's view, from the cosmopolitan perspective of "new views & broader principles . . . given to fit
the natural expansion of the times." And as reaching "a degree of civilization higher than any yet attained" depends on an interplay between
new perspectives and fundamental concepts, we should, in Douglass's
view, "welcome to our ample continent all nations, kindreds, tongues
and peoples, and as fast as they learn our language and comprehend
the duties of citizenship, we should incorporate them into the American
body politic."[18]

LABILE JUSTICE AND THE SCIENCE OF LIBERTY – EMERSON'S HIGHER LAW THEORY

When the Fugitive Slave Law was passed, Emerson sarcastically mar-
veled that such a "filthy enactment" could have been "made in the 19th
Century, by people who could read & write." Though earlier he had
had his doubts about Thoreau's espousal of civil disobedience, Emerson
now joined Thoreau, rejecting the citizen's duty to obey the Fugitive
Slave Law – "I will not obey it, by God."[19] Disconcerted by the public
scorn heaped on William H. Seward's higher law argument against the
Fugitive Slave Law, Emerson began assembling the material for a treatise
on the higher law:

A few months ago, in my dismay at hearing that the Higher Law was reckoned
a good joke in the courts, I took pains to look into a few law-books. I had often
heard that the Bible constituted a part of every technical law-library, and that
it was a principle in law that immoral laws are void. I found accordingly, that
the great jurists, Cicero, Grotius, Coke, Blackstone, Burlamaqui, Montesquieu,
Vattel, Burke, Mackintosh, Jefferson, do all affirm this.[20]

Emerson obtained these authorities for his higher law position from an
anonymously published pamphlet, "The Higher Law Tried by Reason
and Authority," which, as he discovered, had been written by an acquaintance, Ainsworth Rand Spofford. Verbatim extracts from Spofford's
essay cover the pages of Emerson's WO Liberty journal and inform
the jurisprudence of all of Emerson's most ardent antislavery lectures.
Emerson confessed his "unblushing plagiarisms" in an 1851 letter, stating
that in formulating his critique of the Fugitive Slave Law he had "only
succeeded in reproducing" Spofford's.[21]

The higher law process described by Spofford begins in individual
moral inspiration and surges outward toward an engagement with public

debate and political action. Like Spofford, Emerson was grateful that the Fugitive Slave Law had at least had the republican benefit of stimulating widespread debate:

The only benefit that has accrued from the law is its service to the education. It has been like a university to the entire people. It has turned every dinner-table into a debating club, and made every citizen a student of natural law. When a moral quality comes into politics, when a right is invaded, the discussion draws on deeper sources; general principles are laid bare, which cast light on the whole frame of society.[22]

Higher law advocates, such as Spofford, Emerson, Douglass, and Charles Sumner, took hope from the fact that the Fugitive Slave Law had reinfused public discussions of American justice with the broader abstractions of the higher law tradition – republican notions of public virtue, liberal accounts of human rights, and the notion of moral progress. These advocates shared a recognition that what Seward called the "public conscience" could be reformed through cultural as well as political intervention. Inspired by the idea that this law fatally violated fundamental moral norms, individuals could bring the subject forward in speeches, lectures, sermons, novels, and poems illuminating the incongruity. And they could defy the law. If successful, this process would give new meanings to old words and coin new ones. New stories would be found to describe justice and citizenship. The perpetual revision of the national story and ethos threatened by the higher law project provoked fears of anarchy in many who urged that such reasoning gives lawmakers "a scope as wide as the winds." "Cut loose from . . . restraints," they could find "a charter . . . in the casuistry of theologians, the dicta of modern philosophers, and the suggestions of metaphysical theorizers." "Transcendental" was a favored term of derision for such labile notions of justice.[23]

For Emerson, the moral terms of constitutional consensus were part of an abstract argot of justice inherited from the past but not circumscribed by history or race, a fluid, universal political poetic in which diverse peoples could articulate new visions of justice. It is appropriate that Emerson's WO Liberty journal was discovered in the papers of the first President of the NAACP, Moorfield Storey. Emerson's higher law approach not only influenced Storey but was shared by Storey's mentor, Charles Sumner, one of the great leaders of political antislavery and Reconstruction.[24]

Emerson's vision of higher law has been largely ignored or dismissed by scholars and critics. Prominent historians have caricatured Emerson and the Transcendentalists as escapists who, feeling themselves too pure for the vulgar realities of politics, sought to convert what was a failure of moral and political character into a spurious kind of nobility.[25] Wanting to "reprimand" Emerson for transcendentalism's incompatibility with "political activism," John Carlos Rowe has given Emerson's alleged apolitical individualism a recent airing.[26] In Rowe's version, Emersonian idealism is unsuitable for any practical politics because its privileged notion of inspiration detaches the individual from society and renders social concerns trivial and political action unnecessary. Emerson's efforts at political engagement are thus fatally undermined by his transcendentalist ethos of private inspiration.[27] But how does one then account for the fact that the movement from individual inspiration to political dialogue and action described by Emerson in his antislavery addresses – the movement from conscience to consent – has been an animating principle of the seminal political and constitutional events of American history? The American Revolution, the Civil War amendments, women's suffrage, and the Civil Rights movement – all move from the inspiration about the vague certainties of rights, justice, and civic virtue to the messy, uncertain political and cultural processes of consensus formation. The Emersonian "detachment" Rowe condemns is essential to any revision of the nation's ethos. The ethical and critical perspective capable of deviating from habitual norms including, among other things, racial prejudice, requires a degree of detachment: "He only who is able to stand alone is qualified for society."[28] Emerson's separation of the "just man" from "society" in such addresses as "New England Reformers" (1844) is not a retreat from social and political engagement but an acknowledgment of the distance necessary for innovations in justice.[29] For Emerson as for Kant, the reflective distance of abstraction and impartiality is not hierarchical, rising above the mêlée, but lateral, preserving openness to novel experiences, events, and other points of view.[30]

Oddly, Rowe's account of the apolitical flaw of Emerson's transcendentalism is apolitical itself. Rowe hardly glances at the political and legal figures with whom Emerson was grappling. Relying on an index to Douglass's autobiographies instead of a critical consideration of the substance of his jurisprudential views, Rowe finds a gulf separating Douglass (the good example of a politically engaged advocate) and Emerson (the bad example of a politically disabled elitist).[31] When one compares the substance of Douglass's and Emerson's higher law visions, however, the gulf between Emerson and Douglass and the illusion that the tension between private conscience and public consent betokens an apolitical perspective disappears.[32]

Another way to dismiss Emerson is simply to find the signs of racism in his writing and then to discard his thought because it is complicit in the ascriptive tradition identifying the American nationality as white, Anglo-Saxon, and Protestant. Anita Patterson disavows such a project, then proceeds to undertake it. In the final analysis, Patterson finds that Emerson's "defense of rights and his racism are intimately and deliberately connected" – no aspect of Emersonian idealism escapes race. While Emerson's idealism and "defense of rights should have nothing to do with racism," in fact his "recuperation of American democracy . . . was shaped and indeed made conceptually coherent only through his recourse to racialist language and ideology." In Emerson, democratic universals collapse into race, as does national identity.[33] Accepting these conclusions, one cannot distinguish Daniel Webster's argument in favor of the Fugitive Slave Law from Emerson's in opposition to it. Emerson's bitterly ironic castigation of Webster becomes nonsensical, as both believe in an identity of rights and race. That Patterson's characterization would lump Emerson and Webster together and obliterate the subtler distinctions between Emerson and Stowe highlights the basic flaw in her approach: her failure to situate Emerson's jurisprudence in its higher law context.[34] Particularly glaring is Patterson's avoidance of Emerson's antislavery lectures, his WO Liberty journal, and his influence on the antislavery movement.

No student of the nineteenth century can be surprised by Patterson's detection of racialist or racist aspects in Emerson's thinking. In this, Emerson's case is far from unique. George Bancroft, for example, castigated Taney's *Dred Scott* opinion in a letter to Francis Lieber, suggesting that Western jurisprudence had never before heard of "the existence of slave races," and, in his *History of the United States*, Bancroft joyfully espoused the Declaration's "faith in natural equality and the rights of man." Yet, he also subscribed to the romantic Herderean conception that "the child inherits the physical and moral characteristics of the race to which it belongs."[35] Similarly, Emerson scoffed at Taney's reference in *Dred Scott* to "servile races," offering a quotation from Augustine Thierry's *History of the Norman Conquest* to the effect that the Saxons had been a servile race when the Normans conquered them. Yet, Emerson would on occasion figuratively tie notions of liberty, equality, and self-government to a mythic Anglo-Saxon identity.[36]

Despite such moments, it is a mistake to discard Emerson's thought as racist.[37] The practical impact of Emersonian thought on the anti-slavery movement described by Len Gougeon and Albert Von Frank and the critical recuperation of Emersonian politics begun by Sacvan Bercovitch urge us to avoid dismissing Emerson's politics and jurisprudence as elitist escapism or racism.[38] Emerson's participation with Douglass, Sumner, Storey, and others in shaping a more inclusive, cosmopolitan vision of American justice and citizenship, a vision that informed the Civil War amendments, the Civil Rights Act of 1875, and the NAACP's first major litigation victory *Buchanan v. Warley* (1917), militates against such cavalier dismissals. In addition, our discovery of race in Emerson's thought should not lead to a literalist's insistence that every sign of race carries the same racist freight. Such an unnuanced approach misses the corrosive ironies in Emerson's invocations of race in the wake of the Fugitive Slave Law and obscures the anti-identitarian aspects of his notion that the proper form and function of government are derived through experimental applications of moral reasoning and consensus.

Once an ardent admirer of Webster, Emerson viewed Webster's endorsement of the Fugitive Slave Law as epitomizing the error of affirming a people's political and ethical mission in the figural guise of their shared ancestry.[39] Well versed in "God-like" Dan's stirring invocations of the national family in support of Union, Emerson drew on the trope of consanguinity to excoriate Webster's capitulation to the slave power in his "Address to the Citizens of Concord" (May 3, 1851). With bitter humor, Emerson turns Webster's praise of the national family's shared blood into an ironic explanation of his moral debility: "Webster perhaps is only following the laws of his blood and constitution." His failure of moral character is "inevitable from his constitution. All the drops of his blood have eyes that look downward. It is neither praise nor blame to say that he has no moral perception, no moral sentiment, but, in that *region,* to use the phrase of the phrenologists, a hole in the head." Instead of instilling in Webster the highest examples of American leadership through consanguinity, blood bears Webster down into the primitive mire of brute power where the strong make law as it suits their interests and desires (what Emerson in a later address terms the choice of "Might" over "Right"). The phrenological evidence used by such American ethnologists as Samuel Morton to support claims of black inferiority becomes in Emerson's hands an ironic sign of Webster's born-in-the-blood inferiority.[40]

Naming blood as the source of Webster's moral debility, Emerson highlights how Webster's figurations of national identity have replaced the ethical basis of American law. Throughout his densely ironic address, Emerson repeatedly joins the terms "blood" and "constitution" to signify that homologies of identity and law rule out justice. Law as a tribal inheritance precludes conceptions of law as created and reformed through human agency and consensus. Emerson describes the failure of Webster's tribe to separate identity and justice as the product of white animality – the "metaphysical debility" of those "ready to go on all fours" to "back this law" – converting the racist figure of black animality into a trope for Webster-like ascriptions of justice to race. To prefer the certainties of blood ("quadruped law") to the uncertainties of a universal language of conscience and consent is, in Emerson's irony, atavistic.[41]

Lest we miss the irony of his blood trope, Emerson notes near the outset that "we owe to the late disgraces" of Daniel Webster and the Fugitive Slave Law the "benefit" of learning that what we "hear and repeat" on Independence Day is "nonsense." The Fugitive Slave Law should disabuse us, Emerson suggests, of any illusions we have about the nation's ability to achieve justice. We prefer blood to spirit, identity to justice: "The fact comes out more plainly [as a result of the enactment of the Fugitive Slave Law], that you cannot rely on any man for the defense of truth, who is not constitutionally, or by blood and temperament, on that side."[42]

How then, considering his ironic treatment of blood, are we to read Emerson's distinct echo of Webster's repeated theme of "One people"?:

The destiny of this country is great and liberal, and is to be greatly administered. It is to be administered according to what is, and is to be, and not according to what is dead and gone. The Union of this people is a real thing, an alliance of men of one stock, one language, one religion, one system of manners and ideas. I hold it to be a real and not a statute Union. The people cleave to the Union, because they see their advantage in it, the added power of each.[43]

If read literally, Emerson's reference to "one stock" (blood is a good, progressive, creative model for civic union) conflicts with his previous excoriation of Webster as an animal man driven by blood (blood is a bad atavistic model for civic union). Even if there were no signs of irony in this address, one would suspect from reading other Emerson essays and addresses that, in the latter example, "blood" is a term of denigration because Emerson tends to replace various historical determinisms with human agency – the will to choose. For instance, in "The Transcendentalist"

(1843), Emerson criticizes the "materialist" who would be governed by "history . . . and the animal wants of man," and, in "Man the Reformer" (1841), Emerson asks, "What is man born for but to be a Reformer, a Re-Maker of what man has made."[44] What, then, do we make of Emerson figuring national unity as blood here? Given his care in creating an elaborate ironic riff on Webster's famous invocations of the national family, the idea that Emerson has merely lapsed into the prevalent Anglo-Saxonism of his era would seem highly unlikely.

The best way to crack this conundrum is to approach Emerson's "one stock" as converting Webster's literal figure of ancestry and blood into a metaphor for national unity created through moral consensus. The phrase "an alliance of men of one stock, one language, one religion, one system of manners and ideas" contains apparent tensions between blood (one stock) and volition (alliance) and between blood and the discursive tools of volition (language, religion, a system of manners and ideas). If Union is chosen, as Emerson indicates it is (the Union exists because people "cleave to" it), then what kind of commonality makes that choice possible? If we read Emerson's "one stock" as drawing on animal husbandry for a symbol of the common blood necessary for union, then his insistence on consent is nonsensical (as is his earlier use of animality to figure Webster's moral debility). The commonality expressed in the trope of "one stock" must be something other than blood. With Webster's oratory in mind, we are quick to note that Emerson does not illustrate "one stock" with any image of shared family heritage and that he does not identify the kinship involved in "one stock" with any allusion to a mythic Anglo-Saxon past or the shared blood of revolutionary forebears. Instead, "one stock" is amplified by unities of language, religion, and a system of manners and ideas – concepts that may be tied to but are also distinguishable from blood. So the question becomes on what basis do we distinguish these terms from a shared racial ancestry?

The answer to that question can be found in Emerson's aversion to the idea that the past can and should direct the jurisprudential constructions of the present and future. In contrast to Webster's slavish deference to the past ("Mr. Webster is a man who lives by his memory, a man of the past, not a man of faith or of hope"), the course of American government and law should be dictated, says Emerson, "according to what is, and is to be, and not according to what is dead and gone." For Emerson, the determinism of blood dovetails with an imprisonment in the past (as exemplified by Webster) and renders one incapable of "faith" in "self-government" – of "extemporising a government."

Webster turns out to be the type of person Emerson had criticized in "The Conservative" (1841), one who chooses the past over the future and memory over hope.[45]

Once severed from determinisms of blood and history and connected to the process of extemporizing government and law, the unities of language, religion, manners, and ideas can be seen as the shared terms of justice and citizenship that enable individuals of different backgrounds to choose union. As defined by Emerson's reference to these discursive tools of political and ethical choice, "one stock" represents not blood but an inclusive moral consensus as to just law, civic virtue, the duties of citizenship, and the individual's fundamental rights. In this context, the unity of religion that Emerson refers to is not a sectarian insistence on a particular religion, but a broader cosmopolitan language of justice, a civic religion capable of making Jews, Catholics, Unitarians, Congregationalists, atheists, and others "one stock" for public, political purposes, enabling them to create heterogeneous political alliances that the diverse membership deems to be fundamentally just. By turning "one stock" from a literal ascription of national identity to blood into a trope for a diverse moral consensus, Emerson suggests that it is the justice we enact and not our heritage that defines us. To drive the point home, Emerson points out that the Union's continued existence is dependent upon the citizenry's moral consensus. Once that moral consensus is abrogated, the Union is at an end: "as soon as the Constitution ordains an immoral law, it ordains disunion." As for Thomas Paine, the bonds of kinship cannot hold together, in Emerson's view, what dissensus on the fundamental terms of justice tears apart.[46]

Blood and ancestral tradition continue to be affecting figures, nostalgic tropes for a past that never existed, but their days are numbered as the pool of consenting members grows more diverse and the racialist tropes either lose their constituency or become so attenuated as to be unrecognizable as denotations of race or tribe. Prophesying that slavery "will yield at last, and go with cannibalism, tattooing, inquisition, dueling, burking," Emerson not only classes it with other primitive remnants of the tribal past but also suggests that tribalism, in its blind deference to the past, perpetuates such remnants.[47]

Rejecting the determinisms of race and history but being a creature formed by notions of race and history, Emerson turns to abstraction for a vision of justice that does not simply reiterate prior articulations: "Abstract! The more abstract the better . . . it is not their climate, not their race, not their government, or their employment, which determines the

destinies of men but their credence. As is their way of thinking and belief, will their power and fortune be, and their influence on mankind."
Notably, Emerson speaks of belief here in the plural. The belief of the individual constitutes this plurality, but it is the plurality of belief that gives
it force, that amounts to an "influence on mankind." Such collective
belief deviates from the determinisms of race and history, for Emerson,
by virtue of its abstraction, its insistence on considering the principles of
justice as transcending the peculiarities of race, history, climate, and all
the other indices of identity. Severing justice from identity enacts human
agency in such a way as to leave future generations a tangible legacy –
the example of change. Indeed, the Constitution creates the possibility
of change through the abstractness of its language. Emerson notes, for
example, that the Constitution does not have "the word slave in it." In
the crisis of conscience created by slavery's legal existence, this vagueness saves the Constitution by opening it to the inventive antislavery
readings of Frederick Douglass, Salmon Chase, Charles Sumner, and
others who make "very good argument . . . that it would not warrant the
crimes that are done under it." In demystifying the Constitution as a
body of language with which one can either do good or evil, Emerson
does not seek to replace the instruments of politics and law with the
substance of moral revelation (as a Garrisonian insistence on God's government would do). Instead, Emerson's skepticism of attempts to fix the
Constitution's meaning ("to nail the stars to the sky") corresponds with
his appreciation of the creative potential of constitutional language in
the hands of those able and bold enough to put such tools to innovative
use–those who ply "the science of liberty which begins with liberty from
fear."[48]

Turning to abstraction as a way to see beyond the blinders of race and
history, Emerson avoids particularized images of black suffering and
vulnerability.[49] Though he acknowledged after the passage of "the de-
testable statute of the last Congress," that, as a "lover of human rights," he
wanted to give "substantial help and hospitality to the slave . . . defending
him against his hunters," Emerson notably resists the prevalent and persuasive rhetorical trope of the shivering fugitive. Eschewing images that
in their typicality do not challenge or transform their audience's conceptions of justice and citizenship, Emerson's antislavery rhetoric maintains
a more abstract level of common, because unspecified, humanity. For
Emerson, images of victimhood tend to generate in the national imagination the "theatrical attitude" of the rescuer of unfortunates rather than
the self-transformation necessary for real change.[50] Emerson's erasure

of black images from his antislavery writing may well be additional proof of his racism, but, if so, it is ironically his racism that frees his view of the Constitution from the containment of race.[51]

Even his infrequent images of black Americans are marked by their abstractness, featuring the attributes of human agency rather than the visual signs of race. For example, in his 1851 "Address to the Citizens of Concord," Emerson imagines the fugitive slave as the

man who has taken the risk of being shot, or burned alive, or cast into the sea, or starved to death, or suffocated in a wooden box, to get away from his driver; and this man who has run the gauntlet of a thousand miles for his freedom, the statute says, you men of Massachusetts shall hunt, and catch, and send back again to the dog-hutch he fled from.

Though each of these images appears to derive from specific slave narratives (e.g., the box image alludes to Henry Box Brown's narrative and the image of running a thousand miles for freedom refers to William and Ellen Craft's narrative), by failing to name or describe the individuals, Emerson abstracts a central image of those narratives into symbols for a consciousness subject to pain and capable of courageous resolve.[52] Emerson's fugitive slave resists visualization. We get no details of his appearance; his features, hair, and skin color are left obscure.[53] The brevity and abstractness of this digest of fugitive slave narratives corresponds to Emerson's statement that "man is man." The principle that "man is man" will not tolerate the greater imagistic specificity in which the racist views of the era cut against the universal perspective recognizing in the black fugitive a man "fit for freedom." Similarly, in a later address, alluding to the "crying facts" of slavery, Emerson avoids a certain kind of imagistic specificity:

when the poor people who are the victims of this crime, disliking the stripping and peeling process, run away into states where this practice is not permitted, – a law has been passed requiring us who sit here to seize these poor people, tell them they have not been plundered enough, and must go back to be stripped and peeled again, and as long as they live.[54]

The overtly metaphoric quality of the verbs "stripped" and "peeled" both conjure a horrifying visual image (obliquely alluding to the slave narrative of John Brown) and block a simple visualization of the plight of the fugitive slave.[55] Instead of a straightforward image of an individual, Emerson's trope of "stripped" and "peeled" both recognizes particular suffering and turns toward a consideration of the horrifying objectification of slavery as a system. The more abstract point of view is not occluded by the racialism of such easy images as the shivering fugitive and perceives black Americans as human agents capable of framing moral action and resolve and meriting participation in the ethical language of democratic politics.

In his WO Liberty journal, Emerson mulled over various ways to articulate the alternative to blood and history he had in mind as a jurisprudential "extemporizing." Here Emerson experiments with formulations emphasizing the creative aspect of higher law jurisprudence:

As to visionary and abstract, you will forgive me if I do not see any harm in that. I think we need that: It is curious now liberty is grown passive and defensive; slavery alone is inventive and aggressive. Slavery reads the Constitution with a very shrewd and daring and innovative eye. Liberty is satisfied with literal construction. The Declaration of Independence is an abstraction. Everyman is an abstractionist on Sunday morning. The gospel of Christ is an abstraction; and by debate and study, new views and broader principles are given to fit the natural expansion of the times. That is the sole consolation to the wounds inflicted, in evil times, on the commonwealth; that in the glare of passion the foundations of law are searched, and *anew* become matters of the science of liberty.[56]

Given Emerson's conception of constitutional jurisprudence as a visionary reading of the country's foundational documents and abstract principles, the sympathy evoked by the image of the shivering and supplicant fugitive is too easy, too passive. Such images are too conventional to engender the creative process Emerson has in mind, and the emotion conjured by such images is too close to paternalistic understandings of justice and citizenship. The merciful impulse, by itself, does not bring about a reinvention of the national character and charter. Something more is required. If abstraction and innovation in contrast to "literal" (read strict) construction is our goal, as Emerson declares, then higher law justice is plainly not something to be seen in a static image or felt in our reaction to that image. Higher law justice is aggressively pursued and created in an interaction of inspiration and conversation ("debate and study") through which "new views and broader principles" are continually found "to fit the natural expansion of the times."

Opening the Constitution's basic concepts to new meanings does not require us to reject past formulations of fundamental principles but instead indicates that the fulfillment of those principles, whose impetus is to keep us moving, lies in the new incarnations of justice we create. Emerson's description in "The Conservative" of how conscience is put into practice foreshadows his conception of constitutional reform:

"although the commands of the Conscience are *essentially* absolute, they are *historically* limitary. Wisdom does not seek a literal rectitude, but a useful, that is, a conditioned one, such a one as the faculties of man and the constitution of things will warrant." As "The Conservative" suggests, reform is not a matter of rejecting the past but a creative conjunction of "Past and Future, of Memory and Hope."[57] Thus, Emerson's emphasis on the mutability of our practice of justice does not obviate the continuity of the substantive ideals informing that practice. Indeed, as Emerson points out in "Circles," one needs continuity of principle in order to recognize and direct the alterations and modifications of one's practice: "this incessant movement and progression which all things partake could never become sensible to us but by contrast to some principle of fixture or stability in the soul."[58] Justice and its component concepts, such as freedom, equality, and the rule of law, are permanent, though we revise our concrete instantiations of these concepts all the time. Some of our revisions fail (e.g., Prohibition) and are subsequently rejected, and some are only partially successful (e.g., the Civil War amendments) and are subject to further revision, but the inspirational ideal of justice remains constant, as do many of the concepts we attribute to it.

Emerson's call for a visionary and inventive approach to the Constitution coheres with the creative transformation of language he praises in "The Poet" (1844). With a bit of judicious tinkering, one can usefully merge the creative standard Emerson sets for the poet with his articulation of the jurisprudential standard he has in mind for the creative jurist who possesses "a great imaginative soul, a broad cosmopolitan mind." Understanding that "Liberty is aggressive," this jurist is not "content with standing on the defensive"; he does not "stop" at the "form" of law but "exerts original jurisdiction," reading its "meaning; neither may he rest in this meaning, but he makes the same objects exponents of his new thought." Whereas we typically err in "ador[ing] the forms of law, instead of making them vehicles of wisdom and justice," the visionary jurist realizes that all legal "symbols are fluxional; all [law] is vehicular and transitive, and is good, as ferries and horses are, for conveyance, not as farms and houses are, for homestead." Neither implicit metaphor in the terms "foundationalist" and "anti-foundationalist" captures the "vehicular" higher law jurisprudence Emerson has in mind. Emerson's jurisprudence is neither tied down nor does it float free without direction or source. Its source is not a foundation. It is a spark of energy surging outward, an inspiration that movement and change must be undertaken despite the uncertainty of the outcome.[59]

Ironically, though he distances Emerson's thought from "social or communal efficacy," Richard Poirier comes as close as any scholar to registering the potential jurisprudential relevance of Emerson's approach to language. Indeed, Poirier is aware of the divergence between Emerson's view that "every text is a reconstruction of some previous texts of work, work that itself is always, again, work-in-progress" and the strict construction touted by Robert Bork and others that fetishizes a past that never existed. In describing Emerson's conception of repetition with a difference ("The same work gets repeated throughout history in different texts, each being a revision of past texts to meet present needs, needs which are perceived differently by each new generation"), Poirier comes close to restating Emerson's visionary constitutionalism in which "new views and broader principles are given to fit the natural expansion of the times." Poirier's Emersonian appreciation that language, "if it is to represent the flow of individual experience," must have "a saving uncertainty and vagueness" parallels the Fourteenth Amendment's sponsors' praise of its "indefiniteness of meaning." The amendment's abstractness, Senator Jacob Howard urged, would ensure that it would be capable of growth from one era to the next. Emerson brings to the constitutional crisis of his day an improvisational approach to language skeptical of the fixity or finality of any expression. He approaches the Constitution in a proto-pragmatist fashion as a text continually in the process of being made and remade by aggressive, visionary readers and authors, anticipating William James's association of the mutability of language and the changes in our idiom of justice. The outcomes in this creative process are mere resting places, temporary pauses while the energy for another revision gathers. Like the figure of the soul and the heart in "Circles," justice (believed in but never fully known) generates a surge of energy bursting the confinement of past articulations, "which also runs up into a high wave, with attempt again to stop and to bind. But the heart refuses to be imprisoned; in its first and narrowest pulses, it already tends outward with a vast force, and to immense and innumerable expansions."[60]

DOUGLASS'S COSMOPOLITAN CONSTITUTIONALISM

Frederick Douglass cut an oratorical figure strikingly different from the shivering fugitive imagined by Seward, Stowe, and others.[61] Observers frequently singled out among his many oratorical talents his uncanny abilities of impersonation. An article appearing in the *National Era* (July 28, 1853) vividly recalled a performance in which Douglass had, nine years earlier, perfectly imitated Henry Clay, John Calhoun, and Daniel Webster:

Douglass put them all upon the stage before us really as Shakespeare could have done it then, or the Witch of Endor now. Half an hour we held our places, fidgeting at first, then frightened, into the cutting consciousness of a somehow participated culpability in the villainies charged home upon our Constitution and our color; then, carried out of ourselves, exchanging those quick glances that telegraph the unknown depths of men's spirits compelled into the light, till time and space and every law of mortal matter yielded, and we swept away into that strange region where inspired thought clothes itself with ideal forms, and not a pulse or breath breaks the enraptured vision . . . It was even terrible to our sympathies, so deeply enlisted, to witness the daring of that unlettered slave, attempting the personation of Clay, Calhoun, and Webster, in action, thought, and utterance . . . His astounding power of transformation, his perfect clearness of discrimination, and his redundant ability in the execution, more than justified the audacity of the design. To see one man with all the varied capacity of these three, mixing them up, without confusion or mistake, in the puppet-show of his imagination, and playing upon them at his pleasure, was verily a sight to see.

The account begins with the sharpest of contrasts – the Great Triumvirate and the fugitive slave. The provocative import of Douglass's performance derives from his "astounding power of transformation." At first frightened then liberated, brought by Douglass's performance into "cutting consciousness" of "culpability in the villanies charged home upon our Constitution and our color," the audience's sense of responsibility is accompanied by a sense of human lightness in Douglass's transformations. These caste-defying transformations constituted a political/ethical acrobatics in which the dark and worldly gravity of blood and race are replaced by the light and ideal forms of human flexibility and universal human recognition. In presenting the reversibility of the social and legal order (one thinks of Douglass's famous chiasmus – "You will see how a man was made a slave and how a slave was made a man"), Douglass's performance reminded his audience that, as Emerson put it, "man" is born "to be a Reformer, a Re-Maker of what man has made."[62]

This bravura performance dramatized a transformed Capitol in which Douglass was imaginatively present to do battle with the Great Triumvirate, arguing for the spiritual fate of the Republic and the cause of real democracy. That Douglass's magical transformation from fugitive slave into a national leader seemed plausible to many Americans, including many committed to white supremacy, at least partially explains his iconic power as an emblem of republican citizenship.

Antislavery politicians and jurists, such as Joshua Giddings, Thaddeus Stevens, John Marshall Harlan, and Salmon Chase, touted Douglass's very existence as a rebuke to racist proscriptions of citizenship both before and after the war. In an 1850 debate on the distribution of public lands in Oregon, Giddings used Douglass to condemn the proposed exclusion of African Americans. "[O]n what principle of justice," Giddings asked, did Congress propose "to exclude such men?" During the debates on Reconstruction, Stevens replied to a congressman's assertion of racial inferiority that he would match Frederick Douglass with the congressman any time. Justice Harlan thought of Douglass as a national leader with the abilities to make him "a great Senator." And Chief Justice Salmon Chase praised Douglass's leadership and "wish[ed] he could come to Congress from his District." Some antislavery advocates were drawn in particular to Douglass's indomitability. In response to Thomas Carlyle's assertion that any black man not getting out of his way would find himself in the stocks (foreshadowing the black humor of Mark Twain's model citizen and white supremacist, Pap Finn, who makes a similar pledge), Elizur Wright wryly noted that Carlyle would find the project unexpectedly difficult on meeting a Douglass, "who has worked his way from chattlehood up to the side of the ablest of white Sanhedrin Doctors and Senators." Douglass's rise had a satisfying edge to it, marking him as a republican hero: an emblem of resistance to tyrants.[63]

Douglass's prominence as a symbol of the nation's constitutional crisis can be seen in a drama critic's jibe that the taste for "Americanizing" French and English plays was so dominant in 1859 that he would "not be surprised to see *Othello* placarded, one of these days, as *Fred Douglass, or the Moor of Syracuse*." We need "not dwell on the downright injustice done a dramatic author" by these vulgarizations, the critic continues, because "The dramatic author is a kind of Pariah, having no rights which a [stage] manager is bound to respect." Echoing Justice Taney's notorious statement in *Dred Scott* that the black Americans have no rights that the white man is bound to respect, the critic sneers at the grip the constitutional crisis has on the nation's literary imagination.[64]

In Southern papers, Douglass stood for murder and amalgamation. He was classed with Henry Ward Beecher, William Lloyd Garrison, Wendell Phillips, and other "fearful agitators," whose influential examples and incendiary doctrines were to be intercepted and barred from the region.[65] "Startling Development," a Richmond *Enquirer* article, December 16, 1856, describes in racially charged terms the disgusting and dangerous spectacle of white elites being led by Douglass's oratory to break down the race barrier. The *Enquirer* laments that Northerners would "countenance . . . exhibitions of abolition madness and infamy," such as Douglass's boast "that white and black people were disappearing" in a rising tide of racial mixture. Douglass's message was rendered more shocking by the fact that his avid

audience was the very cream of the Fremont party in Chicago. Men of high social position were there with their wives and daughters . . . These representatives ogling the sooty beauties and ogled by the colored dandies in return; these persons, embracing the wealthy and tone of Chicago society, were there, listening with delighted hearts to treason, and threats of murder and civil war.

The image of the *Enquirer* article comes nearer to the truth than its overt racism might lead one to expect. Premised on boundary crossings, personal transformations, and heterogeneous compacts, Douglass's cosmopolitan politics clearly countenanced social and political amalgamation. As Michael Lind observes in *The Next American Nation*, the idea of racial amalgamation was "the very center of the vision of the future expressed" by Douglass.[66] Not bound by fixed categories of identity, Douglass's mutability was his most powerful and threatening quality as a symbol of justice and citizenship. His ability to metamorphose from one state of being to another formed an influential higher law analogue for an American people and Constitution that could similarly shift shape, composition, and dimensions.

Given Douglass's prominence, it is noteworthy that the intersection of his cosmopolitanism and his higher law constitutionalism has been passed over by scholars. A recent, landmark study by Ross Posnock recovering the cosmopolitanism of twentieth-century black intellectuals implies the need for an inquiry into this outlook's nineteenth-century lineage.[67] And the shrewd contextual analysis Douglass's politics has received from Waldo Martin, Eric Sundquist, Robert Levine, Priscilla Wald, among others, suggests the rewards of giving his jurisprudential views similar attention. Eric Sundquist's epic study, *To Wake the Nations*, for instance, finds in Douglass's recuperation of the "language of liberty" a revealing fluidity and promising revisability, but Sundquist is more interested in the revolutionary thematics of Douglass's position than the constitutional hermeneutic it suggests. Robert Levine's densely textured and rich study of Delany and Douglass offers a nuanced account of the fractious reciprocity of Douglass's "assimilation *through* self-assertion" (to borrow W.E.B. DuBois's phrase) and Delany's nationalistic Afrocentrism. But where Levine's study focuses on the dialogic formation of competing and overlapping representative identities in Douglass and Delany, the focus of this study is on the relation of power and identity to justice in both men's work. This is, I believe, the most salient distinction between them: law and social organization boil down to power for Delany, where for Douglass they are sustained by the fluidities of consent.[68]

Our way into Douglass's cosmopolitan constitutionalism begins with a brief outline of the versions of antislavery constitutionalism available to Douglass and a sketch of Douglass's rejection of the Garrisonian condemnation of the Constitution. William Wiecek has usefully distinguished between two types of antislavery constitutionalist – the moderate constitutionalists, representing the mainstream of political abolitionism, and the radical constitutionalists, seeking to guard the higher law inspiration of the antislavery movement against proslavery political compromises. Instead of looking backward as proslavery readings did, radicals and moderates both looked forward to what the Constitution might be, and both rejected the apolitical approach of the Garrisonians.[69]

Hoping that slavery would die without federal support, the moderates sought to detach the Constitution from slavery. From the viewpoint of such moderates as William Seward, Charles Sumner, Thaddeus Stevens, and Salmon P. Chase, the constitutional bifurcation of state and central governments may have reserved a space for slavery as a matter of local law in the Southern states, but the Constitution required the federal government to protect the essential liberties and rights of all persons within its jurisdiction. The moderates' program included barring the extension of slavery into the territories (where the federal government had exclusive jurisdiction), eradicating slavery in Washington, D.C., and using federal patronage and federal appointments in the states to work against slavery. Moderate antislavery constitutionalism derived considerable emotional authority from abundant (though selective) quotation of the framers' antislavery sentiments, convincing many that their intent had been antislavery all along despite the Constitution's imperfect announcement of that goal.[70]

Radical antislavery constitutionalists, such as Alvan Stewart, William Goodell, Lysander Spooner, Gerrit Smith, James McCune Smith, Jermain W. Loguen, and Amos Dresser, read the Constitution as making slavery everywhere illegitimate. Radicals critiqued the racist limitations of the Republican mainstream while remaining in correspondence with and lending support to the more radical of the Republican leadership, such as Sumner and Stevens. Radicals eschewed major-party politics in order to push the higher law critique further than the moderates could within those party structures. The radicals' approach to the Constitution boiled down to a hermeneutical imperative to read the nation's charter as enacting justice, not oppression, which entailed reading the document against its grain at times in order to square it with basic moral norms. As read by the radicals, the Constitution was and would always be a higher law Constitution.[71]

As a Garrisonian, Douglass rejected both the moderate and radical positions, reading the Constitution as fatally proslavery. Over time, however, he began to chafe at certain aspects of the Garrisonian position. For example, though Garrison valued Douglass as an eloquent witness against slavery, he sought to limit Douglass's contribution to the straightforward narration of his story. Garrison's instruction to Douglass to simply "Tell his story" may have derived in part from racial prejudice and envy, but it derived as well from the apolitical, even anarchic aspect of Garrison's religious higher law approach, which sought to replace a flawed human law not with a better human law but with God's law. One does not construct, negotiate, plan, or structure God's law – one simply bears witness to and obeys it. The denial of human agency and cosmopolitan movement inherent in this absolutist approach would provoke Douglass as much as the objectification involved in being displayed as a victim of slavery.[72]

When Douglass returned from his first trip to England, his Garrisonian allies found him full of heterodox ambitions and ideas that could not be contained.[73] From the perspective of "a denizen of the world," Douglass came to recognize that, for individual moral inspiration to have effect, it must enter public discourse in such a way as to create a new moral consensus – as Emerson put it, "although the commands of the Conscience are *essentially* absolute, they are *historically* limitary."[74] In attempting to achieve justice, we act on a moral impulse deriving, we believe, from eternal moral principles, but acknowledge at the same time that the implementation of that moral impulse in consensual politics and law is temporal. The eternal truths of the higher law unfold within the "constant evolution of moral ideas" for which we are responsible, not God:

The idea that man cannot hold property in man, that all men are free, that human rights are inalienable, that the rights of one man are equal to those of another, that governments are ordained to secure human rights did not come all at once to the moral conscience of men, but have all come very slowly in the thoughts of the world.[75]

Meeting with considerably less racism in Britain, Douglass could see that racism was a piece of human manufacture and the key impediment to a revised social and legal order. Conceived while Douglass was abroad, the project of *The North Star* was to unmake this majority racism and to replace it with a cosmopolitan discourse of ethics and law.

As editor of the *North Star*, Douglass was drawn into conversation with a broader range of antislavery views. He engaged radical and moderate arguments that, contrary to the Garrisonian position, the Constitution should be embraced as an egalitarian, antislavery charter. Gerrit Smith confronted Douglass with William Goodell's contention that a straight-forward reading of the Constitution's Preamble justified the eradication of slavery: "To promote the general welfare" could not be consonant with "crushing the laboring, the producing class, in half the States of the Republic," and securing "the blessings of Liberty" had to require the "overthrow" of "the deadly antagonist of liberty, to wit, slavery."[76] Encounters with Smith and others compelled Douglass "to re-think the whole subject, and to study, with some care, not only the just and proper rules of legal interpretation, but the origin, design, nature, rights, power, and duties of civil government." While Garrison's "No Union" argument remained rooted in a regionalist view of slavery, quarantining the South's evil to protect the North's moral purity (a dubious purity given race pro-scription in the North), travel and broader intercourse with antislavery advocates pushed Douglass's views in a cosmopolitan direction.[77]

On May 7, 1851, at the Syracuse meeting of the American Anti-Slavery Society convention, Douglass shocked the meeting and the ranks of anti-slavery by summarily announcing his adoption of a radical reading of the Constitution. Douglass described his new point of view to Gerrit Smith: "I am only in reason and conscience bound to learn the intentions of those who framed the Constitution *in the Constitution itself*."[78] We should not let the seeming transparency of this statement obscure the aggres-sively creative hermeneutic Douglass is indicating. Strictly remaining within its four corners, one cannot produce coherent interpretations of the Constitution's many ambiguities. By focusing on its express but ab-stract wording (which does not contain the terms "slave" or "slavery") *and* presuming that it favors justice, Douglass can exclude from the Con-stitution extrinsic historical evidence that does not comport with present conceptions of justice (e.g., that many of the framers owned slaves or that the Constitution's slavery clauses were part of a deal with the Southern states to ensure ratification). And excluding such negative extrinsic evi-dence, in turn, enables Douglass – an ex-slave and disfranchised black

American – to read the document's abstract terms as comporting with present conceptions of justice and to rewrite its history as endorsing a more just vision of American society.[79] As he points out in an April 1852 address, by presuming "that the Constitution" favors "liberty" (a reasonable position given the express wording of the Preamble), one can dismiss evidence that some framers, contrary to the principle of liberty, "desired compromises [favoring] slavery." With such evidence out of the way, the conclusion becomes ineluctable that the framers intended the Constitution to be capable of expansion so as to "secure the equality of *all* the people."[80] In Douglass's revised view, the framers had anticipated that changes in the national moral consensus would redirect readings of the national charter. The parallel of Douglass's self-transformations to the fluidity he ascribes to the Constitution, though implicit, cannot be missed.

Many themes and figures in Douglass's pre-conversion writing anticipate his antislavery constitutionalism. The first of these is his use of various kinds of movement to figure the interpenetrating processes of personal and political transformation. In "The Slumbering Volcano" (1848), Douglass gives a telling sketch of Madison Washington's revolt aboard *The Creole* (an example he would pursue at greater length in his novella, *The Heroic Slave*):

About twilight on the ninth day, Madison, it seems, reached his head above the hatchway, looked out on the swelling billows of the Atlantic, and feeling the breeze that coursed over its surface, was inspired with the spirit of freedom. He leapt from beneath the hatchway, gave a cry like an eagle to his comrades beneath, saying, *we must go through.* (Great applause.) Suiting his action to the word, in an instant his guilty master was prostrate on the deck, and in a very few minutes Madison Washington, a black man, with woolly head, high cheek bones, protruding lip, distended nostril, and retreating forehead, had the mastery of that ship, and under his direction, that brig was brought safely into the port of Nassau, New Providence.[81]

This passage rather neatly breaks into two parts, the prelude to action, which is described in universal terms as the inspiration of a nature not at rest but in motion, and the sequel, which describes the resultant transformation: a reversal of both personal and political fortunes. Douglass figuratively connects natural movement (the mobility of ocean and wind) to Madison Washington's surging physical movement and vocalization of revolt in a "cry like an eagle." The result is a personal and political transfiguration: the black Washington becomes the republican hero. Each of the elements in this figurative matrix has higher law significance: the movement of the wind and water represents the "natural" moral sense inspiration that slavery is wrong, that freedom is man's natural state. The consequent action and cry of Washington puts private, personal inspiration into political play, articulates it and gives it meaning, thereby changing the course of events and altering the person and his political standing. Douglass frequently recurs to a symbolic pattern in which "natural" and private inspiration, forceful but inchoate, leads to action or dialogue that, in turn, not only confirms and glosses the inspiration but also results in a personal and political transformation.

In *My Bondage and My Freedom*, for instance, Douglass reports that as a boy he was "fill[ed]" with "wonder and admiration" by the sight of sailboats scudding along the broad expanse of the Chesapeake Bay. As a child inspired by this sight, he has yet to put the feeling, the swelling in his chest, to any particular symbolic use. That is to say, the potential meanings and significances of this affective response are as yet embryonic. The image returns when, after a period of relative freedom in which Douglass gains literacy, he is leased to the slavebreaker, Covey, whose particularly oppressive version of slavery calculatedly seeks to imbrute the slave, eliminating any buoyancy in his mental life. Suffering under Covey's tyranny, Douglass again is inspired by the sight of sailboats on the Bay. But what before had simply moved him with a raw sensation of *joie de vivre* without any particular denotative or connotative significance, is here charged with very particular political and personal meanings. The "beautiful vessels" become symbols of freedom that "terrify and torment" Douglass by forcing him to recognize his "wretched condition." The sights of "the glad ship" and the "gentle gale" painfully inspire Douglass with kinesthetic feelings of motion as liberty.

While still held "fast in [his] chains," he conceives of flying, swimming, running, sailing to freedom, but the immediate sequel to this poetic vision is Douglass's thrashing of Covey.[82] The boat metaphor suggests a universal truth – as boats on water are always in motion, sometimes violent motion, human existence is a matter of constant, sometimes violent, movement and transformation. Slavery is defined in its most anti-human aspect, in the person of Covey, as an attempt to eliminate this movement (as Emerson says of proslavery readings of the Constitution which attempt to "nail the stars to the sky"). The childhood wonder of Douglass's earlier vision is not negated, explained, or replaced by this later, more pointedly political reading of the symbolic significance of the sailboat image; the prior experience instances a basic affective relation between the human being and his universe. As one becomes more articulate, one's experience becomes more symbolically ductile: one sees the different uses to which it can be put. Here the wind-powered craft indicate the way human knowledge and expertise can draw upon the natural inspiration (the wind itself and the idea of what the wind can do) to achieve movement, to go somewhere new. Similarly, in drawing a parallel between the two sailboat experiences, Douglass suggests the means by which a childhood inspiration can with insight and learning continue to fuel a lifelong process of movement and personal transformation. More than a simplistic emblem of freedom ("free as the wind"), Douglass's images of natural movement ascribe a process of inspired change as fundamental to human existence and human association.

Douglass's two uses of the sailboat image also limn a corresponding republican distinction between the inspirations of the moral sense possessed by all human beings and the implementation of such inspiration in political discourse and action. As for the framers and his antebellum antislavery colleagues, Douglass's higher law argument begins with the faculty of moral cognition. This indwelling and universal faculty of moral perception enables even an untutored child to intuit the wrongness of slavery (think here of Jefferson's ploughman who is the equal to the professor in moral cognition). But Douglass's higher law conception emphasizes the personal and political transformation entailed in moving from private moral inspiration to dialogue and action.

In his famous account of learning to read, Douglass describes how prior to examining Caleb Bingham's popular reader, *The Columbian Orator*, his indwelling moral sense had intuited the wrongness of slavery but the political and jurisprudential import of these feelings remained mysterious and ephemeral: "interesting thoughts of my own soul . . . frequently flashed through my mind, and died away for want of utterance." This early moral intuition, like his first experience of the sailboats on the Chesapeake Bay, awaits a change in Douglass for its consummation. It lies fallow while Douglass develops to the point where he can draw upon its significance. Acquiring literacy in natural rights rhetoric from *The Columbian Orator*, "enable[s]" Douglass "to utter [his] thoughts, and to meet the arguments brought forward to sustain slavery."[83] What was a private inspiration, now can be articulated, now can fuel dialogue and action. His early affective response to slavery helps Douglass recognize the concepts he tells us he is just learning. As he becomes literate in the higher law lexicon of human rights and consensual governance, the prior intuitions of his childhood render this lexicon already familiar though new. In turn, his new literacy reveals the political and ethical

significance of his preliterate moral feelings. Those early feelings, untutored and spontaneous, prove the inherence of the higher law dictates
of the moral sense and confirm his humanity (defined as a being with
a moral sense), thus establishing his entitlement to the inherent rights
accorded by higher law. Both the inherence of the rights and his entitlement to them are demonstrated by his preliterate capacity to intuit their
existence and subsequent ability to articulate them.

Using the critical tools of Lacanian psychology and Derridian post-
structuralism, Henry Louis Gates's analysis of Douglass's literacy (his
"priority of voice") misses Douglass's emphasis on a dialogue of pre-
and post-literate states of mind and that dialogue's political and jurisprudential significance. The contemporary theoretical argument that language precedes or subsumes consciousness or human experience guiding
Gates's interpretation would have been anathema to Douglass, denying
the preliterate subjectivity that both warrants and is warranted by later
access to the tools of literacy. Douglass's hope for a consensually based
model of human association depends on a belief in a universal faculty
of moral cognition (the hardware) that precedes the processes of education and socialization (the software), reflecting the moral sense theory of
Hume, Smith, and others. Gates may feel that the superior perspective
provided by such twentieth-century theory cuts Douglass loose from this
bit of faith, but such analysis misrepresents the process of moral cognition central to Douglass's politics and jurisprudence and erases a core
component of his universalism.[84]

The reciprocity of prior intuition and later articulation is crucial to
understanding how the sorrow songs, a figure seemingly bound to racial
identity, provide a lesson in cosmopolitanism. Douglass describes how
one experiences most fully the poignant beauty of these songs within the
private aesthetic and emotional terms created by the circle of slavery:
"The hearing of those wild notes always depressed my spirits, and filled
my heart with ineffable sadness." But, while one is within that circle,
the songs' public and political significance cannot be fully understood:
"I did not, when a slave, understand the deep meanings of those rude,
and apparently incoherent songs. I was myself within the circle, so that
I neither saw nor heard as those without might see and hear. They told
a tale which was then altogether beyond my feeble comprehension."
Thus, though the songs give Douglass his "first glimmering conceptions
of the dehumanizing character of slavery," it is only after he has access to
different perspectives furnished by literacy and travel (for example, his

hearing "the same *wailing notes*" in Ireland during the famine of 1845–46)
that Douglass can fully comprehend and articulate the universal political
significance of their beauty. Though historical facts focus our attention
on the "the grievous wrongs" of the particular people singing, the insight
that they are wrongs, as Douglass observed in an address comparing the
plight of the Irish to that of the slave, is universal: "A sense of human
wrong and oppression has ONE language the world over."[85]

By suggesting that others, the "truly spiritual-minded men and
women," may go, hear these songs, and be moved by them, Douglass
does not suggest that white spectators who "are strangers to our feelings"
will thereby have the experience of those within the circle.[86] While the
slaves' particular and situate experience remains private and incommensurable, a sympathetic outsider can participate in the songs' public and
political import. This import can only be fully understood, in Douglass's
account, from the cosmopolitan perspective of one outside the circle,
the perspective from which one appreciates the poetry of another time,
country, milieu, or people. Crossing such boundaries of private context
(the domain of identity) is simultaneously the basic figure for Douglass's
transformation from slave to man and more broadly an epistemological
trope for the process of shifting one's perspective through movement, education, dialogue, and debate, enabling one to derive a universal political
discourse of justice and citizenship.

The dualism in Douglass's vision of human development between
certain inspiration and transformative practice sets the basic pattern for
Douglass's cosmopolitan constitutionalism. By beginning from a leap of
faith that liberty and justice are the genius of American law, Douglass's
creative interpretation of the Constitution reads the movement, mutability, and transformation that define cosmopolitan existence into the
nation's charter.[87] Our collective efforts to read the Constitution more
justly represent the process of self-transformation that Douglass embodies writ large.

Douglass's cosmopolitan vision of the Constitution is most provocatively advanced in his famous address "What to the Slave is the Fourth
of July?" (July 5, 1852). When one considers this speech, the absence of
a detailed analysis of Douglass's constitutional jurisprudence becomes
particularly striking. Literary scholars reading Douglass's autobiographical narratives have tended to overlook the correspondence between the
personal transformations of Douglass's life story and the national transformation his address urges.[88] An important exception is Priscilla Wald's

Constituting Americans. Wald understands that the border between the political and the personal in Douglass is elusive and that Douglass's speech, like his narratives, presents a self in transition, a self "contingent upon and embodying the fate of an uncertain and unstable We the People."[89]

To help us see how radical Douglass's speech is in its direful figuration of the nation's moral condition and its hopeful vision of a mutable Constitution, we can observe, in passing, the contrast offered by the speeches of the Great Triumvirate on the Compromise of 1850, speeches that form the milestone for the decade's proslavery constitutionalism. In debating the best way to save the Union, Clay, Calhoun, and Webster self-consciously drew authority to speak from the notion that they were representative of the constituent elements of the country (Calhoun speaks as a Southerner, Clay claims the moderate insight of a border state denizen, and Webster speaks "not as a Massachusetts man, nor as a Northern man, but as an American").[90]

By contrast, Douglass's outsider status gives him a different vantage on the significance of the Fourth of July. Though "It is the birthday of *your* National Independence, and of *your* political freedom," Douglass claims authority to speak on this occasion by virtue of "the distance" he has traveled to get to "this platform" from "the slave plantation, from which I escaped" and "the difficulties" he surmounted "in getting from the latter to the former."[91] This journey allows Douglass to perceive and credibly announce both the nation's failure and promise, making him representative not of the Union as it has been, but of what it can become. Where Calhoun, Clay, and Webster seek to arrest the forces of change, calling for the restoration of a prior equilibrium between the sections ("harmony and fraternal feelings," "brotherly love and affection," and the preservation of "the great American family"), Douglass flatly announces that change is inevitable. The republic, according to Douglass, is like a river. Until it dries up, it is in continual motion. The only question is what its course will be. Douglass finds hope in the fact that the nation's relative youth ("she is still in the *impressionable* stage of her existence") may enable the necessary transformation, a transformation made more radical by virtue of the guilt that must be confronted.[92] Where Calhoun condemns the North for violating the fixed terms of a sacred deal between the sections, Douglass praises the deal struck by "the fathers of this republic" as intentionally left open: "With them, nothing was '*settled*' that was not right."[93]

But the most thunderous contrast can be heard in Webster's and Douglass's characterizations of the United States. Webster's peroration pleads for the sake of a great and just nation:

It is a great, popular, constitutional government, guarded by legislation, law, and judicature, defended by the holy affections of the people. No monarchical throne presses these States together; no iron chain of despotic power encircles them; they live and stand upon a government, popular in its form, representative in its character, founded on principles of equality, calculated to last, we hope, forever. In all its history it has been beneficent. It has trodden down no man's liberty; it has crushed no State; is has been in all its influences benevolent and Beneficent – promotive of the general prosperity, the general glory, and the general renown.

The irony of Webster's touting of American beneficence in a speech urging there is no conceivable moral ground on which to deny the return of fugitive slaves could hardly have been lost on Douglass.[94] Douglass crushes this exceptionalist, self-satisfied illusion with a blistering summation of the hypocrisy entailed in this vision of the Union:

What, to the American slave, is your 4th of July? I answer: a day that reveals to him, more than all other days in the year, the gross injustice and cruelty to which he is the constant victim. To him, your celebration is a sham; your boasted liberty, an unholy license; your national greatness, swelling vanity; your sounds of rejoicing are empty and heartless; your denunciations of tyrants, brass fronted impudence; your shouts of liberty and equality, hollow mockery; your prayers and hymns, your sermons and thanksgivings, with all your religious parade, and solemnity, are, to him, mere bombast, fraud, deception, impiety, and hypocrisy – a thin veil to cover up crimes which would disgrace a nation of savages. There is not a nation on the earth guilty of practices, more shocking and bloody, than are the people of these United States, at this very hour.

To illustrate these charges, Douglass offers the "fiendish and shocking" "spectacle" of the internal slave trade, "the sound of the slave-whip," the separation of families, the brutal exposure of the women to be sold. The Fugitive Slave Law epitomizes the vile direction the nation has taken in substituting power for notions of morality and consent: "[Slavery] is now an institution of the whole United States. The slave power is co-extensive with the star-spangled banner and American Christianity."[95]

Where Webster's oration closes with the dulcet tones of justice and equanimity in an attempt to retune the national harmony and restore the *status quo*, Douglass's speech shatters the complacencies of the nation's self-image with the discord of slavery. The aim of Douglass's jeremiad is to precipitate a transformation of the nation's self-conception and its interpretation of the Constitution. To spur such self-transformation, Douglass must decisively interrupt the exceptionalist tendencies in American thought ("I remember, also, that, as a people, Americans are remarkably familiar with all facts which make in their own favor"). One of the most powerful and insidious of these tendencies is the attempt by Webster and others to avoid the present crises of constitutional conscience by retreating into fantasies of a shared ancestry's heroic past. To drain the affective pull of such images, Douglass contrasts proud claims of revolutionary era ancestry (so often invoked by Webster and other politicians) with recognition that revolutionary ideas have no genealogy: "It was fashionable, hundreds of years ago, for the children of Jacob to boast, we have 'Abraham to our father,' when they had long lost Abraham's faith and spirit. That people contented themselves under the shadow of Abraham's great name, while they repudiated the deeds which made his name great."[96] The ideas and actions of each generation of citizens, not blood, make a republic's development worthy of celebration.

By abruptly pivoting from his withering condemnation of the nation's hypocrisy to praise the Constitution as "a GLORIOUS LIBERTY DOCUMENT," Douglass pushes his audience into an acrobatic recognition of the co-existence of slavery and freedom, power and consent: "In *that* instrument I hold there is neither warrant, license, nor sanction of the hateful thing; but, interpreted as it *ought* to be interpreted, the Constitution is a GLORIOUS LIBERTY DOCUMENT. Read its preamble, consider its purposes. Is slavery among them? Is it at the gateway? or is it in the temple? It is neither." Against the heinous particularities of American slavery, Douglass juxtaposes his and his audience's always present ability to reread the nation's charter in the interests of justice. Thanks to the abstractness and openness of the Constitution, we can continue to author the Union and its organizing principles through our reinterpretation of the national charter:

Now, there are certain rules of interpretation, for the proper understanding of all legal instruments. These rules are well established. They are plain, common-sense rules, such as you and I, and all of us, can understand and apply, without having passed years in the study of law. I scout the idea that the question of the constitutionality or unconstitutionality of slavery is not a question for the people. I hold that every American citizen has a right to form an opinion of the constitution, and to propagate that opinion, and to use all honorable means to make his opinion the prevailing one.

Amateurism is as central to Douglass's jurisprudence as it was to the founding fathers. The average citizen, in Douglass's view, has the ability and the responsibility to revise the basic charter by reading it to conform to what he or she sees as "the evolution of moral ideas." In stating that "I hold that every American citizen has a right to form an opinion of the constitution, and to propagate that opinion, and to use all honorable means to make his opinion the prevailing one," Douglass champions the agency of the citizen-jurist who forms an opinion of the Constitution and garners the public support necessary to render his/her interpretation effective.[97]

Douglass's vision of amateur constitutional interpretation implies an ongoing negotiation of the governing moral consensus animating and directing the national charter. As only justice is "final" and the human agents creating that justice are imperfect, a society's civic virtue lies in the continuing revision of this consensus, not in fictions of arrival like that touted by Webster (or later Justice Taney in *Dred Scott*) in which the framers' consensus as to the Constitution's meaning is held up as forever definitive. What James Otis feared in a contractually based legal and political order, "will not the compact be ever forming and never finished, ever making but never done," Douglass embraces, in part, because the contractualism implied in the citizen-jurist's ability and duty to make his/her construction of the Constitution the prevailing one is predicated upon human agency, dialogue, and consent, not race.[98] If based on moral agency, not race, Douglass and the disfranchised people he represents clearly qualify for citizenship and participation in revising the nation's basic charter.

The constitutional transformation Douglass hopes his speech will help to engender, however, is not simply a matter of changing slaves into cit-izens. One could say that that is almost a happy by-product of another transformation Douglass is more directly concerned with here. The aim of his speech's vitriol is to convert the self-satisfied members of a mythic Anglo-Saxon clan into citizens: political beings who define their politi-cal and legal association not by consanguinity but through consent and moral agency. Douglass powerfully recasts the national narrative as a continuing confrontation of the challenge to read justice into the terms of the national charter despite our history of injustice. In rising to this challenge, we confront the grievous failures of our history as well as the promise of our express dedication to justice, liberty, and equality. With the flaws of history abutting the promise of the Constitution's abstract terms, Douglass's ironic or double vision of the Constitution and its relation to the national narrative was and continues to be an important contribu-tion to American constitutional jurisprudence. Jurists, such as William O. Douglass and Leon Higginbotham, have turned to Douglass's vision (and the Fourth of July speech in particular) to interpret the meaning of the Civil War amendments.[99] Thurgood Marshall's separate opinion in *Bakke*, though it does not cite Douglass, is deeply indebted to the constitutionalism of Douglass's "What to the Slave is the Fourth of July" address, mirroring its double vision of failure and promise.[100]

The frame of reference for Douglass's view of the Constitution is distinctly cosmopolitan:

No nation can now shut itself up from the surrounding world, and trot round in the same old path of its fathers without interference . . . Long established customs of hurtful character could formerly fence themselves in, and do their evil work with social impunity. Knowledge was then confined and enjoyed by the privileged few, and the multitude walked on in mental darkness. But a change has now come over the affairs of mankind. Walled cities and empires have become unfashionable. The arm of commerce has borne away the gates of the strong city. Intelligence is penetrating the darkest corners of the globe . . . Wind, steam, and lightning are its chartered agents. Oceans no longer divide, but link nations together. From Boston to London is now a holiday excursion. Space is comparatively annihilated. Thoughts expressed on one side of the Atlantic are distinctly heard on the other.[101]

This passage anticipates the 1853 *National Era* article recounting how Douglass's impersonation of the Great Triumvirate conveys his audience from a "cutting consciousness" of guilt "into the light, till time and space and every law of mortal matter yielded, and we swept away into that strange region where inspired thought clothes itself with ideal forms." The description of Douglass's performance echoes Douglass's image of a transformed cosmopolitan world. In both Douglass's speech and the journalistic description, boundaries are annihilated, and separations deemed natural and inevitable fall before the expanding human capacity for transformation and communication. The manners, intelligence, and eloquence of Clay, Calhoun, and Webster can no more be shut off from Douglass's appropriation than a portion of the modern world in Douglass's description can effectively isolate itself.

In his most overtly race-focused address, "The Claims of the Negro Ethnologically Considered," Douglass directly confronts the supposed barrier posed by race to his cosmopolitan constitutionalism. Douglass begins where his "What to the Slave is the Fourth of July" address ends – with a cosmopolitan image of the world that breaks down the delusions of race:

It is somewhat remarkable, that, at a time when knowledge is so generally diffused, when the geography of the world is so well understood – when time and space, in the intercourse of nations, are almost annihilated – when oceans have become bridges – the earth a magnificent hall – the hollow sky a dome – under which a common humanity can meet in friendly conclave – when nationalities are being swallowed up – and the ends of the earth brought together – I say it is remarkable – nay, it is strange that there should arise a phalanx of learned men – speaking in the name of *science* – to forbid the magnificent reunion of mankind in one brotherhood.

Douglass's cosmopolitan perspective on the American Constitution derives from a basic moral premise that "[T]he reciprocal duties of all to each, and of each to all" depend upon the "unity of the human race." Corollary duties and rights, the mutual obligations and entitlements that justly order our social and political relations, begin from some recognition of shared humanity. Speaking as a "denizen of the world" as well as a "citizen of a country rolling in the sin and shame of Slavery," Douglass challenges the scientific race thinking of Nott, Glidden, Morton, Agassiz. The intended constitutional bearing of an address ostensibly about race becomes clear in Douglass's attack on the aid and comfort given by the polygenesis argument of Nott, Morton, and others to such proslavery laws as the 1854 Kansas/Nebraska Act. More telling because contained in an address focusing on the prevalent race thinking of his era, Douglass makes clear that his aim is to eradicate racial categorizations of human identity from the discourse of justice and politics:

Human rights stand upon a common basis; and by all the reason that they are supported, maintained and defended, for one variety of the human family, they are supported, maintained and defended for *all* the human family; because all mankind have the same wants, arising out of a common nature. A diverse origin does not disprove a common nature, nor does it disprove a united destiny. The essential characteristics of humanity are everywhere the same.

To grant that various racial groupings of human beings are "naturally different in their moral, physical, and intellectual capacities," Douglass points out, makes "plausible a demand for classes, grades and conditions, for different methods of culture, different moral, political, and religious institutions, and a chance is left for slavery, as a necessary institution." "Human rights," by contrast, are part of the public language of justice enabling political intercourse and association between people of "diverse origin[s]." To participate in cosmopolitan political and ethical intercourse does not entail denying either a claim for the particular effect the sorrow songs have on African Americans or the symbolic importance of a search for ancestral connections between African Americans and ancient Egypt. Communication and negotiation across the lines of identity may alter one's conceptions of justice but such change has no necessary impact on one's sense of origin.[102]

The key to cosmopolitan recognitions of shared humanity is agency. The power to choose and act on choice is fundamental to notions of consensual association as well as moral responsibility. Agency can be forcefully demonstrated either in words or deeds. Early in his antislavery career, Douglass recognized that the failure of higher law argument to overturn proslavery readings of the Constitution made violent resistance unavoidable: "Find out just what any people will quietly submit to and you have found the exact measure of injustice and wrong which will be imposed upon them, and these will continue till they are resisted with words or blows, or with both."[103] The phrase "quiet submission" combines language and physical response, suggesting that tyrannical denials of humanity are underwritten by passivity in words or actions, an effacement of agency. It follows that resistance may be voiced through revolutionary violence as well as speech. As exemplified in Douglass's fight with Covey, violence can be an elemental form of higher law protest, forcing a cosmopolitan recognition of one's humanity.[104]

In framing his decisive moment of insurrection, Douglass singles out the importance of a talisman, a root, given him by a sympathetic slave, Sandy Jenkins ("a genuine African"), to shield him from Covey. Though skeptical, when Covey does not seek to punish him for running off, Douglass admits that, for a moment, the magic of the root seemed real. In the *Narrative*, Douglass describes his subsequent violent resistance of Covey as "fully test[ing]" "the virtue of the *root*." The latter phrase is significant on a number of levels. The root is a species of conjure or voodoo and a symbol of African identity. The word "virtue" derives from the Latin *virtus*, denoting strength as well as morality, aptly signaling a central paradox of the revolutionary era's higher law tradition: human agency or power is necessary for the achievement of the moral norms deemed to be inherent. Announcing Douglass's decisive moment of resistance (one thinks of Patrick Henry's famous declaration "Give me liberty or give me death") as the test of the "virtue of the *root*," the *Narrative* comes close to syncretically fusing the African identity symbolized in the root with the universals of higher law virtue.[105]

In the longer and more detailed depiction of this scene in *My Bondage and My Freedom*, however, Douglass subtly moves away from any suggestion that the racial identity signified by the "root" has anything to do with his triumph over Covey. In the second version, he deletes his previous characterization of the fight with Covey as "fully test[ing]" "the virtue of the root" and additionally associates Covey with "the black art[s]" *and* with regressive slaveholder religion, teaching passivity and obedience to slaves. Pared of the suggestion that a racialized "root" is being tested and not Douglass's "virtue," his later version unmistakably emphasizes the universally human quality of his own agency, his own power of self-transformation: "I now forgot my roots, remembering my pledge to *stand up in my own defense* . . . I was resolved to fight." What was too ambiguous for Douglass in the metaphor of "the virtue of the root," a figure which threatened to obscure within an illusion of racial identity the primary importance of his choice, his will, he makes explicit here. His choice and his acts in resisting Covey's tyranny evidence his humanity from a universal perspective not a "roots" perspective. Enacting his agency through resistance is the source of a rebirth: "I was a changed being after that fight. I was nothing before; I *was a* MAN NOW." And Douglass's rebirth through resistance parallels the birth of the American nation out of the Declaration of Independence. What defines the man and the nation is the ability as agent to choose and act. In *My Bondage*, Douglass sums up the meaning of his fight as the discovery that "A man without force, is without the essential dignity of humanity. Human nature is so constituted, that it cannot *honor* a helpless man, although it can *pity* him; and even this it cannot do long, if the signs of power do not arise."[106] Douglass's conception of agency as definitional of civil recognition coincides with an important theme in American law that requires agency as the prerequisite for the imposition of legal responsibilities and liabilities: each is premised on the other. As would be captured sixty years later in the famous analysis of Wesley Hohfeld, American jurisprudence is thoroughly grounded in a logic correlating power and liability, rights and duties, agency and responsibility.[107]

Though he attempted to deny any change in his attitude toward Douglass, Covey's greatly altered behavior toward Douglass after the fight betrayed an important difference. Bravado aside, Covey's fearful refusal to risk a second thrashing indicated that, at least on a primitive level, he had been forced to recognize Douglass as a being possessing the feelings to resent a wrong and the agency to redress violently that wrong. Transforming himself in the fight, Douglass also succeeded in forcing some recognition of his humanity on his enemy. The fight with Covey foreshadows the war against slavery, and, of course, as a practical matter, the North's victory was not simply a matter of antislavery higher law sentiments. The brutal communication of war did not eradicate racism in the vanquished South or the victorious North. And to some extent, Reconstruction was less a new deal with the former slaveholders than the positivist dictate of the victor to the vanquished. Yet, as Bruce Ackerman has forcefully argued, the Civil War amendments depended for their enactment on a shift in the nation's higher law consensus.[108] And there can be little doubt that the fundamental conceptions of justice and citizenship expressed in those amendments shifted in the direction urged by Douglass and Emerson.

Reconstruction efforts to revise the national charter drew on the continuing labors of a literary/legal, black/white antislavery partnership, including writers, such as Emerson and Douglass, and lawyers and political leaders, such as Samuel R. Ward, William Howard Day, John Mercer Langston, Gerrit Smith, Salmon Chase, Thaddeus Stevens, and Charles Sumner. The pattern of reciprocal influence across race lines within this coalition can be seen in Chase's urging Langston to consider emigration as a solution to racial proscription and in Douglass's advising Chase to reject emigration (Chase and Langston eventually adopted Douglass's position).[109] Public recognition of this partnership often came in a derogatory form. The New York *Herald* termed it a conspiracy, recommending that William H. Seward, Gerrit Smith, Frederick Douglass, Salmon Chase, Charles Sumner, Joshua Giddings, Henry Wilson, Henry Ward Beecher, and Horace Greeley be hanged for their complicity with John Brown's raid on Harper's Ferry.[110]

For Emerson, Douglass, and Sumner, Reconstruction offered an opportunity, in Emerson's words, "to restore the spirit of the American Constitution & not its forced & falsely construed letter." "We can see that the Constitution & law in America," Emerson noted, "must be written on ethical principles, so that the entire power of the spiritual world can be enlisted to hold the loyalty of the citizen, & to repel the enemy as by force of Nature." Unless the conflict between justice and injustice, between freedom and slavery, between equality and caste were resolved, Emerson wrote, "the war will not be extinguished." As Sumner put it, "Where Human Rights are set at nought, there can be no tranquility." Like Douglass, Emerson appreciated the war as a kind of ethical fire consuming the dross incorporated into the nation's charter: the war "sweeps away all the false issues on which it began, & arrives presently at real & lasting questions" – "Let it search, let it grind, let it overturn, &, like the fire when it finds no more fuel, it burns out. The war will show, as all wars

do, what [is] wrong is intolerable." Emerson shared with Douglass and
Sumner a conviction that Reconstruction must not only abolish slavery
but must include black Americans as equal civic participants:

nothing satisfies all men but justice, let us have that, & ...let us stifle our
prejudices against commonsense & humanity, & agree that every man shall have
what he honestly earns, and, if he is a sane & innocent man, have...an equal
vote in the state, and a fair chance in society...This time, no compromises,
no concealments, no crimes...that cannot be called by name, shall be tucked
in under another name, like, "persons held to labor," meaning persons stolen,
"held", meaning held by hand-cuffs, when they are not under whips.

Echoing Douglass's constitutional hermeneutic, Emerson wanted "to
write the moral statute into the Constitution, & give the written only a
moral interpretation." Reframing the national charter in ethical terms
would enable the nation to re-combine "firmly & durably." As Sumner
put it, the "Republic" would "cease to be a patchwork...and will become a Plural Unit, with one Constitution, one liberty, and one franchise."[111]

As the most prominent African American of his day and his era's
greatest orator, Douglass provided powerful evidence that the human
recognition triggering citizenship had to be redefined in non-racial terms.
Douglass's success in puncturing the boundary of race offered a parable
for the justice of erasing the internal divisions and boundaries of race
from the Constitution. When Douglass argued regarding the Nebraska
controversy that "Liberty must stick no stakes, and draw no lines short
of the outer circle of the republic" and that "Liberty and justice, as laid
down in the preamble of the U.S. Constitution, must be maintained in
the outermost parts of the republic," every reader had in some truncated
form or another the transformations of Douglass's life story in mind.
The ex-slave's rejection of boundaries was doubly significant of personal
and national transformation. Rejecting the trope of the map because it
expresses a stultifying reverence for past political compromises and the
internal boundaries drawn thereby, Douglass replaces the map riven with
internal divisions with the Emersonian figure of the circle that becomes
firm and rigid only to be broken outward by a new surge of energy.
Always being redrawn, the circle is a figure of inclusion, an abstract
geometrical figure better suited for the abstractions of equality and liberty
than the internal flaws in the national map created by compromising
those inclusive abstract principles, such as the Missouri Compromise
parallel of 36 degrees and 30 minutes. In his person and his oratory,

Douglass pushes the constitutional ambit of citizenship outward into a circular form, giving the mutable qualities of Emerson's figure new jurisprudential meaning and a living exemplar.[112]

By looking at Douglass's connection with Sumner, we can glimpse Douglass's influence on a more cosmopolitan conception of the Constitution. A review of their correspondence provides direct evidence of their alliance. When Douglass turned away from Garrisonianism toward antislavery constitutionalism, he announced the change to Sumner, explaining that he had broken out of the confinement of the Garrisonian "school," which was "too narrow in its philosophy and too bigoted in spirit to do justice to any who venture to differ from it."[113] We can overhear the intimate and confident tone of confederates in Douglass's later suggestion to Sumner that he change two items in a recent speech that "grated a little on my ear." The first is Sumner's comment that Garrison originated the present antislavery movement. Douglass had been at some pains to show that the antislavery genealogy is much longer and more international than Sumner's comment suggests, stressing thereby an innate and universal higher law intuition that slavery is evil. Also he objected to Sumner's "guarded disclaimer touching the social elevation of the colored race."[114] Such disclaimers betokened a curb or limit on the fluidity of social and political relations between the races, a limit Douglass sought to destroy.

The symbolic import of Douglass's association with Sumner for his era's conception of justice and citizenship is suggested by the newspaper reports of Sumner's famous 1866 Senate address entitled "The Equal Rights of All." Sumner intended this address to orient the Reconstruction Congress's approach to suffrage and other citizenship rights of the freedmen. Citing a wide range of literary, philosophical, and legal precedents from Kant, Condorcet, and Milton to Justice Story and the framers, Sumner urged: "Thus is Equality the Alpha and the Omega, wherein all other rights are embraced. Men may not have a natural right to certain things, but most clearly they have a natural right to *impartial laws*, without which justice, being the end and aim of government, must fail. Equality in rights is the first of rights." As Douglass and others had, Sumner contends, against the racist ethnology of his era, that we are all of "one blood." Raising the specter of Douglass-like higher law violence in the person of "Toussaint l'Ouverture, a black of unmixed blood, who placed himself at the head of his race, showing the genius of war, and the genius of statesmanship also," Sumner warns that African Americans will not stand still for the continuing injustice of legal caste. Leading newspapers covering the speech stressed the noticeable presence of Douglass and other black Americans in the galleries overlooking Sumner's attempt to act as midwife at the birth of a redeemed national ethos of equality, a political and legal order purged of identity and race. The Pittsburgh *Commercial* noted that

The great event of the day and of the session in the Senate was Mr. Sumner's speech. The galleries were crowded to excess, as they have not been on any occasion before in a long time. Frederick Douglass was in the gallery, one of the most attentive listeners, and evidently the best-placed man in the Chamber, as he heard the distinguished champion of his race plead so eloquently in its behalf.

A New York *Tribune* article suggested the connection between Douglass's and Sumner's efforts for equality by pairing the interview Douglass and a delegation of black men had with President Johnson with Sumner's "grand vindication of the fundamental principles underlying republicanism." The *Tribune* article suggests the two-pronged approach of their Partnership – Sumner on the inside, Douglass on the outside – both seeking between them to push recalcitrant, even hostile, politicians in the right direction. Each offered a symbolic vindication of the other's argument, and together they symbolized for their era the possibility of a transracial mix of conscience and consent.[115]

Douglass exemplified the identity-neutral definition of citizenship Sumner describes in his address "Are We A Nation?" In this 1867 address, Sumner asks what constitutes a nation. To answer that question he turns to a set of definitions of nation and finds that "These definitions all end in the idea of unity under one government. They contemplate political unity, rather than unity of blood or language." We should pause here to savor the rare fresh air of genuine political discourse filtered of the private and proprietary languages of race and tribe, languages that by definition cannot constitute the consensual ethical norms enabling public political discussion and decision across such divisions. As Emerson contended before the war that the "one stock" of America is created through choice ("people cleave to [it]"), Sumner here pushes for a consensual definition of the republic as the political community of those choosing it. "Various accents of speech and various types of manhood, with the great distinction of color, which we encounter daily, show that there is no such unity [of identity] here," but Sumner concludes, that "is not required." Though he does not mention Douglass by name on this occasion, Sumner considered

Douglass as giving the lie to "The preposterous pretension, that color, whether of the hair or of the skin, or that any other unchangeable circumstance of natural condition" may justly be made the condition of citizenship.[116]

At several key points in the Reconstruction debates, Sumner overtly uses Douglass as a symbolic measure of the nation's movement toward an identity-neutral definition of citizenship. For example, Sumner offered a notorious bit of racial discrimination suffered by Douglass as illustrating the need for his Civil Rights Bill. "[R]eturning home after earnest service of weeks as secretary of the commission to report on the people of St. Domingo and the expediency of incorporating them with the United States," Douglass, in Sumner's words,

was rudely excluded from the supper-table, where his brother commissioners were already seated on board the mail steamer of the Potomac, just before reaching the President, whose commission he bore. This case, if not aggravated, is made conspicuous by peculiar circumstances. Mr. Douglass is a gentleman of unquestioned ability and character, remarkable as an orator, refined in manners and personally agreeable . . . And yet, with this mission, and with the personal recommendations he so justly enjoys, this returning secretary could not be saved from outrage even in sight of the Executive Mansion.

Sumner argues that Douglass's experience is typical, and "If Frederick Douglass" can be "made to suffer, how much must others be called to endure."[117] Appropriately, Sumner here defends Douglass's right to travel. The right of mobility that Sumner sought to protect in his Civil Rights legislation (which would have, had it been successful, protected access to modes of transport, public entertainment, and accommodation) for all African Americans is symbolically central not only to Douglass's life story but to a vision of the American nation as engaged in a cosmopolitan cultural and political dialogue of diverse peoples.

Douglass is no mere yardstick in Sumner's speeches; he is also an agent whose endorsement of revisions of the basic rules of citizenship and justice is an important sign of the black consent that is necessary to make such adjustments truly representative of a universal moral consensus. In a speech on the Fourteenth Amendment, Sumner indicated the profound weight he attached to the argument of Douglass and other black advocates. In this speech, Sumner presented to the Senate a petition by Douglass and George Downing arguing for equality before the law. Douglass and Downing "pray Congress 'To favor no Amendment of the Constitution which will grant or allow any one or all of the States of this Union to disfranchise any class of citizens on the ground of color.'" Sumner derives a special kind of significance from "the testimony of these very intelligent representatives of colored fellow-citizens." "They speak with peculiar authority," says Sumner. In their expression of "the interest they necessarily have in the question," these black advocates instantiate their qualifications for citizenship more strikingly than any who have merely inherited citizenship status; in that expression, they become representatives, claiming their rightful role in the national political dialogue about the shape and direction of the reconstructed Constitution – "They speak for the freedmen."[118] Thus, Sumner offered Douglass's agreement with his Civil Rights Bill as probative that it would push the nation in the direction of justice, and he cited as particularly persuasive the support for his Civil Rights Bill offered by "an article in the last New National Era, of Washington, a journal edited by colored persons – Frederick Douglass is the distinguished editor."[119]

Perhaps the ultimate symbolic connection of Sumner, Douglass, and Emerson can be found in the fact that Douglass led and Emerson was a pallbearer in Sumner's funeral procession. This procession symbolizes the end of a literary/political partnership that, despite subsequent failures, succeeded in revising fundamental conceptions of citizenship and justice.[120] The constitutional revision that Frederick Douglass, Emerson, Sumner, and others helped to inspire and direct revealed that the nation's charter was far more capacious and fluid than had hitherto been understood or conceived – grounded in a shifting consensus of justice.[121] The Civil War amendments evidenced the revolutionary feeling in the victorious North, which was "temporarily determined to stop at nothing short of a complete and thoroughgoing reformation." As Charles Lofgren has noted, the proponents of the Thirteenth Amendment conceived of it as "intended to serve more than imply the interests of blacks. It would eliminate forever the divisive issues of slavery and race . . . Still more fundamentally, by eliminating legally defined caste and class, the Amendment would remove 'the last moral stain from our national escutcheon – the only disgrace from our flag,' as the *Chicago Tribune* put it."[122] Devised to overturn *Dred Scott*, the Thirteenth and Fourteenth Amendments provide a unitary context for the legal treatment of blacks and whites, and reimbue the defining documents of American government with the moral authority of the higher law tradition. The Fifteenth Amendment recognized, as Emerson had hoped, that "every man shall have . . . an equal vote." Even after their post-Reconstruction retrenchment, the Thirteenth, Fourteenth, and Fifteenth Amendments continued to give African Americans the right to argue for their rights. These amendments, in Douglass's view, put "the supreme law of the land on the side of justice and liberty," giving discrete political minorities a powerful tool with which to advocate for full citizenship and justice.[123]

CHAPTER 4

The positivist alternative

To appreciate fully the higher law arguments of Douglass, Sumner, and Emerson, we have to consider the positivist rejoinders of opponents and some allies. A wide variety of Northern and Southern intellectuals, authors, jurists, and politicians found in the very existence of slavery, war, class and race domination ample proof that neither conscience nor consent but power actually structures and organizes law and society. Northern judges deeply convinced of slavery's immorality, for instance, set aside their own higher law scruples as irrelevant to the professional duty of the judiciary to enforce the political will of the majority expressed in legislation:

Slavery is wrong, inflicted by force and supported alone by the municipal power of the state or territory wherein it exists. It is opposed to the principles of natural justice and right, and is the mere creature of positive law. Hence, it being my duty to declare the law, not to make it, the question is not, what conforms to the great principles of natural right and universal freedom – but what do the positive laws and institutions command and direct.

The antebellum judiciary's thoroughgoing legal positivism (taking its name from the superior *position* of the lawmaker and defining law as the rule a superior lays down to an inferior) was just one expression of a general nineteenth-century suspicion that coercion was the governing principle of human associations.[1]

We find this positivist intuition animating the fiction of the "old Southwest Humorists." For example, in the first story of Augustus Baldwin Longstreet's *Georgia Scenes* (1835), "Georgia Theatrics," a cultured narrator comes upon a rustic plowboy thrashing about in a pastoral forest opening. The boy mimes a brutal fight in front of the Lincoln County courthouse, complete with the voices of the spectators who have gathered to enjoy the spectacle. The fight ends when the imaginary opponent cries, "Enough! My eye's out!" Mistaking the reenactment for the event itself, Longstreet's narrator, Hall, is appalled that "this heavenly retreat" would be disfigured by "such Pandaemonian riots," calling for the boy to assist him "in relieving your fellow mortal, whom you have ruined forever!" The black humor of the tale derives from the contrast of civilized and uncouth perspectives, and the suspicion that, in some circumstances, the latter may prove more germane than the former. Though Hall comforts himself (and the reader) that this "Dark Corner" of "vice and folly," Georgia's Lincoln County, is contained by the civilizing forces of Christianity and education, the boy's vitality and vigor, the gripping authenticity of his ferocious language and gestures, betray Longstreet's appreciation that the values of combat may be more important to the boy's existence than those symbolized by the imaginary courthouse passively overlooking the fight.[2]

Unrestrained by Hall's civilization, Sut Lovingood, George Washington Harris's malignly comic creation, even more bluntly declares the coercive and hierarchical nature of existence:

Whar thar ain't enuf feed, big childer roots littl childer outen the troff, an' gobbils up thar part. Jis' so the yeath over: bishops eats elders, elders eats common peopil, they eats sich cattil es me, I eats possums, possums eats chickins, chickins swallers wums, an' wums am content tu eat dus, an' the dus am the aind ove hit all.

Self-interest and power are the only reality; any other explanation is elitist pretense or sentimental fraud. Foreshadowing Jim Crow law's blend of positivism and racism, Sut's view of power is alloyed with race hate ("hook-nose Jews," "pot-gutted, ball-heded Baptis' bull nigger," the "bald faced, roach-maned, wall eyed Irishman") and with contempt for all representatives of moral authority ("wimmen," parsons, and judges) and cosmopolitan intercourse and fraternity (the pedlar and the freemason). The quotidian brutality of Sut's world and unbreakable narrowness of his perspective is intended to make the antislavery universalism of such texts as James Russell Lowell's *The Biglow Papers* (1847–67) seem laughably fantastic. Sut expressly mocks higher law pretensions, lamenting that the "injuns" did not foredoom "higher law," "abolishunism," "Bloomer bit – britches," "Greeley," and "Sumner" by wiping out their Puritan forebears on arrival. The only real "higher law" is that displayed by a billy goat "buttin the cow herself out ove her slop tub, so that he could wet his own beard in her supper. That wer 'higher law,' warnt it?"[3]

Though different in tone and affect, "Benito Cereno" (1855), Herman Melville's allegory of slavery and sectional conflict, also presents higher law as a delusion blinding those who hold it to the positivist nature of human relations. Boarding the *San Dominick*, a decimated Spanish ship containing a tattered white crew and starving complement of slaves, Amasa Delano (an experienced yet terminally provincial New England mariner) cannot read the increasingly apparent signs of slave revolt. In part, Delano's racism obscures the possibility of black revolt and "misrule." He wavers between viewing the slaves as loyal pets and savage predators. But racism is not solely responsible for Delano's mental paralysis.[4]

Delano's perception is also disabled by a singularly durable kind of innocence, which fantasizes equitable relations despite the increasingly apparent signs of a brutal dominion. The viewpoint allowing Delano to survive the *San Dominick*'s horrors with his sunny democratic optimism intact is akin to the exceptionalism enabling Daniel Webster to claim that "In all its history [the American nation] has been beneficent" and "has trodden down no man's liberty" in a speech sanctioning the denial of liberty to millions. The higher law convictions behind Delano's "republican impartiality" in doling out food and water to the ship's inmates without regard to race seem, in Melville's tale, to require a repression of the anti-democratic, anti-egalitarian realities of power actually governing life aboard the *San Dominick* and, by implication, in the U.S. and throughout the world. Higher law exceptionalism prevents Delano from seeing not only that Babo and Benito Cereno are emblematized in the ship's stern-piece, which features "a dark satyr in a mask, holding his foot on the prostrate neck of a writhing figure, likewise masked," but also that he too takes his place in that emblem of power when in the climactic moment of the tale he grinds the rebel leader, Babo, under his heel.

The parallel Melville draws between the image of the Yankee and the slave and the stern-piece's feudal emblem offers a clue to his tale's torturous and persistent suspense – the story resists unmasking its characters because the ordering principle of human association is not changed by the identity of who is on top. Though power changes hands, the relation is always the same. Our reluctance to see Delano, Babo, and Don Benito as interchangeable is due to our own Delano-like blindness to the realities of power and our mistaking of cultural and racial kinship with Delano for a form of association different from and superior to power. Acknowledging power does not entail a denial of the importance of race to Melville's tale but redefines the import of race in terms of the possession or lack of power. What unites Cereno and Delano, after all, is not race, culture, religion, or politics, but technological know-how: the ability to circumnavigate the globe. In Melville's tale, the inequalities of technological power between the first and third worlds, what Ernest Gellner and others have termed the "big gap," render the possibility of communication and consensus among the haves and have nots inconceivable.[5]

Before and after the Civil War, many Americans viewed the mere possession of such prowess as a racial inheritance metaphysically licensing various forms of racial domination at home and abroad. An 1875 New York *Times* article, "Shocking the Negroes," provides a particularly apt representation of the symbolic connection white Americans increasingly saw between their material, economic, technological, cultural, and scientific prowess and their racial identity. The story, which is quoted from the Lexington (Kentucky) *Gazette*, describes a "right funny scene" occurring when two Negroes cut down a tree, breaking a telegraph wire to the vengeful anger of the telegraph operator who

ordered the Negroes . . . to mend the wire. Each seized end and end, but the moment they came in contact there was a sharp electric shock, and they let go. It was raining and the battery was strong. However, the Negroes didn't know where the shock came from and tried it again . . . Frightened and bewildered they brought the wires together again and again; each time to their great astonishment, an electric shock convulsed them. And when the train started there sat the operator under the shelter of the depot still egging the Negroes to fresh efforts.

Developed by Samuel Morse before the war, the magnetic telegraph promised to unite the world, to build a bridge between nations and cultures, and was touted as such by James Gordon Bennett in the New York *Herald*. But Bennett and Morse shared more than a desire for technologies of communication bridging differences. They shared a vision of the United States that merged the terms of citizenship and justice with racial identity. "Shocking the Negroes" offers a perfect post-Reconstruction emblem of this vision – the alien darker people forever outside of the ambit of technological and material power that joins white people and excludes everyone else. The cruel humor of such scenes has close ties to the broad farce of the minstrel show and the comedy of monstrous likenesses furnished in freak shows. Underlying such humor is an implicit realism about power – the nastiness of life without it, and the utility of racism to keeping it.

The Civil War brought some to a fatalist acceptance of power akin to that expressed in "Benito Cereno." After witnessing the chaotic sacrifice of the nation's "best citizens" in the war to end slavery, Oliver Wendell Holmes, Jr., came to view higher law as the delusion of fanatics (like

Garrison) and sentimentalists (like Stowe) and the antithesis of the rationality required to minimize the cost of the inescapable Darwinian struggle for survival. Holmes's positivism is notoriously expressed in his opinion in *Buck v. Bell* (1926), upholding Virginia's authority to require sterilization of individuals deemed to be mentally deficient. Being found mentally defective and subject to mandatory sterilization, Carrie Buck protested that the Virginia law violated the due process and equal protection clauses of the Fourteenth Amendment – the greatest achievement of the antebellum higher law argument.[6] Noting that "We have seen more than once that the public welfare may call upon the best citizens for their lives," Holmes's rejection of her argument was blunt and harsh:

It is better for all the world, if instead of waiting to execute degenerate offspring for crime, or to let them starve for their imbecility, society can prevent those who are manifestly unfit from continuing their kind. The principle that sustains vaccination is broad enough to cover cutting the Fallopian tubes . . . Three generations of imbeciles are enough.[7]

Just as the nation's "best citizens" had to bend to the will of the majority in wartime, Carrie Buck would have to yield to the will of Virginia's political majority. That this political majority had exercised its power rationally was enough to sustain the law. For Holmes, there was no political, epistemological, or metaphysical standpoint outside the context of power relations from which to gauge the ethical propriety of the law.[8]

Probably better than any white American, Martin Delany appreciated the degree to which power governed social and political association in nineteenth-century America despite pretensions to the contrary. In his novel *Blake*, Delany uses a slaveholder, Major Armsted, to express the fact that it is power, not race, that animates slavery. Major Armsted apprehends that he holds human beings as slaves and that the historical customs and traditions that judges and lawyers refer to in justifying the system of slavery constitute the mere habiliments of a power relation dedicated to the self-interest of the slaveholders. When Judge Ballard, a Northerner, inquires as to how the Major can own slaves when he claims for them "the common rights of other people," the Major replies that "I would just as readily hold a white as a black in slavery, were it the custom and policy of the country to do so. It is all a matter of self-interest with me." Far from antithetical, Major Armsted's comments express Delany's view of the critical importance of power both to the law of slavery and to the promise of emancipation: one only possesses such "inalienable" rights as one can enforce and protect. While Delany preserves higher law argument as the orienting faith of a culturally diverse political union, his assertion (in sharp contrast to Douglass) of the ultimate necessity of majority power expresses a positivist skepticism of Douglass's higher law conception of heterogeneous political consent.[9]

Given Delany's willingness to serve in the Union army and to work within the American political system in Reconstruction, when the possibility of genuinely consensual relations seemed plausible, we might term his positivism "strategic" along the lines suggested by Gayatri Spivak's notion of "strategic essentialism."[10] Viewed in this fashion, positivism becomes a tool Delany is willing to use to accomplish his political aims or to set aside when better options seem to present themselves. However, while apt, this qualification does not moot the critical distinction between power-based and consent-based conceptions of political and legal order so clearly distinguishing Delany and Douglass before the war. In addition, as we consider the contradictions between ethics and power in Delany's political program, we may well wonder whether one can be strategic about power in the same way one may be about race.

In effect, the higher law argument advanced by Seward, Chase, Sumner, Emerson, Stowe, Douglass, Lowell, and others in the years leading to the Civil War summoned such positivist replies as Harris's vicious antithesis Sut Lovingood, Melville's tautology of power, Holmes's fatalism, and Delany's nationalism. This pattern of higher law call and positivist response is not unusual. Throughout American history, higher law's moments of greatest influence have provoked strong positivist reactions. The higher law successes of the relatively brief revolutionary and Reconstruction eras were followed by decades of positivist retrenchment.

As the above examples suggest, the type of positivism we are examining here is not the mere acknowledgment that law depends on force for its effect – all law, including higher law, requires the exercise of state power to be effective; instead, what distinguishes these examples is the degree to which they focus on the possession of power as the controlling principle for law and society. Sut Lovingood, Oliver Wendell Holmes, Jr., Roger Taney, and Martin Delany variously inhabit a political realm where nothing is larger, more important, or more determinative than the biases, desires, and general outlook of the majority. The idea that the entity with the greatest quantum of power could ever be effectively regulated by any larger principle, such as the higher law notion of universally accepted moral norms of civil recognition and responsibility seems, from the perspective of the above examples, a utopian pipe dream. Of course, while this conclusion has been bitterly justified by much of the course and content of American history, it is a concession that those interested in broader conceptions of justice, such as the advocacy of minority rights, cannot accept.

That the Civil War amendments, by contrast, represent "higher law-making" and not positivism has been well argued by Bruce Ackerman. Ackerman grants the plain fact that most law is constitutionally legitimate if it bears the imprimatur of the political majority, but he notes that, in some instances, such as the adoption of the Constitution itself and the Civil War amendments, consent must be as close to universal as is possible. When revising the fundamental terms of citizenship or the composition of the republic, lawmakers derive their authority from a far broader higher law consensus about justice. Resisting a simplistic characterization of the Civil War amendments as an anti-democratic imposition of Northern morality on a still defiant South (identifying the South with its ardently proslavery white populace), Ackerman shows how amendment process, which defied certain requirements of positive law (Article 5's prescriptions for passage of constitutional amendments), garnered as near to a universal consensus as was practicable, entitling the amendments' advocates to claim to speak for "We the People."[11] There would seem to be little doubt that a shift in the nation's moral consensus begun in the antebellum higher law movement did in fact occur. The objection to slavery and the denial of fundamental civil equality to people on the basis of race would seem to be as close to a universal civic value as can be had today in the U.S.[12]

In this chapter, we will survey some of the diverse forms positivism took in the official and unofficial precincts of nineteenth-century American jurisprudence, and, through an examination of certain representative figures and texts, we will trace the fate of the higher law argument for black citizenship in a social and political universe that seemed increasingly defined by power. Our survey will begin with a comparison of the cosmopolitan positivism of Martin Delany and the racist positivism of Roger Taney's *Dred Scott* opinion, proceed to sketch Holmes's career and biography as illuminating the positivist trajectory of nineteenth-century legal theory, and conclude with an examination of the terrible comedy of African American citizenship in Jim Crow America as observed by Mark Twain. Though insightfully analyzed by scholars of legal and political history, such as Morton Horwitz, James Herget, and R. Jeffrey Lustig, most literary and cultural histories neglect the import of legal positivism for nineteenth-century American culture.[13] This chapter will help to correct this critical omission and form a bridge between the antebellum higher law arguments of Douglass and Sumner and the post-Reconstruction higher law arguments of Charles Chesnutt and Moorfield Storey.

THE COLOR OF POWER: MARTIN DELANY
AND ROGER TANEY

To understand the unexpected kinship between the jurisprudential views of Martin Delany, a black nationalist, and Chief Justice Roger Taney, the ultimate expositor of a proslavery Constitution, we need to begin by observing the emergence of a split within black abolitionism between Douglass's cosmopolitan constitutionalism and Delany's cosmopolitan positivism, a split that has not been adequately identified by previous scholarship.[14] Though Delany most emphatically differed from Douglass in terming his antislavery constitutionalism a "blind absurdity," many critics and scholars have neglected this distinction because they looked for the conflict between Douglass's integrationism and Delany's nationalism to fall on the issue of racial identity.[15] Indeed, the very labels applied to Douglass and Delany – "integrationist" and "nationalist" – suggest that the conflict between the men must be about race. However, an examination of 1850s black abolitionism reveals a conflict in its approach to law, not in its generally cosmopolitan approach to race.

The different uses black abolitionists made of the figure and theme of energy disclose an initial view of this jurisprudential contrast. For example, William Howard Day's editorial on the inaugural address of Franklin Pierce features an appreciation for "President Pierce's idea" of "*energy*" as a figure for both individual and national reformation, but he quarrels with Pierce's crass substitution of material energy or power (e.g., territorial expansion) for "advances in education, in general intelligence, and in a strict sense of justice":

There *is* an energy silent as the grave, and yet powerful enough to bring life from dull clods – *innate* energy; in a national sense, energy or force of character. There *is* an energy like that of flame, sparkling, crackling, dazzling, dying. We have had an energy without; but have not had its counterpart within. Increment without has not been based upon a fixed, pure principle within. Things understood, agreed upon by the Fathers of the Government have been boldly disregarded, and a one-sided, selfish policy made the basis of nearly all our increase since.[16]

Pierce's address does not adequately reflect, in Day's view, the necessary reciprocity between an internal process of principled self-transformation and an external process of acquiring power. The correspondence between "inner" and "outer" energy that Day describes calls to mind Frederick Douglass's life story, which begins with a process of inner transformation but proceeds through his fight with Covey to the acquisition of the signs of power. The former without the latter is immature and unrecognizable, and the latter without the former is corrupt and brutal. An editorial on the Kansas–Nebraska bill in *Frederick Douglass's Paper* gives this higher law electricity a distinctly Emersonian ring, calling for "living men" to lead a constitutional reformation:

The bold and dashing Reformer, who walks to and fro, with the besom of destruction in his right hand – whose business seems to be to scatter, tear, and slay, meets with opposition from almost every quarter. He lives in the tempest . . . He comes with his flaming sword, and must penetrate, if he would be successful in the end, the incrustations of ignorance, in which he finds imbedded, man's mental and moral organism. It requires a strong nerve, and potent arm, determined will, moral courage, strong powers of analysis, depth and breadth of comprehension, indomitable perseverance, correct judgement, and a worldwide heart, full of hope and love, to make an effectual Reformer, one whose tongue should sting like a thousand scorpions, and whose pen should manufacture words of fire, clothed with superhuman energy, and almost unearthly power. We want more living men; of dead men, we have enough already.[17]

Though the reformer's energy is figured as violence and destruction– scattering, tearing, slaying, penetrating, stinging – the energy is not material but "superhuman," "an unearthly power." A catastrophe must be generated, hence the explosive and violent quality of such antislavery jeremiads as Douglass's address "What to the Slave is the Fourth of July," but the targeted upheaval begins internally, working from the inside out to effect a change in the external world of law and power.

By contrast, in arguing for emigration or revolution, Delany's *Blake* and David Walker's *Appeal* offer images of energy that are less figurative, more straightforwardly about the possession of power. The hero of Delany's novel, Henry Blake, is described as a powerful man, "a great leaper" whose "speed" is "unfaltering," who surmounts or strikes down all obstacles – including fatally wounding an assailant and killing a pack of vicious dogs. Blake incarnates the external energy of violent revolution and retribution – the kind of power David Walker has in mind when he asks white Americans: "[w]ill you wait until we shall, under God, obtain our liberty by the crushing arm of power." Though Delany and Walker do not deny that the exercise of material power (such as physical, military, or economic might) should be guided by moral character, they emphasize the former and not the latter, a rhetorical distinction with jurisprudential significance.[18]

Black advocates of a higher law constitutionalism, such as Douglass, Day, and John Mercer Langston, viewed the energy of self-transformation as a synecdoche for the moral electricity of reform that would catalyze the nation's conscience and lead to a concomitant change in its fundamental law; early nationalists, such as Martin Delany, Henry Highland Garnet, and their revolutionary precursor, David Walker, tended in a positivist fashion to figure transformative energy as the external, material power requisite to force a change in circumstances for black Americans. To put the contrast another way, Douglass wants the "*signs* of power" (my emphasis); Delany wants power. In Douglass's formulation, "*signs* of power" betoken moral agency and strength of character, qualifying one to participate in forming the moral consensus that legitimates and regulates the American legal and political order. The failure of moral suasion to alter the nation's racist policy, from Delany's point of view, made it clear that the only legal order capable of inscribing and protecting black Americans' rights would be grounded not in consent ("rights by sufferance") but in majority power.[19]

The jurisprudential split within black abolitionism most plainly emerged in the middle of the prewar decade when, frustrated by the lack of political movement and economic opportunity, black abolitionists began to consider other options, such as black industrial schools and emigration.[20] Signed by Frederick Douglass and other leading black abolitionists, "An Address to the Colored People of the United States" (1853) endorsed "complexional institutions" as a useful instrument in the quest for full integration into the body politic. The address notes that, despite the obvious progress made by black Americans toward standing "on a common platform with our fellow-countrymen" in a "final triumph of right over wrong, of freedom over slavery, and equality over caste," "we are as a people, chained together . . . one in general complexion, one in common degradation, one in popular estimation." As a result, "although it may seem to conflict with our views of human brotherhood, we shall undoubtedly for many years be compelled to have institutions of a complexional character, in order to attain this very idea of human brotherhood."

The instrumentalism underwriting the idea of complexional institutions as a means of racial uplift also suggested the emigrationist program. Emigration, in many ways, was merely an extended, grander version of the same wisdom – what one could accomplish with an economic or educational venture could be accomplished on a much grander, global scale with the creation of a nation. Within weeks of the 1853 Rochester convention endorsing the industrial school idea, Delany called for an emigrationist convention to meet in Cleveland a year later.[21] At the emigrationist convention, H. Ford Douglas, Delany, and others argued that emigration offered the only sure means of achieving freedom and franchise because, in the new nation, majority power would be theirs.[22] Though born out of a shared frustration and instrumentalist logic, complexional institutions and emigration signified different jurisprudential projects. Douglass embraced the industrial school, as it would not only improve the quality of black life but also would display the capacity of black Americans for full citizenship and participation in the larger civic dialogue determining the course and content of American law. Delany endorsed emigration as a direct means of acquiring the power that, in his view, dictated legal and political order. Reasoning "logically and politically, leaving morality right out of the question," in *The Condition, Elevation, Emigration, and Destiny of the Colored People of the United States* (1852), Delany contended that the Constitution would never embrace full citizenship for black Americans: "We are politically, not of them, but aliens to the laws and political privileges of the country. These are truths – fixed facts, that quaint theory and exhausted moralising, are impregnable to, and fall harmlessly before." In the heat of 1850s antislavery politics, there was considerable movement back and forth between these positions.[23]

The evolution of John Mercer Langston's antislavery advocacy illuminates the jurisprudential nature of the divergence between emigration and "complexional institutions." Langston began, like all abolitionists, from the higher law position that slavery was an unmistakable violation of universal moral law. Impatient with the inefficacy of moral suasion, at a convention in 1849 Langston voted with the majority of delegates to distribute five hundred copies of a pamphlet containing two landmark calls for black revolt – David Walker's 1829 *Appeal* and Henry Highland Garnet's 1843 *Address to the Slaves* (which had been rejected by the convention which first heard Garnet's address as too militant). But Langston's call for a more aggressive version of antislavery was accompanied by integrationist arguments against the legal proscriptions of interracial marriage. And, as we can see in his proud proclamation in 1850 that "Colored men have acted in all the mighty movements of the world for Freedom," his revolutionary ardor had a distinctly universalist cast. During this early phase of his antislavery career, Langston did not feel any contradiction in simultaneously emphasizing the necessity of complexional institutions for racial uplift, the entitlement of black Americans to full membership in the American polity, *and* the utility of emigration.[24]

However, as he studied law, the attraction of a consensual model of political and legal association waxed and the appeal of emigration waned. By the time of Delany's emigrationist convention in Cleveland, August 24–26, 1854, Langston's legal studies had led him to reject emigration. He had come to embrace higher law constitutionalism, like that of Salmon Chase, one of his Ohio mentors. When called to speak by Delany, Langston admitted his change of heart. He no longer believed white American prejudice impermeable and permanent. "A colored man of science, learning, and industry," he asserted, "could gain, and would be as much respected here as the white man." His subsequent election in 1855 to the office of Township Clerk in Brownhelm, Ohio seemed to vindicate this decision, signifying the possibility of genuine political discourse across racial lines.[25]

As one of the nation's first and foremost black lawyers and legal educators, Langston always insisted on the importance of racial identification as an acknowledgment of the historical situation black Americans had been placed in by racist law and custom.[26] But he recognized that the acquisition of power through emigration was, of itself, inadequate to the accomplishment of a just social and political order, which requires the creation of a race-neutral language of consensual ethical norms of social and political association. In a letter that Charles Sumner presented to the Senate as support for his Civil Rights bill, Langston calls for mutual respect and recognition, not patronage and charity (the paternalistic morality that accompanies some versions of positivism), urging an identity-neutral moral consensus as the basis for public forms of association and interaction.[27] When we look at Langston's and Douglass's advocacy of complexional institutions and other race-centered means of uplift and compare it to Delany's advocacy of emigration, we do not find a dispute about the political importance of race identification – both sides of the constitutionalist/positivist coin emphasized the particular historical position from which they spoke and argued as black Americans. Rather, in espousing emigration, nationalists abandoned higher law notions of moral consensus as offering a viable alternative to the possession of power. That ideas about race do not form the chief distinction between the nationalists and the constitutionalists can be observed by comparing Douglass's "The Claims of the Negro

Ethnologically Considered" with Walker's *Appeal* and Delany's essay on black freemasonry.

The physical traits such racist ethnologists as Josiah Nott, George Gliddon, and Samuel Morton read as signs of racial inferiority, Douglass interprets as the products of domination. To illustrate, Douglass offers the resemblance of poor Irish to the plantation slave:

these people lacked only a black skin and woolly hair, to complete their likeness to the plantation Negro. The open, uneducated mouth – the long, gaunt arm – the badly formed foot and ankle – the shuffling gait – the retreating forehead and vacant expression – and, their petty quarrels and fights – all reminded me of the plantation, and my own cruelly abused people . . . Now, while what I have said is true of the common people, the fact is, there are no more really handsome people in the world, than the educated Irish people. The Irishman educated, is a model gentleman; the Irishman ignorant and degraded, compares in form and feature, with the Negro!

Ignoring the influence "the condition of men" has on "their various appearances," racist ethnologists self-servingly mischaracterized the signs of domination as signs of race to justify the continuation of the oppression inscribing those marks of deterioration in the first place. Consequently, their semiology of race is more accurately viewed as a record of racial domination rather than as an analysis of racial nature. This is not to say that Douglass denies the existence of biological markers indicating kinship and racial descent. The conspicuous resemblance between African Americans and their Egyptian ancestors entitles the "[t]he Negro race," in Douglass's view, to claim "a direct relationship . . . to *that grandest of all the nations of antiquity, the builders of the pyramids.*" But Douglass expressly distinguishes the pride of origins useful in combating racism from a commitment to racial purity, praising hybridity instead as both healthy and inevitable. Indeed, the only signs of "racial inferiority" Douglass entertains are those characterizing the purebred: "it is clearly proved . . . that those nations freest from foreign elements, present the most evident marks of deterioration."[28]

By asserting that his claim of kinship with the Egyptians is as "natural" as Samuel Morton's, Douglass ironizes nature, simultaneously alluding both to biologically derived resemblance *and* the processes of education and cosmopolitan intercourse apparently natural to human existence that lead Morton and Douglass to appreciate the achievements of another people and another era. Douglass's attack on the conventional separation between the biological and the cultural, cautioning us that nature is always "marked" by nurture, is subordinate, however, to his primary aim of severing the claims to civil recognition and human rights from the accidents of nature or history. Racial affiliation, whether biological, cultural, or both, does not alter the "common basis" of "[h]uman rights" and the fact that "[t]he essential characteristics of humanity are everywhere the same."[29]

David Walker's *Appeal* is no more consistent with the merger of racial identity and politics than is Douglass's ethnology address. One of the earliest and most militant of the black abolitionists, Walker was born in Wilmington, North Carolina to a free mother and a slave father. Though many details of his early life are obscure, we know that Walker became literate and traveled widely in the South before moving to Boston in the mid 1820s, where he set up a used clothing store for sailors. In 1828, he began working for the first black weekly newspaper, *Freedom's Journal*, and lecturing against slavery. His *Appeal* appeared in 1829 and went through two additional printings in the following year. Southern reaction was predictably hostile, and in Georgia a considerable reward was offered for Walker's death. Just weeks after the third edition of his pamphlet came out, Walker was found dead in the doorway of his shop.[30]

Though plainly concerned to address the political plight of a discrete racial group united by oppression and common ancestry, his *"beloved Brethren*," the *Appeal*'s vitriolic critique is not delimited by notions of identity. Walker rejects colonization ("America is as much our country, as it is yours") and attacks slavery as a violation of universal higher law – "God almighty" not any group or race "is the *sole proprietor* or *master* of the WHOLE human family." The irrelevance of race to justice will be recognized, in Walker's view, by anyone "who can dispense with prejudice long enough to admit that we are men, notwithstanding our *improminent noses* and *wooly heads*." Walker's comparativist description of the particular wretchedness of American slavery lambastes, among other things, the rigid confinement and isolation of black Americans within a racial identity. Although he proudly states that he "would not give *a pinch of snuff* to be married to any white person" and castigates any "man of color" who would "marry a white woman" "just because she is *white*," Walker censures anti-miscegenation laws as evidence of the unique heinousness of American slavery and prophesies racial amalgamation ("for the Lord knows, that there is a day coming when [whites] will be glad enough to get into the company of blacks"). Foreshadowing Douglass's ethnology address, Walker praises his African heritage as a valuable contribution to world culture. Because, like Douglass, Walker attacks slavery from a universal moral standpoint and conceives of cultural value in a cosmopolitan fashion, his approach cannot be distinguished from Douglass's on the basis that Walker's politics are identitarian and Douglass's are not.[31]

The difference between the two advocates is far more subtle – a matter of rhetorical emphasis. Walker argues for consensual political relations between white and black Americans based on the recognition of a common humanity, but he also prominently features an apocalyptic vision of "the crushing arm of power" as setting things right. The angry and prophetic tone of Walker's *Address* tends to herald power and violent retribution more than it does the democratic processes of consent. The degree to which revolutionary violence in Walker's apocalyptic vision ends the possibility of democratic conversation is suggested by Walker's favored trope of resistance – the cutting of throats. Walker looks to God's power to correct the unjust relations between the races, and his repeated invocation of justice through violence suggests a positivist kinship between his advocacy and that of Delany and Henry Highland Garnet.[32]

The mix of positivist jurisprudence and cosmopolitan perspectives on race, morality, and culture in early black nationalism can be clearly observed in Delany's essay *The Origin and Objects of Ancient Freemasonry* (1853). Arguing for the legitimacy of colored masons, Delany commends the fraternity as an international, ecumenical organization (including Unitarians, Trinitarians, Greek Orthodox, Jews, and Moslems) open to all who agree that there is a God and that man is created in his image: "All men, of every country, clime, color and condition, (when morally worthy,) are acceptable to the portals of Masonic jurisprudence." Even those held in slavery qualify for membership by virtue of their "longing aspiration for liberty" and "manly determination to be free." "[O]riginally intended for the better government of man," the fraternity is founded on and designed to advance such higher law conceptions as liberty and equality. The symbols of geometry and carpentry function as a cosmopolitan argot for the diverse masonic brotherhood and as an emblem of the universality of justice. Delany proudly claims freemasonry as an African contribution to world culture:

whence sprung Masonry but from Ethiopia, Egypt, and Assyria – all settled and peopled by the children of Ham? . . . Was it not Africa that gave birth to Euclid, the master geometrician of the world? and was it not in consequence of a twenty-five years residence in Africa, that the great Pythagoras was enabled to discover that key problem in geometry – the forty-seventh problem of Euclid – without which Masonry would be incomplete? Must I hesitate to tell the world that, as applied to Masonry, the word – *Eureka* – was first exclaimed in Africa? But – there! I have revealed the Masonic *secret*, and *must stop!*

To reject the legitimacy of colored masons is, in Delany's account, simultaneously "to deny a child the lineage of its own parentage" and to subvert freemasonry's universalist higher law basis.[33] Thus far, one would be hard pressed to locate a juristically significant difference between Douglass's ethnology address and Delany's freemasonry address.[34]

The divergence appears in Delany's positivist solution to racism within the masonic fraternity. Instead of insisting on consensual relations among masons of different races in accord with their universal language of justice, Delany recommends "an independent jurisdiction of Masonry" among "the colored men of the United States" as there is among "the Scotch and Irish." Stating in a prefatory letter to the St. Cyprian Lodge of Masons in Pittsburgh that "it is within the power of the Grand Lodge of England to . . . establish our validity," Delany looks to the English Lodge, much as David Walker looks to God, for a superior authority to recognize black masons by fiat. Delany's remedy for black masons suggests that, in practice, justice and citizenship cannot be based on a universal moral consensus. At this point, we may well wonder how to make "plumb, level and square" Delany's positivism and his higher law universalism.[35] Delany hints at an answer to that question in his attack on a former member of Congress, Jacob Brinkerhoof, who sought to bar the descendants of slaves from the masonic order. By contrasting Brinkerhoof's expertise in "legal" rather than "Masonic jurisprudence," Delany limns the familiar distinction between lower and higher law.[36] Delany's recommendation of separate lodges for black masons does not imply a disbelief in the universal norms of higher law, just a pragmatic acceptance that, as regards lower law, power governs (a positivist conception Delany shared with Blackstone and the English Whigs, who felt that higher law universals are expressed, practically speaking, only in revolution; see chapter one). Calling for a separate lodge signals Delany's dismissal of higher law constitutionalism's distinction between, in the words of the Fourteenth Amendment's author, "*conventional* rights," which "are subject to the control of the majority" and "the rights of human nature," which are subject only to the control of universally accepted moral norms, such as equality and freedom.[37]

By putting Delany's *Blake; or the Huts of America* (1859–62) side by side with Chief Justice Roger Taney's opinion in *Dred Scott* (1857), we can examine the range of black and white positivist alternatives to the higher law constitutionalism as well as Delany's cosmopolitan rejoinder to Taney's racist positivism. And we can see more clearly the relation and conflict between Delany's universalism and his positivism.[38]

Delany's novel presents the story of an African American founding father, Henry Blake, who seeks to overthrow slaveholding power in the United States and the Caribbean and to establish a Pan-African republic in Cuba. The novel follows Blake as he spreads the message of revolt among American slaves and participates in the formation of a revolutionary political consensus among the leading people of color in Cuba. Until recently, most scholars treated Delany's novel as an interesting footnote in the extraordinary career of an early black nationalist.[39] Eric Sundquist and Robert Levine, by contrast, have initiated a detailed analysis of *Blake*'s revolutionary ethos and its contribution to American culture.[40]

Blake is, as Paul Gilroy has pointed out, Delany's response to Harriet Beecher Stowe's *Uncle Tom's Cabin*, but *Blake* is also Delany's emphatic dissent from *Dred Scott*.[41] When *Dred Scott* was published, Delany was particularly arrested by Taney's justification of slavery that, at the time of the Constitution's framing, black Americans had "no rights which the white man was bound to respect."[42] Delany repeats Taney's phrase several times in different contexts. Judge Ballard, Delany's representative Northerner, uses Taney's words to express a national proslavery consensus: "It was a just decision of the Supreme Court [that] persons of African descent have no rights that white men are bound to respect!" And Blake's Cuban compatriots view "American Laws" that have declared them to "have no rights that a white is bound to respect" as a spur to revolt, "Why have we so long submitted to [such laws]?"[43] The judge's desire to keep the power that defines membership in the American polity and the Cuban revolutionaries' ambition to take it indicate Delany's perception of the interdependence of power and citizenship. Though angered by Taney's ascription of power to the white race, Delany concludes (more forthrightly than Taney himself) that, without power, one neither has rights nor membership in the body politic.

Prior to writing *Blake*, Delany had urged that the apparent connection between power and citizenship would work to the advantage of African Americans willing and able to emigrate to "those places where the black and colored man comprise, by population, and constitute by necessity of numbers, the *ruling element* of the body politic." In his influential emigration address, "The Political Destiny of the Colored Race" (1854), Delany used words that he would later put in Blake's mouth to describe the appropriate site for emigration as a place where "if we but determine it shall be so, it *will* be so" – where the emigrants' numerical strength would establish and protect their "legitimate claims to inherent rights, bequeathed to [them] by the will of Heaven."[44] Delany rejected the idea that domination was brought on by the inferiority of the oppressed community, and he belittled as "sheer nonsense" the notion that some inherent racial antipathy preceded or accounted for such oppression. He contended that the crime of racial oppression in America, like the class and ethnic domination that he had observed in the histories of other nations, occurred because there was motive, the oppressors' interest in self-aggrandizement, and opportunity, an unequal distribution of political and economic power. Dismissing inherent racial defects and natural racial aversion, Delany held that black Americans were dominated because they were vulnerable and their subjugation served the self-interest of those in power. Racial difference was simply a fortuitous instrument of power.[45]

Having severed racial identity and power in his previous analyses of slavery, in *Blake* Delany imagined what an alternative to Taney's body politic would look like. Near the end of the novel, Blake preaches revolution to a variegated collection of maroon and free Africans, Creole, mestizos, Cubans, and black Americans. They range in complexion from "pure" black to white, and they bring to the revolution a wide variety of languages, cultures, and religions. Blake calls on this plurality to "rise against our oppressors and strike for liberty": "'On this island,' said Blake, 'we are the many and the oppressors few; consequently, they have no moral right to hold rule over us, whilst we have the moral right and the physical power to prevent them. Whatever we determine shall be, will be.'" The scene presents Delany's cosmopolitan yet positivist alternative to Taney's racist positivism. What joins this diverse majority is not race, but shared political values.[46] In Blake's observation that in Cuba "we are the many and the oppressors few" and, as a result, the oppressors have neither the "moral right" nor the "physical power" to continue their oppression, Delany repeats but reverses the terms of Taney's equation of power and citizenship, revealing the artifice of Taney's attribution of historic oppression to black inferiority and challenging the assumption of continued white ascendancy. But Delany's acceptance of majoritarian power as the *sine qua non* of citizenship and justice undermines the higher law ethics that ground his condemnation of Taney and threatens to abandon present and future minorities to a positivist view of citizenship rights as the entitlement of power.

DRED SCOTT

Eleven years after it was begun, Dred Scott's legal quest for freedom arrived at the Supreme Court of the United States in 1856. Though it could easily have confined the decision to the facts of this one case, the Court used the question of Scott's citizenship as a means to address the claims of all African Americans, free and enslaved, to the status and rights of citizenship. In what was the authoritative opinion of a plurality decision, Chief Justice Taney disposed of Dred Scott's citizenship argument through an inquiry into the traditional vocabulary of national membership. According to Taney's constitutional etymology, the words "people of the United States," "citizens," and "sovereign people" are "synonymous terms" historically denoting those "who hold the power and conduct the Government through their representatives." In other words, citizenship is an attribute of political power: those without such power may not be considered citizens because those with power will not permit it. Not surprisingly, given Taney's view that the possession of power is the primary qualification for citizenship, a people who have been "subjugated by the dominant race" and "considered as a subordinate and inferior class of beings" cannot be "constituent members of this sovereignty." Though John C. Calhoun emphasizes the sovereignty of the state, not the citizen, his vision of the Constitution as a bargain between sovereigns shares Taney's emphasis on power (see chapter one). The mere fact of slavery, for both Southerners, signals a weakness fatal to the enslaved population's claims of civic recognition.[47]

If the constitutional issue in *Dred Scott* could have been resolved simply by reference to the fact that political power has always resided with a white majority unmistakably expressing its recognition of slavery in such federal law as the Constitution's slavery clauses, the Fugitive Slave Act of 1850, and the Kansas–Nebraska Act of 1854, one may well wonder why Taney's opinion takes more than a hundred pages when a couple of pages would have sufficed. Fully aware that, given the North's increasing political power (a shift famously recognized in Calhoun's speech against the Compromise of 1850 – see chapter one), legal positivism would permit change inimical to the South, Taney's endorsement of power was neither straightforward nor unvarnished.[48] Indeed, *legal positivism* is too narrow a term to characterize Taney's varied jurisprudence. While Taney's deference to legislative power in *Charles River Bridge v. Warren Bridge* (1837) (upholding a state legislature's charter against a private corporation's breach of contract claims) looks like legal positivism, Taney's aggressive invalidation of legislation (the Missouri Compromise) in *Dred Scott* does not. These divergent opinions represent an intricate vision of political power, including protection of the South as a separate sovereignty, sometimes states' rights, sometimes federal power, and on occasion freedom of contract and commerce.[49] A pithy, Holmes-like announcement that law is the expression of power was not suitable to Taney's complex aim in *Dred Scott* of positing the white majority's power to enslave the black minority while denying the Northern majority's power to dictate to the Southern minority on the issue of slavery.

In addition, the higher law tradition had, as yet, too firm a grip on Taney and the jurisprudential imagination of his era to permit a bluntly positivistic opinion. By glossing the manufacture of black exclusion as historical legacy and natural inherence, Taney attempts to distinguish his *Dred Scott* holding from a mere deference to power. Given that the furor (both pro and con) aroused by his opinion focused on the question of whether it served justice, Taney's attempt to euphemize his positivism proved well considered, if not entirely successful.[50]

Taney's historical approach is ostensibly justified by his strict constructionist hermeneutic, an interpretive approach that reads the Constitution as one would a code, simply putting the lawmakers' will and intent into effect.[51] Thus, the desideratum of constitutional interpretation, in Taney's view, lies in procuring "the best lights we can obtain on the subject, and [administering the Constitution] as we find it, according to its true intent and meaning when it was adopted." Such an approach kills off any notion that the concepts of the Constitution have a life of their own and are available for subsequent expansion, contraction, reinvention, or re-illustration. For Taney, borrowing Paul Kahn's words, the Constitution and the Declaration were "the finished products of history," "not vehicles for the expression of contemporary meanings," as Emerson and Douglass saw them:

No one, we presume, supposes that any change in public opinion or feeling, in relation to this unfortunate race ... should induce the court to give the words of the constitution a more liberal construction in their favor than they were intended to bear when the instrument was framed and adopted ... Any other rule of construction would abrogate the judicial character of this court, and make it the mere reflex of the popular opinion or passion of the day.

The past, in Taney's approach, becomes an analogue for the divine foundation of law. The past's remoteness imparts moral authority to historical public opinion, and cultural etymology becomes a simulacrum of higher law moral intuition. Dressed as history and tradition, past exercises of power take on the permanent and unchanging air of such ahistorical truths as the higher law principles of freedom and equality.[52]

But Taney's history was suspect, and he knew it.[53] Like a nervous tick, his constant repetition that no one in the framers' generation doubted "for a moment the correctness" "in morals and politics" of slavery and race proscription betrays an anxiety that his historical account's distortions will be apparent. Indeed, as Justice Curtis demonstrates in his dissent, Taney's picture of history was, at least in part, a fiction. African Americans had actually enjoyed the privileges and immunities of citizens in many states at the time of the Constitution's framing, including the right to vote.[54] Also, Taney's backward glance, in its repeated emphasis on the universality of the framers' racism, attempts ahistorically to substitute a single point in the past for broader historical inquiry. As both Douglass and Emerson pointed out, such inquiry would expose the fact that, as Douglass put it, "if you read the history of the Norman Conquest, you will find that this proud Anglo-Saxon was once looked upon as of coarser clay than his Norman master, and might be found in the highways and byways of old England laboring with a brass collar on his neck, and the name of his master marked upon it."[55]

Brushing aside contrary facts, Taney attempts to use his historical fiction to seal the Constitution off from the current cultural and political revival of higher law:

[The Declaration] then proceeds to say: "We hold these truths to be self-evident: that all men are created equal; that they are endowed by their Creator with certain inalienable rights; that among them is life, liberty, and pursuit of happiness; that to secure these rights, governments are instituted, deriving their just powers from the consent of the governed."

The general words quoted above would seem to embrace the whole human family, and if they were used in a similar instrument at this day, would be so understood. But it is too clear for dispute, that the enslaved African race were not intended to be included, and formed no part of the people who framed and adopted this Declaration; for if the language, as understood in that day, would embrace them, the conduct of the distinguished men who framed the Declaration of Independence would have been utterly and flagrantly inconsistent with the principles they asserted; and instead of the sympathy of mankind, to which they so confidently appealed, they would have deserved and received universal rebuke and reprobation.

Taney's phrase, "too clear for dispute," represents in Pierre Bourdieu's terms the cultural reflex of orthodoxy to the heterodox challenge: an iteration of what goes without saying necessitated by the higher law challenges posed by Seward, Sumner, Stowe, Douglass, Emerson, and others seeking to revise and expand the essential terms of American democracy.[56] Indeed, Taney concedes that higher law argument had made his job more difficult by shifting the nation's moral consensus so that it was hard "to realize the state of public opinion in relation to that unfortunate race, which prevailed . . . when the Constitution of the United States was framed and adopted."[57] From a fragment found in his papers attributing the sectional crisis to a novel appealing to "fanatics" through exaggerated "pictures" of "the evils of slavery," we can infer that Taney had Stowe and her allies in mind when he admitted in *Dred Scott* that, if drafted in 1857, the words "all men are created equal" would be understood to embrace "the whole human family." Taney's contemporaries certainly saw *Dred Scott* as a rebuttal to the higher law arguments of Stowe and others. A Richmond *Enquirer* article, "Supreme Court vs. The Abolitionists," praised Taney's opinion as thwarting such "perverted portraitures of Southern slavery" and "assumptions of an authority paramount to the Constitution."[58]

Perhaps sensing that his history lesson would prove insufficiently persuasive to insulate the framers' edicts from contemporary revision, Taney additionally characterizes white power as a natural or God-given inherence. The white race, Taney points out, is "separated" from the "unhappy black race" "by indelible marks" of racial difference.[59] In a "supplement" he drafted to respond to public hostility aroused by his *Dred Scott* opinion, Taney refers to the African race as "made subject" to "white dominion" by "the order of nature" in order to justify the legal condition of slaves without apparently replacing higher law with positivism.[60] But Taney's attempt, in his opinion and its supplement, to disguise power as nature fails because his visual figures of inherent racial difference betray human fabrication.

Taney's reliance, in *Dred Scott*, on the visible "impressions" of racial difference unravels as his deference to power gets the better of his trope, and the purportedly natural signs of racial difference wind up revealing the authorial hand of white Americans who have "stigmatized" and "impressed such deep and enduring marks of inferiority and degradation" upon black Americans. Whether inscribed by the judge's pen or the overseer's lash, racial stigmata bear the impress of the majority's power. In his supplement, Taney alternatively attempts to use the moral sense psychology central to the framers' higher law beliefs to cloak power, bizarrely converting *Dred Scott*'s "indelible marks" of racial difference into a mental "impression made *on the white race* in this country," an impression "so deep" that "it appears indelible."[61] *Dred Scott*'s "impressions," the visible signs of race, are thus transformed in the supplement into a visualization of the mind of white America and its inherent racial prejudice. When read together, Taney's figurations of racial difference unintentionally resemble Douglass's ethnology address, blurring the distinction between the physical marks of race (erasable through intermarriage and, hence, necessitating the anti-miscegenation laws that Taney cites in *Dred Scott*) and the mental marks of culture revisable through cosmopolitan dialogue. In Taney's contradictory figures, race threatens to vanish altogether, leaving behind only the human agency and self-interest manufacturing such barriers.

In visually figuring American constitutional law as a "sad reflection" of British justice, a diminished thing administered by puppets not people, Delany rebukes Taney's attempt to render slavery natural. Delany reverses the polemic thrust of Taney's trope of visibility, his impressions and indelible marks of racial difference and white power:

> "It is indeed a sad reflection," said Blake, "to contrast the difference between British and American jurisprudence. How sublime the spectacle of the colossal stature (compared with the puppet figure of the Judge of the American Supreme Court), of the Lord Chief Justice when standing up declaring to the effect: that by the force of British intelligence, the purity of their morals, the splendor of their magnanimity, and aegis of the Magna Charta, the moment the foot of a slave touched British soil, he stood erect, disenthralled in the dignity of a freeman, by the irresistible genius of universal emancipation."
> "Let us then," said Placido, "make ourselves respected."
> "So far as Cuba is concerned, we are here for that purpose," replied Blake.
> "And if we say it shall, it will be so!" added Madame Cordova.
> "Then it shall be so!" declared Blake.[62]

Although Delany's "sad reflection" denotes a thought process, it also conjures a distorted mirror image in which the American copy of British justice has recognizable lineaments but is morally deformed and dwarfed, a reflection in which the republican terms of American political self-esteem are turned upon themselves. Instead of constituting a better type of democracy, the American scheme seems radically flawed in comparison to the British achievement of higher law jurisprudence.

The particular subject of Delany's praise is Lord Mansfield's opinion in *Somerset v. Stewart* (1772), which involved a slave who escaped and was recaptured in England. The Court of the King's Bench released Somerset on the ground that, since English law did not sanction slavery, he could not legally be held against his will.[63] The case was widely interpreted as a landmark precedent establishing that slavery offended natural law and could only exist as an institution of local positive law (i.e., legislation). Lord Mansfield's opinion became famous for a statement attributed to it that slavery was "so odious, that nothing can be suffered to support it but positive law."[64] The case provided antislavery constitutionalists, such as Chase and Sumner, with an argument that the nation's charter permitted slavery only as it existed by the authority of local law – in the absence of state law authorizing it, slavery was inconsistent with the Constitution. And it provided Delany with proof that Taney's version of constitutional history (no one doubted "for a moment the correctness" of slavery) was distorted and selective. Two of the Supreme Court Justices hearing Dred Scott's case argued that, under the *Somerset* rationale, Scott was emancipated when he resided with his master outside of the slave states.[65]

In Delany's figuration, the "colossal stature" of Lord Mansfield and the puppet figure of Justice Taney (who does not even merit the title of "Justice") incarnate in images of relative material power the moral grandeur of the higher law tradition personified by Mansfield and the moral inadequacy of Taney's racist jurisprudence. But, in attempting to turn Taney's visual figuration of justice as race against him, the visual figures of Delany's tribute to *Somerset* recapitulate the tension in Mansfield's jurisprudence between his respect for the moral principles of the higher law tradition and his positivist deference to the lower law of local sovereigns. Delany's characterization of the "spectacle" and "splendor" of British justice suggests an appreciation of the glittering trappings of power, and his visualization of the ideal natural law judge who stands for the moral principle of "universal emancipation" as a colossus, comes close to substituting power for morality. By contrast, the New York *Tribune*, which by 1857 embraced the higher law constitutionalism of Frederick Douglass and others, described Taney not as merely weak but as marked by physical features signifying his guilt. Because "the body to some extent intimates the character of the soul that inhabits it," Taney (a "tricky lawyer" not an "upright judge") "walks with inverted and hesitating steps," his "forehead is contracted," "eye sunken," and "his visage has a sinister expression." Taney's voice was barely audible when he read his opinion not because he was infirm, but because he was aware of its wickedness.[66] Though he aims to replace Taney's "deep and enduring marks of inferiority" with the moral "splendour" of universal emancipation, the prominence of power in Delany's figuration of justice threatens to overwhelm his appeal to higher law.

Parallel conversations in *Blake* between autarchs of American slavery and among their rebel enemies reveal that, while power is necessary to either a denial or a grant of citizenship, race is not. In the dialogue of Judge Ballard and Major Armsted, the themes of law and power that

Taney conflates in *Dred Scott* are separated into the voices of two white characters, who, as their appellations suggest, represent the American legal order and the military might enforcing that order. Delany satirizes the legal profession's formalist reasoning in Judge Ballard's use of legal deduction ("the right to buy implies the right to hold, also to sell") to overcome his "conscientious scruples" against the slave trade. Appropriately, it is the military figure, Major Armsted, not the man of law, who unmasks the fraud involved in such rationalizations. The Major's honest appraisal of slavery as the exercise of domination without basis in any inherent racial difference ("I would just as readily hold a white as a black in slavery") exposes the hypocrisy of the jurist, whose conscience supposedly pulls in one direction while his professional dedication to an apt historical understanding of the law conveniently requires that he serve his own personal and public interest in racial domination.[67]

By contrast, the various conversations Delany imagines among rebels in the American South and Cuba demonstrate how an ethical and political consensus may be established in open dialogue by a culturally diverse group of men and women. Delany enthusiastically touts the creative power of such dialogue to reject a continuity of oppression and to create a more just social and legal order: "If we say it shall, it will be so!"[68] The political, not tribal, nature of this Pan-African republicanism becomes clearest at the precise moment when the claims of racial kinship are most prominent – Blake's time with the maroon rebels in the Dismal Swamp. This episode gives Blake an opportunity to receive the blessing of the "High Conjurors," Gamby Gholar, Maudy Ghamus, and others, "who dwell in the swamp outside the power of slaveholding America." Speaking in dialect, practicing conjure and other African rites, the "High Conjurers" preserve and exemplify an African heritage, and their endorsement would seem to stamp Blake's leadership with an identitarian seal of authenticity. However, these men are also patriots who fought in the American Revolution, and they share with Blake neither dialect nor cultural markers of Africanity. Instead of authenticity, the High Conjurors' conversation with Blake exemplifies a distinctive syncretism, a cross-cultural fusion of Anglo-American higher law rhetoric and the tropes of an African communalism.[69]

Similarly, the group discussions led by Blake and Placido in Cuba locate the Pan-African community's cultural identity in its liberation philosophy. Turning Taney's attempt to preserve the racial homogeneity of the American republic into a liability, Delany's revolutionary poet,

Placido, lauds the cosmopolitan ability of the African people to assimilate the "civilized customs" of any nation or race. Placido's paradox-
ical formulation of the ability to transcend race as the Africans' racial
gift holds particular political (and economic) promise for the revolutionary community, as it will open the community to diverse influences
and practices.[70] This paradox is anticipated in "The Political Destiny of
the Colored Race," where Delany avers that the value of cultural tolerance comprises one of the lessons the people of African descent will teach
the world in the area of law and jurisprudence: "in plain language, in
the true principles of morals, correctness of thought, religion, and law
or civil government, there is no doubt but the black race will yet instruct
the world."[71]

However, by shifting Blake's consensus-building process from the
American South to Cuba, where the Pan-African coalition comprises
a majority, Delany's narrative leaves the jurisprudential question of minority rights in a majoritarian legal system unanswered. This problem is
foreshadowed in "Political Destiny," where Delany's espousal of a universalist definition of justice is accompanied by an emphasis on the importance of sovereignty to African American liberty: "A people, to be free,
must necessarily be *their own rulers*; that is, *each individual* must, in himself, embody the *essential ingredient* – so to speak – of the *sovereign principle*
which composes the *true basis* of his liberty." In *Blake*, Delany's fictional
rebels candidly recognize the prerequisite of force for the acquisition of
citizenship status: "On this island," said Blake, "we are the many and
the oppressors few; consequently, they have no moral right to hold rule
over us, whilst we have the moral right and physical power to prevent
them. Whatever we determine shall be, will be." The political power of
the majority is essential to the reality envisioned by the revolutionaries.
With power, their rights rhetoric becomes more than a polemic device:
it becomes an intellectual framework for a new legal order recognizing
people of color and open to all who oppose racial oppression. But rule by
majority consent, as Francis Lieber pointed out, is just the rule of power
in another guise, and only awaits a divergence between the political
majority and a discrete minority to expose its oppressive potential.[72]

The acute conflict between the universalist aspirations of Delany's
republicanism and his positivism emerges in his treatment of a pair of
terms – sufferance and suffrage. In Delany's view, for a minority to possess citizenship rights without the power to insist on those rights is to exist
"only by sufferance, and subject to enslavement at any time." Taney's
comment in *Dred Scott* that, historically, free blacks had "no rights or

privileges but such as those who held the power and Government might choose to give them" provided constitutional justification for Delany's mistrust of the moral commitment of a benevolent majority.[73] As further support for his positivistic skepticism, Delany offers the example of free blacks in Canada who have a second-class status despite their possession of the right of suffrage. Suffrage proves to be, as Judge Ballard observes, a "mere privilege – a thing permitted" and not "franchise" or full citizenship, which is "a right inherent, that which is inviolable – cannot be interfered with." In Ballard's formulation of "a right inherent," as in Blake's description of the Cuban rebels' majority power ("consequently, they have no moral right to hold rule over us, whilst we have the moral right and physical power to prevent them"), power and human rights are interdependent. We call certain rights "inherent" because we are confident that we can enforce them. A privilege is a thing granted and thus withdrawable, but a right is something taken by force and guaranteed by the continuing possession of power.[74]

The definitional intersection between sufferance and suffrage lies in their connotations of consent. Sufferance indicates the majority's consent to the minority's freedom, civil standing, and enjoyment of basic rights and privileges, such as suffrage; suffrage suggests the minority's consent to and participation in a government in which most decisions are made by the majority. Absent from white sufferance and black suffrage, in Delany's view, is any figure of power to ensure the rights of the minority, which, consequently, must aspire to majoritarian power of its own. Rejecting sufferance and suffrage, Delany replaces consent with power.[75] Thus, though he accepts universal ethical norms as an identity-neutral political discourse in which diverse individuals and groups can negotiate new forms of civil association (e.g., his Cuban rebels accept diversity of religious beliefs as part of a universal conception of justice), Delany finds that this kind of dialogue only has practical value where it is accompanied by majority power.[76] Throughout *Blake*, Delany's positivism shadows his appeals to moral universals as the basis of legal and political association. Delany ignores the fact that the "right" behavior of those in power (e.g., the religious tolerance of his Cuban majority) is merely a happy coincidence of power and morality unless the majoritarian political system is regulated by some notion of universal moral consensus. The morality of religious tolerance, after all, inheres by definition not in any sectarian notion of divine will or some clear vision of fixed moral absolutes but in the ethical superiority of a heterodox and heterogeneous consensus from which no one is excluded – sufferance and suffrage.

HOLMES'S FATALISM

In Oliver Wendell Holmes's transformation from a young Union army officer fired with abolitionist zeal into a jurist deeply skeptical of moral accounts of law, we can follow the antebellum rebirth and post-Reconstruction retrenchment of higher law argument. An examination of the increasing centrality of power to Holmes's influential jurisprudence tends to reorient one's sense of his era's legal doctrines. From the perspective offered by Holmes's career, Jim Crow law begins to look less like a capitulation to racism, than a capitulation to power in the name of race. Thus, a brief glance at Holmes is worthwhile here, despite the fact that an adequate treatment of his jurisprudence is well beyond the scope of this study.

Some would object that portraying Holmes as a positivist flattens the great jurist, who, among other things, championed the first amendment against legislative incursion and extolled an experimental approach to law closely related to progressive politics and pragmatist philosophy. Though it is true that Holmes's multifaceted jurisprudence defies any simple categorization, the point here is not to confine all of Holmes's thinking to one of its strands but to pick out that strand and see what it suggests about his era's jurisprudence.[77] That positivism *is* one of the strands of Holmes's thought is apparent even from a cursory reading of his opinions, legal theory, and letters, and it has been well documented by numerous scholars.[78]

Years after the Civil War, Holmes recalled that as a young man he was set "on fire" by Emerson's transcendentalism and so "deeply moved by the Abolitionist cause" that "a Negro minstrel show" shocked him. In January 1861, Holmes, then a Harvard undergraduate, attended an abolitionist meeting in Boston at which Ralph Waldo Emerson and Wendell Phillips were to speak. Holmes came not only as an auditor but armed with a billy club, as part of Phillips's and Emerson's bodyguard (a role prophetically connecting force and moral reform). A few months later, Holmes left Harvard and enlisted in the Union Army, seeking to scourge the notion that "men own other men by God's law" and conceiving of the Civil War as "a crusade in the cause of the whole civilized world . . . the Christian Crusade of the 19th century."[79] But the war's drudgery and senseless sacrifice of human life shook Holmes's confidence in the project of humanitarian reform.[80] For Holmes the veteran, "the word 'abolition' is associated not with young men of deep sympathies and generous sentiments but with communists, Christian Science, the Catholics on Calvin, Calvin on the Catholics, Trotsky on Stalin, Prohibitionists, Emma Goldman."[81] Dismissing reformers as "do-gooders," Holmes caustically remarked,

If there is a thing I loathe, it is the sentimental squashiness of a big minority of our time – Religious squeams about taking human life . . . the notion that war is about to be abolished by the sacred influence of woman and all the rest of it. The Universe is predatory . . . all life except the very lowest is at the expense of other life . . . I do despise the upward and onward.[82]

Holmes's war experience inclined him toward a social Darwinist view of life as combat, a view that also seemed apt for his new profession, law, which consisted of a bloodless kind of warfare:

[I]n the last resort a man rightly prefers his own interest to that of his neighbors. And this is true in legislation as in any other form of corporate action . . . The more powerful interests must be more or less reflected in legislation; which, like every other device of man or beast, must tend in the long run to aid the survival of the fittest.[83]

Legislation was a weapon in the struggle between classes and races. In limiting the chaos and carnage of competition, law might reflect the majority's habitual moral norms and taste for order but that did not change the fact that it was the majority's political power that wrote and enforced the law.

Holmes's early legal scholarship contradicted legal formalism – the notion that judges could resolve cases with an almost mathematical predictability by logically applying bright line rules to abstract factual categories. In *The Common Law* (1881), Holmes famously announced that "The life of the law has not been logic: it has been experience."[84] Judge-made law was a messy process expressing the community's slowly evolving and sometimes inconsistent customs and traditions. Holmes found law to be characterized by a "paradox of form and substance": while the form of legal development appeared logical, the substance of law was the changing vision of the community's self-interest. "The secret root from which the law draws all the juices of life" is in fact "considerations of what is expedient for the community" and not some ahistorical legal "ideal" – whether logical or moral.[85] The fundamental "requirement of a sound body of law," for Holmes, "is that it should correspond to the actual feelings and demands of the community, whether right or wrong."[86] The early Holmes of *The Common Law* saw social custom, "the unconscious result of instinctive preferences and inarticulate convictions," as the real foundation of legal authority.[87] Thus, Holmes rejected strict liability (which holds one liable for another's injury without reference to one's mental state) not for any supposed violation of natural rights but because it offended the community's traditions.

Law evolved as society evolved, and the ponderous bulk of historic custom furnished not only the material of legal standards and decisions but also a salutary buffer between the potentially anarchic dictates of individual conscience and the tyrannical demands of those with power. Law expressed the community's power, but the medium of that expression, a vast and largely inert body of traditional concepts and figures, clogged the too quick or too extreme exercise of that power. Holmes's account of the traditional basis of law was anticipated by earlier conceptions of the common law's peculiar authority. John Adams, for instance, argued that the common law's preeminence could be traced to its grounding in tradition: "customs... form the common law; they have been used time out of mind, or for a time whereof the memory of man runneth not to the contrary."[88] Though custom was obviously a diachronic concept, Adams and many who followed him tended to figure it as an elemental and ageless basis for law.

In the nineteenth century, the most significant challenge to the common law authority of judges was posed by the codification movement. Advocates of codification contended that state legislatures had the democratic power to encompass *all* legal doctrine within written codes. Conservative members of the bar and bench countered that, of the branches of government, the judiciary alone was unaffected by the partisan turmoil of politics.[89] Speaking for many judges and lawyers, James Coolidge Carter, a prominent New York jurist, rejected the codification advocates' conception of law: "Legislation should never attempt to do for society that which society can do, and is constantly doing for itself. As custom is the true origin of law, the legislature cannot, *ex vi termini*, absolutely create it. This is the unconscious work of society." From "the deeper and more philosophical" point of view, legislation should be seen, according to Carter, as "simply affixing the public mark and authentication upon the customs and rules already existing, or struggling into existence, in the habits of the people."[90] For those doubting the practicability of morally derived law and fearing the unchecked prerogative of legislative majorities, the figure of an independent judiciary executing a body of common law that had evolved from the historic customs of the American people represented an attractively apolitical alternative to either the higher law or positivist models.[91]

However, as the political investments involved in judge-made law, such as the Supreme Court's nullification of a progressive income tax, became increasingly conspicuous, the notion of judicial disinterest lost credibility. As Morton Horwitz notes, by 1897, when Holmes wrote "The Path of the Law," "the power of custom as a mediating category had begun to disintegrate" in the face of economic depression and violent conflicts between labor and capital. In his landmark essay, Holmes reverses de Tocqueville's observation in *Democracy in America* that "scarcely any political question arises in the United States that is not resolved sooner or later into a judicial question," asserting that all adjudication is "a concealed, half-conscious battle on the question of legislative policy."[92] The political majority articulates its policies in law, and judges interpret and enforce those legal expressions of political power. The judge's role was not to "Do justice" but to "play the game according to the rules."[93] Seeking to dispel the "confusion between morality and law," Holmes points out that "A man who cares nothing for an ethical rule which is believed and practised by his neighbors is likely nevertheless to care a good deal to avoid being made to pay money, and will want to keep out of jail if he can." This is not to say, Holmes notes, that there is no connection between morality and law. Viewed historically, "The law is the witness and external deposit of our moral life." However, such a perspective belongs to historians, not politicians who write and judges who enforce and "bad men" who obey the law. For those involved in its processes, law as law begins and ends in force. Law expresses the majority's power to implement public policies serving its interests, limited by morality, says Holmes, only to the extent that if the legislature were to pass an "extreme" law, deviating wildly from the "habits" of the people, "the community would rise in rebellion." Perhaps the most striking contrast between this positivist strand of Holmes's legal theory and the higher law constitutionalism of Douglass, Sumner, and Emerson lies in Holmes's characterization of moral norms, from *The Common Law* to "The Path of the Law," as "deposit," "habit," the "unconscious result of instinctive preferences and inarticulate convictions."[94] In Holmes's description, agency and consent are erased from the cultural production of legally effective moral limits.

Holmes's deference to legislative sovereignty in his famous *Lochner* dissent puts the theory announced in "The Path of the Law" into practice. In *Lochner*, the Court struck down a New York law limiting the number of hours per week that employers could require of their bakery employees, holding that the law unconstitutionally abridged the freedom of contract between bakeries and their employees. Holmes attacked the Court's substitution of its own economic theory and notions of fundamental justice for the will of the New York legislature. As Taney had before him in *Charles River*, Holmes accepted the legislature's power to interfere with contractual relations. Even though personally inclined to accept his brethren's laissez-faire capitalism, Holmes ironically pointed out that the "Fourteenth Amendment does not enact Mr. Herbert Spencer's Social Statics":

This case is decided upon an economic theory which a large part of the country does not entertain. If it were a question whether I agreed with that theory, I should desire to study it further and long before making up my mind. But I do not conceive that to be my duty because I strongly believe that my agreement or disagreement has nothing to do with the right of a majority to embody their opinion in law.[95]

When the legal issue involved race, however, Holmes tended to drop the tone of judicial deference. In *Bailey v. Alabama* (1911), which in its day was compared to *Dred Scott* and *Plessy v. Ferguson* (1896), Holmes's dissent sounded surprisingly moralistic and formalist. *Bailey* involved Alabama's peonage law, which, according to the description of the U.S. Attorney for the Western District of Louisiana, operated "to give the large planters of the state absolute dominion over the Negro laborer."[96] The law converted a black laborer's breach of his employment contract (e.g., failure to work for the full term of the contract) into a criminal fraud for which the laborer could be sentenced to prison and "hard labor." The state would then lease the laborer to local plantation owners. In a sharp departure from his own injunction against legal formalism, Holmes's dissent relies on an abstract analysis of legal categories without any consideration of the factual circumstances of the case: "We all agree that this case is to be considered and decided in the same way as if it arose in Idaho or New York . . . The fact that in Alabama it mainly concerns blacks does not matter."[97] At odds with his usual insistence that contractual duty and morality are distinct ("The duty to keep a contract at common law means a prediction that you must pay damages if you do not keep it – and nothing more"), Holmes's *Bailey* dissent preaches that "Breach of contract without excuse is wrong conduct, even if the contract is for labor, and if a state adds to civil liability a criminal liability to fine, it simply intensifies the legal motive for doing right."[98]

Race was apparently provocative enough to transform Holmes from a self-conscious but skeptical tool of legislative power into a true believer, finding the legal oppression of black Americans to be justified by their native inferiority. Thus, the incapability of blacks to adhere to such a basic moral norm as the keeping of contractual obligations implicitly justified for Holmes laws that in essence re-enslaved them.[99] However, despite this shift in Holmes's tone and the racism that probably animated it, the outcome Holmes urged in cases like *Bailey* fundamentally comports with his deference to the majority's legislative dictates. As G. Edward White notes, "If the political and economic dominance of whites in southern states combined with racial antagonisms to result in laws that were 'bald discriminations' against blacks solely on account of their race, Holmes felt that was the way law worked."[100]

The emergence of Holmes's positivism suggests a juristic perspective on the advent of Jim Crow that studies focusing primarily on race and racism have tended to overlook.[101] That the imperialism and racism sweeping the country at the turn of the century were accompanied by positivist explanations of law and society was not coincidental. Racist biology, sociology, anthropology, history, journalism, and fiction were handy means of underwriting the oppressive exercise of power at home (through legal and extralegal means) and abroad (through military adventure). Such intellectual efforts as Nathaniel Shaler's theories of racial difference and black retrogression, Thomas Dixon's white supremacist fiction, William Graham Sumner's social Darwinism, and Holmes's legal positivism meshed smoothly in the Jim Crow era to present a picture of American law and society as inevitably ruled by the power of the superior people – a vision suggested by a New York *Times* editorial noting that "the suppression of the Negro vote" was no longer denounced in 1900 as "in the reconstruction days" because "[t]he necessity of it under the supreme law of self-preservation is candidly recognized."[102]

A particularly telling sign of the era's alloy of racism and positivist jurisprudence can be found in the restoration of Taney's reputation. In 1909, William E. Mikell, a professor of law at the University of Pennsylvania, praised Taney as "the greatest *expounder* of the Constitution that ever sat on the Supreme Court bench."[103] Such revisionists described higher law objections to *Dred Scott* as "murderous roar," "partisan malice," and "open nullification." As Don Fehrenbacher reports, "In scores of articles and books, the militant opponents of slavery from William Lloyd Garrison to Thaddeus Stevens became virtually the chief villains of their age – men who in their extremism precipitated an unnecessary war and in their vindictiveness imposed a tragically draconian peace."[104] And the higher law vision of African Americans as, in

Charles Sumner's words, "the heroes of our age" who "in their very efforts for Freedom . . . claim kindred with all that is noble" was eclipsed by images of black retrogression – the Negro as beast or minstrel buffoon. Dred Scott, for example, is described in Frederick Trevor Hill's *Decisive Battles of the Law* (1907) as a kind of hapless minstrel buffoon, a "shiftless, incapable specimen of his race," who, abandoned by his legal master, became a burden to the son of a former master.[105] The very notion of black citizenship seemed a freakish distortion of nature and power from the perspective of Jim Crow positivism – the perspective of Mark Twain's bogeyman, Pap Finn.

As a post-Reconstruction incarnation of an antebellum type, Pap is both Sut Lovingood's progeny and contemporary – one of Twain's many parallels signaling that the jurisprudence of the *Dred Scott* era had been reincarnated as Jim Crow. Pap's drunken rant on law and government in *Huckleberry Finn* (1885) expresses the predominance of will in late-nineteenth-century jurisprudence. Pap begins by seeing himself as a victim of law: "Call this a govment! Why, just look at it and see what it's like. Here's the law a-standing ready to take a man's son away from him – a man's own son, which he has had all the trouble and all the expense of raising . . . A man can't get his rights in a govment like this."[106] Here, Twain burlesques how higher law conceptions of natural rights spring to the lips of anyone who has been legally inhibited in the satisfaction of his appetites. Pap's grievance takes a different tack when he considers a free black man from Ohio that he has observed:

Oh, yes, this is a wonderful govment, wonderful. Why, looky here. There was a free nigger there, from Ohio, a mulatter, most as white as a white man. And what do you think? They said he was a p'fessor in a college . . . They said he could *vote*, when he was at home . . . when they told me there was a State in this country where they'd let that nigger vote, I drawed out. I says I'll never vote agin . . . I says to the people, why ain't this nigger put up at auction and sold? – that's what I want to know. And what do you reckon they said? Why they said he couldn't be sold till he'd been in the State six months, and he hadn't been there that long yet. There, now – that's a specimen. They call that a govment that can't sell a free nigger till he's been in the State six months . . . [107]

No longer the oppressed outsider who cannot "get his rights," Pap speaks for a majority angered by the way the law obstructs or checks its will. His incredulity that the black "p'fessor" can vote is framed by the reader's disgust that Pap can. In his vulgar positivism, Pap makes Twain's case for an ethical conception of law in which the political will of the majority is regulated by the rule of law and universal moral norms – an argument that had begun to seem distinctly quixotic by the mid 1880s.

BLACK COMEDY: BLACK CITIZENSHIP AND JIM CROW POSITIVISM

The harshly comedic aspect of black citizenship from the perspective of Jim Crow positivism is suggested by John Mercer Langston's account of becoming a member of the Ohio State Bar. Looking back on the antebellum beginning of his legal career, Langston (a real life version of Pap's "mulatter" "p'fessor" from Ohio) recalled that, on passing the bar exam, the Ohio Chief Justice ordered him to rise. Then, through "a beautiful hocus pocus arrangement," he was "construed into a *white man*" and sworn in. After taking his oath, Langston boldly asked why he had been asked to stand and "was told that it was material to know by sight what [his] color was."[108] Langston's term "hocus pocus" draws a parallel between the solemn rituals of the bar and the magic act or side show which present the marvelous, the anomalous, and the bizarre and leave the audience wondering whether what it has witnessed is illusion or reality, genuine or fake. By the time Langston recalled his magical transformation into white citizen and lawyer, black citizenship seemed a cruel illusion to some and a kind of side show eccentricity to others.

As a black lawyer, Langston was doubly freakish. Twain's bleak satire of Jim Crow positivism, *Pudd'nhead Wilson*, captures the way that law and litigation become a comic theater of the aberrant when viewed from the perspective of the *gemeinschaft* white America pretends to be. Only the odd disputes of anomalous characters find their way into courtrooms. *Normal* disputes are resolved not by law but by reference to the supposedly homogeneous community's social code. The most peculiar aberration of all is constitutional litigation in which a curiosity, such as Langston or Homer Plessy, claims membership. The strangeness of such characters inheres partly in their apparent mutability (white enough to pass, they can be "hocus pocused" white or black), but the oddity of their assertion of citizenship derives from a positivist constitutionalism deeming law the rule of the strong and power a racial inherence. The outsider's claim of civic recognition and justice is met by the same gaze of tribal normalcy and power marking the outsider as a freak in the first place. Before we turn to Twain's satiric "photograph" of American justice, we need to set the stage by briefly examining the forms and figures Taney-like positivism took in the Jim Crow era.

On March 2, 1875, Reconstruction's last political initiative came to fruition when the President signed Senator Charles Sumner's Civil Rights Act. The law forbade racial discrimination in public places of accommodation, such as restaurants, hotels, and theaters and provided both criminal and civil penalties for violations. Endorsed by Douglass and Langston, whose endorsements Sumner touted in Senate debates, the Act was designed to promote a racially fluid public sphere. In keeping with the cosmopolitan constitutionalism Sumner shared with Douglass and Emerson, his bill anticipated that the nation's sense of justice and citizenship would be positively transformed by public intercourse between the races.[109] A dead letter long before the Supreme Court held it unconstitutional in 1883, Sumner's bill was, from its inception, widely evaded by citizens and scorned by the press and judiciary.

One gets a good feel for the cultural disposition effectively nullifying Sumner's bill by surveying the New York *Times*'s coverage of the Civil Rights Act. Given its purported political moderation as a paper of record and Republican, antislavery antecedents, the *Times*'s mocking coverage of the Civil Rights Act's demise exemplifies the very jurisprudential and political shift it records. In its editorials, the *Times* predicted both that the Act would prove impotent in the face of contrary social attitudes and that the Supreme Court would invalidate the law:

A white man may be compelled to sit and eat his dinner at the same table with a negro, and perhaps there is no good reason why he should object to take his meals in that way. But compulsion of this kind is not apt to produce a feeling of cordial friendship, and the social relations of two opposite races are seldom improved by bringing coercion to bear upon either one or the other.

Sumner's bill foolishly denied a basic fact of human nature – that each prefers his own – what Franklin Giddings termed "consciousness in kind."[110] Public reaction to the Act seemed to confirm the *Times*'s prognosis. Rather than accept integration, hotels in Alexandria and Baltimore closed. In Chattanooga, several hotels began operating as private boarding houses, and, in Cincinnati, a barbershop refused service to a black man holding a copy of the Act in his hand.[111] Courts repudiated the law. A federal district court judge in North Carolina declared, "no law can say all men shall be equal socially." And a New Orleans judge declared that the Civil Rights Act could not conceivably or rationally mandate "social rights" in the face of contrary majority prejudice and, as a consequence, held that it did not bar segregation – an astonishing bit of judicial nullification of the Act's express terms.[112]

Violence and laughter set the tone for the white majority's rejection of, in the *Times*'s ironic phrase, "Mr. Sumner's legacy to the American nation."[113] A *Times* report on the evasion of the Act in Richmond, Virginia reported that an Episcopal minister, neatly complying with the era's stereotypes, avoided any confrontation with a black woman try- ing to attend his church by simply dismissing the congregation without holding services. Predictably less fastidious, the "unsympathetic Irish" of the Catholic congregation at St. Peter's Cathedral roughly ejected would-be black parishioners. Describing these attempts at integration as "ludicrous," the correspondent predicts "that the Civil Rights bill will be utterly routed by laughter and ridicule."[114]

Tales of the Act's futility in the *Times* are revealingly framed by other stories capturing the darkly comic flavor of the era's trend toward power and race and away from conscience and consent as explanations of law and society. Consider, for instance, an account of the Civil Rights Act's absurdity, which is immediately followed by an article on the formation of a Freaks' Union. The article on the Civil Rights Act lampoons the very notion of black Americans claiming damages for injuries to "person and estate" by reason of racist exclusion from places of public accom- modation. The joke of such claims, for the correspondent, is illustrated by the fact that the experience of even such a worthy black American as Frederick Douglass (who is represented none too subtly as a marked exception to the clownish norm of his race) is one long litany of insult and outrage. Consequently, a suit for damages for a single instance of racial discrimination becomes laughable. The following item on the formation of a "Freaks' Union" unintentionally amplifies the message and humor of the civil rights article. "The Freaks of Nature" reports that:

It is noteworthy that the "Freaks" decline to recognize tattooed persons and Circassian girls as fit members of their union. This is undoubtedly because tattooed persons and Circassian girls are works of art, and hence the supply can always be proportioned to the demand, whereas the true "Freak" is born, not made, and cannot be supplied to order in unlimited quantities.

The Freaks, according to this report, recognize that identity is innate ("the true 'Freak' is born, not made") and paradoxically that identity must be policed to obtain and preserve power (in this case, economic power). Part of the humorous reaction assumed by both stories derives from the imitation by human oddities of "normal" (white) social and political association – both the blacks' efforts to mingle and the Freaks' efforts to exclude constitute comic copies of different but related aspects of white America. In both cases, the uncanny resemblance together with the obvious distortions and differences give the parallel its comic charge. The minstrel figuration of black citizenship and the exemplary oddity of the freak converge in the majority's assumption that a society's law invariably reflects an identity that is inherent yet enforced. From this identitarian *and* positivist view, the freedom to mingle depends upon the policing of identity – both of which are regulated and protected by law.

The pairing of these two articles suggests the general association of minstrelsy and freak shows in Jim Crow America. Minstrelsy incorporated freaks, freak shows incorporated elements of minstrelsy, and both forms of entertainment were often presented in the same venue. P.T. Barnum's American Museum not only offered freaks and minstrel shows but dramatic renditions of Stowe's *Uncle Tom's Cabin* as well. Minstrelsy's Jim Crow, with his grotesque exaggerations of black appearance, life, and culture and the sideshow's William Henry Johnson, an African American suffering from microcephaly, the most successful freak of the era, both traded on the white public's fascination with and horror at human variety and anomaly.[115] In both minstrelsy and the freak show, physical anomalies were paired with exotic cultural differences to create an ostensibly absolute sense of difference. The popular "Wild Men of Borneo" were a pair of dwarf brothers from Ohio transformed into rare exotics from a strange world, and a brother and sister with microcephaly from San Salvador were fashioned to look "Aztec" and presented as "The Last of the Ancient Aztecs." Yet, the minstrel figure's or freak's recognizable similarity with the audience was also indispensable. As the missing link "between human and brute creation," Johnson needed to be both like and unlike his audience. The general thematic connection of minstrel and freak shows to the *Times*'s coverage of the Civil Rights Act lies in the inevitability these texts seem to furnish for the majority's exclusion of the odd human specimen from the body politic. Marked by glaringly inherent deficiencies, the minstrel figure or freak betokens natural segregation – a neat bit of symbolic hocus pocus in which the political power circumscribing civic recognition and inclusion effaces itself.[116]

Twain satirizes such displacements of positivist agency onto nature in his short piece, "Recent Carnival of Crime in Connecticut," which appeared in the *Times* on May 14, 1876. Twain's story ostensibly explains the cause of a recent crime spree in Connecticut. In the story, a grotesque dwarf materializes in Twain's study. Though "this little person was a deformity as a whole," yet like all freaks "this vile bit of human rubbish, seemed to bear a sort of remote resemblance to me!...a far-fetched, dim suggestion of a burlesque upon me, a caricature of me in little." The dwarf proceeds to give Twain a brutally frank account of his failure to act ethically toward others, "every sentence an accusation, and every accusation a truth." Focusing on Twain's selfish, dishonest, and cruel interactions with strangers, the dwarf represents the ethics of the public sphere. Noisome and galling, Twain's dwarf embodies the irritation that white America feels for higher law conceptions, tending to obstruct or regulate its will. The dwarf explicitly connects conscience to race by citing, as the ultimate example of the torture a conscience can inflict, the case of a man who thinks he has killed a mulatto child. Like the dwarf, the African American is an annoying, at times, harrowing reminder of the majority's failings, its capitulation to power. By killing the dwarf, his "master," Twain, the "slave," ironically heralds the depletion of the higher law vision's cultural and legal authority.

The return of Taney-like positivism in the official jurisprudence of the era is plainly evident in the Supreme Court's treatment of the Civil War amendments – the Fourteenth Amendment in particular. Whatever else they do or do not do, the Civil War amendments write into the Constitution a check on the political power of the majority when the fundamental rights of minority members are at stake. Though variously dressed as tradition, God's will, or nature, the Court's evisceration of this seminal revision of the Constitution is the starkest testament of the rise of positivist jurisprudence. Though tonally quite different from the vulgarities of the minstrel or freak show, these cases similarly focus on the oddity of the individual litigant claiming citizenship. For instance, when Myra Bradwell complained that Illinois's refusal to admit her to the State Bar because she was a married woman violated the Fourteenth Amendment's equal protection clause, Justice Joseph P. Bradley referred, as Taney had before him, to history and nature – both of which demonstrated the "wide difference in the respective spheres and destinies of man and woman." Threatening to disrupt the "harmony" of the "family institution," Bradwell becomes the jurist's version of the sideshow's bearded lady or the minstrelsy's buffoonish black gentleman. That the majority (which Bradley confidently assumes shares his vision of domestic felicity) would permit Myra Bradwell's licensure is as inconceivable to Bradley as the majority's refusal to re-enslave the mulatto professor is to Pap Finn.[117] Similarly, when Chae Chan Ping challenged the Chinese Exclusion Act of 1882, Justice Stephen Field (who had joined in Bradley's *Bradwell* concurrence) offered the "differences of race" in justification of the law. The strange "customs and usages" of Chinese immigrants made their continuing access to the U.S. undesirable. Field admitted that the Act's violation of rights under prior treaties was in some sense immoral, but declared that morality was not the Court's business.[118] Both *Bradwell* and *Chae Chan Ping* read the law through implicit citizenship narratives in which the identity of the majority is normative and inextricably tied to its power to create and protect that identity. Any other principle ordering society would represent an inconceivable relinquishment of identity and power.

When one turns to the line of Supreme Court decisions undermining the Civil War amendments' protection of African American citizenship, the identitarian and positivist turn in the jurisprudence of citizenship takes a less overt form. In the *Slaughterhouse Cases* (1873), Justice Samuel Miller read into the Fourteenth Amendment a division between national and state citizenship. Distinguishing the two types of citizenship, Miller found that most civil rights were issues of state, not federal, citizenship and exclusively within the jurisdiction of state law, subverting the Fourteenth Amendment's removal of black citizenship rights from the control of local majorities.[119] Ten years later, in the *Civil Rights Cases*, the Court held that the Civil Rights Act's proscription of private discrimination was invalid on its face because Congress's power under the Fourteenth Amendment was confined to prohibiting discriminatory state action. The cases at issue involved the exclusion of African Americans from public accommodations, such as a hotel, the dress circle of a theater, and the ladies' car of a train, in direct violation of the Act. Ignoring that coaches, cabs and theaters are licensed and regulated by the state (as Justice Harlan pointed out in dissent), Justice Bradley held that these victims of discrimination had merely suffered private wrongs to their social rights, wrongs that were not recognized by the Fourteenth Amendment. In his famous comment that the time had come for African Americans to cease being the "special favorites of the laws," Bradley politely registers the unnatural, freakish quality of legislative attempts to imbue black Americans with the mantle and rights of citizenship, as well as white America's impatience with this higher law experiment. Henceforth, race relations would assume a less artificial and more natural (i.e., hierarchical) aspect.

Justice John Marshall Harlan's dissent focused on what he deemed was the majority's circumvention of the intent of the Thirteenth and Fourteenth Amendments.[120] For Harlan, the Civil War amendments explicitly rejected the doctrines of *Dred Scott*, including Taney's suggestion that the opinion "entertained by the most civilized portion of the white race" of black inferiority was constitutionally relevant to the adjudication of black rights and citizenship.[121] After the Civil War amendments, the rule of law dictated that majority's racism yield to a new, more inclusive conception of citizenship. As his dissent in *Plessy v. Ferguson* (1896) would make plain, Harlan had at least some success in setting aside his own racism in obedience to what he saw was the intent of the law and the superior moral authority upon which that law was based. Countering the *Plessy* majority's engrafting of the separate but equal doctrine on the Fourteenth Amendment's equal protection clause, Harlan openly averred his opinion that whites were and would remain the superior race but denied that that opinion had any constitutional relevance.[122]

Conceding that Harlan's dissent in the *Civil Rights Cases* was "learned, candid, and able," the *Times* commented, "The tendency during the war period was toward the construction which he favors," but since then "a reaction has set in." Harlan was out of step with an era rejecting "[e]fforts . . . to give great elasticity" to the Fourteenth Amendment's protection of citizenship rights. An apt choice of words, "great elasticity" is precisely the value at stake in higher law conceptions of a mutable and ever more inclusive moral consensus as the legitimating principle of American law. "In the temper which the people have now reached in dealing," said the *Times*, it was simply obvious that the Fourteenth Amendment "did not authorize such legislation as the Civil Rights act." So clear had this consensus become that Harlan's dissent presented "considerations that do not occur to the ordinary mind." In effect, this comment makes Pap Finn an exemplar of the "ordinary mind," a mind that cannot conceive of race-neutral citizenship any more than it can conceive of a legal order not directed by power.[123]

Liberal Southerners, such as George Washington Cable and Mark Twain, were appalled by the *Civil Rights Cases*. Cable responded in a famous essay, "The Freedmen's Case in Equity," which appeared in *Century Magazine* for January 1885, with selections from *Huckleberry Finn*. As his title suggests, arguments against Jim Crow had to be framed as appeals to equity, the ethical norms judges apply when legal doctrine leads to patently unjust results. "The Freedmen's Case in Equity" derived, in part, from Cable's first-hand experience of Jim Crow train travel, when he observed the indignity and discomfort suffered by a well-dressed and polite black woman and her young daughter who were forced to occupy a train car shared with filthy convicts. The injustice of this discrimination was particularly galling because of the law's asymmetry – had the girl been white and the black adult her hired guardian, they would not have been forced into such distasteful company. In January 1885, after a similar experience on a Southern train, Twain angrily wrote to his wife of the insulting remarks made by a white boy about a black woman "who was better dressed and had more brains and breeding than several generations of the white boy's family could show."[124] Twain and Cable's rejection of Jim Crow resembles Harlan's "color-blind" approach to citizenship and foreshadows Charles Chesnutt and Moorfield Storey's conception of public deportment as a consensual language that enables diverse individuals and groups to coexist and that preserves a separation between the terms of civic recognition and those of racial or cultural identity.

By 1894, however, both Twain and Cable had come to doubt that Jim Crow could be stopped by moral suasion and liberal criticism. Cable's novel, *John March, Southerner* (1894), published the same year as *Pudd'nhead Wilson*, exhibits this change in its racist language and bleak tone. In 1884, Cable was so sensitive to the use of the term "nigger" that he convinced Mark Twain to change the title of one of his readings from "You Can't Teach a Nigger to Argue" to "How Come a Frenchman Doan' Talk Like a Man?" Ten years later, in *John March*, Cable uses "nigger" frequently, as well as racist caricatures of black appearance. In Cornelius Leggett's ungrammatical and foolish paraphrase of Cable's "The Freedman's Case in Equity" essay, Cable merges the African American as higher law hero and the minstrel buffoon.[125] Jim Crow's triumphs in the South and the nation as a whole made the very notion of constitutional checks on the majority's will and bias seem doubtful to Cable and Twain.[126] *Pudd'nhead Wilson* is Twain's pessimistic rejoinder to both Harlan's dissent in the *Civil Rights Cases* and his own suggestion in *Huckleberry Finn* of the possibility that a higher law mix of conscience and consent could ground human association despite the pressures of history, the traditions of slavery and racism, and the positivist workings of majority will.

Perhaps the most striking aspect of Twain's vision of law in *Huckleberry Finn* lies in its treatment of conscience. Twain seems to posit and withdraw authority for the moral imperative as a basis for law and society. Twain's derisive treatment of a judge bent on reforming Pap mocks the weepy sentimentalism of Stowe's "conscience" and reflects his era's Holmesean skepticism of moral reform. After reaching Pap through "sympathy" and persuading him to forego strong drink, Pap, the judge, and the judge's wife share tears of joy as Pap pledges that he will "turn over a new leaf." The judge says, "it was the holiest time on record" and invites Pap to stay with them. While the judge and his wife sleep, Pap slips out, gets drunk, returns, and leaves their spare room in such a condition that "they had to take soundings before they could navigate it." In view of Pap's precipitous fall from the wagon, the judge, in Huck's words, "reckoned a body could reform the ole man with a shot-gun, maybe, but he didn't know no other way."[127] Pap is the perfect exemplar of Holmes's "bad man" who "does not care two straws" about morality. The function of law in this view is to constrain effectively people like Pap, for whom the law is only "a prophecy that if he does certain things he will be subjected to disagreeable consequences by way of imprisonment or compulsory payment of money."[128]

But Twain's novel also contemplates the possibility that moral consensus may govern some human relations. In contrast to the saccharine "sympathy" of the judge and his wife, the deeply felt compassion between Huck and Jim bears hopeful results in Huck's decision to do the "wrong" thing by aiding his friend's escape from slavery. Twain prepares us for Huck's ultimate crisis of conscience with a prank. Early in their raft trip, Huck amuses himself by deceiving Jim that their actual separation in a dense fog was nothing but an apparition in a dream. Simply and honestly describing his grief at Huck's loss and joy at his return, Jim emerges from the objectification of Huck's joke and the infantilization of his minstrel-like characterization, as a responsible adult sensitively and successfully reprimanding a mischievous but good-hearted child. Huck responds: "I didn't do him no more mean tricks, and I wouldn't done that one if I'd knowed it would make him feel that way." "With Huck's apology," as Brook Thomas notes, "their relationship promises to be one of free and equal individuals bound together by mutual benefit and trust." As long as Huck and Jim remain on the raft, separated from a political sphere animated by racism and power, their connection can be governed by an interracial moral consensus, not force.[129]

At the novel's famous climax in chapter 31, Huck worries that his moral commitment to Jim is a breach of divine law as well as the custom of his slaveholding community:

Providence slapping me in the face and letting me know my wickedness was being watched all the time from up there in heaven, whilst I was stealing a poor old woman's nigger that hadn't ever done me no harm, and now was showing me there's One that's always on the lookout, and ain't agoing to allow no such miserable doings to go only just so fur and no further.

Huck's confused apprehension that he may be violating the command of an all-powerful sovereign registers the epistemological quandary of following a direction that deviates from customary morality and law. In Huck's case, higher law inspiration does not come in the form of the clear-cut obligations of social convention or divine instruction, but rather emerges from reflection, internal debate, and conversation. Instead of a straightforward recognition of divine absolutes, Twain's higher law is a horizontal and uncertain matter of mutable human experience and connection. Because Huck and Jim have together created a relation based on and governed by their moral consensus, Huck can only say "obedience"; he cannot "do the right thing:" "Somehow I couldn't seem to strike no places to harden me against him, but only the other kind. I'd see him standing my watch on top of his'n, stead of calling me, so I could go on sleeping; and see him how glad he was when I come back out of the fog." He tears up the letter he had written revealing Jim's whereabouts, deciding to conform his words to his actions and his feelings: "All right then, I'll *go* to hell."[130]

The novel's notoriously downbeat ending, however, makes the fugitives' moral contract seem a utopian irrelevancy. The supple tool of the powerful (in this case the slaveholder, Miss Watson), the law has already freed Jim, mooting Huck's civil disobedience and implying the impotence of higher law notions of conscience and consent, which must assume shape within the context of racist custom and power in order to have legal effect. Huck and Jim cannot finally escape law or the social customs of the powerful, a thematic conclusion that Twain makes even more forcefully in *Pudd'nhead Wilson*'s satire of Jim Crow positivism.

As we have seen, the cultural and juridical context of the Civil Rights Act's demise suggests a figurative affinity between black citizenship and freak and minstrel show caricature. This connection comes to a kind of literary culmination in *Pudd'nhead Wilson*, Twain's prince and pauper story of exchanged racial identities, the climax of which is a murder trial solving not merely the identity but the race of the culprit.[131] Twain's satire inverts the function of the alien, who reveals that the majority's self image and its freakish opposite are not natural facts but social convention and legal manipulation, "a fiction of law and custom." While many of its legal themes have received astute critical scrutiny by Eric Sundquist, Brook Thomas, and others, *Pudd'nhead Wilson* deserves another look, as the novel has not been placed in the genealogy of positivist accounts of American law and citizenship.[132]

Pudd'nhead Wilson begins with an image expressive of the white majority's self-conception – 1830s Dawson's Landing – "a snug little collection of modest one- and two-storey frame dwellings whose white-washed exteriors were almost concealed from sight by climbing tangles of rose-vines, honey suckles, and morning-glories." Complete with cats lolling in the sun, these houses "prove title" to being homes by virtue of their typicality – the way they meet the reader's expectations for a homey rural village, fulfilling a nostalgic ideal of home and community characterized by an outward humility and conformity that assures the reader of an underlying social homogeneity.[133] In sharp contrast to the rapid economic development characterizing late-nineteenth-century America, Dawson's Landing's growth is organic and incremental. As indicated by the uniformity of their dwellings, the townsfolk are not separated by great disparities of wealth. They are bound by familial connections and common affection. In short, Dawson's Landing represents the idyllic agrarian past that many in postwar America longed for, a nostalgic image of a happy *gemeinschaft* antedating the fractious *gesellschaft* of the century's waning decades (before urbanization, industrialization, the massive influx of immigrants, trade unionism, and monopolies, and before there were black citizens). Decidedly not cosmopolitan, Dawson's Landing has few outsiders and no class of people within the community whose exact identity and place are unknown. As a consequence, the distinction between private and the public has little import, and the governing ethos of both spheres is a tribal code of social norms and customs, not the rule of law. Law is reserved for handling outsiders and freaks.

After conjuring Dawson's Landing as a homogeneous rural village where everyone has a known identity and role, Twain introduces the two sets of freaks whose careers in Dawson's Landing will illuminate the workings of the majority's norms of identity and behavior. The Italian (Siamese) twins are born freaks, exotic outsiders. Chambers and Tom, the black and white babies switched at birth, are made freaks, like the side-show's tattooed men and Circassian women.[134] The Italian twins' strangeness is overt, but Tom and Chambers's oddity is initially invisible until exposed by the climactic trial of the novel. The passing (as white) and reverse passing (as black) of Tom and Chambers indicates the unsettling possibility that, despite (or rather because of) the one-drop rule of racial identity, the majority might be infiltrated by an emergent class of strangers – racial oddities. In the trial concluding the novel, the two sets of twins/freaks prove to be fungible – Tom and Chambers are substituted for the Italians – and this interchangeability blurs the distinction between the outward markings of the born freak (blood) and those of the made freak (tradition). These freakish markings or, rather, our perception of them, whether the Italian twins' overt difference or Tom's and Chamber's unconscious minstrel imitations of each other's racial station, constitute the external and internal checks used to police the majority's self-definition.

In the introductory "whisper" (in which Twain as sideshow talker or blower hawks the genuineness of the legal marvels of his entertainment – a veritable "photograph of law"), Twain's adoption of an ancient line of Italian nobility foreshadows the novel's central concern with identity and political power.[135] The joke of Twain's "adoption" lies both in its impossibility and in the commonness of such impostures. In forms less obvious than that of the Duke and King in *Huckleberry Finn*, but no less artificial, we all, in Twain's view, tend to inflate our origins. Twenty years later, Horace Kallen's famous essay, "Democracy versus the Melting Pot," observes that one cannot choose one's grandparents. Descent is not consensual – it is beyond manufacture.[136] But for Twain such a perspective naively overlooks the role power plays in creating the norms and categories of descent as well as the many types of artifice, of which passing is only one extreme example, through which identity is altered. Descent, in Twain's satire, is subject to as much manipulation, embellishment, and fraud as side show advertisements for the Wild Men of Borneo. Roxy's switching of Tom and Chambers constitutes a radical manufacture of identity. In a less dramatic instance, Roxy's account of her own blood lines, like Twain's adoption of the Italian nobility, illustrates the showmanship of descent – the stories we tell of ourselves and our origins, which acquire greater authority in each repetition and generation. Whether Roxy's account of her own noble ancestry or Judge Driscoll's touting of his noble blood line, each story has practical weight only to the degree that one has the power to insist on its cultural/political authority. Hence the Judge's account of his birthright has the gravity of property, standing, and law behind it, and Roxy's is weightless. The difference between the two stories lies in the relative power of the storyteller, not their factual basis. Roxy's account is no more implausible than (indeed is produced by) the romantic Cavalier pretensions of the Old South that Twain loved to skewer.[137] The ethnicity Kallen would laud as a source of cultural variety is, for Twain, a sorry but largely unavoidable trap of identity thinking permanently containing the possibility of political discourse within delusions of blood and tradition.

The identitarian paradigm of Dawson's Landing is governed by the inherited code of its leading citizens. A set of principles for behavior and social standing trumping other standards, whether legal or religious, the code consists of rules "as strict as any that could be found among the printed statutes of the land," requiring that a gentleman

keep his honour spotless. Those laws were his chart; his course was marked on it; if he swerved from it by so much as half a point of the compass it meant shipwreck to his honour; that is to say, degradation from his rank as a gentleman. These laws required certain things of him which his religion might forbid: then his religion must yield – the laws could not be relaxed to accommodate religions or anything else.

Ostensibly, this code, as an ethic, is premised on the notion of individual agency – it is up to each gentleman to keep his honor spotless (a none-too-subtle pun suggesting the interplay between ideas of race and ideas of morality in which the former replace the latter). Yet the code is also a matter of blood. Thus, when the Judge first hears that his nephew Tom has been insulted, he assumes Tom will follow his "true old blood" by demanding a gentleman's satisfaction on the field of honor. The gentle-man the Judge imagines his nephew to be would follow the code not as a matter of choice but as the natural outcome of breeding. Tom's cow-ardice and his turning to legal process for redress of his assault signal *both* moral weakness and bad blood. Twain's satiric target here is the self-delusive paradox of identitarian moral norms, which are a matter of both choice and blood – a paradox that enables the majority to see itself simultaneously as morally upright and as naturally determined.[138] One of the sharpest pricks of Twain's satire lies in his depiction of the uncon-scious and unblinking acceptance of the code as nature by such diverse and intelligent characters as Roxy and Wilson. That neither recognizes the fact that the code cannot be nature if outsiders like themselves can exemplify it suggests Twain's skepticism about any hope for an escape from the false consciousness of identity.

Twain uses the duel between Luigi and Judge Driscoll to illustrate how the code works and its symbolic import. Duels have the prominent func-tion of demarcating community in Dawson's Landing. Participation in a duel signifies the duelists' mutual recognition of each other's member-ship in the social order. This recognition receives social sanction from official (the duelists' seconds) and unofficial witnesses (e.g., Roxy). By contrast, summary punishment like Representative Brooks's beating of Charles Sumner on the floor of the Senate or Colonel Sherburn's murder of Boggs in *Huckleberry Finn* is a treatment expressly reserved for dogs – human creatures beneath civic respect and inclusion. Meeting Luigi on the field of honor, Judge Driscoll treats him as a candidate for citizenship, granting him access to one of the insiders' rituals of membership. As in *Huckleberry Finn*'s feud between the Grangerfords and Shepherdsons, one recognizes the humanity and worth of one's neighbors by attempting to kill them – the nobility of the act depends upon the opponent's possession of a like homicidal power. Duels also rank the members of the social order by virtue of their relative ability to kill or maim each other. Both the establishment of membership and one's rank within the social order depend on power.

By contrast, to attack one's opponent in a legal forum in Dawson's Landing is to denominate that person an outsider, a freak, a subhuman creature not deserving of the duel's recognition. After being persuaded by Tom's false portrait of Luigi as a dishonorable, Italian assassin, the Judge attacks the twins in the ensuing election campaign "as adventurers, mountebanks, side-show riff-raff, dime-museum freaks . . . back-alley barbers disguised as nobilities, pea-nut peddlers masquerading as gentlemen, organ-grinders bereft of their brother-monkey." The last insult of the Italian organ grinder and his "brother-monkey" alludes inadvertently to the racial twins, Tom and Chambers, the white slave owner and his "brother-monkey" slave who have traded places. The Judge concedes that, in light of his new view of the twins as freaks, he can see that Tom was right to take Luigi to court.[139] Appropriately, the techniques of the courtroom turn out to be those of the side show, in which the wonders of strange beings are exhibited: hot-blooded Italian assassins, a white black man, and a black white man.

As Twain knew from his close observation of the legal process, whether a civil trial for negligence or a criminal trial for assault, the determination of legal responsibility is not simply a matter of tracing the chain of causation.[140] If it were, trials would go on forever following causation backward in a regression of who did what and who begat whom to the original trespass of Adam and Eve. Instead, the radius of liability is limited by a set of conventions. For instance, the requirement in criminal law of the guilty mind limits the inquiry into causation to those who either intended or recklessly enabled the criminal event. In negligence actions, just beginning to come to the fore in the latter decades of the nineteenth century, the doctrine of proximate cause limits liability to acts closely enough connected to the injury to justify liability based on certain notions of justice (blame only the blameworthy) and certain concepts of social control (penalize those who had the best chance of averting the harm). Of course, what sounds reasonable in the abstract produced in practice results comically highlighting the arbitrary nature of such circumscriptions of responsibility. Twain (and his co-author, Charles Warren) mocked such judicial determinations of responsibility in *The Gilded Age* (1873), describing a steamboat disaster killing twenty-two and injuring scores – the "verdict" was "familiar," heard "all the days of our lives – 'NOBODY TO BLAME.'"[141]

In an 1870 article, Nicholas St. John Green, a friend of Holmes, examined the distinction in negligence actions between proximate and remote cause. Like Holmes and Twain, Green distrusted the notion that courts objectively differentiate between proximate and remote causes, establishing legal liability in a disinterested and non-discretionary fashion. In Green's view, "To every event there are certain antecedents [and] it is not any one of this set of antecedents taken by itself which is the cause. No one by itself would produce the effect. The true cause is the whole set of antecedents taken together."[142] In Green's realistic view, the determination of which cause will be denominated "proximate" owes a great deal to the political and social outlook and expectations of the judge deciding how to circumscribe the causal inquiry.

The events of *Pudd'nhead Wilson* begin and end in trials revealing an intersection of causation and identity that in turn illuminates the homology of race and power in post-Reconstruction notions of justice and citizenship. The first of these is Percy Driscoll's plantation justice. Missing a small amount of money, Driscoll summons his slaves to a crude ad hoc trial for theft. The criminal procedure of the plantation is rough and ready. Driscoll simply repeats his command to name the thief four times and gets his confession after threatening the worst conceivable punishment, the "equivalent of condemning them to hell," to sell them all down the river.[143] By merely selling the thieves in Dawson's Landing, Driscoll is satisfied that he has been quite merciful, noting his leniency in his diary to serve as a judicial precedent of sorts for his heir. By contrast, Roxy, who in this case is innocent, is still deeply frightened by the prospect that on another occasion her son might be sold down the river. In direct response to Driscoll's threat, Roxy switches the babies. Percy Driscoll's trial is, thus, a critical event in the causal chain eventually leading to Judge Driscoll's murder and the climactic trial which results in Roxy's son being sold down the river. Driscoll's investigation begins and ends with the social conventions supporting and justifying his position in society: his property is his by unquestionable right; those persons denominated as black (including those who are visibly white, such as Roxy and her child) are appropriately held in a state of complete subjection; he may do with his slaves as he sees fit; and so on. Of course, as Twain suggests in an editorial aside to the reader, a broader examination of causation might illumine the slaves' petty theft as a just rejoinder to the larger theft of slavery.[144]

The novel's climax comes with the criminal trial of the Italian twins for the murder of Judge Driscoll. As foreigners (and freaks) with a recent history of conflict with the Driscolls, they are the likely suspects, until their lawyer, Wilson, can offer an even better candidate and more spectacular freak–the "what is it" of the white black man who has passed as Percy Driscoll's heir. As in Driscoll's plantation justice, the murder trial goes no further than ascertaining identity and act–that Tom is in fact Chambers, Roxy's son, and that he killed the judge. The governing social conventions of Dawson's Landing that inevitably control the determination of causation preclude any further inquiry. That the institution of slavery through Percy Driscoll's "God-like" power to sell Roxy or her baby down the river bears any responsibility for the chain of events cannot be considered. Instead, the court, as an emblem for American society, simply cuts off the search for causation and responsibility at the point that most comfortably resolves the issue in dispute, namely the discovery of the black criminal.

Lest any reader too comfortably rest on the fact that Wilson's intelligence and scientific method reveals the man who committed the murder, Twain finishes the legal proceedings with a twist symbolizing how American justice manipulates legal doctrines when it serves the majority's interest to do so. Percy Driscoll's creditors succeed in getting the court to do what it would not do in finding Tom guilty, that is, look back at the entire causal sequence in the interests of a larger sense of justice rather than merely adjudicating identity and act. The creditors argue that Tom had been their property all along and "that if he had been delivered up to them in the first place, they would have sold him and he could not have murdered Judge Driscoll, therefore it was not he that had really committed the murder, the guilt lay with the erroneous inventory." Like Driscoll's slaves, the punishment Tom ultimately receives for his murder of Judge Driscoll depends upon his racial identity and not his actions. Given his rediscovered identification as property, Tom cannot be held accountable for his actions in the same fashion as if he "were white and free." "To shut up a valuable slave for life" does not make common sense to the community, and he is accordingly freed from prison and sold down the river.[145] In a frank satiric allegory of the fate of the Fourteenth

Amendment, Twain's version of American legal process captures how the Supreme Court opinions of the era wax eloquent on the higher law and take a broad vision of justice when property rights and freedom of contract are at stake, but read the Constitution's protection of citizenship rights restrictively when the claimants are women or minorities.

The trials of *Pudd'nhead Wilson* reveal that the determination of fault and racial identity intersect in an homology of power and race. Both are matters of convention. Tellingly, the climactic murder trial is a relatively informal dialogue between the attorneys and the community. Almost no formal legal procedure stands between the storytelling lawyers and their audience – which prominently includes the gallery of townspeople as well as the jury. Unlike *The Gilded Age's* trial of Laura Hawkins, there are no evidentiary objections, motions *in limine*, or *in camera* meetings with the judge to obscure the emotional impact of the attorneys' tales. Each lawyer casually testifies to certain facts without being sworn, taking the stand, or justifying to the court the necessity of such an irregular procedure. By emphasizing the centrality of the gallery's response to the attorneys' tales and eliminating legal procedure, Twain goes further than he had gone in *The Gilded Age* to break down the concept of law and adjudication as an autonomous realm: a construct of code, cases, and the rule of law. He creates in its place an even more emphatic vision of adjudication as theater, and legal judgment as audience approval.

In his magic show ("black magic" as Tom and Roxy call it), Wilson deploys the carny trick of fingerprint identification as a kind of entertainer casting a "spell upon the house"-

"Upon this haft stands the assassin's natal autograph, written in the blood of that helpless and unoffending old man who loved you and whom you loved. There is but one man in the whole earth whose hand can duplicate that crimson sign" – he paused and raised his eyes to the pendulum swinging back and forth – "and please God we will produce that man in this room before the clock strikes noon!" Stunned, distraught, unconscious of its own movement, the house half rose, as if expecting to see the murderer appear at the door, and a breeze of muttered ejaculations swept the place.[46]

Wilson's performance becomes even more theatrical when he asks people in the gallery to participate in testing his magical ability to recognize fingerprints. As Wilson repeatedly demonstrates his uncanny ability, the gallery responds with "A deafening explosion of applause." Even the Judge confesses his amazement at Wilson's hocus pocus ("This certainly approaches the miraculous"), turning a white man black and a black man white: "'*A* was put into *B*'s cradle in the nursery; *B* was transferred to the kitchen and became a negro and a slave' – (Sensation – confusion of angry ejaculations) – 'but within a quarter of an hour he will stand before you white and free.'"[147] Through the trial's overtly theatrical quality, Twain suggests the futility of a legal standard that does not play to the crowd. Whether the rise of Wilson's reputation in Dawson's Landing is due to his success in turning Tom black or in revealing the real criminal is not clear, but his ability to please the crowd by discovering a reality that reconciles the crowd's expectations with the facts is a figure for legal reconciliation of the Constitution to the cultural norms of Jim Crow positivism.

CHAPTER 5

Charles Chesnutt and Moorfield Storey: citizenship and the flux of contract

Given the avalanche of positivist precedent, legal and literary, covered in the previous chapter, one may well wonder that the higher law argument survived the crush, but it did. Indeed, the post-Reconstruction era's increasing positivism seems to have intensified the efforts of a wide variety of reformers and intellectuals to articulate an ethical basis for American society and law. Higher law reasoning persisted in the woman's rights movement, populist and progressive politics, anti-imperialism, trade unionism, and advocacy for full black citizenship. Drawing on traditional conceptions of American citizenship as embodying, to borrow James Ketner's words, "the ideal of volitional allegiance," these late nineteenth-century reformers often portrayed contract as the mode and sign of just human relations. Booker T. Washington, for example, made the mechanism of commercial contract central to his program for racial uplift. If equipped to compete, Washington urged, black Americans would be able to find security and freedom transcending race in economic partnership with white America. For feminists, such as Elizabeth Cady Stanton, Susan B. Anthony, and Victoria Woodhull, the symbol of free and equal contract illuminated the way marriage was mired in anticonsensual notions of gender status and role. Stanton and others felt that making marriage more genuinely contractual would strike a blow for all women.[1]

But these reformers were hardly alone in using the language of contract. In 1861, Sir Henry Maine famously observed that the history of progressive societies was characterized by a shift "from Status to Contract," and many eighteenth- and nineteenth-century intellectuals considered contract to be the appropriate and inevitable means of structuring human association. For Adam Smith, Jeremy Bentham, and John Stuart Mill, contractual freedom was "the fundamental and indispensable requisite of progress."[2] William Graham Sumner, the Yale sociologist famous for his laissez-faire and social Darwinist approach, expressed the prevailing turn-of-the-century appreciation of contract as promoting a free and fluid community and untrammeled individual development:

> In our modern state, and in the United States more than anywhere else, the social structure is based on contract, and status is of the least importance . . . [I]t seems impossible that anyone who has studied the matter should doubt that we have gained immeasurably [through the shift from status to contract], and that our farther gains lie in going forward, not in going backward. The feudal ties can never be restored. If they could be restored they would bring back personal caprice, favoritism, sycophancy, and intrigue. A society based on contract is a society of free and independent men, who form ties without favor or obligation, and co-operate without cringing or intrigue. A society based on contract, therefore, gives the utmost room and chance for individual development, and for all the self-reliance and dignity of a free man.[3]

A conservative judiciary echoed these sentiments, using the concept of liberty of contract to symbolize certain ethical limits to the power of democratic majorities. While, early in the nation's legal history, bench and bar increasingly tended in a positivist direction, higher law began a second life in such liberty of contract cases as *Calder v. Bull* (1798) and *Dartmouth College* (1819) (see chapter one). These cases suggested that, in certain circumstances, the judiciary would check the legislature's power to interfere with private contracts. When reduced to its essential contours, contract conjured for John Marshall and many others a primary scene of free and consensual relations among peers that was antecedent to all law.[4] While often necessary, limiting or obstructing contract was serious business, as such regulation could easily circumvent basic freedoms. Prewar liberty of contract precedents prepared postbellum judges to discover in the Fourteenth Amendment's due process clause a protection of the right of individuals and businesses to enter into contractual relations free from governmental interference. This reading of the Fourteenth Amendment gave liberty of contract a powerful constitutional purchase, and, between 1885 and 1937, courts used liberty of contract to invalidate numerous laws.[5] When striking down legislative infringements on the liberty of contract, such as wages and hours regulations passed by progressive state legislatures, the judiciary was as capable as any reformer of waxing eloquent about the higher law requirement that law comport with such universal norms as freedom and equality.

For example, in the *Butchers' Union* case, Justice Bradley described liberty of contract as "an inalienable right" "formulated as such under the phrase 'pursuit of happiness' in the Declaration of Independence." The foundational principles governing "our intercourse with our fellow-men" include the right "to pursue any lawful business or vocation in any manner not inconsistent with the equal rights of others, which may increase [our] prosperity or develop [our] faculties, so as to give to them their highest enjoyment."[6] Bradley verges here on portraying contract not as a mere type of freedom but as the very essence of free human relations, including the freedom to change one's identity and place in society and to alter the consensual arrangements structuring a free society. A striking irony of the liberty of contract cases from our historical perspective is that, in supporting such innovations as the trust and the merger, the judiciary furthered a process of commercial aggregation and modernization that rendered contract as a sign of genuine mutual assent less not more important in many everyday commercial transactions. In buying an airline ticket, for instance, who negotiates in any meaningful fashion the terms and conditions of the airline's responsibilities?

Charles Chesnutt and Moorfield Storey, constitutional lawyer and first President of the NAACP, presciently sensed that contract as a mode of human association would continue to exert its strongest influence in the everyday deals struck between friends, business partners, political associates, spouses, and in commercial transactions between individuals – those connections where the social web is woven, in distinction to the faceless commercial transactions of the modern era. For Chesnutt and Storey, by deeming contractual freedom central to traditional notions of justice and citizenship, the judiciary paradoxically incorporated an agent of flux in its attempt to conserve the economic status quo against the threat of redistributive legislation.[7] Chesnutt's literary manipulation of the liberty of contract doctrine in *The Marrow of Tradition* (1901) precisely anticipates Storey's successful use of the doctrine in the landmark precedent of *Buchanan v. Warley* (1917). In Chesnutt's and Storey's hands, liberty of contract protected something far grander than mere economic exchange – it protected a mode of voluntary human relations mutable and capacious enough to include personal development, social mobility, and political change while still according with ideals of fairness and equality. With logical extension, the traditional value of contractual freedom could be used to validate such non-traditional forms of social association as interracial marriage. Viewed more broadly as a means of and trope for human relations, contract had the potential, in Chesnutt's and Storey's view, to reframe social and political coexistence in terms of moral agency not heredity – practice not identity.[8]

Despite deforming the Fourteenth Amendment's due process clause from a shield of minority rights into a guard of corporate interests and economic freedom, judicial invocations of the liberty of contract doctrine

happily retained in the precincts of official jurisprudence some notion
that the ethical norms of the higher law tradition properly restricted the
political power of the majority. Chesnutt and Storey saw that, by yoking
the traditional ethos supporting American law to the innovative processes of contract, liberty of contract could be used to push the nation's
constitutional jurisprudence toward a vision of justice as grounded on a
negotiated and inclusive moral consensus. Such a transformation would
comport with the jurisprudential ideal expressed in Lincoln's statement
that "'No man is good enough to govern another without that other's
consent. I say this is the leading principle – the sheet-anchor – of American republicanism'" – a passage both Chesnutt and Storey were fond
of quoting.[9]

Though they arrived at their shared vision independently, coming to
it from different backgrounds, the correspondence between Chesnutt's
and Storey's use of liberty of contract was hardly accidental.[10] Both were
trained in law and committed to reforming American race relations. And
both were influenced by the previous generation's higher law conception of the national charter. Chesnutt described the Civil War amendments coming out of that reform effort as "the most glorious onward
step in the cause of human liberty that history discloses."[11] Chesnutt's
and Storey's views of liberty of contract bear a particularly close resemblance to the formulation of conscience and consent in Charles
Sumner's, Frederick Douglass's, and Ralph Waldo Emerson's cosmopolitan constitutionalism.

In Sumner's view, the American republic should combine a form of
government where, quoting Kant, "'*every citizen* participates'" (Sumner's
emphasis) with a national unity derived, practically as well as ideally,
from political consent, not "blood."[12] Douglass stressed the fundamental
importance of founding the nation's law on consent rather than force,
expressly framing citizenship as an consensual exchange of participation
and responsibility for inclusion:

I am here to advocate a genuine democratic republic [and to] blot out from it
everything antagonistic of republicanism declared by the fathers – that idea was
that all governments derived their first powers from the consent of the governed;
make it a government of the people, by the people and for the people, and for
all the people, each for all and all for each; blot out all discriminations against
any person, theoretically or practically, and make it conform to the great truths
laid down by the fathers; keep no man from the ballot box or jury box or the
cartridge box, because of his color – exclude no woman from the ballot box because of her sex. Let the government of the country rest securely down upon the
shoulders of the whole nation; let there be no shoulder that does not bear up

its proportion of the burdens of the government. Let there [be] no conscience, no intellect in the land not directly responsible for the moral character of the government – for the honor of the government.[13]

The absence of contract was central to Douglass's account of slavery's unconstitutionality. If the free and mutual assent defining contract were always an implied higher law prerequisite for enforceable civil obligations, then the Constitution's apparent requirement that the fugitive slave "shall be delivered up to whom such service and labour may be due" became incoherent: "Why, sir, due!... There is nothing *due* from the slave to his master in the way of service or labour. [The slaveholder] is unable to show a contract." The idea of a constitutionally cognizable obligation, Douglass said, "implies an arrangement, an understanding, by which, for an equivalent, I will do for you so much, if you will do for me, or have done for me, so much."[14] In a similar vein, Emerson saw the era's increasing contractual orientation as both the sign and means of slavery's demise – slavery and contract were mutually exclusive, and contract was pushing slavery out.[15] All three made the notion of voluntary exchange, dialogue, and assent central to their notions of just human relations.

Chesnutt and Storey regarded Sumner, Douglass, and Emerson as heroes of the antebellum and Reconstruction effort to ground the Constitution on principles of justice rather than the possession of power.[16] Chesnutt viewed Douglass's career as an irrefutable argument for freedom of personal development and the principle that human relations must be consensual to be just. With Douglass in mind, Chesnutt read the Civil War amendments as creating a "safe harbor of constitutional right" in which consensual governance combined with the freedom and equal opportunity of every American "to develop such powers as he possessed." And Chesnutt shared Douglass's conception of the Constitution developing in tandem with the free development of the body politic.[17] In an address presented at a centenary celebration of Emerson's birth, Storey described Sumner and Emerson as endowed with the rare ability to look beneath the surface of established institutions and divine their true moral nature.[18] Emphasizing both the ethical imperative to impel law in the direction of justice and a faith in the human processes of consent to achieve that goal, Storey's successful liberty of contract argument in *Buchanan v. Warley* drew from and extended the higher law reasoning of Ainsworth Rand Spofford, Emerson, and Sumner.

In addition to sharing higher law antecedents, Chesnutt's and Storey's approach to liberty of contract drew support from such counterintuitive allies as William Graham Sumner, James Coolidge Carter, a conservative jurist, and the *Plessy* majority (see below, page 206). These figures' conception of tradition's determinative influence on the legal and cultural norms governing social interaction became, in Chesnutt's and Storey's hands, the basis of an unexpectedly cosmopolitan vision of law and society.

The importance of contract for turn-of-the-century American literature has become a subject of considerable critical interest.[19] In *American Literary Realism and the Failed Promise of Contract*, Brook Thomas, for example, convincingly argues that the Age of Realism can only be fully understood in relation to the Age of Contract. From the contractual paradigm dominant in late nineteenth-century commerce and politics, American literary realists, such as Mark Twain, William Dean Howells, and Henry James, extract a utopian possibility of organizing society through an exchange of promises. This exchange of promises replaces status relations with consensual ones (e.g., Huck's promise not to trick Jim reestablishes their relationship on the basis of "mutual benefit and trust" instead of status) and replaces transcendental moral sanctions with "no higher sanction" than those created by the promises themselves. By recording the persistence of status in race, gender, and class relations, Thomas argues, realist depictions also expose the extent to which contract's promise was unrealized.[20]

The recovery and analysis of contract as a cultural and literary figure, such as Thomas's, can be furthered by an examination of the specific correspondence between Chesnutt's and Storey's use of liberty of contract doctrine – a correspondence which has been passed over by critics and scholars. Storey, whose extraordinary life and career connects the abolitionist tradition to the NAACP and other reform movements of the early twentieth century, has received scant scholarly attention, being the subject of only one sustained piece of recent historical scholarship (much remains to be explored in Storey's connections with such figures as Oliver Wendell Holmes, Jr., William James, W. E. B. DuBois, and James Weldon Johnson).[21] And, while his career and work have received considerable recent critical and scholarly attention, Chesnutt's invocation of liberty of contract has been neglected.[22]

While due in part to disciplinary differences, scholarly neglect of Chesnutt's and Storey's use of contractual freedom as a consensual alternative to the racist coercions of Jim Crow may also manifest a critical suspicion that consent will ultimately prove inseparable from coercion.[23] The oppression we observe in our own historical moment may well make us wonder whether the appearance of genuine consent does not await a still distant transition from the "reign of necessity" to the "reign of freedom."[24] And, to the extent that reformers in the Jim Crow era touted contract or consent, one might with considerable justification suspect that they were deluded. Alert to the Althusserian warning that people consent to their own coercion, Sacvan Bercovitch charts in considerable detail how nineteenth-century invocations of the "rhetoric of consensus" hid the substitution of a form of intellectual and material domination for actual consent.[25] However apt, such observations do not obviate the distinction between consent and coercion. In fact, such comments depend for comprehension on the preservation of that distinction. Without a sense of the difference between consent and coercion, we cannot recognize the coercion we "consent" to, and we cannot tell the difference between Bercovitch's "*rhetoric* of consensus" and actual consensus.

Well-founded convictions, such as Patricia Williams's, that allusions to consent and social contract are often part of "strategies of evasion or control" do not relieve us of the burden of discerning what is (and to what degree it is) genuinely consensual from what is not. Such critics remind us how difficult, even at times impossible, it may be in certain circumstances to ferret out the difference, but, unless one is prepared to accede to a deterministic vision of human society, the ethical imperative to distinguish between what is consensual and what is coercive persists. Making such an effort, Douglass sharply attacked Henry Clay's characterization of his emigration proposal as "transporting the free people of color, *with their own consent*, from the United States to the coast of Africa." Because consent "savor[s] of justice, of humanity, of respectful consideration for the feelings and wishes of '*the free people of color*,'" Clay's claim is particularly egregious. "[T]he virtue of '*consent*' depends," Douglass notes, "much upon the mode of gaining it. If a highway-robber should at the *pistol's mouth* demand my purse, it is possible that I should '*consent*' to give it up." Thus, Douglass's critique does not ignore the ways that coercion may be mixed with or disguised as consent (as in Ahab's assertion, "I do not order ye; ye will it") but insists on the possibility of genuinely mutual assent. Following Douglass, Chesnutt and Storey appropriate liberty of contract, not as an end in itself, but, borrowing Patricia Williams's words, in order to "expand" the doctrine "into a conception of civil rights, into the right to expect civility from others" in return for granting the same.[26]

The postmodern "bad tools" paradigm offers a good example of the error resulting from a cavalier dismissal of the consent/coercion distinction.

In this analytic template, instruments, such as contract, which have been or can be used to oppress are rejected as means of structuring or revising social and political relations. Carla Kaplan, for instance, finds that, though contract "generally appears as a progressive form of social relations" (i.e., a consensual means of creating and adjusting the terms of human relationships), its twin fictions of freedom and equality actually hide the "social domination" it invariably engineers. Though her reading of *Incidents in the Life of a Slave Girl* acknowledges Harriet Jacobs's apparent embrace of contract, Kaplan sees Jacobs as ultimately scorning to take down the master's house with the master's wicked tools.[27] As Gerrit Smith pointed out in persuading Frederick Douglass not to jettison the Constitution, throwing away the hammer for striking one's thumb mystifies the tool, imparting the agency of the builder to the implement of construction.[28] Like any tool, contract, of itself, does nothing – it is a language of intent (promises, statements of capability and agency, actions and words betokening assent) that may be used by powerful parties to expand their fortunes at the expense of the weaker parties or may be used between equals to structure their relations as equitably as they deem possible. Curiously, Kaplan admits that freedom and equality do sometimes exist without considering whether a contract between such relatively free and equal parties would perpetuate domination, and, if not, what that fact does to her conception of contract as inherently oppressive.[29] Kaplan's argument would discard a tool that in its most basic form of primary agreements between individuals as to the nature and regulation of their relations cannot be discarded. Indeed, she makes no effort to delineate the alternative, non-contractual device capable of structuring social relations in the interests of justice.[30]

A general distrust of contract as an example of tainted Enlightenment universalism has tended to obscure the political and jurisprudential utility of contract for African American authors, such as Jacobs, Douglass, Harper, Chesnutt, Washington, DuBois, and others, who found in the notion of a shared language of proper behavior and just social and legal relations a means of civic exchange and negotiation.[31] For instance, even when focused on racial solidarity, as in "The Conservation of Races," DuBois shares with Chesnutt, his literary colleague, and Storey, his legal colleague, a desire to recover from Jim Crow positivism an anti-identitarian language of consensual political, legal, and social association in distinction to the identity-centered norms animating the private sphere of family, race, and tribe. This chapter will examine the promise contract held for these advocates of black citizenship and the contribution their version of contractual freedom made to higher law conceptions of justice and membership.

To situate Chesnutt's and Storey's liberty of contract conception, we need first to consider progressive criticism of the doctrine and the judiciary creating it. Viewing law as the majority's positivistic means of reallocating the benefits and burdens of capitalism through legislation, progressive jurisprudence grew out the class conflict disrupting the nineteenth century's final decades.[32] Progressive jurists, such as Professor Gerard Henderson, conceived of citizenship rights as the product of legal enactment. Henderson argued that "modern jurisprudence . . . rejected" the concept of rights "springing out of the nature of man, independent of the law and anterior to it." In Henderson's Holmesean view, the term "rights" simply signifies that the state will use its power to protect certain interests. Citizenship rights were solely the creation of legislative power and, as a result, were open to legislative revision.[33]

Despite the fact that most legislation regulating commerce and business survived judicial scrutiny, the period's judge-made law was exemplified, for progressives, by a string of decisions killing legislation aimed at righting economic wrongs. Courts in general and the Supreme Court in particular seemed bent on preventing the political majority from tempering the excesses of gilded age capitalism and the human suffering it created. Particularly notorious were the *Lochner* case (in which the Supreme Court struck down a law limiting the hours bakery employees could work as an unconstitutional abrogation of the employees' and employers' contractual freedom), the Sugar Trust case (in which the Supreme Court failed to find any violation of the Sherman Anti-Trust Act because it deemed the corporations involved in the sugar refining combination not to be engaged in interstate commerce), and the Income Tax Cases (in which the Court struck down the progressive income tax passed by Congress as an unconstitutional violation of the fundamental right of private property).[34] Trade unionists were appalled by the Court's invalidation of the Erdman Act, which prevented railroads from discriminating against union labor, and the Court's rejection of federal legislation regulating child labor betokened, for many, a grotesquely callous indifference to the economic plight of the working class.[35] Roscoe Pound, a prominent progressive jurist and important precursor of legal realism, contended that, in such cases, the Court used fictions of equality and freedom to thwart intelligent social reform. Legislatures, not courts, had the means to gather and analyze the facts of a given social problem. Invalidations of legislation in the name of freedom and equality simply discarded legislative expertise and balked the political will of the people.[36]

Widely viewed as serving the interests of a wealthy minority at the expense of the majority, the Supreme Court's invalidations of progressive legislation unleashed a torrent of popular criticism of the Court unheard since the 1857 *Dred Scott* ruling. Governor Sylvester Pennoyer of Oregon, for instance, declared "Our constitutional government has been supplanted by a judicial oligarchy."[37] Gustavus Myers's sharply polemic *History of the Supreme Court of the United States* (1912) detailed the Justices' corporate connections and financial interests as support for his contention that the Court's decisions simply served to legitimate their own economic and class interests.[38] Charles A. Beard criticized the Court's "usurpation" of political power. Beard's book *An Economic Interpretation of the Constitution of the United States* (1913) studied the broad economic interests at play in the framing and adoption of the Constitution. Beard attacked the denial of economic self-interest entailed in the Constitution's checks on the majority's political power and in the judiciary's conception of the common law as a disinterested expression of moral tradition.[39] Roscoe Pound also inferred a troubling connection between the judiciary's self-image as neutral arbiter of moral tradition and its preservation of unequal economic power. Pound pointed out, for example, that the presumption of equality between employers and employees in such liberty of contract cases as *Lochner v. New York* was clearly a "fallacy to everyone acquainted at first hand with actual industrial conditions." For Pound, the principle behind such formalist abstractions was "an individualist conception of justice, which exaggerates the importance of property and of contract [and] exaggerates private right at the expense of public right."[40]

A set of now forgotten progressive novels vividly attacked the judiciary and its liberty of contract doctrine. David Graham Phillips's *The Fashionable Adventures of Joshua Craig* (1909), Isaac Kahn Friedman's *The Radical* (1907), Henry O. Morris's *Waiting for the Signal* (1897), Frederic Upham Adams's *President John Smith* (1897), and Robert Herrick's *A Life for a Life* (1910) depicted judicial invocations of tradition as a screen for the plutocratic oppression of the working class.[41] Like Myers and Beard, Friedman's novel *The Radical* portrays the judiciary's social background and economic interests as inevitably shaping its opinions and interpretation of the law.[42] Phillips's *The Fashionable Adventures of Joshua Craig* portrays the justices of the Supreme Court as creatures of fashionable society, who cater in their opinions to the "recognized social favorite."[43] In Herrick's *A Life for A Life*, the law is characterized as a corpulent language "full of affidavit and citation, testimony and points of law," which, in effect, suffocates the people's claim "in a flood of language." Probing the fat lawyers' briefs and the swollen record of the novel's climactic case with "a long bony finger," the cadaverous aspect of the Chief Justice corresponds with the Court's role as compassionless agent of corporate interests.[44]

Yet, even when most critical, these novels imply an alternative vision of the United States as a redeemer nation able to exemplify for the rest of the world how a political and legal order can continue to move toward greater justice. The judiciary was to be rebuked for its conservation of an unjust legal and social order, and its tyranny replaced with a more equitable social and political arrangement that would be divined by the majority. In his very odd amalgam of political tract and fiction, *President John Smith* (1897), Frederick Upham Adams, for instance, attacks tradition-based common law, the "aged enemy of the people," as a form of superstition. Judges urge that it is safest for things to remain as they have ever been, in Adams's view, to block genuine self-rule, which would be marked by its experimentalism: "Progress has no greater foe than precedent." As a reliable guide for legal and social reform, Adams needs no "higher authority than the majority" who "can be safely entrusted with the regulation of their affairs and the shaping of their prosperity and happiness." By getting rid of judicial review, the cornerstone of counter-majoritarian conceptions of the Constitution, Adams would withdraw the Supreme Court's ability to impose its anti-democratic will. Adams's revised constitution denies the judiciary jurisdiction over any law "passed by the people of the United States." Appropriately expressing his positivism, though ethically discordant, Adams draws on Taney's infamous language from *Dred Scott* to announce his progressive approach to justice and citizenship:

The great issue of 1900 will be: "Shall the Constitution of the United States be so amended or revised that the rights of the Majority shall be preserved? Shall the majority rule?"

To-day the majority has no right which a fortified minority is bound to respect. The people of the United States are powerless to enact legislation for the redress of their grievances.

Adams's passage replaces disfranchised black Americans with the political majority as the victim of judicial tyranny. Like Delany and Taney before him, Adams defines rights as critically dependent upon power, framing the core concern of his novel as those rights which anyone, including a "fortified" or economically powerful minority, is "bound to respect." Adams justifies his faith in majority rule by deeming the majority to be an oracle of higher law impulse – that is, his positivism is justified by a faith in the innate goodness of the sovereign, not a commitment to the political ethics of agreement and consent. Released from plutocratic oppression, the majority will justly rule because they are inherently just and the only dissenters will be the wealthy elite whose evil dominion has been foiled.[45]

In addition to their positivism, these progressive novels were disfigured by identitarian appeals to a genuine American people. Adams, for instance, defines Americanism as the willingness to defy the status quo in the interests of justice, but the hero of Adams's novel, *President John Smith*, is not only a man of the people but a genuine American who can trace his roots to the original John Smith.[46] Moving in a different racialist direction, Friedman's description of the Supreme Court in *The Radical* associates the justices' cool rationality with their whiteness in the symbol of the marble columns of the Supreme Court building – "A screen of Ionic columns, hewn out of Potomac marble, made the background for the Supreme bench where sat enthroned the nine justices." The justices are "enthroned" – a none-too-subtle sign of the Court's anti-democratic aspect – and appear not to be warm-blooded denizens of an emotionally redolent physical world but pale creatures of intellectual abstraction who are appropriately installed in a building marked, in Friedman's terms, by the severity and chaste aspect of its geometrical forms and symmetry. Friedman's description overtly separates the Court (and the white Americans represented by the justices) from "the people," who are figured by Friedman as of "swarthy hue," unlike the cool, pale marble and white faces of the Court.[47] Ultimately, in their mix of majority power and majority identity, these novels offer little comfort to one seeking a social and legal order founded on neither force nor identity. Rejecting both the positivism and identitarianism of such progressive visions, Chesnutt and Storey seized on the hated liberty of contract doctrine to make their argument for an identity-neutral form of moral tradition that could form a consensual language of public association and legal order.[48]

The liberty of contract decisions despised by progressives assumed that the judiciary, as the disinterested and autonomous savant of majority custom, was imbued with a peculiar authority to moderate or check legislation contrary to traditional principles of American law and society. The notion that the judiciary's common law decisions constituted revelations of an apolitical body of majority tradition was offered by a largely conservative legal profession as an alternative to codification. Codification threatened to reduce all law to the will of political majorities, an outcome feared by many, in part, because of the likelihood that such majorities would enact legislation redistributing economic power.[49] Prominent conservative jurists, such as James Coolidge Carter, argued that the common law decisions of judges interpreting a body of immemorial social norms and principles furnished the only repository of non-political law capable of objectivity and disinterested justice in contrast to the turbulent conflicts of self-interest that characterized the political landscape. Developing and changing slowly over time as part of an organic process, custom was not subject to the artificial interventions of fleeting political majorities; Carter styled it "the imperishable record of the wisdom of the illimitable past reaching back to the infancy of the race, revised, corrected, enlarged, open to all alike, and read and understood by all."[50]

To illustrate the determinative force of tradition, Carter revealingly drew upon notions of etiquette and deportment:

A man must not appear shabbily dressed, or in a state of intoxication, or set a bad example. Offenses like these disappoint expectation and create in others irritation and resentment. The ordinary rules of etiquette and fashion obtaining in social circles have a similar foundation and sanction. Social customs like these are often spoken of deprecatingly as merely conventional, or capricious, or whimsical. They do indeed differ greatly in importance from those of which the law takes notice, and very different degrees of culpability are attached to the violation of them. Such obligations, however, are, in their *nature*, the same as those of the law, the difference being in the rigour with which they are enforced.

Once one conceives, as Carter does, that social obligations are enforced by sanctions "more powerful than those of the law," it follows that legislation is powerless to compel a community to act contrary to its traditions. Chesnutt puts this view in the mouth of the sympathetic Judge Straight in *The House Behind the Cedars*, "[C]ustom *is* law ... Right and wrong ... must be eternal verities, but our standards for measuring them vary with our latitude and our epoch. We make our customs lightly; once made, like our sins, they grip us in bands of steel; we become the creatures of our creations." For Carter, the Civil War amendments and Civil Rights Acts of 1866 and 1875 epitomized "the impotence of written law brought into conflict with custom."[51]

As either the cultural premises inevitably informing judicial and legislative definitions of justice and citizenship rights or as a set of behavioral expectations enforced by social censure, the language of tradition offers access to the force of law. *Plessy v. Ferguson* (1896) offers an apt example of Carter's conception of the determinative force of custom. The *Plessy* majority expressly grounded its decision in majority tradition:

> In determining the question of reasonableness [the legislature] is at liberty to act with reference to the established usages, customs and traditions of the people, and with a view to the promotion of their comfort, and the preservation of the public peace and good order. Gauged by this standard, we cannot say that a law which authorizes or even requires the separation of the two races in public conveyances is unreasonable.

In the Court's view, the constraint of the Constitution by tradition is inevitable: in "the nature of things" the Fourteenth Amendment "could not have been intended to abolish distinctions based upon color."[52] By figuring tradition as nature, the Court not only exhibits the historic need of mainstream American culture to imagine law as organic and innate and to represent its edicts and rulings in the emotionally resonant language of the higher law tradition, but it also evokes an appeal to the contemporary social Darwinist image of a slowly evolving social order.

Social Darwinism lent intellectual credence to judicial descriptions of tradition as a bedrock immune to legislative interference. Using Herbert Spencer's philosophy to argue against legislative intervention in the processes and outcomes of free trade, William Graham Sumner embraced the imperviousness of social customs and traditions:

> Every one of us is a child of his age and cannot get out of it. He is in the stream and is swept along with it. All his science and philosophy come to him out of it. Therefore the tide will not be changed by us. It will swallow up both us and our experiments... That is why it is the greatest folly of which a man can be capable to sit down with a slate and pencil to plan out a new social world.

Not surprisingly, social Darwinism was a congenial philosophy for those who had accumulated wealth in the absence of governmental regulation or redistribution.[53] Legislation could not effect an immediate shift in social behaviors and norms that had evolved over centuries. Anticipating Sumner's comments in *Folkways* (1906) that "legislation cannot make mores" and "stateways do not make folkways," the Court in *Plessy v. Ferguson* found legislation "powerless to eradicate racial instincts" or otherwise to challenge the contrary traditions of the majority.[54]

From its title to its conclusion, Charles Chesnutt's great political novel is centrally concerned with the force of tradition on the legal and cultural norms governing social interaction, but *The Marrow of Tradition* challenges the vision of tradition as a static monolith presented by Carter, Sumner, and *Plessy*. From an early age, Chesnutt had doubted the impermeability of tradition, particularly valuing the power of literature to revise custom and thereby necessitate and enable a revision of the nation's law.[55] The symbolic complexity of the title's visualization of tradition as a bone's cross-section – a dark, vital core surrounded by a hard, white shell – indicates that Chesnutt conceives of tradition as a duality. The apparently dead and stone-like fixity of the carapace – tradition according to Carter, Sumner, and *Plessy* – hides the living consensual process within it, creating, revising, and questioning its terms and applications. The title's reference to the "*marrow* of tradition" summons the ethical, philosophical, and emotional core of a shifting moral consensus styled as tradition that forms the basis for judging the legitimacy of the legal system's claims to justice.

The central event of Chesnutt's novel is drawn from the Wilmington, North Carolina riot of 1898, an anti-democratic *coup d'état* seeking to disfranchise the local black majority. Part of the late nineteenth-century retrenchment of Reconstruction, the Wilmington *coup's* twin themes were "Negro domination" and "white supremacy." "Negro domination" referred to the visible presence of black citizens in local government, a presence that glaringly emblematized for certain whites a loss of economic and political control, which loss in turn violated the principle of white supremacy.[56] The white supremacist program of election fraud, lynch law, and race riots represented Jim Crow positivism in its most raw aspect, stripped of even the semblance of political or legal procedure.[57] Ironically, Chesnutt uses a set of conversations among Major Carteret, Captain McBane, and General Belmont (the "Big Three") to depict the threat of Jim Crow positivism to black citizenship and political dialogue between the races.[58] In formulating a plan to steal black suffrage through mob violence and the manipulation of white public opinion, the "Big Three's" discussions form an unpleasant analogy for the political colloquy among white Americans reversing Reconstruction and the Civil War amendments.

The military appellations of the "Big Three" indicate not only their respective places within the hierarchy of Southern society but also the role armed force will play in effecting their ends. Each of these characters represents a different facet of a racist alliance, combining legal process (represented by Belmont, a lawyer), the press (represented by Carteret, a newspaper editor and publisher), and white vigilantism (represented by McBane, a foreman of convict labor). Though the "Big Three" nominally set aside class differences in the interest of "white supremacy," their divergent manners illustrate the various forms the same positivist ambition can take. Conceiving of their *coup* as a restoration of power to its rightful aristocratic heirs, the descendants of the First Families of Virginia, Carteret must disguise his positivism in terms that meet "the approval of his conscience, even if he had to trick that docile organ into acquiescence. This was not difficult to do in politics, for he believed in the divine right of white men and gentlemen, as his ancestors had believed in and died for the divine right of kings." Representing the *herrenvolk* alternative to Carteret's aristocratic notions, McBane, the son of an overseer, is not so delicate.[59] McBane names the positivistic truth that Carteret's pretensions of gentility obscure: "We may as well be honest about this thing. We are going to put the niggers down because we want to, and think we can; so why waste our time in mere pretense? I'm no hypocrite myself, – if I want a thing I take it, provided I'm strong enough." Racial domination is a contest of wills without moral justification. It has nothing to do with questions of culture or breeding; it is the creation of a congruence of desire and power. Appreciating both the political utility of Carteret's aristocratic traditionalism and McBane's more accurate perception about the essential nature of their project, General Belmont will not permit "fine scruples to stand in the way of success" yet accedes to the practical necessity of maintaining the semblance of something more than the naked truth of domination. As a lawyer and politician, Belmont understands that the language of tradition, with its higher law component, must be manipulated so as to garner public support for the aims of the "Big Three." General Belmont's calculus takes into account the fact that the power of the "Big Three" is largely dependent on the consensus of a national majority without which they are just another insular minority.[60] As the best alternative to the racist positivism of the "Big Three," Chesnutt's novel offers liberty of contract.[61]

Distinguishing Chesnutt from his realist contemporaries, Brook Thomas has argued that "Chesnutt's fiction exposes the failure of contract – especially the newly negotiated 'contract' between North and South – to generate an equitable situation for people of color."[62] Knowing that the failure of *a* contract (the Civil War amendments) is not the failure of contract, Thomas finds additionally that Chesnutt's faith in a transcendental morality qualifies his confidence in contractually created norms of human association. But Thomas's distinction draws too hard a line between contract and higher law, tending to reduce all higher law argument to the Garrisonian variety of government by God. As we have seen, the higher law constitutionalism inspiring both the

American Revolution and the Civil War amendments combines notions of conscience and consent. Contract proved indispensable to those politically engaged higher law arguments conceiving of justice as the product of human agency, not divine intervention. For such higher law advocates as Chesnutt (who takes one of his novel's chapter titles from the higher law maxim *fiat justitia ruat coelum* – "let justice be done though the heavens fall") and Frederick Douglass, the governance of society had to be consensual both to be just and to allow for the change and development that characterize free human existence. Where Twain's *Pudd'nhead Wilson* bleakly suggests in Tom's fate that status distinctions (race) inevitably trump the implementation of even the most basic dictates of conscience (the criminal law's prohibition of murder), Chesnutt's novel rediscovers the contractual nature of ethical relations we tend to assume are status driven, such as marriage and family.

Early in *The Marrow of Tradition*, a confrontation between two of the Carteret's black employees illustrates the centrality of contract to the novel's social and political struggle and the significance of the transition from status to contract for both races.[63] Mammy Jane's fond and respectful deference to her employers exemplifies the sentimental tie of status described by William Graham Sumner as the antithesis of the modern relation of contract – a throwback to a time when "society was dependent, throughout all its details, on status."[64] By contrast, the Carterets' young nurse typifies the contractual form of relation. Her identity and place in society are in flux and the mechanism by which she structures her rights and duties within that society is contract, not personal affection or sentimental reverence for an old social order. Her deal with the Carterets is contractual: "It was purely a matter of business; she sold her time for their money." Negroes of the old school, such as Mammy Jane and her grandson Jerry, are stuck – their identities, roles, and forms of social connection are fixed. However, the "new negroes" despised by Mammy Jane as well as the Carterets are in motion, using contract to climb "the ladder of life."[65] As exemplified by the notably unnamed young nurse, contractual relations are not about who you are, where you come from, or who your parents are. Contract is about what you do or what you will do. Unlike the cultural pluralism touted by Horace Kallen a few years later, in which who you are determines what you do, contract tends to identify parties in terms of performance and action.[66] Indeed, as this encounter between Mammy Jane and the young nurse suggests, defining oneself by contract (for example, identifying the young nurse by profession and not by status-driven titles such as Major, Aunt, Uncle, or Mammy), implicitly allows for identity to shift as one changes positions or takes on new contracts, new connections.

In praising the old-style Negroes, Major Carteret represents "the sentimentalists among us" who in Sumner's words "seize upon the survivals of the old order" attempting "to save and restore them."[67] Unlike the "new negroes," Mammy Jane does not attempt to "overstep the mark" – she accepts the transcendental givens of status. Ironically, however, in extolling Jane's deference to status, Carteret describes the "old ties" as an exchange of "dependence and loyal obedience on the part of the colored people" in return for "protection and succor" by the whites. The old paternalistic contract that Carteret lauds, protection for subservience, turns out to be fraudulent. The Major's failure to protect Jerry Letow, his loyal vassal and Mammy Jane's grandson, suggests that the paternalist consideration for the old contract was illusory all along. But more telling is Carteret's inconsistent assertion of nature and consent in describing the "old ties." If the superior class rules the inferior by dint of nature, then exchange and consent do not enter into their relations. There are no deals, no contracts, just a naturally positivistic social order of the kind expounded by George Fitzhugh and Taney's *Dred Scott* opinion. That contract enters Carteret's racist and positivist vision of a permanently hierarchical American society exhibits the degree to which the model of status has become obsolete as an explanation of Southern society and the degree to which his ethical pretensions constrain him to introduce some notion of contract as a sign of the moral agency of both master and servant.[68] His conscience requires some admission of agency and consent, though his racism seeks to regulate and confine those principles within a natural, divinely ordained hierarchy.

Any analysis of how contract functions in this scene must consider whether a reader's affective preference for sweet Mammy Jane over the curt young nurse may betoken a reservation on Chesnutt's part about contract as a basis for human relations. The ultimate worthlessness of the familial bond asserted between Mammy Jane and the Carterets should make us suspect that a negative reaction to the young nurse's bluntly contractual approach is part of Chesnutt's irony. After all, a reader's preference for Mammy Jane is shadowed by the fact that Carteret prefers her as well. In addition, Chesnutt frames Mammy Jane's appeal with her grandson's repulsiveness. Jerry Letow is one of those Negroes Sutton Griggs described as "[t]he cringing, fawning, sniffling, cowardly Negro" left behind by slavery and being replaced by "a new Negro, self-respecting, fearless, and determined in the assertion of his rights."[69]

Chesnutt wants his Northern, white readers to be more comfortable with Mammy Jane, drawing out their implicit allegiance with Major Carteret's views of race, in order to crush their complacency with the novel's tragic turn of events. Aside from such affective ironies, Chesnutt's point concerning the young nurse's "chip on the shoulder stage" is not that her contract with the Carterets is not barren of the kind of emotional connection enriching human association, but that it is a *stage*, a step in the direction of a truly consensual and equal exchange that then can form the basis of a redeemed emotional connection. Chesnutt does not drive a wedge between contract and affective relations, such as family, but ties them closer together; he critiques the hypocrisies of the old contract not to replace them with cold, economically driven connections but to advance relations in which affect is tied to consent and reciprocity. Thus, Chesnutt juxtaposes the Carterets' relation with Mammy Jane with the "old-fashioned" yet genuinely reciprocal bond of mutual affection characterizing Mr. Delamere's relation with Sandy Jenkins – a bond that does not prove counterfeit as Mr. Delamere saves Sandy, his contractual connection, at the expense of his grandson Tom, his blood connection.[70]

Even the novel's most dramatic evocation of family and transcendent morality frames kinship and moral certainty within a contractual pattern of offer and counter-offer. In the novel's climax, the estranged half-sisters, Janet Miller and Olivia Carteret, finally face each other. Janet's only child has been killed in the riot incited by the Big Three, and, ironically, the riot has also put the Carteret's only child in desperate need of Dr. Miller's medical expertise, for which Olivia has come to plead. Despite her loss, Janet sends her husband to aid the Carteret baby. In its renunciation of the "strict justice" or fair trade of a son for a son, Janet's compassion at first glance might seem to transcend or reject contract. However, when contrasted with Harriet Beecher Stowe's analogous visualizations of higher law in the deaths of little Eva and Uncle Tom, the contractual dimensions of Chesnutt's depiction become apparent. Stowe's icons of divine justice move in a vertical direction – they ascend. The movement in Chesnutt's scene of elemental justice is horizontal – a confrontation and negotiation between equals, between sisters. At death, Eva and Tom engage at the last moment in backward-glancing, one-way communications, final thoughts from a traveler on the verge of heaven. By contrast, Janet's compassion is staged as a counter-offer to Olivia's offer of familial recognition and money in return for medical care. Responding "*that you may know* that a woman may be foully wronged, and yet may have a heart to feel, even for one who has injured her, you may have your child's life, if my husband can save it," Janet prominently terms her gesture of compassion as an act that is to be perceived and understood by another – "that you may know." And, though Janet's comment is ostensibly intended as the final word between the sisters, it inevitably summons an acknowledgment by Olivia – "God will bless you for a noble woman!" Through Janet's insistence on and Olivia's now humbled acceptance of the ethical basis for human connection, the sisters have come to an understanding and consequently to the brink of an ethically grounded and emotionally rich kinship. As a result, Olivia declares that their communications are not at an end but at a beginning.[71]

By imagining Janet's compassion as part of an exchange, instead of portraying it as a gesture arrived at in private meditation, Chesnutt represents higher law inspiration as dialogic. For Chesnutt, a sense of justice impels one to conversation, broadly conceived as including action as well as speech, and that conversation has the potential to create the ethical consensus and reciprocity required for any worthy interpersonal bond. Whether Janet and Olivia will have future consensual relations grounded in mutual respect is left open, as Chesnutt's sign of the uncertain future of American race relations. Contrasting this open-ended conclusion with Uncle Tom's apotheosis (Tom's ascent into heaven is as certain as Legree's descent into hell), we can see that Chesnutt's scene, unlike Stowe's absolutist, top-down version of higher law justice, stresses the relations that the living create with each other and the principles they enact to render those relations just.

The sisters' climactic exchange reveals, among other things, that Janet's black mother was legally married to Olivia Carteret's white father. This disclosure is part of a chain of events, prominently including the Big Three's use of an inflammatory black newspaper editorial attacking the repression of interracial romantic relations. The editorial signals Chesnutt's intent to turn liberty of contract from a commercial doctrine into a broader conception of social and political intercourse:

The article was a frank and somewhat bold discussion of lynching and its causes. It denied that most lynchings were for the offense generally charged as their justification, and declared that, even of those seemingly traced to this cause, many were not for crimes at all, but for voluntary acts which might naturally be expected to follow from the miscegenation laws by which it was sought, in all the Southern States, to destroy *liberty of contract*, and, for the purpose of maintaining a fanciful purity of race, to make crimes of marriage to which neither nature nor religion nor the laws of other states interposed any insurmountable barrier.[72]

In this passage, Chesnutt paraphrases an editorial by Alex Manly, the black editor of the Wilmington *Record*, responding to Rebecca Latimer Felton's racist diatribe before the Georgia State Agricultural Society.[73] Felton, the first woman senator from Georgia, proclaimed the increasing danger of rape for rural white women left home alone while their husbands worked on the farm. She argued for lynch law as a deterrent, saying that white Southerners should "lynch a thousand a week if necessary." In reply, Manly decried the obvious injustice of "mak[ing] it appear that the negroes were the only criminals," suggesting that a non-racist attack on crime "would find [the] strongest allies in the intelligent negroes themselves, and together the whites and blacks would root the evil out of both races." Contrary to the image of the black beast rapist enunciated by Felton and Senator Ben Tilman, theorized as the product of racial retrogression by Charles Carroll in *The Negro A Beast* (1900), and fictionalized by Thomas Dixon in *The Leopard's Spots* (1902) and *The Clansman* (1905), Manly offered the image of consensual sexual relations between the races.[74] Manly provocatively replaced the image of the "big burly, black brute" with handsome, well-deported men who "had white men for their fathers" and were not only "not 'black and 'burley,' but were SUFFICIENTLY ATTRACTIVE FOR WHITE GIRLS OF CULTURE AND REFINEMENT TO FALL IN LOVE WITH THEM, as is very well known to all."[75]

Though muting the incendiary quality of the Manly original, Chesnutt's paraphrase adds a jurisprudential dimension completely missing from Manly's comments. Chesnutt's version draws an explicit analogy between the anti-miscegenation laws restricting romantic freedom and commercial regulations, such as labor laws, impinging commercial freedom. Given that liberty of contract is a legal term of art, it is hardly surprising that Manly does not raise it in protesting the repression of interracial romantic relations. But its absence in the Manly original illumines Chesnutt's rhetorical strategy in introducing liberty of contract in a novel where it will not be recognized (or pigeonholed) as a particular legal doctrine but will be read more expansively as a notion of basic justice. By reframing liberty of contract in this fashion, Chesnutt returns the judicial doctrine to its supposed source in a cultural tradition. Reinstalled in a broader cultural context, the doctrine can become the subject of literary reinvention in which it is imagined anew and illustrated with new stories, transforming the countermajoritarian concept developed by conservative jurists to defend the property of a wealthy minority from redistributive legislation into a larger principle of liberty protecting all forms of contractual relation without regard to racial identity. In effect, as Walter Benn Michaels suggests, Chesnutt lauds liberty of contract as a form of resistance to race.[76] The novel's insistent figurations of family resemblance (e.g., Janet and Olivia are often mistaken for each other) point to the hypocrisies of pretending that Jim Crow protects any "purity of race." Giving the lie to such racist pretense, these resemblances remind us that even our most status-driven conceptions of society, such as family, are supposed to begin in consent. Far from being antithetical, consent and descent should be seen as interrelated, so to speak, as the latter properly flows from the former.

Recovering the higher law conception of republican virtue in the era of Jim Crow positivism, Chesnutt's version of liberty of contract highlights the connection between traditional morality and consensual forms of association. Thus, though Chesnutt's editorial censures the "offense" of sexual relations outside of marriage, it invokes the traditional value of liberty of contract to indicate that nothing in the notion of contract, which derives its legitimacy from the consent of the parties, racially delimits such romantic connections. Interracial marriage contracts offend anti-contractual notions of status, such as the status-based rules of contractual incompetence vitiating the agreements of slaves and married women before the Civil War amendments and the married women's property acts. As George Fitzhugh well understood in lambasting the proslavery argument that the Constitution was a bargain protecting the South's peculiar institution, nothing in contract, of itself, will stop or qualify such innovations as revising the deal to include a new party (see chapter one). Unlikely or new forms of romantic partnership do not in their newness or uniqueness distort the rules of contract, which rely on notions of human agency and consent. The reciprocal promises, rights, and obligations that constitute a valid contract and that tradition deems important to a good marriage are not disturbed by members of opposed clans marrying each other (whether Twain's Shepherdsons and Grangerfords or Chesnutt's Merkells and Browns). Such novel alliances trouble notions of identity, not contract. The marriage of Julia Brown and Sam Merkell is precisely the kind of novel-yet-traditional relation enabled by contract in contrast to identitarian conceptions of society. Their romantic partnership comports with traditional insistence on marriage and instances the fluidity of contractual relations, which, without "artificial" legal interference, will "naturally" include race mixture and other forms of social innovation. That the dishonest and even criminal denial of this marriage lies at the root of the novel's chain of events – its suppression providing

Carteret with the necessary funds to conduct the campaign for black disfranchisement – is Chesnutt's representation of the anti-traditional, artificial interference with liberty of contract characterizing Jim Crow positivism.

Although contract does not explicitly arise in his analysis of nativist modernism (which meets its most challenging and intricate moment in the marriage contract that must be disguised as incest to preserve the fantasy of a national race), Walter Benn Michaels implicitly draws on contractual notions of human association as the contrasting perspective from which one recognizes the exogamy-as-endogamy paradox of American modernism. Michaels's observation of a modernist insistence "that what people and things do or mean is a function of what they are," an insistence "on identity as the determining ground of action or significance," is countered by literary deployments of contract.[77] As Chesnutt's manipulation of liberty of contract suggests, contract as a process of forming social relations tends in an anti-identitarian direction. The more a society is formed by contract the less it does or can rely on notions of identity as a ground for being. Contract as a trope for and a process of human connection tends to frame identity as choice and action.

In a later novel, *Paul Marchand, F. M. C.*, written in 1921 but only recently published, Chesnutt indicates his continuing faith in consent as the mechanism for just human relation in sharp distinction to identitarian notions of blood. In *Marchand*, the eponymous hero is a white man who has been raised as a quadroon. At the novel's climax, Marchand reverses the switch engineered by his parents, as he rejects his white inheritance, turning it over to the decent "black" heir who never knows of his own "black" blood. On discovering his "true" identity as a white man, Marchand rejects blood notions of identity and chooses the alliances formed not by blood but by choice, particularly his marriage to a mulatto woman. While it is tempting to see Chesnutt as replacing one determinism with another, substituting Marchand's acculturation as a mulatto for nature, Marchand's character does not support such a reading. Without denial of or regard for his supposed racial identity as a mulatto, Marchand's cosmopolitan education abroad has given him the skills – the manners, speech, business acumen, and worldly standards of honor and respect – to take his place as the head of an aristocratic white family. Rather than being unable to assume a white identity (like Chambers at the end of Twain's *Pudd'nhead Wilson*), Marchand does not choose to be white. Out of a horror at the injustice of racial labels that would bastardize his children and negate his marriage, he rejects

Jim Crow America for a cosmopolitan life in Europe where social and civil relations are consensual. The alternative of choosing his white inheritance would place "race" above "justice or humanity" and privilege "pride of blood" above the consensual relations established by mutual affection.[78]

In *Marrow*, Chesnutt appropriately uses train travel from one section of the country to the other to emblematize liberty of contract as a mechanism of social mobility in which individuals meet and negotiate their connections in a shared consensual language of public deportment and culture. Such public accommodations were the subject of Charles Sumner's ill-fated Civil Rights Act of 1875. Chesnutt's version of train travel also clearly responds to *Plessy v. Ferguson*.[79] In the "Journey Southward" chapter, Chesnutt accepts and inverts the justices' deference to liberty of contract and tradition in accepting the constitutionality of legal segregation, turning their logic against their result and rendering their notion of consensually established norms of social and legal recognition as the basis for a racially heterogeneous and cosmopolitan society.

Chesnutt uses a realistic description of Jim Crow train travel to expose the harsh realities repressed by the *Plessy* court's ruling and to counter a curious bit of judicial storytelling offered by the majority in justification of its opinion's fairness:

We consider the underlying fallacy of the plaintiff's argument to consist in the assumption that the enforced separation of the two races stamps the colored race with a badge of inferiority. If this be so, it is not by reason of anything found in the act, but solely because the colored race chooses to put that construction upon it. The argument necessarily assumes that if, as has more than once been the case, and is not unlikely to be so again, the colored race should become the dominant power in the state legislature, and should enact a law in precisely similar terms, it would thereby relegate the white race to an inferior position. We imagine that the white race, at least, would not acquiesce in this assumption.[80]

In addition to its rather startling erasure of the discriminatory intent and effect of Jim Crow, this little shoe-on-the-other-foot fantasy about what it would be like for whites to face a separate-but-equal law passed by a black legislature is distinguished by the Court's use of an imaginative reversal to test the law's impartiality. By pretending to trade places with Homer Plessy, the Court seeks to demonstrate the equity of Louisiana's separate train car statute, implicitly warranting that legal segregation complies with the higher law injunction to do unto others as you would have them do unto you. This fable exposes the High Court's apprehension that its decision must comport with a cultural idiom of justice, a traditional idiom that includes such figures and concepts as "fair play," "poetic justice," and "fair trade." And the Court's fictive speculation reflects the affective power of reversal narratives as a test of American justice, such as Lydia Maria Child's *A Romance of the Republic* (1867) (in which white and black babies are switched and later, through a twist of fate, the racist grandfather of the white child mistakenly returns him to slavery), Gertrude Dorsey Brown's short story "A Case of Measure for Measure" (1906) (in which a group of white masqueraders made up as blacks find their make-up will not come off), Chesnutt's short story "Mars Jeems's Nightmare" (1899) (in which through conjure a white man is turned black and gets thereby a taste of his own despotic medicine), Twain's *Pudd'nhead Wilson* (1896), and the NAACP's first litigation triumph *Buchanan v. Warley* (1917) (in which black civil rights are presented in the form of a white property owner's liberty of contract).[81]

Having no quarrel with the *Plessy* Court's supposed commitment to the traditional value of fair play, Chesnutt is highly critical of its dishonest legal formalism, which hides the discriminatory reality of Louisiana's separate train car statute behind a blanket assumption of equivalent accommodations. Speaking for the Court, Chesnutt's white train conductor praises Jim Crow as a beautifully symmetrical system of mirror images, but the appearance of the car exposes the fraud involved in such claims:

It was an old car with faded upholstery, from which the stuffing projected here and there through torn places. Apparently the floor had not been swept for several days. The dust lay thick upon the window sills, and the watercooler, from which he essayed to get a drink, was filled with stale water which had made no recent acquaintance with ice.

The false impartiality of Jim Crow law is most tellingly revealed by the appearance of McBane in the "colored" coach. Having displaced Dr. Miller by alerting the conductor to the light-skinned doctor's race, McBane underscores his dominance by coming into the colored car to smoke and spit. In response, Dr. Miller tests the fairness of the *Plessy* rule by reminding the conductor that the law supposedly applies to black and white alike. Predictably, the law fails this test. At its positivistic root, the law of segregation, like McBane's behavior, is not founded upon a traditional respect for legal or moral impartiality – the Anglo-American rule of law in which legal stricture applies to governor and governed. The rule of law proclaimed by Justice Harlan in his *Plessy* dissent holds no sway for the majority's jurisprudence of power.[82]

Inferring the liberty of contract theme behind the Court's aversion to the forced commingling of the two races on terms unacceptable to either, Chesnutt uses liberty of contract and the traditional norms of deportment that he knows give shape and color to the Court's aversion to undermine its holding. At its core, the *Plessy* ruling depends on the orthodoxy of James Coolidge Carter and William Graham Sumner that law is powerless to alter contrary social traditions. According to the Court, "social prejudices may [not] be overcome by legislation," and "an enforced commingling of the two races" will not secure equal rights for African Americans. Instead, "If the two races are to meet on terms of social equality, it must be the result of natural affinities, a mutual appreciation of each other's merits and a voluntary consent of individuals." Reading this passage, one needs no psychic powers to sense the justices shuddering at the thought of unkempt, loud, ill-mannered black folks being forced by the Fourteenth Amendment's equal protection clause upon a group of well-dressed, polite, well-spoken white people. Laws that "commingl[e] ... the two races upon terms unsatisfactory to either" violate the traditions authorizing the Constitution itself – the norms of deportment that constitute the "terms" of our social contract. Yet, because that contract is "voluntary" and the cultural language of deportment is not the natural or exclusive property of any class, Chesnutt sees in lawyerly fashion that the Court's own terms indicate a test case where white and black want to ride together, a test case demonstrating that the separate train car statute impermissibly violates liberty of contract.[83]

In Chesnutt's test case, two well-deported and highly educated individuals of different races – Dr. Miller and Dr. Burns – want to ride together, but their freedom to do so is curtailed by Jim Crow law. The travelers, Miller and Burns, share the language, tastes, and interests of "men of culture." Additionally, as colleagues, their association is grounded in professional "capacity, with which color is not at all concerned," as Dr. Burns, puts it. Reacting to legal segregation as "an outrage upon a citizen of a free country," Dr. Burns's anger is shaped by higher law notions of freedom of consensual intercourse – precisely the traditional value invoked by *Plessy* to uphold segregation. As prejudice will later block his desire to have Dr. Miller by his side in an operation on Major Carteret's son (foreshadowing the final medical emergency of the novel), the Jim Crow train law curtails Dr. Burns's freedom of association, in *Plessy*'s language, to commingle with another on terms satisfactory to both.[84]

Seeking to engender majority opposition to a practice contrary to its own higher law traditions, Chesnutt's depiction of Jim Crow law draws

both on the republican tradition emphasizing the consensual combination of individuals in a political community and the liberal natural rights
tradition stressing the private rights of individuals. The abridgment of
Miller's and Burns's ability to ride together and later to act together in an
ad hoc professional partnership represents the way in which identity as
politics obstructs genuine republican combination. And Jim Crow law is
precisely the kind of majoritarian abridgment of individual rights, here
the doctors' individual rights of free association and freedom of movement, with which the liberal natural rights tradition is most concerned.
The scene opposes freedom and racial classification, in part, because
Chesnutt perceived that liberty is the central countermajoritarian value
of a constitutional tradition that James Madison described as preventing legal measures from being "decided, not according to the rules of
justice and the rights of the minor party, but by the superior force of an
interested and overbearing majority."[85] The existence of "rights beyond
the reach of the majority," as Francis Lieber had argued before the war,
constitutes "liberty, not the power of the majority."[86] Chesnutt's constitutionalism depends on the assumption that, as Moorfield Storey put it
in objecting to progressive attacks on the doctrine of judicial review, the
"object of the constitution" is "to restrain the power of the majority and
to protect the rights of the individual against its tyranny."[87] For Chesnutt
and Storey, "American constitutionalism is *meant*," as H. N. Hirsch puts
it, "to be countermajoritarian; the Constitution and the Supreme Court
are meant to serve as a break upon the legislative process and to protect
the rights of minorities."[88]

As a conception of social and political relations, liberty of contract,
in Chesnutt's view, helpfully presupposes a public language of moral
norms and proper behavior which diverse individuals can use to negotiate the terms of their association. Public notions of proper deportment,
for Chesnutt, comprise an important (and inevitable) part of the language of social and political connection.[89] Described by James Coolidge
Carter as "the coin of the realm," a phrase unintentionally highlighting
the element of exchange that Chesnutt finds hopeful in notions of deportment, these standards are capable of enabling public intercourse among
people of very different backgrounds and with highly divergent domestic
arrangements and practices.[90] William Miller's friendship with Dr. Burns
is but one example of the kind of social fluidity enabled by this form of
public intercourse. Lee Ellis, the middle-class Southern Quaker's son
who proves to be the better suitor for the aristocratic Clara Pemberton,
provides another example of the beneficial social movement created

through an acceptance of ethical principle and thoughtful deportment in lieu of inherited status as the basis for social connection.

Chesnutt's version of deportment as a language of political inclusion draws upon an African American literary tradition, including William Wells Brown, Frederick Douglass, Harriet Jacobs, Frances Harper, W. E. B. DuBois, Pauline Hopkins, and many others. Generally speaking, the political and jurisprudential values of deportment have been misprized by critics and scholars variously troubled or embarrassed by what they see as a distasteful assimilation of or capitulation to the cultural standards of the white middle class. As Hazel Carby notes, early in the twentieth century a reaction set in against the politics and moral code of "uplift" that dominated the 1890s. Critics such as Sterling Brown, Arthur Davis, and Ulysses Lee dismissed work deemed assimilationist, such as Harper's *Iola Leroy*, and this theme was picked up later in the work produced out of the 1960s black arts movement, such as Addison Gayle's literary history, which similarly excommunicates Harper's novel.[91] Signs of current critical distaste for anything smacking of bourgeois assimilationism abound. For instance, in an aside, Henry Louis Gates's dismisses Chesnutt's criticism of early black writing as mere "middle-class respectability and gentility."[92] And we can divine a kindred discomfort with Chesnutt's middle-classness in Richard Brodhead's otherwise very sensitive reconstruction of the context for Chesnutt's conception of authorship. Brodhead suggests a conflict between the novelist's early intuition that literature offers a means of advocating "black causes" and his conception of "high-cultural" literature, a conception influenced by his taste for the bourgeois life. The conflict Brodhead assumes between political cause and "high culture" obscures the intersection between these categories in Chesnutt's concept of liberty of contract as a metaphor for a broader conception of public intercourse. As a consequence, the higher law component of "higher culture" which connects Chesnutt to Douglass, Harper, and Jacobs (figures Brodhead sees as distinct from Chesnutt) is ignored.[93] As Claudia Tate has pointed out, "By adopting what from our late-twentieth-century vantage point are conservative bourgeois values," black authors, such as Harper and Chesnutt, "ironically offer a radical repudiation of race and class origins as the absolute determinants for qualifying the characters' personal esteem, access to virtue, and success."[94]

Although an adequate analysis of assimilation, its varieties and positive and negative aspects, is well beyond the scope of this study, we need to make a couple of observations in looking at the use of deportment by Chesnutt and his nineteenth-century precursors as a kind of public contractual language. First, we should note that, by definition, contract is a pattern of exchange in which something or some performance of mine becomes yours and vice versa. To the extent that assimilation takes a contractual pattern, it becomes a process of reciprocal influence. By contrast, assimilation is usually attacked as a kind of one-way merger in which an outsider is economically or politically forced to shed a former identity and melted into a homogeneous (white) body politic and its culture. The source of valid complaint in such attacks lies not with the fact of cultural mixture but with the fact of coercion, for which assimilation is simply the token. Consensual exchanges of cultural influence would seem entirely unobjectionable (except, of course, to the tyrant using race to maintain power or the racist seeking to preserve cultural purity). Second, the quest for a consensual heterogeneous political union requires the discovery of a public political language common to all groups and individuals in which differing perspectives and interests can be negotiated. By rendering a common language impracticable, a blanket objection to assimilation thwarts consensual politics and jurisprudence.

To rebut arguments that in the system of slavery the "Negro is governed by those *naturally* superior," Harriet Jacobs offers her own good character, which is distinguished by such universally valued attributes as compassion, honesty, and bravery.[95] Her dignity and poise constitute a continuing argument for civil recognition and respect. But Jacobs not only presents herself in the terms of proper deportment she shares with her white audience, she also modifies those behavioral norms by insisting on the quality of her character despite the breach of sexual etiquette involved in her out-of-marriage liaison with the aptly named Mr. Sands.[96] As Hazel Carby observes, "Jacobs's confession was at once both conventional and unconventional," carefully negotiating between "satisfying moral expectations and challenging an ideology that would condemn her as immoral." Carby's analysis captures the politically necessary paradox of the traditional-yet-novel approach of the minority advocate who would invoke traditional norms while revising the tradition.[97] As Chesnutt after her, Jacobs seeks not only to wear the garb of custom successfully (the clothing, manners, proper speech, and behavior of citizenship) but also to retailor it so that it accommodates an expanded version of the American community and the realities facing the marginalized and oppressed.[98]

Significantly, Jacobs's vision of a race-neutral contractual exchange of proper deportment for civil recognition comes to her most vividly, as it

had Douglass, in England, where she has the cosmopolitan experience
of social fluidity and treatment according to her behavior not her
complexion:

For the first time in my life I was in a place where I was treated according to my
deportment, without reference to my complexion. I felt as if a great millstone
had been lifted from my breast. Ensconced in a pleasant room, with my dear
little charge, I laid my head on my pillow, for the first time, with the delightful
consciousness of pure unadulterated freedom.[99]

The exchange of "unadulterated freedom" for proper deportment is
clearly a fairer bargain than the trade of degraded status for complexion. Extolling deportment as a passport to social and legal recognition,
Jacobs seeks to reclaim the founding fathers' republican correlation of
character and citizenship and redefine the democratic requirement of a
consensually established public morality as race-neutral.

Deportment became more important after the Civil War amendments
ostensibly opened the door to black civic participation, and, later, as Jim
Crow laws, such as that endorsed in *Plessy*, explicitly circumscribed black
citizenship on the basis of social conventions. Frances Harper's novel of
Reconstruction, *Iola Leroy or Shadows Uplifted* (1892), focuses on the figure
of the noble mulatto to disrupt facile associations of moral convention
and racial identity.[100] Iola's fine character and manners are part of an
African American literary tradition concerned "to establish the 'capacity
of the Negro,'" arguing against what Kwame Anthony Appiah terms the
doctrine of "extrinsic racism" that presupposes "that the racial essence
entails certain morally relevant qualities."[101] As black blood "is on trial
before the world," Harper moves the narrative focus back and forth between mulatto characters, such as Iola, and dark-skinned characters, such
as Lucille Delany and Dr. Carmicle, who present nobility of character
in a darker complexion: "Every person of unmixed blood who succeeds
in any department of literature, art or science is a living argument for
the capability which is in the race." Seeking to correct "one of the great
mistakes of our civilization," "that which makes color, and not character, a social test," Harper's novel works with the traditional vocabulary
of manners and proper behavior to eliminate race from the customary
terms of American franchise. Praising law as the "great distinction between savagery and civilization" and accepting the important role of
custom as the substratum of legal authority and public policy, Harper
echoes such legal conservatives of her era as James Coolidge Carter and
anticipates Chesnutt.[102]

Chesnutt uses Dr. Miller's mixed response to the company of "a jolly, good natured crowd" of black farm laborers who are "noisy, loquacious, happy, dirty, and malodorous" to dramatize the unfairness of the Jim Crow social bargain for the well-deported African American on precisely the same assumptions guiding *Plessy*.[103] Miller's reaction to the laborers, though sympathetic, is qualified by his aversion:

They were his people, and he felt a certain expansive warmth toward them in spite of their obvious shortcomings. By and by, however, the air became too close, and he went out upon the platform. For the sake of the democratic ideal, which meant so much to his race, he might have endured the affliction. He could easily imagine that people of refinement, with the power in their hands, might be tempted to strain the democratic ideal in order to avoid such contact; but personally, and apart from the mere matter of racial sympathy, these people were just as offensive to him as to the whites in the other end of the train. Surely, if a classification of passengers on trains was at all desirable, it might be made upon some more logical and considerate basis than a mere arbitrary, tactless, and by the very nature of things, brutal drawing of a color line.[104]

Dr. Miller's transformation from the son of a thrifty, hardworking stevedore into a cosmopolitan, well-read doctor has imbued him with tastes and expectations unfitting him for this rough company. The "democratic ideal" of completely open identification with one's fellow beings gives way in Chesnutt's culturally pragmatic vision to an exchange of civil respect for respectability, the terms of which vary from group to group, and which, while not ignoring the inevitability of social divisions, would redescribe those divisions as penetrable through such personal transformation as that exemplified by Miller (and Chesnutt himself or Frederick Douglass). This civil exchange connects the customary norms of behavior to consensual forms of association. Early in his career, Chesnutt conceived of etiquette as obtaining respect in return for self-respect and "a proper regard for the rights and opinions of others." This contractual conception of etiquette is the social correlative of Chesnutt's later constitutional observation that "duties are dependent upon rights, without rights there can be no duties."[105]

Looking at another Chesnutt novel, *The House Behind the Cedars*, Walter Benn Michaels has argued that "Chesnutt subjects the idea of class difference – the idea that differences in class can matter – to a sustained criticism from the standpoint of race."[106] Dr. Miller's sympathy for and aversion to the black laborers works in the opposite direction, in which race is criticized from the standpoint of consensual social relations. Chesnutt highlights Dr. Miller's distaste for the crowd of laborers in order to separate the various kinds of deportment informing a wide range of social contracts, including that among the laborers themselves, from the overarching citizenship contract, which derives from the universals forming the "democratic ideal." In Dr. Miller's dual reaction, Chesnutt's novel looks to a society that permits social mobility and association on terms that are just because they are consensual. To achieve this vision, the black laborers must be included in the body politic *and* Dr. Miller and Dr. Burns must be able to continue their conversation. Dr. Miller's person and vocation work symbolically in both directions. While his return South to aid "his people" derives from a sense of justice that they must and should be brought within the terms of national franchise, his deportment and education argue for fluid social relations and multiple social contracts and contacts.

W. E. B. DuBois's essay, "The Conservation of Races," distinguishes the role and function of public deportment as a common language of political association from notions of racial or ethnic identity. In this essay, DuBois, who links Chesnutt and Storey, is chiefly concerned to argue for the "race idea" as a means of human progress. As Douglass and Delany had before him, DuBois offers a Herder-like appreciation of racial difference and monadic contribution, valorizing the effort of each race "to develop for civilization its particular message, its particular ideal." In this vein, he finds the better destiny of black Americans lies not in the "absorption by the white Americans" or "a servile imitation of Anglo-Saxon culture" but in "a stalwart originality which shall unswervingly follow Negro ideals."[107] Yet, in making this pitch, DuBois neither endorses multicultural conceptions of identity as the locus of politics nor discards general notions of deportment or other plausibly universal rules and terms of interracial dialogue. Indeed, DuBois separates the particulars of cultural identity from the universal ethical norms and procedures enabling a culturally diverse citizenry to negotiate and consensually determine their political coexistence.[108] DuBois urges that where "there is substantial agreement in laws, language and religion" – the categories we have seen Emerson use to define the "one people" of the American union – "then there is no reason why, in the same country and on the same street, two or three great national ideals might not thrive and develop, that men of different races might not strive together for their race ideals as well, perhaps even better, than in isolation."[109]

By routinely comparing racial to religious difference, Moorfield Storey implies a similar distinction between identity and politics.[110] The observance of public norms of social propriety, legal procedure, and political process does not prevent Jewish-Americans, for instance, from going to shul, celebrating Passover, or fastening mezuzah to their doorposts. Accepting the necessity of shared notions of justice and proper behavior for a consensual political system, DuBois commends the overtly traditional values of honesty, industriousness, and moral propriety, urging earnest, hardworking black Americans to unite "to stop the ravages of consumption among the Negro people . . . to keep black boys from loafing, gambling and crime" and "to guard the purity of black women." And he urges that the American Negro Academy must be "[r]epresentative in character," "[i]mpartial in conduct," and "[f]irm in leadership."[111] Thus, DuBois's proposal expressly joins the norms of social propriety to the basic republican values of representativeness, impartiality (rule of law), and morally courageous leadership.

The minority advocate who has discarded emigration as a solution does not have the luxury of imagining the norms of civilized society as *merely* or *simply* a means of oppression. While wanting to revise the parts or applications of this civic language that in fact operate so as to exclude or oppress individuals or groups, the reformer cannot, as Chesnutt, DuBois, and Storey realized, dispose of the whole project of universalist procedure without succumbing to untenable and regressive fantasies of nationalist isolation.

Chesnutt's novel locates the figure and theme of liberty of contract in the marrow of American jurisprudence, as an innovative site where revision accompanies the invocation of tradition, and where citizenship rights and traditional norms of public association are reshaped through the flux of contract. The NAACP's strategy in *Buchanan v. Warley* (1917) parallels that of Chesnutt's portrait of Jim Crow train travel, focusing on the curtailment not just of black rights but of white freedom as well.[112] *Buchanan* – the NAACP's first major victory – employed a clever reversal by taking the case of a white property owner who was barred from selling his property to a black buyer by a racist Louisville, Kentucky zoning ordinance. The black buyer used the racist statute as a defense against the white seller's lawsuit for performance of the sales contract. The NAACP thus staged its challenge to the Louisville ordinance as a question of interracial liberty of contract. In a bit of juristic passing, the NAACP presented the case for black Americans' civil rights in the guise of a white man's liberty of contract – a private form of social and commercial association – with a black man. Among other ironies, this reversal forced a defense team arguing for separation of the races to represent an African

American. In the precise manner foreshadowed by Chesnutt's use of the liberty of contract doctrine in *Marrow*, *Buchanan* reclaims the due process clause for the purposes of racial equity for which it was originally designed, turning the legal doctrine shielding commercial interests into a guard of African Americans' citizenship rights.

Moorfield Storey was the chief architect of the NAACP's victory in *Buchanan*.[113] Storey was an independent reformer in the antebellum pattern of his mentor, Charles Sumner, who consistently proclaimed that his political program was grounded on notions of principle rather than party allegiance.[114] In the NAACP's early days, Storey was widely considered as the organization's most able constitutional lawyer. James Weldon Johnson, for instance, said of Storey: "[N]o name that we could mention would have such significance to the colored people of the country in arguing these cases before the Supreme Court as your own." Similarly, another NAACP colleague, Mary White Ovington, termed Storey "our ablest constitutional lawyer."[115]

Born in 1845 to a family of Boston Brahmins and educated at Harvard, Storey counted among his friends Oliver Wendell Holmes, Jr., Henry Adams, and William James. In rejecting a deterministic universe and positing the possibility of moral action, Storey's views most resemble, of these three thinkers, James's, but Storey's views were more decisively shaped by the influence of a previous generation of Boston intellectuals, in particular, Sumner and Emerson.[116] Sumner and Emerson embodied, for Storey, a visionary conception of higher law principles as a spur to continuing creative efforts to realize justice. In his biography of Sumner, Storey praises Sumner's "faith in the principles of free government as laid down in the Declaration of Independence . . . he gave his life to secure their practical recognition. They were not to him glittering generalities, but ultimate, practical truths, and in this faith Lincoln and Sumner were one."[117] This passage tellingly combines faith and practicality, signaling something other than an absolutist assertion of a detailed plan denominated as God's law. Rather, what Storey praises here is Sumner's courage in pushing and being pushed by ethical abstractions into new forms of practice where they can lead to such important and far-sighted experiments as the Civil Rights Act of 1875 and Sumner's argument to end school segregation in the 1848 *Roberts* case, which introduced the phrase "equality before the law" into the context of citizenship and race. (Sumner's argument in *Roberts* that equivalent segregated educational facilities did not meet the standard of equality and that legal segregation in and of itself marked the minority member in such a way as to cause psychic damage anticipated the ruling in *Brown v. Board of Education* by more than a century.)[118]

The kinship between Storey's praise of Sumner and the description of higher law we have examined in the work of Ainsworth Rand Spofford and Emerson is not coincidental. In addition to being a friend of the Emerson family, Storey was an ardent admirer of Emerson's work and had in his possession and drew upon Emerson's WO Liberty Journal in composing an address for the centenary celebration of Emerson's birth. In this journal, Emerson, as we have seen, quotes Spofford extensively and describes higher law jurisprudence as a visionary project of experiment and dialogue based on a generative belief in abstract principles of justice. The influence of Emerson's higher law conception on Storey's advocacy of black civil rights may be seen in an address Storey composed the same year as his lecture on Emerson. Quoting from Emerson in "Negro Suffrage is not a Failure" (1903), Storey describes the framers as betraying the higher law basis of their democratic experiment by incorporating slavery into the Constitution:

they lacked the courage to build as well as they knew, when they framed their government. "In the necessities of the hour," to quote the words of Emerson, "they overlooked the moral law, and winked at a practical exception to the bill of rights they had drawn up. They winked at the exception, believing it insignificant. But the moral law, the nature of things, did not wink at it, but kept its eyes wide open." It turned out that this one violation was a subtle poison, which in eighty years corrupted the whole body politic, and brought the alternative of extirpation of the poison or ruin to the republic."[119]

This quote expresses the distaste Storey shared with Emerson and Sumner for compromise of principle – the fearful, conservative hedging of democratic experiments aimed at achieving justice.

Storey's visionary willingness, as Sumner's and Emerson's disciple, to embrace change in the hope of achieving justice is reflected in his nostalgia for the nation's most intense years of conflict – 1840–70:

Ah, what a time it was to live in, when 'the frozen apathy' which Garrison deplored . . . was gradually yielding, and the tide of freedom was constantly rising; when the annexation of Texas with a slave constitution, the Fugitive Slave Law, the repeal of the Missouri Compromise, the expulsion of Samuel Hoar from Charleston, the return of Anthony Burns, the assault on Sumner, the outrages in Kansas and the growing insolence of the slave lords taught the North, as it were line upon line, precept upon precept, what slavery meant to freemen as well as slaves, until secession and the attack on Sumter brought the smouldering fire into fierce life and the conflagration began in which slavery finally perished.[120]

As these comments written in 1914 suggest, Storey enthusiastically embraced the revolutionary aspect of higher law reform well into his later years (in marked contrast to such peers as Holmes, who retrospectively viewed his youthful abolitionist ardor as folly). As Douglass had in "What to the Slave is the Fourth of July," Storey hails the destruction that enables new construction – a new attempt at creating a social and legal order better exemplifying the higher law mix of conscience and consent that gives American law its claim to legitimacy and justice.

The insistence on the universality of consent, for Storey, was the hallmark of higher law republicanism: "Government by the people cannot succeed unless all the people take part in it."[121] Storey excoriated Jim Crow for shutting the door to equal participation in the civil or public sphere. Without universal participation in the political and cultural conversation that forms the moral consensus legitimating law, that consensus becomes an expression not of universal norms of justice but of the majority's will and biases. In a passage closely echoing DuBois's comments in "The Conservation of Races," Storey suggests we reject the false securities of status and accept consensually determined coexistence:

Does a dread of social equality excuse injustice! Society protects itself. Men of very different characters, tastes, associations and incomes live together in every community. Those associate together who like each other, whose tastes and ideas are the same. We all live near fellow-citizens who perhaps speak a different language and certainly lead very different lives from our own. We do not think it necessary to deny their legal rights or to keep them ignorant, lest they invade our houses and marry our daughters; and, unless the colored race is peculiarly attractive to the white, there is no reason why they should not live side by side, as all over our land men live side by side, enjoying the same rights and privileges, but never having social relations with each other or even knowing each other's names.[122]

Here Storey makes the same distinction that DuBois makes in his essay and that Hannah Arendt would make in her controversial essay on school integration in Little Rock, Arkansas – though social discriminations may prove inevitable, such discriminations, including those in the interest of conserving racial or cultural identity, can be distinguished from the sphere of public interaction and political commerce.[123]

In emphasizing the liberty of contract between a white seller and a black buyer in *Buchanan*, Storey focused judicial attention on freedom of consensual relations in the most persuasive form possible for the conservative justices of the Court. As a defense to the white seller's lawsuit for performance of the sales contract, the African American purchaser referred to a provision in the contract providing that he have a legal right to reside at the property in question, pointing out that the Louisville zoning ordinance made performing this term impossible. By design, this strategy uses the *Plessy* Court's shoe-on-the-other-foot reversal test to demonstrate an opposite conclusion. Just as Chesnutt's test case of two doctors being forcibly separated by Jim Crow law illustrated *Plessy*'s error, trading places in *Buchanan* revealed the curtailment of white freedom as well as black franchise.

Supporters of the Louisville statute countered, in an overtly Holmesean move, with the determinative consideration of custom: "The extent to which legislation may modify and restrict the uses of property consistently with the Constitution is not a question for pure abstract theory alone. Tradition and the habits of the community count for more than logic." Hoping for a *Plessy*-like ruling, the opposition cited the friction that would inevitably result from social commingling of the races. In a unanimous decision, the Court disagreed, finding that the statute violated the Fourteenth Amendment by interfering both with black Americans' right to reside where they please and the freedom of contract between white and black Americans. In regard to the argument that the white plaintiff represented by the NAACP did not have the requisite standing to complain of a restriction of black rights, the Court accepted Storey's contention that the plaintiff's right to sell his property was directly involved and necessarily impaired by the challenged ordinance. In sum, the ordinance offered the NAACP a beautiful opportunity to use liberty of contract to push for freedom of social mobility. Though the Court's opinion attempts to mute the fact that its ruling did indeed suggest that some forms of interracial social commerce were constitutionally protected, the briefs of the lawyers for both sides indicate that the case was centrally concerned with interracial social contact and mobility of the sort depicted by Chesnutt's portrait of Jim Crow train travel.[124]

Because the Court was far from ready to entertain a direct challenge to *Plessy*, Storey knew that to win he had to distinguish the facts of *Buchanan* from those of *Plessy* and *Berea College* (which upheld a state law mandating segregated education even for private institutions).[125] He accomplished this by arguing that the separate but equal doctrine announced in previous cases had not worked to exclude black Americans from either transportation or education. Real property, however, was another matter, being deemed at common law inherently unique and not fungible. Unlike a train car or a classroom (which could be mirror images of each other), "every parcel of land has qualities peculiar to itself."[126] The

organic irregularities of land rendered it, unlike objects of human manufacture, potentially desirable in a singular fashion so that no other will
quite do. Though quite conventional in terms of common law precedent, in the context of race relations where one of the express goals
of legal segregation in keeping the races apart corresponds to that of
anti-miscegenation statutes, Storey's argument about land's uniqueness
suggested an obvious parallel to the desirability of any individual as a
potential mate – both are singular, particular, not fungible. Both sides
recognized that miscegenation inevitably becomes an issue when one
urges liberty of contract as a bar to legislative restrictions on consensual
relations between the races.[127] Though in his briefs Storey distinguished
anti-miscegenation laws by urging that marriage is more a relation of
status than it is of contract ("Marriage is primarily a matter of status
and only incidentally a matter of contract"), in oral argument before
the Court, he revealed his disgust at the continuing influence of status
relations in the law of marriage and the racist interference of Jim Crow
with freedom of the marriage contract.[128]

Despite his attempt to distinguish the "social" issue of miscegenation,
in pairing liberty of contract with the ordinance's effect of "preventing
the better and more prosperous element of the colored inhabitants" of
Louisville "from obtaining residences in a better locality," Storey's attack is centrally concerned with the value of social mobility and freedom
of public intercourse. The ordinance was intended, says Storey, "to establish a Ghetto for the colored people of Louisville," confining "those
members of the colored race who are anxious to improve their condition
to undesirable quarters of the city." And, citing Bradley's opinion in the
Butchers' Union case, Storey points out that, in pursuit of a specious concern about racial conflict which may be addressed more directly by laws
against civil disorder, the ordinance unquestionably and impermissibly
infringes on the freedom of property owners to enter into contractual
relations with any ready, willing, and able buyer. In Storey's argument,
the constitutional evil of interfering with contractual freedom parallels
the connected evil of curtailing social intercourse and mobility. Both run
counter to the basic notion of consensual relations animating American
notions of freedom (e.g., the freedom of association guaranteed by the
First Amendment), in which relations are appropriately governed not by
race but by agreed upon notions of moral character and behavior:

No one outside of a court room would imagine for an instant that the pre-
dominant purpose of this ordinance was not to prevent the Negro citizens of

Louisville, however industrious, thrifty, and well-educated they might be, from approaching that condition vaguely described as "social equality." This is not a restriction laid upon a specified class of citizens because they are dirty, shiftless, or otherwise objectionable in their habits. It puts in one class every colored man, no matter how free he may be from all these objectionable qualities, simply because he is colored, and it puts in the other class every white man, even though he may be in every way an "undesirable citizen," simply because he is white.[129]

Storey contends, as do Chesnutt and DuBois, that social norms, such as industry, honesty, and diligence, constitute a race-neutral language of public intercourse that in this context is specifically tied to the contracts, the consensual arrangements, that people of different identities and backgrounds can make. Liberty of contract requires freedom of social mobility.

Defense counsel counters that race antipathy is human nature; hostility and revulsion are the inevitable reaction of whites to the "dread invasion" by blacks into their neighborhoods. This "consciousness of kind" makes it natural that members of both races would be more comfortable living "among their own." Repeatedly and at length, counsel for the defendant urge that this inherent racial antipathy makes interracial contract and contact unlikely and aberrant. Because of this inherent aspect of human nature, it is only in what the defense terms the "twilight zone" of interracial relations that the ordinance will actually cause any perceivable abridgement of freedom. Such rare abridgements of freedom, defense counsel argue, are justified by the fact that in certain circumstances nature trumps choice – freedom of association is and must be limited by nature: "the thing aimed at by all this [Jim Crow] legislation was not that of volition, but something deeper and more important than a matter of choice."[130]

The "twilight zone" of race relations is precisely the cosmopolitan ground where different identities blur together as day and night do at dusk – the site of mixture and intercourse touted by Douglass, DuBois, and others as the liberating, in-between place where the intrepid cross the boundaries of identity. While the figure of twilight intentionally diminishes the scope of this zone, making it sound diminutive and fleeting, it is more properly seen as the ubiquitous public sphere of commerce, travel, politics, and education. The *Plessy* court and the defense team in *Buchanan* err rather fantastically, as Justice Harlan and Charles Chesnutt understood, in "adopting the Southern fallacy" that the interactions in the public sphere, such as "riding in a railroad car or eating in an inn" are private, "social" matters.[131] For its defenders, Jim Crow law appropriately seeks to make this "twilight zone" a no-man's land, but Storey and Chesnutt use the rights claims of its already existing denizens (Miller and Burns, Buchanan and Warley) to challenge such legal proscriptions.

Expressly classing Storey and DuBois with Charles Sumner, counsel defending the Louisville statute argue that such higher law advocates have made the "romantic" error of thinking that the Constitution can incorporate changing notions of social equality.[132] In a fashion similar to the antebellum era's classification of the higher law argument as "transcendental," Jim Crow's defenders discern the genealogy of the higher law argument we have been tracing. The derisive "romantic" label aptly connects the efforts of Emerson, Sumner, Storey, DuBois, Chesnutt, and Douglass to remove the terms of identity from the higher law mix of conscience and consent properly grounding American citizenship and law.

Notes

INTRODUCTION

1 Edwin Corwin, *The "Higher Law" Background of American Constitutional Law* (Ithaca, NY: Cornell University Press, 1955), reprinted from the *Harvard Law Review*, 42 (1928, 1929): 149–85; 365–409. Corwin's essay covers the higher law philosophical and religious background to the Constitution. In a similar vein, though they do not focus on the higher law tradition *per se*, recent scholarly works by Sanford Levinson, David Richards, and Kenneth Karst have argued for the historic importance of a constitutional faith in the justness of American law to such revisions as the Civil War amendments. And political theorists as divergent as John Rawls, Robert Nozick, Alan Gewirth, and Jürgen Habermas have all sought to locate moral principles and a moral vantage point independent of particular laws and institutions so as to allow for an evaluation of those laws and institutions – the core project of higher law jurisprudence.

2 Earl Warren, *"All Men Are Created Equal"* (New York: Association of the Bar of the City of New York, 1970), pp. 13, 11.

3 Ivan Hannaford, *Race: The History of an Idea in the West* (Baltimore: Johns Hopkins University Press, 1996), pp. 8–9, 12, 21, 51.

4 Warren, *Equal*, p. 12. *Regents of the University of California v. Bakke*, 438 U.S. 265, 326–27, 387–95 (1978). Justifying affirmative action as a step toward equality of opportunity, Marshall's *Bakke* opinion centrally rests on a notion of an identity-neutral conception of equality as one of the legitimating goals of the American legal and constitutional system.

5 *Romer v. Evans*, 134 L.Ed 2d 855, 866, 868, 871, 878 (1996); *Dred Scott v. Sandford*, 19 How. 398, 410 (1857). Scalia's dissent makes a point of trying to transform the gay minority into a kind of politically dominant force by referring obliquely to their cultural authority, which authority is signaled by the powerful political support Hollywood tendered to the opponents of the Colorado amendment.

6 Ethan Bronner, *Battle for Justice: How the Bork Nomination Shook America* (New York: Doubleday, 1989), pp. 224–25, 275–76. Of course, many have argued for the salutary influence of such cultural norms on the course of American justice. Such argument lies behind and authorizes the current rediscovery

of the beneficial influence of literature on judges and lawyers in law and literature courses taught in law schools and in continuing education courses for bench and bar.

7 Henry David Thoreau, "Resistance to Civil Government," in *Walden and Civil Disobedience* (New York: Signet, 1960), p. 223.

8 Seyla Benhabib, *Democracy and Difference: Contesting the Boundaries of the Political* (Princeton: Princeton University Press, 1996), pp. 69–74; Stuart Hampshire, *Justice is Conflict* (Princeton: Princeton University Press, 2000), pp. 97–98.

9 Ralph Waldo Emerson, "Circles" in *The Selected Writings of Ralph Waldo Emerson*, ed. Brooks Atkinson (New York: Modern Library, 1950), pp. 285, 288–89; Frederick Douglass, "Pictures and Progress," *The Frederick Douglass Papers*, ed. John Blassingame, 5 vols. (New Haven: Yale University Press, 1982), III: 460; William James, *Pragmatism* (New York: World Publishing, 1969), p. 158.

10 John Dewey, "Freedom and Culture" (1939), in *The Later Works, 1923–53*, ed. JoAnn Boydston, 17 vols. (Carbondale: Southern Illinois University Press, 1986), XIII: 174; Hannah Arendt, *On Revolution* (New York, Penguin, 1963), pp. 126–27, 234–35.

11 See, e.g., David Hollinger, *Postethnic America: Beyond Multiculturalism* (New York: Basic Books, 1995); Martha C. Nussbaum, *For the Love of Country* (Boston: Beacon Press, 1996); Bruce Robbins and Phengh Cheah, *Cosmopolitics: Thinking and Feeling Beyond the Nation* (Minneapolis: University of Minnesota Press, 1998); Paul Gilroy, *Against Race: Imagining Political Culture Beyond the Color Line* (Cambridge, MA: Harvard University Press, 2000), pp. 6–7.

12 Though he tends to dismiss it as an "utopian irrelevancy," Rogers Smith's conception of a "trans-American nationalism" in its emphasis on inclusion and heterogeneity bears the influence of a cosmopolitan perspective. Rogers Smith, *Civic Ideals: Conflicting Visions of Citizenship in U.S. History* (New Haven: Yale University Press, 1997), pp. 472, 473 n. 3, 498 n. 66, 499–500.

13 Wai Chee Dimock, for instance, approaches law as foundationalist and literature as anti-foundationalist. This perspective is inadequate to account for those thinkers, such as Emerson and Douglass, who refuse the dichotomy. *Residues of Justice: Literature, Law, Philosophy* (Berkeley: University of California Press, 1996), pp. 1–10.

14 Saidiya V. Hartman, *Scenes of Subjection: Terror, Slavery, and Self-Making in Nineteenth-Century America* (New York: Oxford University Press, 1997), pp. 5, 6, 13.

15 Matthew Frye Jacobson, *Whiteness of a Different Color: European Immigrants and the Alchemy of Race* (Cambridge, MA: Harvard University Press, 1998), p. 12.

1 HIGHER LAW IN THE 1850S

1 Frederick Bancroft, *The Life of William H. Seward* (New York: Harper, 1900), pp. 251–52; Glyndon Van Deusen, *William Henry Seward: Lincoln's Secretary of State* (New York: Oxford University Press, 1967), p. 122; Merrill D. Peterson,

The Great Triumvirate: Webster, Clay, and Calhoun (New York: Oxford University Press, 1987), p. 467; John M. Taylor, *William Henry Seward: Lincoln's Right Hand Man* (Washington: Brassley's, 1991), pp. 80–81, 84–85.

2 *The Works of William H. Seward*, ed. George E. Baker, 5 vols. (New York: Redfield Press, 1853), I: 51–93.

3 See, below, p. 47.

4 *Works of William H. Seward*, I: 65; John C. Calhoun, "Speech on the Admission of California – and the General State of the Union," in *Union and Liberty: the Political Philosophy of John C. Calhoun*, ed. Ross M. Lence (Indianapolis, IN: Liberty Press, 1992), p. 590; Henry Clay, *Speech of the Hon. Henry Clay, of Kentucky, on taking up his Compromise Resolutions on the Subject of Slavery* (New York: Stringer & Townsend, 1850), pp. 21–22; Daniel Webster, "The Constitution and the Union," in *The Papers of Daniel Webster: Speeches and Formal Writings*, ed. Charles M. Wiltse, 2 vols. (Hanover, NH: University Press of New England, 1988), II: 515.

5 *The Republic*, March 15, 1850, quoted in the New York *Tribune*, March 19, 1850; as Albert Von Frank notes, higher law argument was often termed transcendentalist by those hostile to such arguments. Albert Von Frank, *The Anthony Burns Case* (Cambridge, MA: Harvard University Press, 1998), p. 100.

6 New York *Tribune*, March 20, 1850; Richmond *Enquirer*, March 27, 1857; "Abolition vs. Christianity and the Union," *The United States Magazine and Democratic Review*, 27 (July 1850): 13.

7 *Works of William H. Seward*, I: 74–75.

8 "Abolition vs. Christianity and the Union," *Democratic Review*, p. 11. A similar attack on Seward's invocation of higher law from the Southern point of view is expressed in "The Doctrine of 'Higher Law,'" *Southern Literary Messenger*, 17 (March 1851): 130–42.

9 Drawn from an account of the meeting of the Anti-Slavery Society in Syracuse, New York, May, 1851, Douglass's comments offer a glimpse of the way in which the international aspect of the antislavery movement and an appreciation of the racial and ethnic diversity of the American people pointed toward a cosmopolitan conception of justice and citizenship. At the same meeting, Edmund Quincy, a Boston lawyer, lauded the influence of "foreigners" on American culture and law:

> What would our country have been without "foreigners"? What were the Pilgrim Fathers but "foreigners and interlopers?" . . . For 200 years foreigners have been coming to these shores, and by their direct influence have changed the character and laws of the country. They come by the thousands now, and no one is alarmed. Nothing is said for years on years, till one foreigner appeared to point out the plague-spot of Slavery – a plague-spot which she seeks to cover with all the skill of the Pulpit and the Press. (New York *Tribune*, May 10, 1851.)

10 See below, p. 256, n. 67.

11 *Minutes of the Fifth Annual Convention for the Improvement of the Free People of Colour in the United States, Held by Adjournments, in the Wesley Church, Philadelphia, from*

the First to the Fifth of June, Inclusive, 1835 (Phliadelphia: William P. Gibbons, 1835), p. 26.

12 *Proceedings of the Colored National Convention, Held in Franklin Hall, Sixth Street, Below Arch, Philadelphia, October 16th, 17th and 18th, 1855* (Salem, NJ: National Standard Office, 1856), pp. 30–33.

13 New York *Tribune*, March 19, 1850.

14 Peterson, *The Great Triumvirate*, p. 467; William Furness, a friend of Ralph Waldo Emerson, wrote to Webster urging him to take the ethical high ground in the debate on the issue of fugitive slaves and in effect draw a moral line that the North would not countenance or aid the South in crossing: "There are thousands & tens of thousands in the land thirsting for the words which you alone can speak, & whom those words would crystallize into adamant to resist & break down the slave power. Freedom of thought & speech cannot get into full play without commotion, but it is worth the cost." *The Papers of Daniel Webster: Correspondence*, eds. Charles M. Wiltse and Michael J. Birkner, 7 vols. (Hanover, NH: University Press of New England, 1986) VII: 17.

15 Emerson, "WO Liberty," *The Journals and Miscellaneous Notebooks of Ralph Waldo Emerson*, ed. William H. Gilman *et al.*, 16 vols. (Cambridge, MA: Harvard University Press, 1960–82), XIV: 373–430; Spofford, *The Higher Law Tried by Reason and Authority* (New York: S.W. Benedict, 1851); Hosmer, *The Higher Law in its Relations to Civil Government* (Auburn: Derby & Miller, 1852). For example, the way in which the Fugitive Slave Law summoned Stowe's narrative response was appreciated by John Greenleaf Whittier, the Quaker poet and antislavery activist, who offered "[t]hanks for the Fugitive Slave Law! ... for it gave occasion for 'Uncle Tom's Cabin!'" Thomas Gossett, *Uncle Tom's Cabin and American Culture* (Dallas, TX: Southern Methodist University Press, 1985), p. 165.

16 *Works of William H. Seward* I: 65; New York *Tribune*, March 9, 1850.

17 Henry David Thoreau, "Slavery in Massachusetts" (1854), in *Miscellanies* (Boston: Houghton, Mifflin, 1863), p. 229; Theodore Parker, "The Function of Conscience" (1850), in *The Slave Power* (New York: Arno, 1969), p. 340.

18 *National Era*, August 1, 1850.

19 "The Constitution and its Defects," *North American Review*, 99 (1864): 119–21.

20 Rogers Smith, *Civic Ideals: Conflicting Visions of Citizenship in U.S. History* (New Haven: Yale University Press, 1997), pp. 1–6.

21 Morton J. Horwitz, *The Transformation of American Law: 1780–1860* (Cambridge, MA: Harvard University Press, 1977), p. 21.

22 Moorfield Storey and Marcial L. Lichauco, *The Conquest of the Philippines by the United States, 1898–1925* (Freeport, NY: Books for Libraries, 1971), p. v; Moorfield Storey, *Abraham Lincoln: An Address Delivered at the Shawmut Congregational Church in Boston on February 14, 1909* (Boston: Geo. H. Ellis, 1909), p. 6. Like Storey, Charles Chesnutt was fond of this passage from Lincoln's oratory, quoting it in his biography of Frederick Douglass. Charles Chesnutt, *Frederick Douglass* (Boston: Small, Maynard, 1899), p. 102.

23 Gordon Wood, *The Creation of the American Republic, 1776–1787* (Chapel Hill: University of North Carolina Press, 1969), pp. 53, 118, 119–20. In the utopianist or millennialist aspects of American republicanism, one can see the influence of Puritan forebears and covenant theology, an influence that created an intersection of civic morality and Christian ethics unlike the Continental tradition of Machiavellian republicanism. Bernard Bailyn, *The Ideological Origins of the American Revolution* (Cambridge, MA: Harvard University Press, 1967), pp. 32–33, 140; J.G.A. Pocock, *The Machiavellian Moment: Florentine Political Thought and the Atlantic Republican Tradition* (Princeton: Princeton University Press, 1975), pp. 511–13; Ernest Tuveson, *Redeemer Nation: The Idea of America's Millennial Role* (Chicago: University of Chicago Press, 1968), pp. 92–94.

24 Wood, *Creation of the American Republic*, p. 119.

25 Bernard Bailyn, ed., *Pamphlets of the American Revolution, 1750–1776* (Cambridge, MA: Harvard University Press, 1965), p. 472; Wood, *Creation of the American Republic*, p. 120.

26 Bailyn, *Pamphlets*, pp. 423, 425, 426; Wood, *Creation of the American Republic*, p. 66.

27 Garry Wills, *Inventing America: Jefferson's Declaration of Independence* (New York: Vintage, 1979), p. 301. Bailyn, *Ideological Origins of the American Revolution*, p. 66; Edmund S. Morgan, *American Slavery, American Freedom: The Ordeal of Colonial Virginia* (New York: Norton, 1975), pp. 5–6; Smith, *Civic Ideals*, pp. 72–77. Otis, *Rights of British Colonies*, in Bailyn, *Pamphlets*, p. 441. Of course, as Gordon Wood points out, even as they protested that they were only returning to a shared British past, the revolutionary generation was rushing to something new, incorporating principles of self-rule that could rewrite that history. Wood, *Creation of the American Republic*, pp. 12–14.

28 For Shaftesbury, Locke's dismissal of innate moral ideas was tantamount to a rejection of virtue. Shaftesbury contended, instead, that the heart is the seat of an innate moral sense that determines right from wrong as the visual sense determines beauty from ugliness. Through the benevolent power of sympathy or fellow feeling enabling us to experience another person's pleasure or pain, we can perceive virtue and undertake a virtuous course of action. David Richards, *Foundations of American Constitutionalism* (New York: Oxford University Press, 1989), pp. 83–87; Stephen Buckle, *Natural Law and the Theory of Property: Grotius to Hume* (Oxford: Clarendon Press, 1991), pp. 197–214; Third Earl of Shaftesbury (Anthony Ashley Cooper), *An Inquiry Concerning Virtue or Merit*, in *British Moralists*, ed. L.A. Selby-Bigge, 2 vols. (New York: Dover, 1965), I: 1–67. Francis Hutcheson, *Inquiry Concerning the Original of Our Ideas of Virtue or Moral Good*, in *British Moralists*, I: 68–177. Both Hutcheson and Shaftesbury argued against positivist accounts of natural law as legitimated by the command of a divine sovereign who rewards compliance and punishes disobedience. Shaftesbury, *Inquiry Concerning Virtue*, pp. 15–16, 23–24; Hutcheson, *Inquiry*, pp. 71–72, 90–92. Adam Smith and David Hume extend the moral sense concept by characterizing sympathy

as an activity of the imagination. Imagination enables us to go beyond our own person and understand "another man's suffering." Smith, *Theory of Moral Sentiments*, ed. D.D. Raphael and A.L. Macfie (New York: Oxford University Press, 1976), pp. 316–26; David Hume, *A Treatise of Human Nature* (Oxford: Clarendon Press, 1975), p. 581.

29 *The Portable Thomas Jefferson*, ed. Merrill D. Peterson (New York: Penguin, 1975), p. 542; Wood, *Creation of the American Republic*, p. 69; Richard Sennett, *The Fall of Public Man* (London: Faber, 1986), p. 91. James Wilson, one of the architects of the Constitution, contended that, unlike English law, which was validated by parliamentary power, American law, including the Constitution, was grounded in and legitimated by the citizenry's benevolent feelings. Richards, *Foundations*, pp. 87–89, 138–39.

30 As Jefferson posed the case in his famous letter to Peter Carr, August 10, 1787: "State a moral case to the ploughman and a professor. The former will decide it as well, and often better than the latter, because he has not been led astray by artificial rules." *Portable Jefferson*, p. 425. J.G.A. Pocock points out that the republicans viewed "specialization" as "prime cause of corruption; only the citizen as amateur, propertied, independent, and willing to perform in his own person all the functions essential to the polis, could be said to practice virtue or live in a city where justice was truly distributed." *Machiavellian Moment*, p. 499.

31 Robert Ferguson, *Law and Letters in American Culture* (Cambridge, MA: Harvard University Press, 1984), p. 10.

32 David Hume, *A Treatise of Human Nature* (Oxford: Clarendon Press, 1975), p. 369. For an account of the flaw that resemblance introduces into Stowe's antislavery fiction, see chapter two below.

33 Hume, *Treatise of Human Nature*, pp. 490, 491, 526.

34 *Ibid.*, pp. 513, 533, 579–80.

35 Wood, *Creation of the American Republic*, pp. 562, 606–15; Pocock, *Machiavellian Moment*, pp. 526–27.

36 For example, abolitionist rhetoric juxtaposing the corruption and luxury of the slaveholding class with the civic virtue of the free-soil yeoman farmer (think here of the moral debility of Marie St. Clare in *Uncle Tom's Cabin* in contrast with the hearty morality of the hardworking Rachel Halliday) invokes the republican tradition as well as the liberal emphasis on inalienable individual rights to self-ownership and the fruits of one's labor.

37 Jack N. Rakove, *Original Meanings: Politics and Ideas in the Making of the Constitution* (New York: Knopf, 1996), p. 290; Bailyn, *Ideological Origins of the American Revolution*, pp. 56–57; Harriet Beecher Stowe, *Uncle Tom's Cabin or, Life Among the Lowly* (New York: Norton, 1994), p. 293.

38 [John Dickinson], *An Address to the Committee of Correspondence in Barbados . . .* (Philadelphia, 1766), in *The Writings of John Dickinson*, ed. Paul L. Ford (Philadelphia: Historical Society of Pennsylvania, 1895), p. 262.

39 Though Garry Wills argues that Locke's influence has been vastly overstated at the cost of obscuring other important influences, such as the

moral sense philosophy of the Scottish Enlightenment, as Rogers Smith points out, "a close comparison of the Declaration of Independence and Locke's discussion of valid rebellions, which Wills never undertakes, reveals that Jefferson's contentions met all of Locke's basic criteria and echoed his language." Smith, *Civic Ideals*, p. 526, n. 34.

40 John Locke, *Two Treatises of Government* (Cambridge: Cambridge University Press, 1960), pp. 269–78, 330–33; Bailyn, *Ideological Origins of the American Revolution*, pp. 58–59. For insightful analyses of Locke's place in natural rights theory, one may turn to Richard Tuck, *Natural Rights Theories: Their Origin and Development* (Cambridge: Cambridge University Press, 1979); A. John Simmons, *The Lockean Theory of Rights* (Princeton: Princeton University Press, 1992); Michael P. Zuckert, *Natural Rights and the New Republicanism* (Princeton: Princeton University Press, 1994); and Leo Strauss, *Natural Right and History* (Chicago: University of Chicago, 1953).

41 Thomas Paine, *Common Sense, The Rights of Man, and Other Essential Writings of Thomas Paine* (New York: Meridian, 1969), p. 25; Wood, *Creation of the American Republic*, pp. 282–91, 341–43, 601–02.

42 Tuck, *Natural Rights*, p. 3; Buckle, *Natural Law*, pp. 48–52, 82–83.

43 Locke, *Two Treatises*, p. 142; Rakove, *Original Meanings*, p. 292; Bailyn, *Ideological Origins of the American Revolution*, pp. 77–78; Wood, *Creation of the American Republic*, pp. 292–94, 260–61, 456.

44 Rakove, *Original Meanings*, pp. 289–90; Wood, *Creation of the American Republic*, pp. 453–63, 292, 264; Edward S. Corwin, *The "Higher Law" Background of American Constitutional Law* (Ithaca, NY: Cornell University Press, 1955), pp. 4–5. In *The Federalist*, number 78, Hamilton argues that judicial review protects the people by removing exposition of the nation's fundamental law from the hands of professional (and, hence, interested) politicians and putting it in the hands of an independent judiciary with life tenure. James Madison, Alexander Hamilton, and John Jay, *The Federalist Papers* (New York: Penguin, 1987), pp. 440–42.

45 *Marbury v. Madison*, 1 Cranch. 137, 177–78 (1803). Out of fear of governmental incursions, Americans insisted on recording fundamental principles in a written Constitution but simultaneously resisted the notion that these principles were exhaustively defined and enumerated in that Constitution, "retaining Otis's conviction that 'righteousness should be the basis of law.'" Wood, *Creation of the American Republic*, pp. 295, 262–65; Bailyn, *Ideological Origins of the American Revolution*, pp. 101–04.

46 Smith, *Civic Ideals*, pp. 72–77; Reginald Horsman, *Race and Manifest Destiny* (Cambridge, MA: Harvard University Press, 1981), p. 22; Corwin, *Higher Law*, pp. 24–25; *Portable Jefferson*, p. 577.

47 Paine, *Common Sense*, pp. 66, 49, 39; J. Hector St. John de Crèvecoeur, *Letters to An American Farmer* (New York: Fox Duffle, 1904), p. 51.

48 Otis, *Rights of the British Colonists*, in Bailyn, *Pamphlets*, p. 435; Horsman, *Race and Manifest Destiny*, pp. 23–24.

49 Smith, *Civic Ideals*, p. 73; Jonathan Elliot, ed., *The Debates in the Several State Conventions on the Adoption of the Federal Constitution*, 5 vols. (Philadelphia: Lippincott, 1836), II: 434.

50 St. Thomas Aquinas, *Summa Theologica* (New York: Benziger, 1947–48), Ia, IIae, q. 90, a. 4, q. 91, a. 1 & 2.

51 Richard Niebuhr, *The Kingdom of God in America* (Hamden, CT: Shoe String Press, 1956), p. 55; Lewis Perry, *Radical Abolitionism; Anarchy and the Government of God in Antislavery Thought* (Ithaca, CT: Cornell University Press, 1973), p. 34. One of the most famous sermons from the revolutionary era, Samuel Sherwood's "Scriptural Instructions to Civil Rulers" (1774), offers a defense of the Revolution from the pulpit that could have been taken directly from the political writings of the era:

> Subjects have rights, privileges and properties; and are countenanced and supported by the law of nature, the laws of society, and the law of God; in demanding full protection of justice, from their rulers. And when rulers refuse these, and will not comply with such a reasonable and equitable demand from the subject; the society is dissolved. [W]hen such a melancholy event takes place, that a civil society is dissolved, and men return to a state of nature; they have the same liberty they at first had, to form themselves into society again, in what form, and on what terms they please. (Ellis Sandoz, ed., *Political Sermons of the American Founding Era* (Indianapolis: Liberty Fund, 1990), pp. 383, 388.)

52 *Ibid.*, p. 143; Ronald Dworkin, *Taking Rights Seriously* (Cambridge, MA: Harvard University Press, 1977), p. 134.

53 John Adams, "A Dissertation on the Canon and Feudal Law" (1765), in *The American Intellectual Tradition*, ed. David Hollinger and Charles Capper, 2 vols. (New York: Oxford University Press, 1997), I: 108; Ernest Tuveson, *Redeemer Nation*, pp. 7–11, 24.

54 Perry, *Radical Abolitionism*, pp. 18, 52, 53; Bertram Wyatt-Brown, *Lewis Tappan and the Evangelical War against Slavery* (Cleveland, OH : Case Western Reserve University, 1969), pp. 270–71.

55 Eric Foner, *Free Soil, Free Labor, Free Men: The Ideology Of The Republican Party Before The Civil War* (New York: Oxford University Press, 1970), p. 302.

56 George Bancroft, *History of the United States of America, From The Discovery Of The Continent* 10 vols. (New York: D. Appleton, 1924), II: 269; Francis Lieber, *On Civil Liberty and Self-Government* (Philadelphia: J.B. Lippincott, 1901), pp. 204–05, 208–09.

57 Letter from Jefferson to John Adams, October 28, 1813, in *Portable Jefferson*, pp. 558–59. One cannot read this passage without a keen sense of the incipient romanticism of Jefferson's notion of growth and development, figured, tellingly, in the clothes metaphor Thomas Carlyle would make central to *Sartor Resartus* (1833–34).

58 Though slavery constituted the icon of all that their political theory abhorred, the founders uneasily tolerated it in their midst. Bailyn, *Ideological Origins of the American Revolution*, pp. 232–46. While apt, Edmund Morgan's description of the material importance of slave labor and the

luxury it produced to the founders' republican and rights conceptions does not resolve the theoretical contradiction between their universalist aspirations and their political practice. Racial difference, as Morgan notes in passing, was of critical importance to the founders' ability to defer this contradiction. Morgan, *American Slavery*, pp. 5–6, 381–87.

59 Adam Smith, *Theory of Moral Sentiments* (Indianapolis, IN: Liberty Fund, 1982), pp. 25, 340–41, 140–41, 14.

60 Paine, *Common Sense*, pp. 39–40.

61 Madison, Hamilton, and Jay, *Federalist Papers*, p. 123.

62 *Ibid.*, p. 127. Gordon Wood finds the contrast of localism and cosmopolitanism the framers had in mind usefully illustrated by a pamphlet written by William Beers of Connecticut in 1791. Though Beers was not writing to justify the Constitution, "his insight into the workings of American politics was precisely that of the Federalists of 1787." According to Beers the independent and worthy members of the electorate were dispersed throughout the larger political community. In localities, they were frequently outnumbered by their lesser opponents. The expanding power of the larger political unit would temper the power of faction and demagogic appeals to local prejudice. Political success at this broader, more cosmopolitan level would be more likely founded upon "those points of character which alone can entitle one to universal confidence." Wood, *Creation of the American Republic*, pp. 511–12.

63 Madison, Hamilton, and Jay, *Federalist Papers*, p. 91.

64 Expressly connecting the higher law justification of the Constitution, "Justice is the end of government," to the protection of minorities by a government representing a plurality of interests and backgrounds, Madison asserts in *The Federalist*, number 51, that

> In a free government the security for civil rights must be the same as that for religious rights. It consists in the one case in the multiplicity of interests, and in the other in the multiplicity of sects. The degree of security in both cases will depend on the number of interests and sects; and this may be presumed to depend on the extent of country and number of people comprehended under the same government. (Madison, Hamilton, and Jay, *Federalist Papers*, pp. 321–22.)

65 Francis Wayland, *The Elements of Moral Science* (Boston: Gould and Lincoln, 1854), pp. 180, 189, 197, 208, 219; Lydia Maria Child, *An Appeal in Favor of That Class of Americans Called Africans* (Amherst: University of Massachusetts Press, 1996), pp. xlvi–vii; William Ellery Channing, *Slavery* (New York: Arno, 1969), p. 31.

66 Larry E. Tise, *Proslavery: A History of the Defense of Slavery in America, 1701–1840* (Athens: University of Georgia Press, 1987), p. 237. It should be noted that many scholars, such as Tise, class Channing and Emerson as part of the anti-abolitionist, conservative movement. This vantage is gained primarily by looking at the objections raised and antipathies felt by such thinkers toward Garrisonian abolitionism, which they deemed excessive. See, Tise,

Proslavery, p. 267. However, Tise's judgment neither takes Emerson's antislavery writings into account nor considers the fact that the politically oriented higher law arguments of Sumner, Emerson, and others proved far more successful than Garrison's Christian anarchism in rewriting the Constitution.

67 J.R. Pole, *The Pursuit of Equality in American History* (Berkeley: University of California Press, 1993), pp. 51–54.

68 Benjamin Blake Minor, *The Southern Literary Messenger: 1834–1864* (New York: Neale Publishing, 1905), p. 22; James P. Holcombe, "Is Slavery Consistent with Natural Law," *The Southern Literary Messenger*, 27 (December 1858): 401–21. Many Southerners came to scorn the egalitarian themes of the Declaration of Independence as Jefferson's French sentimentality or his French atheism. See, e.g., Governor Hammond, "Morals of Slavery," *The Pro-Slavery Argument* (New York: Negro Universities Press, 1968), p. 250 and F.A. Ross, *Slavery Ordained of God* (Philadelphia: J.B. Lippincott, 1857), p. 105.

69 As Eugene Genovese has observed, the elimination of abolitionism in the South was attended by an increasing emphasis on humane treatment of slaves as evidence of the benign nature of the institution, reflecting a compulsion to conform slavery to the higher law imperative that such institutions be just. Genovese, *Roll, Jordan, Roll: The World the Slaves Made* (New York: Vintage, 1974), p. 51.

70 Thomas Dew, *An Essay on Slavery* (Richmond, VA: J.W. Randolph, 1849), pp. 7, 24.

71 Morton J. Horwitz, *The Transformation of American Law: 1780–1860* (Cambridge, MA: Harvard University Press, 1977), p. 30.

72 *Proceedings and Debates in the Virginia State Convention of 1829–1830* (Richmond, 1830), quoted in Carl Becker, *The Declaration of Independence: A Study in the History of Political Ideas* (New York: Vintage, 1958), p. 235; Thomas Dixon, Jr., *The Clansman: An Historical Romance of the Ku Klux Klan* (Lexington: University of Kentucky Press, 1970), p. 46.

73 Perry Miller, *The Life of the Mind in America* (San Diego, CA: Harcourt Brace Jovanovich, 1965), pp. 104, 102; Robert Cover, *Justice Accused: Antislavery and the Judicial Process* (New Haven: Yale University Press, 1975), pp. 197–259.

74 *The Antelope*, 23 U.S. (10 Wheat.) 66, 116, 120 (1825); *United States v. Amistad*, 40 U.S. (15 Pet.) 518, 593 (1841); *Prigg v. Pennsylvania*, 41 U.S. (16 Pet.) 539 (1842). Though his holding overtly avoids such sentiments, one can infer Story's higher law sympathies in the way his allocation of *exclusive* authority over slave recapture to the federal government permitted Northern states to refuse to aid slave catchers, which, given the dearth of federal officials in most regions, meant that many fugitives would never be taken. Story's antislavery views and desire to see a correspondence between moral law and positive law were clearly expressed early in his judicial career in the lower court case *La Jeune Eugénie*, 26 F. Cas. (No. 15, 551) 832, 845, 846

(C.C.D. Mass., 1822). In *Prigg*, Chief Justice Taney vehemently objected that Story's view of the exclusive authority of the federal government over the recapture of fugitive slaves and the inaction on the part of state governments permitted thereby violated the bargain struck in the Constitution, which is a kind of partnership contract, binding all of the states to aid in the protection of the slaveholder's property rights. 41 U.S. 539, 627–28.

75 *Jones v. Van Zandt*, 46 U.S. (5 How.) 215, 230 (1847). Salmon Chase would later proudly claim that his client had been the basis for Stowe's portrait of John Van Trompe, an ex-slaveholder who aids Eliza Harris's escape in *Uncle Tom's Cabin*. *The Salmon P. Chase Papers*, ed. John Niven, 5 vols. (Kent, OH: Kent State University Press, 1993), 1: 166.

76 Thomas Wortham, ed., *James Russell Lowell's The Biglow Papers* (DeKalb: Northern Illinois Press, 1977), p. 95; John Greenleaf Whittier, *The Complete Poetical Works of John Greenleaf Whittier* (Boston: Houghton Mifflin, 1894), pp. 186–87; Ralph Waldo Emerson, *The Journals and Miscellaneous Notebooks of Ralph Waldo Emerson*, ed. Alfred R. Ferguson and Ralph H. Orth, 16 vols. (Cambridge, MA: Harvard University Press, 1971), IX: 409; Harriet Beecher Stowe, *The Key To Uncle Tom's Cabin* (New York: Arno, 1969), p. 148; Child, *Appeal*, pp. 207, 36–71, 94.

77 *Calder v. Bull*, 3 U.S. (3 Dall.) 386, 387–88, 399–400 (1798).

78 John E. Nowak, Ronald D. Rotunda, and J. Nelson Young, *Constitutional Law* (St. Paul, MN: West, 1983), pp. 425–43. This is not to say that freedom of contract was an absolute right in the court's view or to overestimate the persuasive power of higher law principles in contract cases.

79 *Dartmouth College v. Woodward*, 17 U.S. (4 Wheat.) 518, 644–48, 643, 713, 707 (1819).

80 *Ibid.*, 17 U.S. 518, 607, 587, 589.

81 Webster's peroration is not included in the Supreme Court reports. These notes of the conclusion to Webster's successful argument were taken by Chauncey A. Goodrich, a professor at Yale and a spectator in the court. Goodrich's impressions are generally corroborated by Justice Story's account of the event. Robert Remini, *Daniel Webster: The Man and his Time* (New York: Norton, 1997), pp. 155–57.

82 *Ibid.*, p. 157, n. 84.

83 Readers will note that Story's recognition that on some level Webster was giving a performance is implied by the comment that Webster clenched his hands "without a *seeming* consciousness of the act." For Story, the success of Webster's performance depended not on some mythic (and more recent) notion of spontaneity and immediacy but on the way Webster touched the commonly understood and shared springs of affect, making the right allusion and the right gesture to accompany that allusion.

84 While Webster's speech on March 7, 1850 endorsing the Fugitive Slave Law received abundant praise (e.g., the *National Intelligencer* declared that it added "fresh luster to the fame of the great orator, and gave fresh proofs of his truly

national and patriotic spirit"), it also provoked a chorus of castigation made more bitter by the sense that Webster had betrayed the ideals he once so nobly embodied. *National Intelligencer*, March 9, 1850. In a curiously passive figuration of Webster, Wendell Phillips characterized Webster's failure as a kind of victimization of Godlike Daniel by an evil Constitution: "Who can blame us for detesting that Moloch Constitution to which the fair face of our statesman is sacrificed?" And many, like Theodore Parker, assigned Webster's higher law apostasy to his desire for the Presidency. Parker called him a traitor: "I know of no deed in American history, done by a son of New England, to which I can compare this but the act of Benedict Arnold." Wendell Phillips, *A Review of Webster's Speech on Slavery* (Boston: American Antislavery Society, 1850), p. 30; Theodore Parker, *Speech of Theodore Parker delivered in The Old Cradle of Liberty* (Boston: American Antislavery Society, 1850), p. 35. At a rally on March 25, 1850 in Faneuil Hall, Samuel Ringgold Ward, a prominent black abolitionist, termed Webster "a Daniel who has deserted the cause of freedom."

85 Spofford, *Higher Law*, pp. 6, 5, 7, 8, 12.

86 *Ibid.*, pp. 12, 14, 24, 25–27, 29.

87 *Ibid.*, pp. 31–32.

88 *Ibid.*, pp. 37, 18. Spofford's acceptance of mutability in the quest for justice anticipates William James's conception of how the idiom of justice changes over time: "Given previous law and a novel case, and the judge will twist them into fresh law . . . Previous truth; fresh facts: – and our mind finds a new truth." James, *Pragmatism* (New York: Meridian, 1969), p. 158. Certainty or fixity of principle is an illusion in law as it is in life, as Oliver Wendell Holmes, Jr., points out. Holmes, "The Path of the Law," *Harvard Law Review*, 10 (1897): 457.

89 Harvey Wish, *George Fitzhugh, Propagandist of the Old South* (Baton Rouge: Louisiana State University Press, 1943), pp. 1–13, 343–44.

90 Boston *Liberator*, March 13, 1857, quoted in Wish, *Fitzhugh*, pp. 126–27.

91 Genovese, *Roll, Jordan, Roll*, pp. 85–86, 504–05; C. Vann Woodward, "Introduction," George Fitzhugh, *Cannibals All!, or Slaves Without Masters* (Cambridge, MA: Belknap Press of Harvard University Press, 1988), pp. ix, xxviii.

92 George Fitzhugh, "The Conservative Principle; or, Social Evils and their Remedies," *De Bow's Review*, 22 (1857): 420–21, 424, 427–28.

93 George Fitzhugh, "The Politics and Economics of Aristotle and Mr. Calhoun," *De Bow's Review*, 23 (1857): 169–70; "Southern Thought – Its New and Important Manifestations," *De Bow's Review*, 23 (1857): 347.

94 Fitzhugh, *Cannibals*, p. 134; "The Conservative Principle," pp. 420–21.

95 Fitzhugh's comments, published within months of the *Dred Scott* decision, offer a prophetic justification for holding the line on slavery: "A social revolution certainly impends throughout free society, and that revolution, directed at first against negro slavery, now proposes to destroy all religion, all government, and all private property, because the principle

and practice of slavery are found to exist in them, and in all other exist-ing human institutions." George Fitzhugh, "The Conservative Principle," pp. 421, 422.

96 In *Dred Scott v. Sandford*, 60 U.S. (19 How.) 393, 410 (1857), Justice Taney is not swayed by changes in public opinion on the issue of slavery, commenting that any other result would "make [the Court] the mere reflex of popular opinion or passion of the day." Similarly, in *Romer v. Evans*, 134 L.Ed 2d 855, 871 (1996), Justice Scalia rebukes those "who think that the Constitution changes to suit current fashions." Public opinion is permitted to influence law in the conservative views of Fitzhugh, Taney, and Scalia by way of a distinction between bad public opinion (mere fashion) and good public opinion (tradition). That is to say, they acknowledge the determinative force of public opinion even as they seek to evade some of its less palatable effects. For example, see Fitzhugh's view of the favorable effect of "public opinion" on the conduct of the "father" as "the universal and natural head and despot of the family." Fitzhugh, "The Politics and Economics of Aristotle and Mr. Calhoun," p. 170.

97 Fitzhugh, *Sociology for the South; or the Failure of Free Society* (Richmond, VA: A. Morris, 1854), pp. 25–26, 89; *Cannibals*, pp. 243, 218–219, 134–35.

98 Fitzhugh, "The Conservative Principle," pp. 427, 457.

99 John C. Calhoun, "Speech on the Admission of California, pp. 571–601; Henry Clay, *Speech of the Hon. Henry Clay*; Daniel Webster, "The Constitution and the Union," in *The Papers of Daniel Webster: Speeches and Formal Writings*, II: 513–51; *The Works of William H. Seward*, I: 51–93.

Dubbed the "Great Triumvirate," Clay, Calhoun, and Webster domi-nated American politics in the decades leading to the slavery crisis in the 1850s. Clay's career as leader of the Whig party included five unsuccessful bids for the Presidency, a term as Secretary of State under John Quincy Adams, and holding the position of Speaker of the House longer than any-one else in the nineteenth century. His moniker, "the Great Compromiser," was based on his role in formulating three landmark sectional compro-mises: the Missouri Compromise of 1820, the Tariff Compromise of 1833, and the Compromise of 1850. Clay was an early and influential advocate of colonization of free blacks. It was a measure of Clay's success in hit-ting the ideal middle ground, politically and culturally, that radicals North and South condemned his compromise plan. Calhoun's illustrious politi-cal career included his years as a U.S. Representative and Senator from South Carolina, and his terms as Secretary of War, Vice President, and Secretary of State. In the years leading to the Compromise of 1850, as Senator from South Carolina, Calhoun warmed to the role of the South's best defender against the growing antislavery feeling of the North. Web-ster served as congressional representative from New Hampshire, Senator from Massachusetts, and as Secretary of State. As important as his political career was, his career as a lawyer was in many ways its equal. The highest paid lawyer of his time, Webster successfully argued before the Supreme

Court a number of landmark cases, including *Dartmouth College, McCulloch v. Maryland*, and *Gibbons v. Ogden*. The holdings of the Court in these cases strengthened the central government at the expense of state governments. Peterson, *The Great Triumvirate*, pp. 1–6, 257, 458, 460.

100 Clay, "Speech," pp. 22, 32.

101 Calhoun, "Speech," pp. 582, 583, 586–88.

102 Webster, "The Constitution and the Union," p. 547.

103 Webster, "Reply to Hayne," in *Papers of Daniel Webster: Speeches and Formal Writings*, I: 325.

104 Quoted in Paul D. Erickson, *The Poetry of Events: Daniel Webster's Rhetoric of the Constitution and Union* (New York: New York University Press, 1986), pp. 53, 71, 183.

105 Webster, "The Constitution and the Union," p. 541. In his reply to William Furness, a friend of Emerson's who had urged Webster to oppose the Fugitive Slave Law, Webster said that he had condemned slavery from his earliest youth, abjuring defense of the institution on the basis of racial difference: "I have ever said that if the black race is weaker, that is reason against, not for, its subjugation & oppression." But Webster holds that Christian suasion, not political opposition, will effectively work to end slavery. *The Papers of Daniel Webster: Correspondence*, VII: 11.

106 *Works of William H. Seward*, I: 51–52.

107 Samuel Fleischacker, *The Ethics of Culture* (Ithaca, NY: Cornell University Press, 1994), pp. 120–21, 209–11.

108 Sounding a very Herderian note, DuBois writes in "The Conservation of Races" that each race "in its own way" develops "for civilization its particular message, its particular ideal, which shall help to guide the world nearer and nearer that perfection of human life for which we all long." DuBois, "The Conservation of Races," in *The American Negro Academy, Occasional Papers* (Washington, D.C.: The American Negro Academy, 1897), pp. 9, 10. As we will see in chapter 5, in contrast to critics who would reduce DuBois's politics to his vision of race, "The Conservation of Races" distinguishes quite clearly between politics and race, between the public language of basic justice and civil recognition in which we negotiate the terms of our cohabitation with others of different backgrounds and the private language of identity.

109 Horsman traces the "emphasis on the Anglo-Saxons as particularly able Germans" back to Tacitus's *Germania*. "In the peoples of Germany," wrote Tacitus, "there has been given to the world a race untainted by intermarriage with other races, a peculiar people and pure, like no one but themselves." In this "pure" race, Tacitus found a high moral code alloyed with a profound love of freedom and individual rights. Their important decisions were made by the whole community. Thus, in its origins, the myth of heroic, freedom-loving Anglo-Saxons tied higher law principles to racial identity. Horsman, *Race and Manifest Destiny*, pp. 178, 12, 25.

110 One of the earliest texts of the emergent discipline of ethnology, Samuel Stanhope Smith's *An Essay on the Causes of the Variety of Complexion and Figure in the Human Species*, first published in 1787 and reissued in 1810, defended monogenesis, the unity of the human species, arguing that racial differences could be accounted for by environment in sharp contrast to the racist polygenesis theories of Morton and the American school of ethnology. Horsman, *Race and Manifest Destiny*, pp. 25, 99

111 J.C. Nott, M.D. and George R. Gliddon, *Types of Mankind, or Ethnological Researches, based upon the Ancient Monuments, Paintings, Sculptures, and Crania of Races, and upon their Natural, Geographical, Philological, and Biblical History: Illustrated by Selections from the Inedited Papers of Samuel George Morton, M.D., and by additional contributions from Prof. L. Agassiz, LL.D.; W. Usher, M.D.; and Prof. H.S. Patterson, M.D.* (Philadelphia: Lippincott, Grambo & Co, 1854), pp. 130, 405. As Horsman points out, the *Types of Mankind* was very popular, going through ten editions between 1854 and 1871. Horsman, *Race and Manifest Destiny*, p. 135.

112 John Van Evrie, *Negroes and Negro "Slavery:" The First an Inferior Race: The Latter Its Normal Condition* (New York: Van Evrie, Horton, 1863), pp. 117, 109–14, 112, 181–84, 188; Horsman, *Race and Manifest Destiny*, p. 135; George Frederickson, *The Black Image in the White Mind* (Hanover, NH: Wesleyan University Press, 1971), p. 61.

113 Foner, *Free Soil*, pp. 269, 274–75, 262–63, 279.

114 Phillip S. Paludan, *A Covenant with Death: The Constitution, Law, and Equality in the Civil War Era* (Urbana: University of Illinois Press, 1975), pp. 68, 76–82, 83, 84; Thomas Sergeant Perry, *The Life and Letters of Francis Lieber* (Boston: James R. Osgood, 1882), pp. 308–09.

115 Francis Lieber, "Leading Truths in Political Economy," *De Bow's Review*, 15 (August 1853): 188.

116 Francis Lieber, *On Civil Liberty and Self-Government* (Philadelphia: J.B. Lippincott, 1901), p. 21. The common law tradition entrusted to an independent judiciary was in Lieber's view "[T]he jewel of Anglican liberty." These judicial sages were usefully poised "between the pure philosophers and the pure men of government," and they oversaw the slowly evolving jurisprudential wisdom of the people. It was perhaps inevitable, given the organicism of this conception of the common law's evolution and the romantic conception that it represented the moral sense of a particular people, that Lieber would figure it as a racial heritage. The particular utility of this racial figure for a higher law theorist concerned about the anarchic potential of devotion to moral abstraction lies in the way the figure incorporates a genetic incrementalism and racial boundedness that clogs quick and heterodox forms of social and political experiment. Lieber, *Civil Liberty*, pp. 218, 167, 229, 213.

117 Perry, *Life and Letters of Francis Lieber*, p. 245.

118 Quoted in Horsman, *Race and Manifest Destiny*, pp. 269–70.

119 Lieber, *Civil Liberty*, pp. 261–62.

120 "Literary Criticism and the Politics of New Historicism," in *The New Historicism*, ed. H. Adam Veeser (New York: Routledge, 1989), p. 222.

121 Audience reaction to plays made from *Uncle Tom's Cabin* seemed to instantiate the transformative power of Stowe's vision of higher law. Reviewing a performance of George Aiken's *Uncle Tom's Cabin* play in the National Theater (in the objectionable Five Points district of Lower Manhattan, which was transformed by the presence of the play, according to one reviewer, into a holy place), the New York *Tribune* recalled that thirteen years before, the Freeman's Hall in Philadelphia had been burned down by a mob composed of people like many of the men and boys who were now seeing *Uncle Tom's Cabin*. Now, the "'b'hoys' were on the side of the fugitive," said the reviewer. "The pro-slavery feeling had departed from among them. They did not wish to save the Union. They believed in the higher law." New York *Tribune*, quoted in *National Anti-Slavery Standard*, August 20, 1853. Whether exaggerated or not, this account of the performance expresses the perception that the cathartic effect of literature can convert the audience from a jurisprudence of power and identity to one of universal moral norms.

122 David Grant makes a good argument for "the value of examining *Uncle Tom's Cabin* in light of the Republican agenda" that would inform the Civil War amendments. As Grant points out, that Stowe "chose to publish *Uncle Tom's Cabin* in an organ of the *political* anti-slavery movement, not in an abolitionist or otherwise moral or religious forum" indicates the political aims of her fiction. Grant, "*Uncle Tom's Cabin* and the Triumph of Republican Rhetoric," *The New England Quarterly*, 71,3 (September 1998): 429–30.

2 THE LOOK OF HIGHER LAW: HARRIET BEECHER STOWE'S ANTISLAVERY FICTION

1 As Joan Hedrick puts it, Stowe "raged against the 'cool way' the press and public lumped together 'all the woes and crimes the heartbreaks the bitter untold agonies of thousand poor bleeding helpless heartwrung creatures with the bland expression its very sad to be sure – very dreadful – but we mustn't allow our feelings to run away with us we must consider &c, &c, &c.' She longed to 'do something even the humblest in this cause.'" Hedrick, *Harriet Beecher Stowe: A Life* (New York: Oxford University Press, 1994), p. 205.

2 Letter, dated January 20, 1853, from Harriet Elizabeth [Beecher] Stowe to Thomas Denman, 1st Baron Denman, Huntington Library, San Marino, California.

3 Lydia Maria Child, *An Appeal in Favor of That Class of Americans Called Africans* (Amherst: University of Massachusetts Press, 1996), pp. xlvi–xlvii, 95–96; as Carolyn Karcher notes, Child praised *Uncle Tom's Cabin* as a "truly great work," doing "much to command respect for the faculties of woman," parts of which bore the signs of Child's direct influence. Carolyn L. Karcher, *The*

First Woman in the Republic: a Cultural Biography of Lydia Maria Child (Durham, NC: Duke University Press, 1994), pp. 389, 336. In an impassioned moment of *Uncle Tom's Cabin*, Stowe has one of her black heroes, George Harris, exclaim, "What laws are there for us? We don't make them, – we don't consent to them, – we have nothing to do with them . . . Don't you tell us all, once a year, that governments derive their just power from the consent of the governed?" Harriet Beecher Stowe, *Uncle Tom's Cabin* (New York: Norton, 1994), p. 96.

4 Robert S. Levine, *Martin Delany, Frederick Douglass, and the Politics of Representative Identity* (Chapel Hill: University of North Carolina Press, 1997), pp. 59–60; "Review of *Dred*," *New Englander*, 13 (November 1856): 515; Richmond *Enquirer*, January 23, 1857; George Frederick Holmes, "Editorial and Literary Department," *De Bow's Review*, 13 (September 1852): 319.

5 Ann Douglas, *The Feminization of American Culture* (New York: Avon, 1977), pp. 2–3, 11–12; Jane Tompkins, *Sensational Designs: The Cultural Work of American Fiction, 1790–1860* (New York: Oxford University Press, 1985), pp. 126, 132; Julia A. Stern, *The Plight of Feeling: Sympathy and Dissent in the Early American Novel* (Chicago: University of Chicago Press, 1997), p. 238. See also, Elizabeth Ammons, "Heroines in *Uncle Tom's Cabin*," *American Literature*, 49 (1977): 163–64, and Gillian Brown, *Domestic Individualism: Imagining Self in Nineteenth-Century America* (Berkeley: University of California Press, 1990), pp. 16–18.

6 Marianne Noble, "The Ecstasies of Sentimental Wounding in *Uncle Tom's Cabin*," *The Yale Journal of Criticism*, 10.2 (1997): 296, 298–99, 304. In response to the criticisms of two of her readers, Glenn Hendler and Michelle Masse, Noble insists that it is not herself but Stowe who insists on separating head and heart. "Further Responses to Marianne Noble on Stowe, Sentiment, and Masochism," *The Yale Journal of Criticism*, 12.1 (1999): 163–65. Noble approves of Martha Nussbaum's use of Adam Smith's figure of the judicious spectator as capturing the truth that the "truly just person does not separate feeling and thinking but understands the two to be intertwined." But then, oddly, Noble describes the Scottish common sense philosophers, whose number prominently included Adam Smith, as the source for Stowe's separation of head and heart, attributing to their influence Stowe's desire to "get head out of the way so that the heart can act." This strikes me as a misprision of both the common sense philosophers and Stowe. As Nussbaum points out, Smith's notion of the judicious spectator yokes feeling to reason. The judicious spectator allows him/herself to register emotionally the particular facts of the case before him/her but also preserves some space for rational reflection on those feelings. A more apt example of this concept could not be found than in the episode in *Uncle Tom's Cabin* in which Senator Bird enters into rational debate with his wife, followed by an immediate confrontation with human distress, which conjures feelings of sympathy and results in further dialogue and action by the man of law in the interest of justice. Martha Nussbaum, *Poetic Justice: The Literary Imagination and Public Life* (Boston: Beacon, 1996), pp. 72–77.

7 Henry David Thoreau provides a quintessential formulation of the higher law question in his famous essay "Resistance to Civil Government": "a government in which the majority rule in all cases cannot be based on justice, even as far as men understand it. Can there not be a government in which majorities do not virtually decide right and wrong, but conscience?" To answer this question affirmatively requires that we be capable of some form of "bridging," so that we can arrive at a plausibly universal moral consensus, such as the present-day consensus that slavery is evil. Thoreau, "Resistance to Civil Government," in *Walden and Civil Disobedience* (New York: Signet, 1960), p. 223. In addition, confident assertions of the unbridgeability or untranslatability of human experience would seem to entail a logical incoherence. To assert that it is fundamentally impossible to bridge the gap between one person's experience and that of another, would seem to assume that one can tell that something has in fact been left behind by the attempt to bridge experiences. Yet, if one has the perspective from which to see that something has been left behind, is not that person in a position to bridge the experiences, seeing each separately and registering what they can and do share? Assertions of untranslatability have been effectively challenged by Donald Davidson's theory of interpretation. Davidson contends that the very idea of closed and incommensurable perspectives is incoherent, for to see languages as untranslatable requires a perspective capable of translating. Davidson, *Inquiries into Truth and Interpretation* (Oxford: Clarendon Press, 1984), p. 198.

8 James M. Cox contends that the religious images of *Uncle Tom's Cabin* were "written directly *against the law*." Cox, "Harriet Beecher Stowe: From Sectionalism to Regionalism," *Nineteenth-Century Fiction*, 38 (1984): 455. Similarly, Lisa Whitney finds that the discourses of sentiment and law are so different as to foreclose any attempt on Stowe's part to marry them in *Dred*. Whitney, "In the Shadow of *Uncle Tom's Cabin*: Stowe's Vision of Slavery from the Great Dismal Swamp," *The New England Quarterly*, 66 (1993): 555.

9 A revolutionary era precursor for Stowe's image of the shivering fugitive can be found in Benjamin Rush's "Address . . . Upon Slave-Keeping" (1773). In this address, Rush attempts to "rouse up your Indignation against Slave-keeping" with the image of "Mothers . . . torn from their Daughters, and Brothers from Brothers" and "the son of a Prince . . . torn by a stratagem, from an amiable wife and two young children," who in the spirit of revolution kills his tyrannical master. [Rush] A Pennsylvanian, "An Address to the Inhabitants of the British Settlements in America Upon Slave-Keeping," in *American Political Writing during the Founding Era: 1760–1805*, ed. Charles S. Hyneman and Donald S. Lutz, 2 vols. (Indiannapolis, IN: Liberty Fund, 1983), I: 227–28. In a 1775 sermon, Levi Hart similarly asks his audience to put themselves "in the place of the unhappy Negroes . . . the time has come for a last farewell, you are destined to different ships bound to different and far distant coasts, go husbands and wives, give and receive a last embrace; parents bid a lasting adieu to your tender offspring." Hart, "Liberty Described and Recommended: in a Sermon

Preached to the Corporation of Freemen in Farmington," *American Political Writing during the Founding Era*, 1: 313–14. In both of these antislavery addresses, pictures of slavery's horrors are designed to rouse the will to action and are appended to rational argument about the contradiction between the American ethos of consensual government and slavery, following the moral sense philosophers' conceptions of psychology and their notions of effective rhetorical practice, which mandated both rational argument and emotional appeal. In the combination of rational argument and passionate appeal through concrete images, Stowe's fiction, like the addresses of her revolutionary forebears, reflected the rhetorical orientation of the Scottish common sense philosophers, who opined that swaying human reason itself was insufficient. To stir people to action one had to move their will and to do that one had to present affecting images. The rhetorical school of Lord Kames and Hugh Blair came to dominance in the early decades of the nineteenth century. Kenneth Cmiel, *Democratic Eloquence: The Fight over Popular Speech in Nineteenth-Century America* (New York: William Morrow, 1990), pp. 35, 40; Gregory Clark and S. Michael Halloran, eds., *Oratorical Culture in Nineteenth-Century America: Transformations in the Theory and Practice of Rhetoric* (Carbondale: Southern Illinois University Press, 1993), pp. 15, 62–63.

10 See above, pp. 26–27.

11 As Julia Stern points out, Josiah Wedgwood designed this "emblem for the London Society for the Abolition of Slavery in 1787, which Philadelphia abolitionists begin to display on their lapels in the years that follow." Stern, *Plight of Feeling*, p. 218.

12 Hedrick, *Stowe: A Life*, pp. 205–06, 208.

13 Thomas Jefferson, *The Portable Thomas Jefferson*, ed. Merrill Peterson (New York: Penguin, 1975), pp. 425; Stowe, *Uncle Tom's Cabin*, p. 472; Hedrick, *Stowe: A Life*, pp. 5, 86; Charles H. Foster, *The Rungless Ladder: Harriet Beecher Stowe and New England Puritanism* (Durham, NC: Duke University Press, 1954), p. 14; Kathryn Kish Sklar, *Catherine Beecher: A Study in American Domesticity* (New Haven: Yale University Press, 1973), pp. 80–1; Forrest Wilson, *Crusader in Crinoline: The Life of Harriet Beecher Stowe* (Philadelphia: J.B. Lippincott, 1941), p. 71; Charles Edward Stowe and Lyman Beecher Stowe, *Harriet Beecher Stowe: The Story of Her Life* (Boston: Houghton Mifflin, 1911), p. 41; Joseph Butler, *The Analogy of Religion, Natural and Revealed, to the Constitution and Course of Nature* (London: George Routledge, 1890).

14 Butler, *The Analogy*, pp. 148–50, 294. Butler's choice of moral over positive precepts is an ancestor of the higher law position of Stowe, Theodore Parker, Thoreau, and others. Parker contended that it was the "function of conscience" to ensure that one obeyed "the natural duty to keep the law of God" which "overrides the obligation to observe" the positive law of the state in certain instances. Like Thoreau, Parker distinguishes between those laws he obeys though they are "inexpedient" and those laws that tread "down the inalienable rights of man to such a degree as this, then I know no ruler but God, no law but natural justice." Parker, "The Function

of Conscience," in *The Slave Power* (New York: Arno, 1969), pp. 303, 340; see also Thoreau, "Slavery in Massachusetts," *Miscellanies* (Boston: Houghton Mifflin, 1893), p. 188. In *Dred*, Stowe defines one's duty to respect any law, even divine law, as deriving from its rectitude, not from the superior divine power that issues the command, reflecting the influence of Shaftesbury and Hutcheson's shared notion that divine precepts govern because they are right in principle, not because God rewards or punishes their obedience. Stowe, *Dred: A Tale of the Great Dismal Swamp*, 2 vols. (New York: AMS Press, 1967), I: 447; see chapter 1, note 28.

15 Stowe, *Uncle Tom's Cabin*, pp. 67, 17–18; see above, pp. 46–47.

16 Stowe, *Uncle Tom's Cabin*, p. 68.

17 *Ibid.*, pp. 91, 69; see above, p. 22.

18 Stowe, *Uncle Tom's Cabin*, p. 69. As Eric Sundquist has pointed out, Stowe's advocacy of sentiment as a challenge to the law of slavery went "beyond the restricted 'women's sphere' of feminine involvement with the politics of slavery advocated by Catherine Beecher." Sundquist, "Slavery, Revolution, and the American Renaissance," in *The American Renaissance Reconsidered*, eds. Walter Benn Michaels and Donald E. Pease (Baltimore: Johns Hopkins University Press, 1985), p. 18. Indeed, Stowe's jurisprudence of feeling transgressed Catherine Beecher's deference to the principles of "social rectitude" embodied in law and custom:

> In Catherine's earlier writings the law of God was roughly congruent with the laws of man. There was no inherent conflict between human institutions and heavenly proscriptions. Yet now in the 1850s Catherine saw a clear difference and possible conflict between heavenly and earthly justice and between religious benevolence and social rectitude. In all cases she maintained that the best rule for men to follow was a worldly rather than a heavenly one. (Sklar, *Catherine Beecher*, p. 247)

19 Stowe, *Uncle Tom's Cabin*, pp. 70, 77; see above, pp. 38–40.

20 Stowe, *Uncle Tom's Cabin*, p. 100.

21 Abraham Lincoln, "Speech on the Dred Scott Decision at Springfield, Illinois," *Speeches and Writings: 1832–1858* (New York: Library of America, 1989), pp. 397–98.

22 Stowe, *Uncle Tom's Cabin*, pp. 96–98. George Harris's dramatic recitation of his oppression establishes his right of revolution much as the Declaration of Independence's litany of the sins of the British Crown purports to justify the American Revolution. As Thoreau put it in his essay "Resistance to Civil Government," "all men" have the "right to refuse allegiance to and to resist the government, when its tyranny [is] great and unendurable." "Resistance," p. 225.

23 Stowe, *Uncle Tom's Cabin*, pp. 94, 128–29, 96–97.

24 *Ibid.*, p. 216. For an example of the flashing eye of the romantic hero, one could turn to the fierce but sympathetic eye of Cooper's noble savage, Uncas. James Fenimore Cooper, *The Last of the Mohicans* (New York: Penguin, 1986), p. 115. Robert Remini, *Daniel Webster: The Man and his Time* (New York: Norton, 1997), p. 157, n. 84.

25 Stowe, *Uncle Tom's Cabin*, pp. 123, 290, 18–26. George Fredrickson, *The Black Image in the White Mind: The Debate on Afro-American Character and Destiny, 1817–1914* (Hanover, NH: Wesleyan University Press, 1971), pp. 110–17.

26 Stowe, *Uncle Tom's Cabin*, pp. 150, 155.

27 In response to Phineas's readiness to use force to oppose the recapture of the Harris family, Simeon says, "It's quite plain thee was n't born a Friend . . . The old nature hath its way in thee pretty strong as yet." Stowe, *Uncle Tom's Cabin*, p. 207

28 In discussing this passage with students and colleagues, I have often found that they are put off by the "Village of the Damned" quality of the Quaker community, its odd absence of dispute making it seem frightening in its own way.

29 In 1837, while living in Cincinnati and pregnant with twins, Stowe had a close encounter with the necessity and attraction of armed resistance, during the mob violence that followed an attack on James G. Birney's antislavery journal. Stowe's response to this incident suggests that she was not only willing to endorse armed resistance but that it held some visceral attraction for her: "For my part I can easily see how such proceedings may make converts to abolitionism, for already my sympathies are strongly enlisted for Mr. Birney, and I hope he will stand his ground and assert his rights . . . I wish he could man [his office] with armed men and see what can be done. If I were a man, I would go for one, and take good care of at least one window." Charles Stowe, *Harriet Beecher Stowe*, pp. 104–05; Hedrick, *Stowe: A Life*, p. 106.

30 Stowe, *Uncle Tom's Cabin*, pp. 105, 169–76, 332, 364.

31 Hedrick, *Stowe: A Life*, p. 258; Wilson, *Crusader*, p. 414. Apparently something happened while Stowe was writing the novel (*Dred*) to make the last sections entirely different. In 1884, James C. Derby recounted a story told by M.D. Phillips, the publisher of *Dred*. Phillips said that Stowe was deeply shocked by the physical assault by Preston Brooks of South Carolina on Charles Sumner on the floor of the United States Senate in 1856. She was so angered by the attack, said Derby, that "instead of carrying some of her characters and making them like little Eva, charming and tender, she introduced the spirit of revenge under the name of the negro Dred." Thomas F. Gossett, *Uncle Tom's Cabin and American Culture* (Dallas, TX: Southern Methodist University Press, 1985), p. 297. The distortions and warps in Dred's mental character signal not only Stowe's perception of the psychological pressure that such an isolated rebel would face but also her discomfort with the image of a black George Washington. Eric Sundquist, *To Wake the Nations: Race in the Making of American Literature* (Cambridge, MA: Harvard University Press, 1993), p.79; Fredrickson, *Black Image*, p. 112–13.

32 Stowe, *Dred*, I: 255.

33 The name of Stowe's second antislavery novel suggests an awareness of the *Dred Scott* case. Stowe wrote the bulk of *Dred* during the summer of 1856, and, according to Don Fehrenbacher, *Dred Scott* began to receive considerable attention in the press after it arrived at the Supreme Court in

February of the same year. Fehrenbacher, *The Dred Scott Case: Its Significance in American Law and Politics* (New York: Oxford University Press, 1978), p. 288. Noel Gerson opines in *Harriet Beecher Stowe* that Stowe changed the name of her maroon rebel from "Dread," a name signifying the terrifying potential of black revolt, to "Dred" as a consequence of the publicity *Dred Scott* received while she was writing her novel. This change suggests Stowe's apprehension of the violent consequences of an unjust decision in *Dred Scott*. Gerson, *Harriet Beecher Stowe* (New York: Prager, 1976), pp. 105–06.

34 Stowe, *Dred*, I: 255–56. In *The Key to Uncle Tom's Cabin* (1853), Stowe emphasizes the manifest injustice of slavery by characterizing it as "absolute despotism, of the most unmitigated form . . . which exists only in some of the most savage countries of the world." The racial terms of the condemnation of slavery betray a problematic association of ethical governance and whiteness. A black revolt against slavery, on such a view, would paradoxically be an action for white principles of justice against the ruling ethos of the darker races. Stowe, *The Key to Uncle Tom's Cabin* (New York: Arno, 1969), p. 233.

35 Stowe, *Dred*, I: 445.

36 *State v. Mann* (1829), 13 N. Car. (2 Devereux) 263, 266.

37 *Ibid.*, 13 N. Car. 263, 267–68.

38 *Ibid.*, 13 N. Car. 263, 268. In the "moral-formal dilemma" that Robert Cover discerns in American antebellum jurisprudence, a judge's moral opposition to slavery would often collide with his positivist approach to the law, which required him as a matter of professional duty to merely apply the declarations of proslavery legislatures. While natural law furnished an overt source of legal doctrine for legislators and provided a theoretical basis for the interpretive preference of judges for the principles of freedom and equality, the judicial natural rights preference was always subordinate to the hierarchic triumvirate of constitution, statute, and case. In Cover's view, Judge Ruffin was "the most eloquent spokesman for a doctrine of stern necessity, requiring an unflinching, conscious disregard of natural justice." Cover, *Justice Accused: Antislavery and the Judicial Process* (New Haven: Yale University Press, 1975), pp. 7, 25–29, 34. Cover also describes the perdurability and persuasive effect of natural rights rhetoric even for judges eschewing the principles of natural justice in order to fulfill their professional roles as expositors of positive law:

> The very persistence of the language of natural law, even within the circumscribed areas [of code and case], had the effect of publicly proclaiming the gap between law as it was and law as it should have been. To speak of slavery as against natural law, even if the legal consequences of the statement were few and undramatic, was to admit the moral blemish on the legal system. (Cover, *Justice Accused*, pp. 34–35, 77–78, 197–256.)

Mark Tushnet substitutes for Cover's moral–formal dilemma a law/sentiment dichotomy central to but covert in Southern slave law, which "treated the opposition between sentiment and law as corresponding to a division between slave relations and market relations." In Tushnet's view,

The emerging rhetoric of judicial opinions in the 1820s developed a distinction between law and morality in order to make irrelevant challenges to new rules as immoral. Judge Ruffin invoked that rhetoric but transformed its goal; rather than simply denying that law was connected with morality, he asserted that law had a restricted jurisdiction, within which its morality could be honored while the morality of sentiment could be respected in the situation presented by State v. Mann.

As interesting and illuminating as Tushnet's analysis is in terms of the structural split hidden and active in Southern slave ideology, it does not address the central object of this study, which considers to what extent and how natural rights theory and rhetoric informed and impelled such dichotomies. Tushnet, *The American Law of Slavery: 1810–1860* (Princeton: Princeton University Press, 1981), pp. 58, 65.

39 "No one can read this decision, so fine and clear in expression, so dignified and solemn in its earnestness, and so dreadful in its results, without feeling at once deep respect for the man and horror for the system." Stowe, *The Key to Uncle Tom's Cabin*, pp. 147–48. As Alfred Brophy puts it, "Stowe sought to understand why the brilliant Justice Thomas Ruffin, who sensed the inhumanity of slave law, nevertheless applied it like 'elegant surgical instruments' to 'dissec[t]' a living human heart.' Her answer provides a window into a complex world of legal logic, humanity, and utilitarian thinking." Brophy, "Humanity, Utility, and Logic in Southern Legal Thought: Harriet Beecher Stowe's Vision in *Dred: A Tale of the Great Dismal Swamp*," *Boston University Law Review*, 78 (October 1998): 1158.

40 Stowe, *Dred*, 1: 372, 209. In his book, *Sociology for the South; or the Failure of Free Society*, George Fitzhugh argues for the natural rightness of his paternalistic theory of authority, comparing the rule of slavery to such benevolent schemes of authority as that of the family. In Fitzhugh's view of the natural hierarchy into which we are all born, the authority of the slaveholder is as "equally right and incumbent" as that of the parent. Fitzhugh, *Sociology* (Richmond, VA: A. Morris, 1854), pp. 25–26, 89.

41 Stowe, *Dred*, 1: 202. The fist and pistol are Stowe's apt symbols of the force of arms that ultimately supports the positivistic view of social and legal order: "Confound it all!" said Tom Gordon,

teach them that you've got the power! – teach them the weight of your fist! That's enough from them. I am bad enough, I know; but I can't bear hypocrisy. I show a fellow my pistol. I say to him, You see that sir! I tell him, You do so and so, and you shall have a good time with me. But you do that, and I'll thrash you within an inch of your life! That's my short method with niggers, and poor whites, too. When one of these canting fellows comes round to my plantation, let him see what he'll get, that's all! (*Dred*, 1: 199–200.)

Like Captain McBane in Charles Chesnutt's *The Marrow of Tradition* and Frederick Douglass's brutal master, Covey, Gordon considers all human relations as at least implicitly determined by power. The hand is the appropriate symbol for positivistic legal and social entitlements because it is the appendage that both strikes and grasps. In *Uncle Tom's Cabin*, Stowe uses the heavy fist of the slave hunter, Tom Loker, and the fist of Simon Legree that "has got hard as iron knocking down niggers" to represent the hard-hearted positivism that recognizes only the rights of the strong, who take what they can. Stowe, *Uncle Tom's Cabin*, pp. 80, 363. In the words of Chesnutt's McBane, "We may as well be honest about this thing. We are going to put the niggers down because we want to, and think we can; so why waste our time in mere pretense? I'm no hypocrite myself, – if I want a thing I take it, provided I'm strong enough." Charles W. Chesnutt, *The Marrow of Tradition* (Ann Arbor: University of Michigan Press, 1969), p. 81.

42 Stowe, *Dred*, I: 247–48; II: 95, 100; I: 443. The paradox in Stowe's fiction that a potential slave rebellion both signals the slaves' right of revolution and the need for more oppressive containment had other historical precedents. The explosion in San Domingo, for instance, reinforced the antislavery arguments of the early American jurist, St. George Tucker, and prompted new repressive legal measures. Inspired by Denmark Vesey's revolutionary example, such African American abolitionists as Henry Highland Garnet and Frederick Douglass urged slaves to break their bonds and the South Carolina legislature tightened its restrictions on free Negroes. Harold M. Hyman, *Equal Justice Under Law: Constitutional Development, 1835–1875* (New York: Harper & Row, 1982), pp. 13–14; Kermit L. Hall, *The Magic Mirror: Law in American History* (New York: Oxford University Press, 1989), pp. 131–32; Gary B. Nash, *Race and Revolution* (Madison, WI: Madison House, 1990), pp. 42–47; Sterling Stuckey, *Slave Culture: Nationalist Theory and the Foundations of Black America* (New York: Oxford University Press, 1987), pp. 98–104; Stuckey, *Going through the Storm: The Influence of African American Art in History* (New York: Oxford University Press, 1994), p. 19; Fehrenbacher, *The Dred Scott Case*, p. 69.

43 Stowe, *Dred*, I: 377–78.

44 In representing Milly, Edward Clayton attempts to reiterate the moral foundation for the legal authority of the master in order to show how the behavior in question violates the proper source of such authority:

"The law guarantees to the parent, the guardian, and the master, the right of enforcing obedience by chastisement; and the reason for it is, that the subject being supposed to be imperfectly developed, his good will, on the whole, be better consulted by allowing to his lawful guardian this power.

"The good of the subject," he said, "is understood to be the foundation of the right; but when chastisement is inflicted without just cause, and in a manner so inconsiderate and brutal as to endanger the safety and well-being of the subject, the great foundation principle of the law is violated. The act becomes perfectly lawless, and as incapable of legal defense as it is abhorrent to every sentiment of humanity and justice."

Like George Fitzhugh, Clayton musters a paternalistic version of the natural law sanction of slavery that argues by analogy to other institutions that recognizably involve domination and hierarchical authority, such as the family. The analogy of the moral duty of the parent to the child is essential to Clayton's argument that the forms and intent of the law of slavery are not the mere workings of power and the will to dominate. The good of the slave provides the moral authority for the legal form of domination. Stowe, *Dred*, 1: 473, 378, 442.

45 Kenneth M. Stampp, *The Peculiar Institution: Slavery in the Ante-Bellum South* (New York: Vintage, 1956), pp. 30, 32.

46 Gossett, *Uncle Tom's Cabin*, pp. 164–65.

47 George Frederick Holmes, "Review of *Uncle Tom's Cabin*," *The Southern Literary Messenger*, 18 (December 1852): 727.

48 George Frederick Holmes, "Review of *The Key to Uncle Tom's Cabin*," *The Southern Literary Messenger*, 19 (June 1853): 328. Of course, many Northerners as well as Southerners were skeptical about the political efficacy of Stowe's fiction. Wendell Phillips, for instance, warned that the emotion roused by *Uncle Tom's Cabin* by itself may well be insufficient to motivate real antislavery action: "There is many a man who weeps over Uncle Tom and swears by the [New York] Herald." Gossett, *Uncle Tom's Cabin and American Culture*, p. 168. The proslavery *Herald* was in its day the most popular and profitable paper in the United States, and its editor, James Gordon Bennett, was well versed in the same moral sense tradition animating Stowe's antislavery fiction.

49 Gossett, *Uncle Tom's Cabin and American Culture*, p. 183.

50 "Fragment of a Manuscript Relating to Slavery in the United States," Ms., Roger B. Taney Papers, Library of Congress.

51 Representative John Bingham, *Congressional Globe*, 36th Cong., 2nd Sess., January 23, 1861, appendix, p. 83.

52 Senator Lyman Trumbull, *Congressional Globe*, 39th Cong., 1st Sess., April 4, 1866, p. 1757; Senator Henry Wilson, *Congressional Globe*, 39th Cong., 1st Sess., January 22, 1866, p. 343; Rep. Jehu Baker, *Congressional Globe*, 39th Cong., 1st Sess., July 9, 1866, appendix, p. 256.

53 See Abraham Lincoln, "Speech at Peoria, Illinois" (1854), "Gettysburg Address" (1863), "Second Inaugural Address" (1865), in *The American Intellectual Tradition*, ed. David Hollinger and Charles Capper, 2 vols. (New York: Oxford University Press, 1997), 1: 463–70, 475, 476–77. Garry Wills, *Lincoln at Gettysburg: The Words That Remade America* (New York: Simon and Schuster, 1992), p.38.

54 Harold Holzer, Babor S. Borbitt, Mark E. Neely, Jr., *The Lincoln Image: Abraham Lincoln and the Popular Print* (New York: Scribner, 1984), p. 170.

55 *Ibid.*, pp. 211–16.

56 David Donald, *Charles Sumner and the Coming of the Civil War* (New York: Knopf, 1960), p. 259. Sumner's "Crime Against Kansas" speech was reprinted in London, in a publication by Nassau W. Senior, the eminent

publicist and economist, entitled "American Slavery: A Reprint of an Article on 'Uncle Tom's Cabin' in the 'Edinburgh Review,' and of Mr. Sumner's Speech of the 19th and 20th of May, 1856." Charles Sumner, *The Works of Charles Sumner*, 15 vols. (Boston: Lee and Shepard, 1872), III: 93. This partnership between Sumner and Stowe can also be seen in their correspondence. For example, in a letter to Stowe of November 12, 1852, Sumner offers Stowe counsel and advice in composing *The Key to Uncle Tom's Cabin*.

57 Charles Sumner, "Freedom National, Slavery Sectional" (1852), *Works*, III: 194; Sumner, "The Antislavery Enterprise: Its Necessity, Practicability, and Dignity" (1855), *Works*, IV: 15.

58 Sumner, "Freedom National," *Works*, III: 181–82.

59 Ibid., Works, III: 184.

3 COSMOPOLITAN CONSTITUTIONALISM: EMERSON AND DOUGLASS

1 Thomas F. Gossett, *Uncle Tom's Cabin and American Culture* (Dallas, TX: Southern Methodist University Press, 1985), p. 165. Giving the novel a cosmopolitan spin it did not fully deserve, Douglass said: "The word of Mrs. Stowe is addressed to the soul of universal humanity. That word, bounded by no national lines, despises the limits of Sectarian sympathy, and thrills the universal heart." *Ibid.*, p. 172.

2 While appreciating the antislavery sentiment engendered by the novel, Douglass and other black abolitionists, such as Robert Purvis and John Mercer Langston, regretted Stowe's racialism. *The Black Abolitionist Papers*, ed. C. Peter Ripley, 5 vols. (Chapel Hill: University of North Carolina Press, 1991), IV: 124; William Cheek and Aimee Lee Cheek, *John Mercer Langston and the Fight for Black Freedom: 1829–65* (Urbana: University of Illinois Press, 1989), pp. 216–17. In addition, such sentiments might prove to be what Emerson disparaged as a mere "theatrical attitude" of mercy without any corresponding revision of the nation's fundamental concepts of justice and citizenship. "Fortune of the Republic," December 1, 1863, in *Emerson's Antislavery Writings*, ed. Len Gougeon and Joel Myerson (New Haven: Yale University Press, 1995), p. 143. All subsequent references to this edition appear parenthetically as *EAW*. Commenting that *Uncle Tom's Cabin* was uncongenial for those "who read Emerson," Julia Ward Howe implied just such a criticism of Stowe. Gossett, *Uncle Tom's Cabin*, p. 166.

3 "What to the Slave is the Fourth of July," July 5, 1852, in *The Frederick Douglass Papers*, ed. John Blassingame, 5 vols. (New Haven: Yale University Press, 1982), II: 386. Subsequent references to this edition of Douglass's writings appear parenthetically as *FDP*.

4 "Lecture on Slavery," January 25, 1855, *EAW*, p. 94. As Robert Richardson notes, Emerson thought of Douglass as an exemplar of the "Anti-Slave," the truly free individual who authors his freedom and character. *Emerson: The Mind on Fire* (Berkeley: University of California Press, 1995), p. 398.

5 Sacvan Bercovitch, *The Rites of Assent: Transformations in the Symbolic Construction of America* (New York: Routledge, 1993), pp. 46, 351–52, 370–72. Interestingly, Bercovitch offers his own "outsider's perspective" as an alternative to the absorbing mythos of the "American Way." That is to say, Bercovitch offers his own cosmopolitan perspective as an alternative to American exceptionalism. As an immigrant, Bercovitch can see what nineteenth-century writers could not – that the United States was "but a certain political system... one of many possible forms of society." *Rites*, pp. 65, 368. It is my contention that, like Bercovitch, Emerson and Douglass were capable of a cosmopolitan perspective rejecting conceptions of justice as the property or special province of the "American Way."

6 Douglass supported national interests insofar as they comported with the dictates of a universal morality: "when there is a supposed conflict between human and national rights, it is safe to go the side of humanity." "Our Composite Nationality," December 7, 1869, *FDP*, IV: 252. And, for Emerson, the Civil War could only be legitimated as an effort to ground the Union in justice. *The Journals and Miscellaneous Notebooks of Ralph Waldo Emerson*, ed. William H. Gilman *et al.*, 16 vols. (Cambridge, MA: Harvard University Press, 1960–82), XV: 301. All subsequent references to this edition of Emerson's journals appear parenthetically as *JMN*.

7 Bruce Robbins and Pheng Cheah, *Cosmopolitics: Thinking and Feeling Beyond the Nation* (Minneapolis: University of Minnesota Press, 1998), p. 101.

8 David Hollinger, *Post-Ethnic America: Beyond Multiculturalism* (New York: Basic Books, 1995), p. 88.

9 *Frederick Douglass's Paper*, for instance, carried a column authored by "Cosmopolite," touting the virtues of cosmopolitan intercourse abroad, particularly with the English. Elisa Tamarkin, "The 'Englishness' of Abolition and the Making of the Black Intellectual," paper presented at the American Studies Association, October 1998, p. 9. In addition, it was an antislavery commonplace to cite world opinion condemning the peculiar institution.

10 For provocative accounts of this historical narrative, see Jürgen Habermas, *The Structural Transformation of the Public Sphere: An Inquiry into a Category of Bourgeois Society* (Cambridge, MA: MIT Press, 1991) and Richard Sennett, *The Fall of the Public Man* (London: Faber, 1976).

11 Hannah Arendt, *Lectures on Kant's Political Philosophy* (Chicago: University of Chicago Press, 1992), p. 43.

12 Immanuel Kant, *Critique of Judgment* (New York: Hafner Press, 1951), §§ 40, 41, pp. 135–40.

13 *Ibid.*, p. 202.

14 Samuel Fleischacker, *A Third Concept of Liberty: Judgment and Freedom in Kant and Adam Smith* (Princeton: Princeton University Press, 1999), pp. 7, 31, 40.

15 Emerson, "Lecture on Slavery," *EAW*, p. 95.

16 "Circles," in *The Selected Writings of Ralph Waldo Emerson*, ed. Brooks Atkinson (New York: Modern Library, 1950), pp. 288, 285. All subsequent

references to this edition appear parenthetically as *SWE*. Emerson, "Kansas Relief Meeting," September 10, 1856, *EAW*, p. 113. Douglass, "Our Composite Nationality," *FDP*, IV: 244. Douglass, "Pictures and Progress," December 3, 1861, *FDP*, III: 460.

17 David Hollinger makes a similar point in *Post-Ethnic America* p. 84.

18 "WO Liberty," *JMN*, XIV: 396, 421. "Composite Nation," *FDP*, IV: 256.

19 *JMN*, XI: 412.

20 For an informative discussion of the WO Liberty journal from which Emerson would draw most of the precedents for his antislavery addresses, see John C. Broderick, "Emerson and Moorfield Story: A Lost Journal Found," *American Literature*, 38 (May 1966): 177–86. Emerson, "Address to the Citizens of Concord," May 3, 1851, *EAW*, p. 59.

21 [Ainsworth Rand Spofford], *The Higher Law Tried by Reason and Authority* (New York: S.W. Benedict, 1851). "WO Liberty," *JMN*, XIV: 374–430. Letter from Ralph Waldo Emerson to Ainsworth Rand Spofford (May 23, 1851), in the Spofford Collection, Library of Congress.

22 Spofford, *Higher Law*, 5–6; Emerson, "Address to the Citizens of Concord," *EAW*, p. 64.

23 New York *Tribune*, March 19, 1850.

24 Though Sumner once professed complete incomprehension as to what transcendentalism meant, it is clear that he and Emerson had kindred views of justice and the Constitution. Both were influenced by William Ellery Channing, a founder of American Unitarianism and the father of organized benevolence in Boston. From Channing, Emerson and Sumner learned to expect upheaval when the *status quo* conflicted with justice. Channing ended his famous sermon, "Unitarian Christianity" (1819), with a call for revolution: "our earnest prayer to God is, that he will overturn, and overturn, and overturn the strong-holds of spiritual usurpation." "Amidst the disappointments which may attend individual exertions," Sumner argued, in words that paraphrased Channing's, "let us recognize ... that whatever is just, whatever is humane, whatever is good, whatever is true ... in the golden light of the Future, must prevail." In a similar vein, Emerson declared that if the war eradicated slavery and grounded "the Constitution & law in America ... on ethical principles," "it will be worth all our calamities." David Donald, *Charles Sumner and the Coming of the Civil War* (New York: Knopf, 1960), pp. 71, 99, 103; Richardson, *Emerson*, p. 47; *JMN* XV: 209.

25 Arthur M. Schlesinger, Jr., *The Age of Jackson* (Boston: Little, Brown, 1945), pp. 382–84; Stanley Elkins, *Slavery: A Problem in American Institutional and Intellectual Life* (Chicago: University of Chicago Press, 1959), p. 147; George Frederickson, *The Inner Civil War: Northern Intellectuals and the Crisis of the Union* (New York: Harper and Row, 1965), pp. 176, 178–79; Anne Rose, *Transcendentalism as a Social Movement, 1830–1850* (New Haven: Yale University Press, 1981), pp. 219–20.

26 John Carlos Rowe, *At Emerson's Tomb: The Politics of Classic American Literature* (New York: Columbia University Press, 1997), pp. 3, 7, 41.

27 *Ibid.*, pp. 19–21. One might explain the divergence between Rowe's Emerson and mine, by arguing that Rowe's reading is justified by the Emerson of the 1840s (e.g., "New England Reformers") and mine by the Emerson of the 1850s. While it seems clear that Emerson's political vision was catalyzed by the Fugitive Slave Act, impelling him to a more active role, I cannot agree that this change betokens a fundamental contradiction in Emerson's thought. Even the 1844 essay, "New England Reformers," which mocks such experiments as Brook Farm, lauds the process of conversation in which the operative moral consensus that shapes law and society is changed. Even if "we" begin with "objections" to the reform project of abolitionism, such objections are part of a dialogic process of conversion:

O friend of the slave . . . understand well that [we object] because we wish to drive you to drive us into your measures. We wish to hear ourselves confuted. We are haunted with a belief that you have a secret which it would highliest advantage us to learn, and we would force you to impart it to us, though it should bring us to prison or to worse extremity. ("New England Reformers," *SWE*, p. 464)

28 "WO Liberty," *JMN*, XIV: 385.
29 "New England Reformers," *SWE*, p. 465.
30 Arendt, *Kant's Political Philosophy*, 42.
31 Emerson's connection to Seward's higher law theme is given a bare footnote in Rowe's discussion, and Emerson's sharp attacks on Daniel Webster are ignored altogether. *Emerson's Tomb*, p. 7.
32 Sacvan Bercovitch has noted such parallels "in phrasing and in concept" between Emerson and Douglass. *Rites*, p. 372. Readers of William McFeely's biography of Douglass may object that any commonalities between Emerson and Douglass are undercut by Emerson's racist hypocrisy, given his blackballing of Douglass's membership in the "Town and Country Club." William S. McFeely, *Frederick Douglass* (New York: Norton, 1991), p. 166. In response, Thomas Wortham has shown "there is nothing in the record to support McFeely's serious charge." Indeed, "[w]hatever Emerson's private feelings regarding race, he did in fact speak in favor of admiting persons of color to membership in the Town and Country Club on 2 May 1849." Thomas Wortham, "Did Emerson Blackball Frederick Douglass from membership in the Town and Country Club?," *New England Quarterly* 65 (June 1992): 295–98.
33 Anita Patterson, *From Emerson to King: Democracy, Race, and the Politics of Protest* (New York: Oxford University Press, 1997), pp. 4–5, 19–21, 138, 153–54.
34 One problem with Patterson's account of Emerson's political theory is that she focuses exclusively on the liberal, Lockean rights tradition. The "double consciousness" merging national identity and individual rights that she tenders as Emerson's is a flattened, two-dimensional conception that would be considerably altered by taking into account the republican, millenialist, and cosmopolitan traditions in Emerson and their potential to dissolve identity. While she avows a social contractarian focus, Patterson makes no mention

of the republican tradition's version of the social contract not merely as a means of protecting individual rights but as a means of instantiating the civic virtue of the body politic. *From Emerson to King,* pp. 154, 204, n. 9.

35 Letter to Francis Lieber, January 24, 1866, Huntington Library, San Marino, California. George Bancroft, *History of the United States of America, From The Discovery Of The American Continent,* 10 vols. (Boston: Little, Brown and Company, 1866), IX: 32.

36 "WO Liberty," *JMN,* XIV: 429. Particularly credible evidence that Emerson's universalism gave way at times to the ascriptive notion that Anglo-Americans had a particular birthright to democratic political ideals can be seen in his reaction to the heckling of a group of proslavery rowdies at an antislavery meeting in Boston. Under provocation, Emerson informed the "young foreigners" that the men they were interrupting were in fact real Americans, real sons of Massachusetts, who implicitly had a birthright to participate in this political forum, unlike "the young people who have endeavored to interrupt this meeting." "Attempted Speech," January 24, 1861, *EAW,* p. 126.

37 Like Patterson, Christopher Newfield finds that Emerson's antislavery advocacy was not merely accompanied by "a liberal kind of racism" but dependent on that racism. Even if we grant Emerson's racism, Newfield's claim that this racism was an essential component of Emerson's views of justice is not tenable. To the extent that Emerson's antislavery views espoused a jurisprudence based on moral agency without regard to race, they do not depend on whatever racist views he may have had. And, conversely, to the extent that his racism compromises his notion of moral agency and consent, such racism has replaced agency with the determinisms of identity. His antideterminist advocacy of human agency and the determinism of his race views cannot, by definition, be conflated but exist, if at all, in contradiction. But we should not accept Newfield's account of Emerson. Newfield argues that the nexus between Emerson's racism and his antislavery views precludes the possibility of black civic participation and political agency, yet Emerson's conception of Reconstruction plainly includes black suffrage: "let us stifle our prejudices against commonsense & humanity, & agree that every man shall have what he honestly earns, and, if he is a sane & innocent man, have . . . an equal vote." *JMN,* XV: 301–02. Newfield asserts that Emerson's "commonplace racism" was uniform and unchanging during his life, but consider the following statements:

> The negro race is, more than any other, susceptible of rapid civilization;
> The negro has saved himself, and the white man very patronizingly says I have saved you;
> Here is the Anti-slave. Here is Man; and if you have man, black or white is an insignificance;
> They have produced some persons of ability. But now, to be sure, we are told, they are not men, but chimpanzees. Montesquieu said, "It will

not do to grant them to be men, lest it appears that whites are not."
EAW, p. 30; *JMN*, IX: 126, 125; *JMN*, XV: 387–88.

While not devoid of the racialist tenor of his era, Emerson's comments on race sharply contrast with proslavery racism. Newfield expressly admits that his argument derives from an absence of evidence "that Emerson ever conceived of the possibility of black–white social equality," but, as Thomas Wortham notes, Emerson "did in fact speak in favor of admitting persons of color to membership in the Town and Country Club on 2 May 1849." Wortham, "Did Emerson Blackball Frederick Douglass," p. 298. And, as Len Gougeon points out, Emerson refused to lecture before the New Bedford Lyceum because of its exclusion of blacks from full membership. *EAW*, p. xxxiii. Newfield, *The Emerson Effect: Individualism and Submission in America* (Chicago: University of Chicago Press, 1996), pp. 195, 201, 196–97.

38 Bercovitch, *Rites*, pp. 307–52; Len Gougeon, *Virtue's Hero: Emerson, Antislavery, and Reform* (Athens: University of Georgia Press, 1990); Albert J. Von Frank, *The Trials of Anthony Burns: Freedom and Slavery in Emerson's Boston* (Cambridge, MA: Harvard University Press, 1998), pp. 96–102, 322–33.

39 As Thoreau puts it in "Slavery in Massachusetts" (1854),

> The question is not whether you or your grandfather, seventy years ago, did not enter into an agreement to serve the Devil, and that service is not accordingly now due; but whether you will not now, for once and at last, serve God, – in spite of your own past recreancy, or that of your ancestor, – by obeying that eternal and openly just CONSTITUTION, which He, and not any Jefferson or Adams, has written in your being.

Henry David Thoreau, *Miscellanies* (Boston: Houghton, Mifflin, 1893), p. 188.

40 *EAW*, pp. 53–72, 66; "The Fugitive Slave Law," March 7, 1854, *EAW*, p. 78.

41 *EAW*, pp. 56, 79.

42 *Ibid.*, p. 55.

43 *Ibid.*, p. 67.

44 *SWE*, p. 87; "Man, the Reformer," January 25, 1841, in *The Portable Emerson*, ed. Mark Van Doren (New York: Viking, 1946), p. 83. All subsequent references to this edition appear parenthetically as *PE*.

45 *EAW*, pp. 66, 67. "The Conservative," December 9, 1841, *PE*, p. 89, 91. In *Justice is Conflict* (Princeton: Princeton University Press, 2000), p. 44, Stuart Hampshire sounds a similar theme:

> The perpetual conflict between conservative thinking, in all its varieties, and the ambitions of reformers, socialists, and liberals comes, in the last analysis, from this single source: ought we to raise continually our consciousness of political possibilities, or ought we to accept the limits of political agency that, as it happens, our history has so far left in place?

46 *EAW*, pp. 67–68.

47 "Lecture on Slavery," January 25, 1855, *EAW*, p. 93.

48 "WO Liberty," *JMN*, XIV: 421; *EAW*, pp. 82, 56.

49 Emerson's emphasis on abstraction stands in sharp contrast to the current critical appetite for the particular, the embodied, for, in short, identity. Marianne Noble, for instance, values Stowe's sentimental images as "a critique of abstract, disembodied notions of personhood." Noble, "The Ecstasies of Sentimental Wounding in *Uncle Tom's Cabin*," *The Yale Journal of Criticism*, 10.2 (1997): 295–320. Similarly, Karen Sanchez-Eppler appreciates what she sees as the attempt of abolitionists and feminists to substitute a corporeal specificity for the incorporeal universals and abstractions used to oppress and exclude. Sanchez-Eppler, *Touching Liberty: Abolition, Feminism, and the Politics of the Body* (Berkeley: University of California Press, 1997), pp. 139–41. While the particular factual circumstances are often of critical importance to any attempt to achieve justice (e.g., how does one decide whether a contract is conscionable without knowing the factual details of the bargaining process and the relative bargaining power of the parties), yet in other circumstances justice can only be served by a measure of abstraction. Samuel Fleischacker offers a fine illustration of the moral necessity of such abstraction:

> In Jerusalem a few years ago, a woman who described herself as an Orthodox Jew threw her body on an Arab teenager to save him from a lynch mob that had just seen him stab and wound a young Jew. A few days later, all the participants in the event except the Arab were gathered together on TV for a bizarre, Oprah-like conversation. The woman who had thrown herself on the stabber repeated several times, in a low voice, that without respect for the due process of law a civilization cannot survive. To which the mother of the stabbing victim cried, "You don't understand the feelings of a mother!" Here concern for abstract principles led fairly obviously to better action than immersion in the particular would have done . . . an abstract ideal of justice enabled her to overcome her particularized reactions – and for that ideal she was willing to risk her life. Sometimes, especially when we face a stranger or an enemy, we can recognize other people's humanity only via the filter of very general principles and procedures, ones which do implicitly express our shared humanity, as Kant insisted, but only by *distancing* us from the particular circumstances in which we find ourselves and the emotions those circumstances evoke. (*A Third Concept of Liberty*, p. 34.)

50 "Leter to Mary Merrick Brooks," March 18, 1851, *EAW*, p. 51; "Fortune of the Republic," December 1, 1863, *EAW*, p. 143.

51 Anne Rose singles out Emerson's abstraction as what made his antislavery advocacy "comparatively desultory." *Transcendentalism*, p. 219. But I contend that Emerson's abstraction and irony give his antislavery argument and his approach to the Constitution its greatest force and continuing value.

52 *EAW*, p. 58. [William Craft], *Running a Thousand Miles for Freedom; Or, The Escape of William and Ellen Craft from Slavery* (London: William Tweedie, 1860); Henry Box Brown, *Narrative of Henry Box Brown* (Boston: Brown & Stearns, 1851).

53 The fugitive slave passage of Walt Whitman's "Song of Myself," though certainly more concretely descriptive than Emerson's passages, works in a similar fashion to establish the humanity of the fleeing slave, in part, by

avoiding the kinds of specific description tainted by racist type. Whitman's poem provides a sense of the fugitive's movements and physical state rather than a picture of his appearance. The highpoint of the Whitman passage is its beautifully flat narration of what the speaker did for the fugitive. Whitman presents this aid without editorial comment, in sharp contrast to Stowe's presentation of the Birds' rescue of Eliza Harris and her son. *Leaves of Grass*, eds. Sculley Bradley and Harold W. Blodgett (New York: Norton, 1973), pp. 37–38.

54 *EAW*, pp. 58, 62, 92.

55 John Brown, *Slave Life in Georgia; a Narrative of the Life of John Brown* (Freeport, NY: Books for Libraries, 1971).

56 "WO Liberty," *JMN*, XIV: 20–21.

57 "The Conservative," *PE*, pp. 94, 89.

58 "Circles," *SWE*, pp. 288–89.

59 "Lecture on Slavery," *EAW*, p. 94; "Fugitive Slave Law," *EAW*, pp. 88, 82; "The Poet," *SWE*, p. 336; "Kansas Relief Meeting," September 10, 1856, *EAW*, p. 113; "The Poet," *SWE*, p. 336.

60 Richard Poirier, *Poetry and Pragmatism* (Cambridge, MA: Harvard University Press, 1992), pp. 17, 11, 94, 17–18; Kenneth Karst, *Belonging to America: Equal Citizenship and the Constitution* (New Haven: Yale University Press, 1989), pp. 54–55; William James, *Pragmatism* (New York: Meridian, 1969), p. 158; "Circles," *SWE*, p. 281.

61 Douglass's oratorical charisma is glimpsed in William H. Ferris's description of a Douglass conclusion,

> his eyes flashed, his face lighted up, his voice rose and swelled like the notes of an organ and rang in stentorian tones over the audience, he moved more rapidly about the platform and his gestures grew more animated . . . Then, stepping to the front of the platform with head thrown back, outstretched arms [his] voice . . . rang out like a clarion. (William H. Ferris, "Douglass as an Orator," *Champion Magazine*, 1 (February 1917): 296–99.)

62 "Man, the Reformer," *PE*, p. 83.

63 New York *Tribune*, May 31, 1850; *Congressional Globe*, 40th Cong., 2nd Sess., 1850, pp. 234–67; the Harlan quote is from an unpublished memoir in the Manuscripts Division of the Library of Congress, 16; *The Salmon P. Chase Papers*, ed. John Niven, 5 vols. (Kent, OH: Kent State University Press, 1993), I: 632; New York *Tribune*, September 4, 1850.

64 *The Albion* (New York), October 29, 1859, quoted in *The Dawning of American Drama*, ed. Jürgen C. Wolter (Westport, CT: Greenwood Press, 1993), pp. 158–59.

65 In this vein the *Natchez Mississippi Free Trader*, May 15, 1857, records the consternation caused in Pedee, South Carolina, by sales of a volume entitled *Lives of Eminent Methodist Ministers*, which on closer examination, proved "to contain the biographies of Henry Ward Beecher, Fred. Douglass, and William Lloyd Garrison."

66 Michael Lind, *The Next American Nation: The New Nationalism and the Fourth American Revolution* (New York: Free Press, 1995), p. 380.

67 Ross Posnock, *Color and Culture: Black Writers and the Making of the Modern Intellectual* (Cambridge, MA: Harvard University Press, 1998). The direction indicated by Posnock's book has been taken up in a recent paper by Elisa Tamarkin on the anglophilism in black abolitionism. Tamarkin examines among other things the column by "Cosmopolite" in *Frederick Douglass's Paper*. "The 'Englishness' of Abolition." And a recent essay by William McFeely, pointing to the crucial importance of Douglass's experience abroad to his political advocacy, argues for an examination of Douglass's cosmopolitanism. "Visible Man: Frederick Douglass for the 1990s," in *Liberating Sojourn: Frederick Douglass and Transatlantic Reform*, ed. Alan J. Rice and Martin Crawford (Athens: University of Georgia Press, 1999), pp. 15–27.

68 Waldo E. Martin, Jr., *The Mind of Frederick Douglass* (Chapel Hill: University of North Carolina Press, 1984); Eric J. Sundquist, *To Wake the Nations: Race in the Making of American Literature* (Cambridge, MA: Harvard University Press, 1993), pp. 108–09, 121; Robert S. Levine, *Martin Delany, Frederick Douglass, and the Politics of Representative Identity* (Chapel Hill: University of North Carolina Press, 1997); Priscilla Wald, *Constituting Americans: Cultural Anxiety and Narrative Form* (Durham, NC: Duke University Press, 1995).

69 William Wiecek, *The Origins of Antislavery Constitutionalism in America* (Ithaca, NY: Cornell University Press, 1977), pp. 19, 202.

70 Eric Foner, *Free Soil, Free Labor, Free Men: The Ideology Of The Republican Party Before The Civil War* (New York: Oxford University Press, 1970), pp. 116–17.

71 Wiecek, *Antislavery Constitutionalism*, pp. 16–17.

72 Waldo Martin observes that Garrison not only sought to restrain Douglass's increasing independence and alliance with antislavery constitutionalists, such as Gerrit Smith, but also to regulate Douglass's interracial friendship with Julia Griffiths (to Douglass's great anger). This last fact is telling as it suggests a correspondence between the passivity enjoined upon Douglass by Garrison and the fear of open heterogeneous relations – both bespeak fear of consensually derived human association (*Mind of Fredenick Douglass*, pp. 27–47). Lewis Perry, *Radical Abolitionism: Anarchy and the Government of God in Antislavery Thought* (Ithaca, NY: Cornell University Press, 1973), pp. 44–46. Frederick Douglass, *My Bondage and My Freedom* (New York: Dover Publications, 1969), p. 361.

73 McFeely, *Frederick Douglass*, pp. 146–47.

74 "The Claims of the Negro Ethnologically Considered," July 12, 1854, in *Life and Writings of Frederick Douglass*, ed. Philip S. Foner, 5 vols. (New York: International Publishers, 1950–75), II: 309. All subsequent references to this edition appear as *LW*. Emerson, "The Conservative," *PE*, p. 94.

75 Quoted in Martin, *Mind of Frederick Douglass*, p. 172.

76 William Goodell, *American Constitutional Law* (Freeport, NY: Books for Libraries, 1971), p. 41.

77 Douglass, *My Bondage*, pp. 397, 399–400.

78 *FDP*, II: 330; "Letter To Gerrit Smith," May 21, 1851, *LW*, II: 157.

79 Adopting Lysander Spooner's interpretive approach in *The Unconstitutionality of Slavery*, Douglass argued that "[T]he language of the law must be construed strictly in favor of justice and liberty" and that "Where a law is susceptible of two meanings, the one making it accomplish an innocent meaning, and the other making it accomplish a wicked purpose, we must in all cases adopt that which makes it accomplish an innocent purpose." *LW*, II: 476.

80 "Antislavery Principles and Antislavery Acts," April 27, 28, 29, 1852, *FDP*, II: 349.

81 "Slavery, The Slumbering Volcano," April 23, 1849, *FDP*, II: 155.

82 *My Bondage*, pp. 137, 220.

83 *Ibid.*, p. 158; *Narrative of the Life of Frederick Douglass*, in *The Classic Slave Narratives*, ed. Henry Louis Gates, Jr. (New York: Mentor, 1987), pp. 278–79.

84 Gates's repression of the moral sense component of Douglass's thought fits with his desire to pit black authors against such giants of Western philosophy as Hume, Kant, Hegel, and Jefferson, all of whom can be quoted at length for their racist sentiments. This oppositional approach tends to obscure certain helpful influences such thinkers had on Douglass, and it implicitly projects an identitarianism onto thinkers who were fundamentally universalist in orientation – instead of black universalists trying to purge the racist error of the philosophical tradition they were drawing upon we get a protonationalist vision of black intellectuals drawing upon themselves, and their *own* tradition to oppose bad white racist authoritarianism. This vision is inaccurate as to Douglass, but it misreads even the most ardent black nationalists of the era. Gates, *Figures in Black: Words, Signs, and the "Racial" Self* (New York: Oxford University Press, 1987), pp. 105–07, 25–26.

85 *My Bondage*, pp. 99, 98; "Persecution on Account of Faith, Persecution on Account of Color," January 26, 1851, *FDP*, II: 291.

86 *My Bondage*, p. 98; "Persecution on Account of Faith," *FDP*, II: 295.

87 Douglass's critique of the centrality of slavery to antebellum America works simultaneously to illuminate the prevalent taint of slavery but also to sharply distinguish the practice of the nation from its abstract higher law principles, which remain at hand for cultural and political revision. "An Antislavery Tocsin," December 8, 1850, *FDP*, II: 260, 261, 268.

88 Relatively little work has been done to draw out the intersections between Douglass's autobiographies and his political oratory. For example, an illuminating and insightful book of essays on Douglass edited by Eric Sundquist contains only a handful of references to any of Douglass's speeches. Sundquist, *Frederick Douglass: New Literary and Historical Essays* (Cambridge: Cambridge University Press, 1990).

89 Wald, *Constituting Americans*, pp. 88–90.

90 John C. Calhoun, "Speech on the Admission of California – and the General State of the Union," in *Union and Liberty: the Political Philosophy of John C. Calhoun*, ed. Ross M. Lence (Indianapolis, IN: Liberty Press, 1992),

p. 590; Henry Clay, *Speech of the Hon. Henry Clay, of Kentucky, on taking up his Compromise Resolutions on the Subject of Slavery* (New York: Stringer & Townsend, 1850), pp. 21–22; Daniel Webster, "The Constitution and the Union," in *The Papers of Daniel Webster: Speeches and Formal Writings*, ed. Charles M. Wiltse (Hanover, NH: University Press of New England, 1988), II: 515.

91 "What to the Slave," *FDP*, II: 360.

92 Calhoun, "Admission of California," p. 600; Clay, "Compromise Resolutions," p. 13; Webster, "Constitution and Union," II: 548; Douglass, "What to the Slave," *FDP*, II: 360, 361.

93 Calhoun, "Admission of California," pp. 599–600; Douglass, "What to the Slave," *FDP*, II: 365.

94 Webster, "Constitution and the Union," II: 550–51, 541.

95 Douglass, "What to the Slave," *FDP*, II: 371, 373, 375.

96 *Ibid., FDP*, II: 366–68.

97 *Ibid., FDP*, II: 385. Perry Miller has observed how, in sharp distinction to the founders' amateurism, law and politics increasingly in the nineteenth century became the province of a specialized class of professionals. Antislavery did much to reclaim the more participatory political model of the founders (even though they might well have been surprised by the directions taken). Perry Miller, *The Life of the Mind in America* (New York: Harcourt Brace, 1965), p. 104.

98 James Otis, *The Rights of the British Colonies Asserted and Proved* (1764), in Bernard Bailyn, ed., *Pamphlets of the American Revolution* (Cambridge, MA: Harvard University Press, 1965), p. 420.

99 For example, in *Jones v. Alfred H. Mayer Co.*, 392 U.S. 409, 446–47 (1968), Justice William O. Douglas refers to Frederick Douglass's essay "The Color Line" as defining the type of discrimination that the Civil War amendments should proscribe. And Judge Higginbotham refers, in *Commonwealth of Pa. v. Local U. No. 542, Int. U. of Op. Eng.*, 347 F.Supp. 268, 270–71 (1972), to Douglass's "What to the Slave is the Fourth of July" to amplify and situate the meaning of the Civil War amendments.

100 *Regents of the University of California v. Bakke*, 438 U.S. 265, 387–402 (1978). It is precisely the continuing influence of the cosmopolitan higher law vision of a mutable Constitution combated by Robert Bork with a return to "original understanding." See *The Tempting of America* (New York: Free Press, 1990).

101 Douglass, "What to the Slave," *FDP*, II: 386.

102 "Ethnologically," *LW*, II: 292, 293, 294, 309, 307.

103 "The Do-Nothing Policy," September 12, 1856, *LW*, II: 403.

104 Henry Louis Gates, Jr. shows how Douglass's strategy of reversal tends to break down the binary oppositions of master/slave, spiritual/material, aristocratic/base, human/beast. *Figures in Black*, pp. 92–93. I would add words/blows to this list.

105 *Narrative*, pp. 297; *My Bondage*, pp. 238, 240; Lawrence W. Levine, *Black Culture and Black Consciousness: Afro-American Folk Thought from Slavery to Freedom* (New York: Oxford University Press, 1977), pp. 56–57, 72–73.

106 *My Bondage*, pp. 241, 242, 246–47.

107 Wesley Hohfeld, "Some Fundamental Legal Conceptions as Applied in Judicial Reasoning," *Yale Law Journal*, 23 (1917): 16.

108 Bruce Ackerman, *We the People: Transformations* (Cambridge, MA: Harvard University Press, 1998), chapters 4–8.

109 Cheek, *John Mercer Langston*, pp. 161, 174; *Chase Papers*, II: 296–97.

110 New York *Herald*, October 20–22, 24, 27–31, November 1–3, 1859.

111 Emerson, *JMN*, XV: 221, 301; Charles Sumner, *The Works of Charles Sumner*, 15 vols. (Boston: Lee and Shepard, 1874), X: 226; Emerson, *JMN*, XV: 298, 300, 301–02, 346; Sumner, *Works*, X: 231. The closeness of Emerson's affiliation with Sumner can be felt in Emerson's account of a wartime trip to Washington, D.C., in which Sumner introduces Emerson into political and ethical discussion with such Republican leaders as William Seward, Henry Stanton, Salmon Chase, and others. *JMN*, XV: 186–200.

112 "The Nebraska Controversy – The True Issue," March 4, 1853, *LW*, II: 277.

113 Martin, *Mind of Frederick Douglass*, p. 47.

114 *LW*, II: 362.

115 Sumner, *Works*, X: 174, 132, 248–49, 265. Henry Highland Garnett's letter of appreciation for Sumner's equality speech (which Sumner includes in the version of his speech published in his collected works) and DuBois's historical recognition of Sumner and Thaddeus Stevens as genuine visionaries of a better constitutional order, indicate the importance of Sumner's partnership to black Americans. Sumner, *Works* X: 265; W.E.B. DuBois, *Black Reconstruction in America: 1860–1880* (1935, reprinted New York: Atheneum, 1992), pp. 191–97. That Sumner selected newspaper quotations featuring the presence of Douglass and other African Americans for inclusion in his collected works indicates his appreciation of the validation these black Americans offered for his constitutional argument.

116 Sumner, "Are We a Nation?," *Works*, XII: 195, 245; Emerson, *EAW*, p. 67.

117 *Congressional Globe*, 42nd Cong., 2nd Sess., January 15, 1872, pp. 381–82.

118 Sumner, *Works*, X: 341–42.

119 *Congressional Globe*, 42nd Cong., 2nd Sess., January 31, 1872, p. 729.

120 As David Donald notes, during the period of his greatest public power, "Sumner renewed his ties with the aging Transcendentalists of Concord, as if to reaffirm the connection between their philosophical and his political idealism." That Sumner provided a kind of link between Emerson and Douglass can be found in the fact that close to the end of his life Sumner enjoined Douglass not to let his civil rights bill fail, and just before his death he asked a mutual friend to "tell Emerson how much I love and revere him." Donald, *Charles Sumner and the Rights of Man* (New York: Knopf, 1970), pp. 71, 573, 586–87. Emerson termed Sumner "Great-hearted man, / noble in person / incorruptible in life / the friend of the poor, / the champion of the oppressed," JMN, XV: 476. In an address published in the New York *Tribune* (May 15, 1868), Douglass said of Sumner, "He has demonstrated anew that one man with the truth on his side is a majority

against all the hosts of darkness, and to-day has the proud satisfaction of seeing his very soul in the image of the nation."

121 Though he does not mention Douglass, William Nelson has observed the seminal influence of the higher law argument Douglass helped in advancing on the framing of the Fourteenth Amendment. Nelson, *The Fourteenth Amendment: From Political Principle to Judicial Doctrine* (Cambridge, MA: Harvard University Press, 1988), pp. 64–67. David Richards notes the important "role" played by Douglass as a "constitutional leader." Richards, *Conscience and the Constitution: History, Theory, and Law of the Reconstruction Amendments* (Princeton: Princeton University Press, 1993), p. 257. The continuing influence of Douglass's approach to the Constitution can be seen in Sanford Levinson's citation of Douglass's ability to "stretch the sense of constitutional possibility." Levinson, *Constitutional Faith* (Princeton: Princeton University Press, 1988), p. 192.

122 C. Vann Woodward, *The Strange Career of Jim Crow* (New York: Oxford University Press, 1974), pp. 4–6; Charles A. Lofgren, *The Plessy Case: A Legal–Historical Interpretation* (New York: Oxford University Press, 1987), p. 61.

123 Douglass, *Life and Times of Frederick Douglass* (New York: Gramercy, 1993), p. 499.

4 THE POSITIVIST ALTERNATIVE

1 Robert Cover, *Justice Accused: Antislavery and the Judicial Process* (New Haven: Yale University Press, 1975), pp. 120–21, 34; James Herget, *American Jurisprudence, 1870–1970* (Houston, TX: Rice University Press, 1990) p. 12.

2 Augustus B. Longstreet, *Georgia Scenes, Characters, Incidents &c. in the First Half Century of the Republic* (Savannah: Library of Georgia, 1992), pp. 5, 4, 6, 3, 70.

3 George Washington Harris, *Sut Lovingood's Yarns* (1847–66, reprinted. New Haven, CT: College and University Press, 1966), pp. 174–75, 140, 130, 223, 274, 317.

4 The details and outline of Melville's story are taken from an historical incident. As Michael Rogin observes, when Melville changed the name of the ship involved, *The Tryal*, to the *San Dominick*, "he was calling attention to the slave seizure of power on Santo Domingo, in the wake of the French Revolution." Rogin, *Subversive Genealogy: The Politics and Art of Herman Melville* (Berkeley: University of California Press, 1979), p. 213. As Eric Sundquist points out, Melville uses Delano's obtuseness to "eviscerate" "northern liberalism for its profound indulgence in racialist interpretations of black character." Sundquist, *To Wake the Nations: Race in the Making of American Literature* (Cambridge, MA: Harvard University Press, 1993), p. 152.

5 "Benito Cereno," in *Great Short Works of Herman Melville*, ed. Warner Berthoff (New York: Harper and Row, 1969), pp. 275, 241, 295. Ernest Gellner, *Postmodernism, Reason, and Religion* (New York: Routledge, 1992). As Eric Sundquist observes, Melville's vision of black revolution does not include moral authority – "It is simply one form of power standing behind

the mask of another waiting in the shadows for its turn." Sundquist, *To Wake the Nations*, p. 180.

6 William E. Nelson, *The Fourteenth Amendment: From Political Principle to Judicial Doctrine* (Cambridge, MA: Harvard University Press, 1988), pp. 64–67.

7 *Buck v. Bell*, 274 U.S. 200, 207 (1927); see also, Walter Berns, "*Buck v. Bell*: Due Process of Law?" *Western Political Quarterly*, 6 (1953): 762.

8 A few years prior to *Buck*, Holmes had written a friend that social progress rested more upon efforts "to build a race" than on "tinkering with the institutions of property: " "I believe that Malthus was right... Every society is founded on the death of men... I shall think socialism begins to be entitled to serious treatment when and not before it takes life in hand and prevents the continuance of the unfit." Liva Baker, *The Justice from Beacon Hill* (New York: Harper, 1991), pp. 601–02; Max Lerner, *The Mind and Faith of Justice Holmes* (New York: Random House, 1954), p. 427. Holmes "took pleasure" in sustaining the Virginia statute, and his decision in that case reflected not only his deference to legislative authority but also his own brand of social Darwinism. *Holmes – Einstein Letters*, ed. James B. Peabody (London: hboxMacmillan, 1964), p. 267. Holmes's opinion in *Buck v. Bell* was reportedly cited at the Nuremburg war crimes trials as support for the defense contention that the alleged Nazi war criminals had acted in accordance with law. Gerard, "Capacity to Govern," *Harvard Journal of Law and Public Policy*, 6 (1989): 501.

9 Martin Delany, *Blake; or The Huts of America* (Boston: Beacon Press, 1970), p. 64.

10 Nell Irvin Painter, "Martin R. Delany: Elitism and Black Nationalism," in *Black Leaders of the Nineteenth Century*, ed. Leon Litwack and August Meier (Urbana: University of Illinois Press, 1988), pp. 162–65; Robert S. Levine, *Martin Delany, Frederick Douglass, and the Politics of Representative Identity* (Chapel Hill: University of North Carolina Press, 1997), pp. 180, 219–37; Gayatri Spivak with Ellen Rooney, "In a Word," *differences*, 1 (Summer 1989): 2.

11 Bruce Ackerman, *We the People: Transformations* (Cambridge, MA: Harvard University Press, 1998), pp. 92, 14, 114, 160–247.

12 A poll taken during the confirmation hearings on Judge Robert Bork's nomination to the Supreme Court, which began on September 15, 1987 and ended with Bork's withdrawal twelve days later, while not dispositive, suggests the striking long-term success of Reconstruction and Civil Rights era higher lawmaking:

Of white southerners polled, 62 percent said they were less inclined to support Bork upon hearing that "he has strongly criticized most of the landmark decisions protecting civil rights and individual liberties." Moreover, 68 percent of white southerners said they were less inclined to support Bork upon hearing that the NAACP opposed him. The same percentage was also less inclined to support him because Bork opposed "a decision striking down a poll tax requirement for voting." Bork's opposition to the public accommodations law pushed to 77 the percentage of southern whites less inclined to support him.

However fair or unfair this poll may have been to Bork, it is a telling indication of the degree to which the national consensus on race, citizenship, and justice had been shifted in precisely the direction urged by Douglass, Sumner, Thaddeus Stevens as well as Thurgood Marshall and the NAACP. Ethan Bronner, *Battle for Justice: How the Bork Nomination Shook America* (New York: Doubleday, 1989), pp. 289–90.

13 Morton J. Horwitz, *The Transformation of American Law: 1870–1960* (Cambridge, MA: Harvard University Press, 1992); Herget, *American Jurisprudence*; R. Jeffrey Lustig, *Corporate Liberalism: The Origins of Modern American Political Theory, 1890–1920* (Berkeley: University of California Press, 1982). Michael Rogin's and Brook Thomas's analyses of Melville's *Billy Budd* provide striking counter-examples exploring the dialogue between the era's legal positivism and its literary conceptualizations of justice. Rogin, *Subversive Genealogy*, pp. 298–316; Brook Thomas, *Cross-Examinations of Law and Literature: Cooper, Hawthorne, Stowe, and Melville* (Cambridge: Cambridge University Press, 1987), pp. 224–50.

14 By establishing the common political ground between the figures as well as the collaborative effects of their public disagreement and debate, Eric Sundquist and Robert Levine have done much to qualify oversimplified contrasts between Douglass and Delany. Sundquist, *To Wake the Nations*, pp. 108–09, 121; Levine, *Martin Delany, Frederick Douglass*. This book supplements these prior studies by examining the precise nature of the divergence between Delany's and Douglass's legal theories and by arguing that this jurisprudential contrast, rather than any difference about racial identity, constitutes the significant difference between the men.

15 In a chapter of *The Condition, Elevation, Emigration, and Destiny of the Colored People of the United States Politically Considered*, entitled the "National Disfranchisement of Colored People," Delany quotes entire the Fugitive Slave Act of 1850, stating that it is a "blind absurdity" for black Americans suffering "the dread consequences" of the racism written into the Constitution to deny that it in fact does make distinctions between people or to assert that it treats all alike. Delany, *The Condition* (1852, reprinted New York: Arno Press, 1968), pp. 147–53, 154, 155.

16 William Howard Day, Editorial on President Pierce's Inaugural, *Alienated American* (Cleveland, Ohio), April 9, 1853, reprinted in *The Black Abolitionist Papers*, ed. C. Peter Ripley, 5 vols. (Chapel Hill: University of North Carolina Press, 1991), IV: 149.

17 "The Reformer," Editorial, *Frederick Douglass's Paper* (Rochester, NY), April 7, 1854, reprinted in *The Black Abolitionist Papers*, IV: 212–13.

18 Delany, *Blake*, pp. 68, 96, 97; David Walker, *Walker's Appeal, with a Brief Sketch of his Life by Henry Highland Garnet, and also Garnet's Address to the Slaves of the United States* (1848, reprinted Salem, NH: Ayer, 1969), pp. 30, 80. Delany expressly found the ethical warrant for his positivist solutions to the problem of racial oppression in the higher law – "the common rights of man, based upon the great principles of common humanity." Delany, *The Condition*, p. 173.

19 Delany, *The Condition*, p. 27

20 William J. Watkins, for example, charged white abolitionists with lacking "the moral courage to *actualize* their ideas" by hiring qualified black employees in "their countinghouses, or workshops, for fear of impairing their business." Editorial, *Frederick Douglass's Paper* (Rochester, NY) February 10, 1854, in *The Black Abolitionist Papers*, IV: 203.

21 William Cheek and Aimee Lee Cheek, *John Mercer Langston and the Fight for Black Freedom: 1829–65* (Urbana: University of Illinois Press, 1989), p. 260.

22 Eric Foner, "Rights and the Constitution in Black Life during the Civil War and Reconstruction," *Journal of American History*, 74 (December 1987): 863, 866.

23 Delany, *The Condition*, pp. 157, 158. The vacillation between power-based and consent-based models of law and society was exemplified in the careers of William Howard Day and George Vashon. Initially a committed higher law constitutionalist, Day endorsed the Liberty and Free Soil parties, led the struggle to overturn Ohio's black laws, and lobbied for black suffrage before the state legislature and the 1850–51 state constitutional convention. But increasingly frustrated by the apparent failure of abolitionist argument to reform the nation's race relations, Day broke with Douglass, joining Martin R. Delany's Western faction at the 1854 and 1856 national emigration conventions in Cleveland. Moving in the other direction, George Vashon championed the precedent offered by the Haitian revolution and was himself a temporary emigrant to the black Republic, but later he criticized Delany's 1854 emigration convention and in 1862 wrote to Abraham Lincoln to express his opposition to the emigration policy outlined by the President in 1862 to settle freed slaves in Central America. *The Black Abolitionist Papers*, IV: 73–76, 79; Cheek, *John Mercer Langston*, pp. 115, 233.

24 Cheek, *John Mercer Langston*, pp. 115, 170, 175–78.

25 An Oberlin teacher had exposed Langston to Emerson's description of self-transformation in which history and tradition are not rejected but reconstructed. The transformative energy suggested by Emerson's vision appealed to Langston as a particularly apt figure for the kind of constitutional reformation he conceived of as his project. With his election as township clerk, Langston felt he not only had potential to reshape his own destiny but also to aid in reshaping the destiny of his community. Cheek, *John Mercer Langston*, p. 231, 261; see also, John Mercer Langston, *From the Virginia Plantation to the National Capitol, or The First and Only Negro Representative in Congress from the Old Dominion* (Hartford, CT: American Publishing, 1894).

26 Cheek, *John Mercer Langston*, p. 218.

27 Introducing Langston as "an excellent speaker and an able lawyer, born in Virginia a slave, educated afterward at Oberlin, in Ohio, and now giving to the neighboring university the fruits of his culture," Sumner read a letter from Langston dated December 26, 1871, containing the following passage: "I would have no colored man 'thrust' himself upon 'white people.' I would have white people and black upon the same *legal* level. And, as far as colored men are educated, learned, virtuous, and influential, I would have

them recognized and treated legally and socially according to their worth."
Congressional Globe, 42nd Cong., 2nd Sess., January 17, 1872, pp. 433–34.

28 Douglass, "The Claims of the Negro Ethnologically Considered," July 12, 1854, in *The Life and Writings of Frederick Douglass*, ed. Philip S. Foner, 5 vols. (New York: International Publishers, 1950), II: 305, 301, 306.

29 *Ibid.*, pp. 296, 307. Douglass's response to Nott, Morton, *et al.*, calls to mind Glenn Loury's response to Mary Lefkowitz's characterization of Afrocentric accounts of classic Greek culture as "rob[bing] the ancient Greeks and their modern descendants of a heritage that rightly belongs to them." Loury retorts, "And here I had been thinking it was *my* heritage too!" "[T]he search for a black Shakespeare or a black Tolstoy [is] unnecessary," because a shared cultural heritage is created through appreciation not consanguinity. Glenn Loury, "Color Blinded," *Arion: A Journal of Humanities and the Classics* (Winter 1997): 183–84.

30 Sterling Stuckey, *Slave Culture: Nationalist Theory and the Foundations of Black America* (New York: Oxford University Press, 1987), pp. 98–137; Leon F. Litwack, *North of Slavery: The Negro in the Free States, 7190–1860* (Chicago: University of Chicago Press, 1961), pp. 232–35.

31 Walker, *Appeal*, pp. 11, 80, 15, 18–19, 24–25, 30.

32 *Ibid.*, pp. 80–81, 15, 44, 74, 87. Like Walker, Garnet recommends violent resistance from the revolutionary era's higher law perspective: "NEITHER GOD, NOR ANGELS, OR JUST MEN, COMMAND YOU TO SUFFER FOR A SINGLE MOMENT. THEREFORE, IT IS YOUR SOLEMN AND IMPERATIVE DUTY TO USE EVERY MEANS, BOTH MORAL, INTELLECTUAL, AND PHYSICAL, THAT PROMISE SUCCESS [to end slavery]," and his revolutionary message is framed as a part of an emerging global moral consensus – "The nations of the old world are moving in the great cause of universal freedom, and some of them at least, will ere long, do you justice. The combined powers of Europe have placed their broad seal of disapprobation upon the African slave trade." From this cosmopolitan perspective, the pantheon of revolutionary heroes includes "Demark Veazie" as well as "Moses, Hampden, Tell, Bruce, and Wallace, Touissaint L'Ouverture, Lafayette and Washington." Garnet, "Address to the Slaves of the United States of America," in Walker, *Appeal*, pp. 95, 91.

33 We should note, in passing, that the universality of Delany's version of freemasonry becomes even more marked when one considers the anti-Catholic history of the organization. Delany, *The Origin and Objects of Ancient Freemasonry; Its Introduction into the United States, and Legitimacy Among Colored Men: A Treatise Delivered before St. Cyprian Lodge, No. 13, June 24th, A.D. 1853–A.L. 5853* (Pittsburgh: W.S. Haven, 1853), pp. 17, 18, 9, 30, 32.

34 As Robert Levine notes, Delany's "argument 'legitimates' blacks' place not only in Freemasonry but also in the Western cultures that attempt to exclude and degrade them." Levine, *Martin Delany, Frederick Douglass*, p. 9. Levine's astute and detailed reading of the similarities and differences between Douglass's ethnology address and Delany's freemasonry address

is, I think, complemented by this examination of the precise jurisprudential distinction between what Levine describes as their different forms of representative politics. The precise nature of the legal stakes involved in their debate would otherwise remain unclear, as would their respective places within the development of American jurisprudence.

35 Delany, *Freemasonry*, pp. 26, 6, 24.

36 In *The Condition, Elevation, Emigration, and Destiny of the Colored People*, Delany similarly separates higher and lower law, dividing all law into three major categories: *spiritual*, *moral*, and *physical* laws (given freemasonry's emphasis on the number three, Delany's three-way division comes as no surprise). Each category of law has its own instrumentality – prayer, moral sense, and power. One prays to get into heaven not for a change in government. To change government one must obtain power. While Delany's general emphasis on the practical application of moral insights resembles Douglass's higher law dualism of inspiration and agency, Delany's jurisprudence sharply differs in the way in which it severs power off from the formation of a moral consensus. Delany, *Freemasonry*, pp. 27–29, 12, 13; *The Condition*, pp. 38, 39.

37 John Bingham, *Congressional Globe*, 34th Cong., 3rd Sess., January 15, 1857, appendix, p. 140. Bingham's distinction between "*conventional* rights" that "are subject to the control of the majority" and "the rights of human nature" anticipates Bruce Ackerman's "dualist" conception of American democracy. In Ackerman's view, the American Constitution includes both normal, everday lawmaking in which no one doubts the authority of the majority to enact law and "higher lawmaking" which requires something tantamount to a declaration of "we the People," that is something akin to a plausibly universal moral consensus, as in the Declaration of Independence's proclamation of self-evident truths. Ackerman, *We The People: Foundations* (Cambridge, MA: Harvard University Press, 1991), pp. 6–7.

38 Delany, *Blake*; *Dred Scott v. Sandford*, 60 U.S. 393 (1857).

39 Dorothy Sterling, *The Making of an Afro-American: Martin Robinson Delany, 1812–1885* (Garden City, NY: Doubleday, 1971), pp. 176–85; Victor Ullman, *Martin R. Delany: The Beginnings of Black Nationalism* (Boston: Beacon Press, 1971), pp. 200–10; Wilson Jeremiah Moses, *The Golden Age of Black Nationalism, 1850–1925* (New York: Oxford University Press, 1978), pp. 149–55; Nell Irvin Painter, "Martin R. Delany: Elitism and Black Nationalism," in *Black Leaders of the Nineteenth Century*, ed. Leon Litwack and August Meier (Urbana: University of Illinois Press, 1988), pp. 157–58.

40 Sundquist, *To Wake the Nations*, pp. 182–221; Levine, *Martin Delany, Frederick Douglass*, pp. 190–215.

41 Paul Gilroy, *The Black Atlantic: Modernity and Double Consciousness* (Cambridge, MA: Harvard University Press, 1993), p. 27.

42 *Dred Scott v. Sandford*, 60 U.S. 393, 407. Taney's opinion posits the history of racial oppression as obviating the possibility of African American citizenship, but his opinion's history lesson is, in fact, a sectional credo,

a Southern polemic couched in the fearful, angry, and defiant sentiments of the antebellum South. Don E. Fehrenbacher, *The Dred Scott Case: Its Significance in American Law and Politics* (New York: Oxford University Press, 1978), pp. 559–61. Delany was certainly not alone in considering Taney's statement that black Americans had "no rights which the white man was bound to respect" a telling indication of the constitutional extent of black vulnerability. In 1862, Frederick Douglass used Taney's words to express his concerns for the legal status of the newly emancipated "freed men" (concerns that proved prophetic of Jim Crow): "Shall they . . . become the slaves of the community at large, having no rights which anybody is required to respect . . . Or shall they have secured to them equal rights before the law." Frederick Douglass, *Life and Writings of Frederick Douglass*, ed. Philip S. Foner, 5 vols. (New York: International, 1952–75), III: 292.

43 Delany, *Blake*, pp. 61, 262–63.

44 Martin Delany, "The Political Destiny of the Colored Race," in *Life and Public Services of Martin R. Delany*, ed. Frank (Frances) A. Rollin (1883; reprinted New York: Oxford University Press, 1991), pp. 333, 338.

45 Delany, *The Condition*, pp. 21, 18, 19, 15.

46 Delany, *Blake*, p. 287. As Paul Gilroy has observed, "The version of black solidarity *Blake* advances is explicitly anti-ethnic and opposes narrow African-American exceptionalism in the name of a truly pan-African, diaspora sensibility. This makes blackness a matter of politics rather than a common cultural condition." Gilroy, *The Black Atlantic*, p. 27.

47 Fehrenbacher, *Dred Scott*, pp. 322–34. *Dred Scott*, 60 U.S. 393, 404, 405. The role of power in Taney's conception of citizenship derives, at least distantly, from the fundamental interrelation of power and rights in early formulations of natural rights theory. Hugo Grotius's theory of rights, for instance, depended on some manifestation of power for recognition of concomitant rights. The example he gave for the origin of the primary right of property was the classical one of the acquisition of seats in a theater. Once they are claimed by physical possession, they become property. The agency and power of the occupant creates the cognizable legal relation. Richard Tuck, *Natural Rights Theories: Their Origin and Development* (Cambridge: Cambridge University Press, 1979), pp. 61–62.

48 Fehrenbacher, *Dred Scott*, p. 234. Many Republicans saw *Dred Scott* as a part of the South's conspiracy with the Buchanan administration to protect and extend the slave system in contravention of the fact that the electoral majority had shifted to the North. Seward and others were convinced that there had been collusion between Buchanan and Taney in formulating the *Dred Scott* outcome. David Zarefsky, *Lincoln, Douglass and Slavery in the Crucible of Public Debate* (Chicago: University of Chicago Press, 1990), p. 81. As Eric Foner notes, even "Two judicious observers of the politics of the 1850s, Roy F. Nichols and Allan Nevins, agree that during the Buchanan administration southern control of all branches of the federal government was virtually complete." Foner, *Free Soil, Free Labor, Free Men: The Ideology of the*

Republican Party before the Civil War (New York: Oxford University Press, 1970), p. 100.

49 *Charles River Bridge v. Warren Bridge*, 36 U.S. 420 (1837); Fehrenbacher, *Dred Scott*, pp. 226–35.

50 As Frederick Trevor Hill observes, though intended as a statement of historical fact, Taney's statement that a black American "has no rights which a white man was bound to respect" engendered considerable "popular wrath": "Thousands of copies of his opinion were printed with those of the dissenting judges . . . and in less than a fortnight Dred Scott had become a national character and his suit for assault and battery a *cause célèbre*." Hill, *Decisive Battles of the Law: Narrative Studies of Eight Legal Contests Affecting the History of the United States Between the Years 1800 and 1886* (New York: Harper and Brothers, 1907), p. 133. James Gordon Bennett's New York *Herald* (March 8, 15, April 14, 1857) praised the decision as "wise, just, and right." The Richmond *Enquirer* (March 17, 1857) saw Taney's holding as reflecting "the destiny of the African and Anglo Saxon races by an observance of the relations between them designed and decreed by divinity." Francis Lieber condemned it as "illegal, unjuridical, unphilosophical, and unethical." *The Life and Letters of Francis Lieber*, ed. Thomas Sergeant Perry (Boston: James R. Osgood, 1882), pp. 308–09. And Frederick Douglass termed the opinion a "vile and shocking abomination" but found a bright side in the fact that the opinion seemed to stimulate the "nation's conscience" rather than lulling it. Douglass, "The Dred Scott Decision," May 11, 1857, in *The Life and Writings of Frederick Douglass*, II: 407–09.

The singularly frank positivism of George Fitzhugh's endorsement of *Dred Scott* stands out. Fitzhugh adopted Taney's definition of citizenship, noting that as

> proved by the Ancient Republics . . . the most perfect social system is that where the slaves number ten to one to the citizens. (We employ the word "citizen," not according to Mr. Seward and Mr. Greely's version of the Higher Law, which would invest with the privilege any "featherless biped," but as defined in the Dred Scott case, and as understood and practiced by the Greeks and Romans.) (Fitzhugh, "Black Republicanism in Athens," *De Bow's Review*, 23, (July–December 1857): 20–26)

51 Taney's opinion implicitly rejects the distinction drawn by Chief Justice John Marshall between Constitution and code: a differentiation crucial to Douglass's antislavery constitutionalism and more recently delineated by Ronald Dworkin as the difference between concepts and conceptions. According to Dworkin, the Constitution employs concepts rather than the conceptions of specific code sections, and a court interpreting a constitutional concept should look at present as well as past specific conceptions of that concept (e.g., the changing examples of what constitutes cruel and unusual punishment). Such an interpretive practice allows the concept to be redefined by the new conceptions of subsequent generations. Dworkin, *Taking Rights Seriously* (Cambridge, MA: Harvard University Press, 1977), pp. 134–36. H. Jefferson Powell's account of the late eighteenth-century lawyers'

approach to "intent" provides historical support for Dworkin's interpretive distinction. According to Powell, for such eighteenth-century lawyers as the framers, a law's intent was to be derived by judicial construction of each age's sense of reasonable meanings and outcomes. "The Original Understanding of Original Intent," *Harvard Law Review*, 98 (March 1985) 899. As J.R. Pole notes, "there was neither historical evidence nor logical support" for Taney's notion that the framers and signatories to the Constitution could not have intended to make the Constitution adaptable to subsequent metamorphoses in the American community. J.R. Pole, *The Pursuit of Equality in American History* (Berkeley: University of California Press, 1993), p. 183.

52 *Dred Scott*, 60 U.S. 393, 405, 426, 403; Paul W. Kahn, *Legitimacy and History: Self-Government in American Constitutional Theory* (New Haven: Yale University Press, 1992), p. 47.

53 Critics jumped on the exaggerations and distortions of Taney's history lesson. Terming the decision the product of "a depraved judiciary," written by "a man profoundly immoral," George Bancroft found Taney's account to show "an open scorn for the facts of history." Bancroft, "The Place of Lincoln in American History," *Atlantic Monthly*, 15 (June 1865): 762. The New York *Tribune* (March 10, 1857) lambasted the Court's version of history:

as early as 1705, Lord Holt had held that the law of England afforded no warrant for holding anybody in Slavery, and that as to this matter, negroes did not differ from other men – a doctrine solemnly reiterated and forever established in the famous case of Somerset, three years previous to the Declaration of Independence . . . so far, indeed, from it being received at the time of the Declaration of Independence as "an axiom" that negroes had no rights, and that anybody might lawfully reduce them to bondage, it was precisely at that period that Christendom fully woke up to the ideal that all men had natural rights, and that negro Slavery was no less a usurpation and an abuse than white Slavery. Nor is there any room to doubt that it was this very idea which the authors of the Declaration of Independence intended to embody in that document . . . The "self-evident truths" with the enunciation of which the Declaration of Independence sets out, were not put forward in that document as truths which had been practiced upon – in which case no declaration of them would have been needed – but as truths that ought to be practiced upon. Understood according to the system of interpretation propounded by our slaveholders' Judges, and the whole Declaration means – nothing.

54 *Dred Scott*, 60 U.S. 393, 407, 571–88; Fehrenbacher, *Dred Scott*, pp. 406–14; New York *Tribune*, March 10, 1857. Taney's version of a uniform white perception of African descendants suppresses the uneasiness that many white Americans felt regarding the continuing existence of slavery in a nation supposedly dedicated to equality and liberty – a discomfort evidenced by a rise in manumissions after the Revolution and the creation of a number of abolitionist societies, "which drew their inspiration from the republican belief in the natural liberty of the person, and their rhetoric from the Declaration of Independence." Pole, *The Pursuit of Equality in American History*, pp. 51–52.

55 Douglass, "What the Black Man Wants," in *The Frederick Douglass Papers*, ed. John Blassingames, 5 vols. (New Haven: Yale University Press, 1985), IV: 65; Emerson, "WO Liberty," *The Journals and Miscellaneous Notebooks of Ralph Waldo Emerson*, ed. William H. Gilman *et al.*, 16 vols. (Cambridge, MA: Harvard University Press, 1960–82), XIV: 429. In a letter to Francis Lieber written while composing his memorial oration on Abraham Lincoln, George Bancroft wondered at Taney's suggestion that blacks were one of the "slave races," asking incredulously "Are slave *races* known to canon law, civil law, common law? or international law? Did ever before a judge from the bench declare the existence of *slave races?*" Letter in Lieber collection in Huntington Library, San Marino, California.

56 *Dred Scott*, 60 U.S. 393, 410. See Pierre Bourdieu, *Outline of a Theory of Practice* (Cambridge: Cambridge University Press, 1977), pp. 163–71.

57 *Dred Scott* 60 U.S. 393, 407. One can get a glimpse of the growing higher law consensus requiring Taney to admit that times had changed in the reactions his opinion drew in the House and the Senate. Of course there were those who supported the opinion, but a number of elected officials were startlingly willing to disavow the opinion, which for better or worse was the law of the land within the constitutional scheme. For example, John Bingham denied the Court's authority to "deprive large numbers of [the people] of their natural rights." Senator Fessenden of Maine stated "I do not hold, either in substance or in form, to any extent to the doctrines of the Dred Scott opinion." *Congressional Globe*, 36th Cong., 1st Sess., April 24, 1860, p. 1839; 35th Cong., 1st Sess., May 5, 1858, p. 1964.

58 Richmond *Enquirer*, March 13, 1857. The Natchez Mississippi *Free Trader* similarly termed Taney's ruling as the "triumph of national principles" over higher law "fanaticism" (May 15, 1857). And the New York *Tribune* saw the opinion as reflecting the "trembling terror" provoked in proslavery politics by the higher law argument of Chase, Sumner, and others (March 17, 1857).

59 Delany's 1852 recommendation of emigration anticipated not only the positivist thrust of Taney's opinion but much of its wording, arguing that "It is useless to talk about our rights . . . Our descent, by the laws of the country, stamps us with inferiority." Delany, *The Condition*, p. 158.

60 Samuel Tyler, *Memoir of Roger Brooke Taney* (Baltimore: John Murphy & Co., 1872), p. 579. George Fitzhugh was among those who set the stage for Taney's use of the rhetoric of nature. Viewing authoritarian schemes of social organization, like slavery and the family, as natural institutions that appropriately reflect an inherent or divinely ordained distribution of power and responsibility, Fitzhugh offered the analogy of ant and bee hives, hoping that, once the reader recognized the similarly social character of human beings, he or she would accept the associated trait of the hive's hierarchical power structure as an innate part of human society as well. Fitzhugh, *Sociology for the South* (Richmond, VA: A. Morris, 1854), pp. 25–26, 177–79.

61 *Dred Scott*, 60 U.S. 393, 416; Tyler, *Memoir*, p. 601.

62 Delany, *Blake*, p. 263.

63 20 Howell State Trials 1. Mansfield's oral decision was not officially reported and that has created a problem of variant versions. See William M. Wiecek, "*Somerset*: Lord Mansfield and the Legitimacy of Slavery in the Anglo-American World," *University of Chicago Law Review*, 42 (1974): 141–46.

64 Kermit L. Hall, *The Magic Mirror: Law in American History* (New York: Oxford University Press, 1989), p. 130; Fehrenbacher, *Dred Scott*, pp. 53–56.

65 Wiecek, "*Somerset*," p. 138.

66 New York *Tribune*, March 17 and 10, 1857.

67 Delany, *Blake*, pp. 60, 64.

68 *Ibid.*, p. 263.

69 *Ibid.*, p. 113.

70 *Ibid.*, p. 262.

71 Delany, "Political Destiny," p. 335. The constitutional promise of Delany's jurisprudence lies in his conception of a governing political ethos that is not fixed at any particular historical moment, as in Taney's constitutional hermeneutics of stasis, but changes over time, reflecting the changing composition and perceptions of the community. As Delany put it in *The Condition*, "The colored people of to-day are not the colored people of a quarter of a century ago, and require very different means and measures to satisfy their wants and demands," p. 8.

72 Delany, "Political Destiny," pp. 329–30; Delany, *Blake*, p. 287; Francis Lieber, *On Civil Liberty and Self-Government* (Philadelphia: J.B. Lippincott, 1901), p. 31.

73 Delany, *Blake*, pp. 288; *Dred Scott*, 60 U.S. 393, 405. Foreshadowing his *Dred Scott* opinion, while serving as Andrew Jackson's Attorney General, Taney characterized the rights of free blacks as "privileges they are allowed [by whites] to enjoy . . . as a matter of kindness and benevolence rather than of right." Fehrenbacher, *Dred Scott*, p. 70. Like Taney, Delany's Judge Ballard finds in the history of American slavery and racism ample proof that, in regard to the "doctrines of human rights," "'free black[s] . . . are liable to enslavement by any white person. They are freemen by sufferance.'" *Blake*, p. 61.

74 Delany, *Blake*, pp. 153, 61–62, 287.

75 Biographically, it might be more accurate to say that Delany gives up on rather than rejects consent. Writing to Frederick Douglass, Delany said: "I care but little, what white men think of what I say, write, or do; my sole desire is, to benefit the colored people; this being done, I am satisfied – the opinion of every white person in the country or the world, to the contrary notwithstanding." *Frederick Douglass's Paper* (Rochester, NY) July 23, 1852. These comments signal Delany's abandonment of forming an interracial political consensus in the U.S. One hears the tone of resignation in Delany's comments to William Lloyd Garrison, thanking him for a generally favorable notice of *The Condition*:

I am not in favor of caste, nor a separation of the brotherhood of mankind, and would as willingly live among white men as black, if I had an *equal possession and enjoyment* of privileges; but shall never be reconciled to live among them, subservient to their will – existing by mere *sufferance*, as we, the colored people, do, in this country. The majority of white men cannot see why colored men cannot be satisfied with their condition in Massachusetts – what they desire more than the *granted* right of citizenship. Blind selfishness on the one hand, and deep prejudice on the other, will not permit them to understand that we desire the *exercise* and *enjoyment* of these rights, as well as the *name* of their possession. If there were any probability of this, I should be willing to remain in the country, fighting and struggling on, the good fight of faith. But I must admit, that I have no hopes in this country – no confidence in the American people – with a *few* excellent exceptions – therefore, I have written as I have done. (Letter from M.R. Delany to Garrison, dated May 14, 1852, in *Liberator,* May 21, 1852)

76 Delany, *Blake*, p. 258; see also, Delany, *The Condition*, p. 36.
77 As Thomas Grey notes, "Holmes is the great oracle of American legal thought, but as with other oracles his message is subject to much dispute." Holmes has been lauded as a great writer, a penetrating critic of legal formalism, and an eloquent herald of progressive politics, and he has been lambasted as an amoral positivist and dismissed as a muddled thinker. Grey makes an effective argument that all the sides of Holmes are best grouped under the heading of legal pragmatism, despite Holmes's own dismissal of William James's version of pragmatism as "humbug." Grey, "Holmes and Legal Pragmatism," *Stanford Law Review*, 41 (April 1989): 787–89.
78 R. Jeffrey Lustig, for example, notes that the "draconian" side of "Holmes's view of law" excluded the "ethical element" and "cut behavior loose from conscience." "Devoid of moral content," law ultimately rests on force. Lustig, *Corporate Liberalism*, pp. 177, 178, 181. See also Henry M. Hart, "Holmes' Positivism – An Addendum," *Harvard Law Review*, 64 (1951): 929; Yosal Rogat, "The Judge as Spectator," *University of Chicago Law Review*, 31 (1964): 213; John Patrick Diggins, *The Promise of Pragmatism: Modernism and the Crisis of Knowledge and Authority* (Chicago: University of Chicago Press, 1994), pp. 349, 353; Herget, *American Jurisprudence*, p. 151; Horwitz, *Transformation of American Law, 1870–1960*, pp. 140–41.
79 It is interesting to note that, though violence did not erupt, Emerson's attempt to speak on January 24, 1861 was routed by hecklers whom Emerson chided as "foreigners" forgetting their places in interrupting the native sons of Boston. Ralph Waldo Emerson, *Emerson's Antislavery Writings*, eds. Len Gougeon and Joel Myerson (New Haven: Yale University Press, 1995), pp. 125, 126; G. Edward White, *Justice Oliver Wendell Holmes: Law and the Inner Self* (New York: Oxford University Press, 1993), pp. 341–42, 32, 36–37, 45; Mark DeWolfe Howe, *Oliver Wendell Holmes: The Shaping Years* (Cambridge, MA: Harvard University Press, 1957), pp. 49, 54, 65.
80 Holmes was wounded three times, and each incident had a darkly comic and anarchic aspect. White, *Holmes*, pp. 52, 72–74, 57–59, 60–61, 62–63; Sheldon Novick, *Honorable Justice: The Life of Oliver Wendell Holmes* (Boston: Little, Brown and Company, 1989), pp. 45–52, 65–68, 71–80, 84–86; Baker, *The Justice from Beacon Hill*, pp. 148–50.

81 George Fredrickson, *The Inner Civil War: Northern Intellectuals and the Crisis of the Union* (Urbana: University of Illinois Press, 1993), pp. 169–70; Saul Touster, "In Search of Holmes from Within," *Vanderbilt Law Review*, 36 (1965): 437, 449.

82 Quoted in Baker, *The Justice from Beacon Hill*, p. 623.

83 Quoted in Novick, *Honorable Justice*, pp. 140–41; Howe, *The Shaping Years*, pp. 220–21; Jan Vetter, "The Evolution of Holmes, Holmes and Evolution," *California Law Review*, 72 (1984): 343, 362–63.

84 Holmes, *The Common Law* (Boston: Little, Brown and Company, 1963), p. 5; James Willard Hurst, *Justice Holmes on Legal History* (New York: Macmillan, 1964), pp. 1, 3; Horwitz, *Transformation of American Law: 1870–1960*, pp. 128–30.

85 Holmes, "Common Carriers and the Common Law," *American Law Review*, 13 (1879) 608, 630–31.

86 Holmes, *The Common Law*, p. 41.

87 *Ibid.*, p. 32.

88 Quoted in Morton Horwitz, *The Transformation of American Law, 1780–1860* (Cambridge, MA: Harvard University Press, 1977), p. 8.

89 Herget, *American Jurisprudence*, pp. 63–66; Perry Miller, *The Life of the Mind of America: From the Revolution to the Civil War* (New York: Harcourt Brace Jovanovich, 1965), pp. 156–64; Horwitz, *Transformation of American Law: 1870–1960*, pp. 117–20, 10; Horwitz, *Transformation of American Law: 1780–1860*, pp. 256–57; Hall, *The Magic Mirror*, pp. 9–10, 15–16, 126–27; Lawrence Friedman, *A History of American Law* (New York: Touchstone, 1985), pp. 407–08, 540.

90 James Coolidge Carter, "The Ideal and the Actual in the Law," *American Law Review*, 24 (1890): 752, 775, 770.

91 Conscience could not be the basis for law because it was too various, too idiosyncratic to produce a consistent and stable system of law. James Coolidge Carter, *Law: Its Origin, Growth, and Function* (New York: G.P. Putnam's Sons, 1907), pp. 141–42.

92 Alexis de Tocqueville, *Democracy in America* (New York: Vintage Books, 1954), p. 156; Holmes, "The Path of the Law," in *Collected Legal Papers* (New York: Harcourt, Brace & Howe, 1920), p. 182.

93 Holmes, "The Path of the Law," pp. 172–73; Francis Biddle, *Justice Holmes, Natural Law, and the Supreme Court* (New York: Macmillan, 1961), p. 71.

94 Holmes, *The Common Law*, p. 32; "The Path of the Law," pp. 161–62, 167.

95 *Lochner v. New York*, 198 U.S. 45, 74 (1905).

96 *Bailey v. Alabama*, 219 U.S. 219 (1911).

97 *Ibid.*, 219 U.S. 219, 245; White, *Holmes*, p. 337.

98 Holmes, *The Common Law*, p. 300; see also "The Path of the Law," p. 164, where Holmes ridicules "the confusion of legal and moral ideas ... in the law of contract"; *Bailey vs. Alabama*, 219 U.S. 219, 246.

99 An extensive study of Holmes's opinions in cases in which civil rights claims were made by black petitioners indicates that Holmes's "consistent

reaction" was to "deny . . . the claimed right, sometimes in dissent against majority support of the right." Yosal Rogat, "Mr. Justice Holmes: A Dissenting Opinion," *Stanford Law Review*, 15 (1963): 254, 255.

100 White, *Holmes*, p. 343.

101 C. Vann Woodward's *The Strange Career of Jim Crow* (New York: Oxford University Press, 1974) and Joel Williamson's *The Crucible of Race: Black–White Relations in the American South Since Emancipation* (New York: Oxford University Press, 1984), for instance, though enormously helpful and revealing in capturing the rising tide of American racism, make no effort to connect that racism to the positivist conception of law.

102 Woodward, *Strange Career*, pp. 73–74.

103 Once termed a "perversion" and "a decision that shocked the moral and judicial sense of mankind," for defenders such as Mikell, Taney's *Dred Scott* opinion was "unassailable in the logic with which it declared unconstitutional the aim and purpose of the Republican party." Senator Fessenden, *Congressional Globe*, 35th Cong., 1st Sess., May 5, 1858, p. 1964; Senator Oliver Morton, *Cong. Globe*, 40th Cong., 3rd Sess., February 8, 1869, p. 991; Mikell as quoted in Fehrenbacher, *Dred Scott*, p. 588.

104 Fehrenbacher, *Dred Scott*, pp. 587–89.

105 Charles Sumner, "Freedom National, Slavery Sectional," in *The Works of Charles Sumner*, 15 vols. (Boston: Lee and Shepard, 1872), III:184; Frederick Trevor Hill, *Decisive Battles of the Law: Narrative Studies of Eight Legal Contests Affecting the History of the United States Between the Years 1800 and 1886* (New York: Harper and Brothers, 1907), p. 116.

106 Mark Twain, *The Adventures of Huckleberry Finn* (New York: Norton, 1977), p. 26.

107 *Ibid.*, pp. 26–27.

108 Under Ohio law of the time, a person of mixed racial heritage, if white enough, could be sworn in as a lawyer. John Mercer Langston, *From the Virginia Plantation to the National Capitol, or The First and Only Negro Representative in Congress from the Old Dominion*, (Hartford, CT: American Publishing, 1894), p. 125.

109 Sumner, *Congressional Globe*, 42nd Cong., 2nd Sess., January 31, 1872, p. 729; *Congressional Globe*, 42nd Cong., 2nd Sess., January 17, 1872, pp. 433–34; Eric Foner, *Reconstruction: America's Unfinished Revolution, 1863–1877* (New York: Harper and Row, 1988), pp. 504–05, 532–34; Richard Kluger, *Simple Justice: The History of* Brown v. Board of Education *and Black America's Struggle for Equality* (New York: Random House, 1977), p. 50.

110 New York *Times*, February 8, 1875; January 24, 1883.

111 New York *Times* March 3, 7, 8, 1875. The *Times* reported on similar incidents in Richmond, Virginia (March 7, 1875), Washington, D.C. and Louisville, Kentucky (March 6, 1875), Trenton, New Jersey (March 16, 1875), and Montgomery, Alabama (March 13, 1875).

112 New York *Times*, May 2, 5, 1875.

113 New York *Times*, March 11, 1875. In a debate on the Act, North Carolina Senator Augustus S. Merrimon turns black Americans' access to the

public sphere into a kind of joke, asking what the Act's "other places of public amusement" means – "Is it a menagerie...a circus...[a] Fourth of July celebration, a barbecue, a harangue, an exhibition of large men, of small men, or of fat men...a collection of monkeys, or a cage of snakes, and such like things?" *Congressional Globe*, 43rd Cong., 1st Sess., May 22, 1874, Appendix, p. 361.

114 New York *Times*, March 7, 1875.

115 Sundquist, *To Wake the Nations*, pp. 259, 281–82; Robert Bodgan, *Freak Show* (Chicago: University of Chicago Press, 1988), p. 134; Eric Lott, *Love and Theft: Blackface Minstrelsy and the American Working Class* (New York: Oxford University Press, 1995), pp. 5–6, 140–41. As Leonard Cassuto observes, "Freaks and freak shows are the visible artifacts of an attempt to cast one group of humans outside the human category, but the fetishistic attention they receive serves alone as ample evidence of the failure of that attempt." Cassuto, *The Inhuman Race: the Racial Grotesque in American Literature* (New York: Columbia University Press, 1997), p. 179.

116 Bodgan, *Freak Show*, pp. 121–29, 134–35, 154–55. Our horror at these exhibitions derives in part from our inheritance of the higher law universalism of Douglass, Sumner, and others, which privileges moral agency, not physical inherence. What our facile feelings of disgust may at times mask, however, is the close relation that can (though does not necessarily) obtain between the sympathetic image of the victim (e.g., the shivering fugitive) and the objectified image of the freak. Sensing this connection, the Natchez *Free Trader*, within days of the paper's coverage of *Dred Scott*, noted the discovery in Ohio of "the skeleton of a man, who when living...stood 20 feet." The paper connected this tall tale to Stowe's novel, noting that "The Buckeyes seem apt at gettin off *gigantic* as well as negro-dramatic tales." In both cases, our supposed common-sense acceptance of natural facts, such as black inferiority, belies the tale, and in both cases, it is precisely the freak show-like exaggeration of nature that gives the tale its entertainment value – the implausible giant and Christ-like Negro. Natchez, Mississippi *Free Trader*, March 6, 1857.

117 *Bradwell v. State of Illinois*, 83 U.S. 130, 131, 136 (1873).

118 *Chae Chan Ping v. U.S.* (The Chinese Exclusion Case), 130 U.S. 594 (1889).

119 *The Slaughterhouse Cases*, 83 U.S. 36 (1873); Otto Olsen, *The Thin Disguise* (New York: Humanities Press, 1967), p. 6, n. 3. *Slaughterhouse* and its offspring, as Frederick Douglass noted, made a "mockery" of the citizenship rights expressly guaranteed to black Americans by the Civil War amendments. *United States v. Reese*, 92 U.S. 214 (1875) (holding that the Fifteenth Amendment did not grant black men the right to vote); *United States v. Cruikshank*, 92 U.S. 214 (1875) (holding that a state's passive promotion or acceptance of the private infringement of black citizens' rights was not prohibited by the Fourteenth Amendment). Douglass, as quoted in Loren Miller, *The Petitioners: The Story of the Supreme Court of the United States and the Negro* (New York: Pantheon, 1966), p. 114.

120 Harlan was raised in a slaveholding family and had a mulatto half- brother who was the offspring of Harlan's father and a slave. Loren P. Beth, *John Marshall Harlan: The Last Whig Justice* (Lexington: University of Kentucky Press, 1992), pp. 2 and 12–13. Entering politics as a Whig, Harlan later became a Know- Nothing. On the eve of the Civil War, Harlan opposed se- cession, but firmly supported slaveholders' rights to their human property. Harlan protested both the Emancipation Proclamation and the Thirteenth Amendment. After the war, however, Harlan came to support the Civil War amendments, repudiating racism and his former Know-Nothing prejudices against Roman Catholics and immigrants; *ibid.*, p. 2; Louis Filler, "John M. Harlan," in *The Justices of the United States Supreme Court 1789–1969*, ed. Leon Friedman and Fred Israel (New York: Chelsea House, 1969), p. 1281.

121 *Civil Rights Cases*, 109 U.S. 2, 31, 32, 36, 57 (1883).

122 *Plessy v. Ferguson*, 163 U.S. 537, 559, 561 (1896). It is worth noting here that Harlan's success in setting aside his prejudices was limited. In trying to illustrate powerfully the injustice of legal segregation, Harlan appealed to the patent unfairness of a "Chinaman" receiving better treatment than a black veteran of the Civil War. While deplorable, such limitations to Harlan's egalitarianism (such as his anti-Chinese bias or his unwillingness in *Cumming v. Richmond County Board of Education*, 175 U.S. 528 [1899] to embrace integrated schools), do not erase the importance of Harlan's contribution to the higher law constitutionalism. For decades, Harlan's dissents were the best authority legal reformers had for a race-neutral interpretation of the rights of citizenship.

123 New York *Times*, November 19, 1883, October 16, 1883.

124 Phillip Butcher, *George Washington Cable* (New York: Twayne Publishers, Inc., 1962), p. 82; Woodward, *Strange Career*, pp. 44–47; Williamson, *Crucible of Race*, pp. 97–100.

125 George Washington Cable, *John March, Southerner* (New York: Charles Scribner's Sons, 1898), pp. 122–23; Butcher, *Cable*, pp. 117–125; Letter from Cable to Twain, October 25, 1884, in Guy A. Cardwell, *Twins of Genius* (East Lansing: Michigan State Press, 1953), p. 105.

126 Woodward, *Strange Career*, pp. 67–74; Williamson, *Crucible of Race*, pp. 111–39.

127 Twain, *Huckleberry Finn*, p. 23.

128 Holmes, "The Path of the Law," p. 173.

129 Twain, *Huckleberry Finn*, p. 72. Brook Thomas, *American Literary Realism and the Failed Promise of Contract* (Berkeley: University of California Press, 1997), p. 5.

130 Twain, *Huckleberry Finn*, pp. 168–69.

131 Twain observes in his novel's companion story of Siamese twins, "The Extraordinary Twins," which is only incompletely removed from the novel by a kind of "literary caesarian section," that the whole point of the original "show" was "to exhibit that monstrous 'freak'" – "the twin-monster." He says he got the idea for the story from "a picture of a youthful Italian 'freak' – or 'freaks' – which was – or were – on exhibition in our cities – a combination consisting of two heads and four arms joined

to a single body and a single pair of legs." Twain, *Pudd'nhead Wilson and Those Extraordinary Twins* (New York: Penguin, 1969), pp. 303, 230.
132 Thomas, *American Literary Realism*, pp. 191–230; Sundquist, *To Wake the Nations*, pp. 225–70; Michael Cowan, "'By Right of the White Election,' Political Theology and Theological Politics in *Pudd'nhead Wilson*," in *Mark Twain's* Pudd'nhead Wilson: *Race, Conflict, and Culture*, ed. Susan Gillman and Forrest G. Robinson (Durham, NC: Duke University Press, 1990), pp. 155–76; Wilson Carey McWilliams, "*Pudd'head Wilson* and Democratic Governance," in *Mark Twain's* Pudd'nhead Wilson *Race, Conflict, and Culture*, pp. 177–89.
133 Twain, *Pudd'nhead Wilson*, pp. 55–6.
134 Bodgan, *Freak Show*, pp. 235–56.
135 Twain, *Pudd'nhead Wilson*, pp. 53–4.
136 Horace Kallen, "Democracy Versus the Melting Pot," *Nation*, 100 (February 18–25, 1915): 214.
137 Twain, *Pudd'nhead Wilson*, pp. 157–58, 138–42; William Dean Howells, *My Mark Twain* (Baton Rouge: Louisiana State University Press, 1967), p. 30.
138 Twain, *Pudd'nhead Wilson*, pp. 138–39, 140–41, 145, 157–58.
139 *Ibid.*, p. 178.
140 Twain considered writing as a professional alternative to law. He had an intense interest in legal procedure and legal doctrine, such as the law of intellectual property. And he had some litigation success in *Clemens v. Such*, urging trademark as a supplement to copyright protection. Throughout his writing one sees the evidence of Twain's close and critical scrutiny of American law (e.g., Twain's parody of American jury trials in *The Gilded Age* [1873], a novel he co-wrote with an attorney, Charles Dudley Warner). *Mark Twain's Letters*, ed. Edgar Marquess Branch, Michael B. Frank, and Kenneth M. Sanderson (Berkeley: University of California Press, 1988), p. 139; Paul Fatout, *Twain Speaks for Himself* (West Lafayette, IN: Purdue University Press, 1978), p. 76; Mark Twain and Charles Dudley Warner, *The Gilded Age* (Indianapolis, IN: Bobbs-Merrill, 1972).
141 Nan Goodman, *Shifting the Blame: Literature, Law and the Theory of Accidents in Nineteenth-Century America* (New York: Routledge, 2000), p. 65.
142 Nicholas St. John Green, "Proximate and Remote Cause," *American Law Review*, 4 (1870): 211.
143 Twain, *Pudd'nhead Wilson*, p. 68.
144 *Ibid.*, pp. 67–68.
145 *Ibid.*, pp. 225–26.
146 *Ibid.*, pp. 217, 218–19.
147 *Ibid.*, p. 221.

5 CHARLES CHESNUTT AND MOORFIELD STOREY:
CITIZENSHIP AND THE FLUX OF CONTRACT

1 See, e.g., Robert Crunden, *Ministers of Reform: The Progressives' Achievement in American Civilization, 1889–1920* (New York: Basic Books, 1982); Richard

Hofstadter, *Age of Reform: From Bryan to F.D.R.* (New York: Knopf, 1955); James H. Kettner, *The Development of American Citizenship, 1608–1870* (Chapel Hill: University of North Carolina Press, 1978), p. 197. Booker T. Washington's famous example of the brick manufacture at Tuskeegee illustrates his version of freedom through economic contract – "We had something which they wanted [good bricks at a fair price]; they had something which we wanted [money]. This, in a large measure, helped to lay the foundation for the pleasant relations that have continued to exist between us and the white people in that section, and which now extend throughout the South.") *Up From Slavery: An Autobiography*, (New York: Carol Publishing, 1989), p. 153. Amy Dru Stanley provides a cogent and well-researched account of the centrality of contract for post-emancipation reformers, such as feminists, in *From Bondage to Contract: Wage Labor, Marriage, and the Market in the Age of Slave Emancipation* (Cambridge: Cambridge University Press, 1998), pp. 4–17, 177–86.

2 Sir Henry Maine, *Ancient Law: Its Connection with the Early History of Society and Its Relation to Modern Ideas* (London: J. Murray, 1930), p. 182; Samuel Williston, "Freedom of Contract," *Cornell Law Quarterly*, 6 (1921): 365, 366.

3 William Graham Sumner, *What the Social Classes Owe to Each Other* (New York: Arno Press, 1972, orig. pub. 1883), pp. 15–16. Of course, women, Indians, African Americans, and many others reading this passage might well and with good reason ridicule Sumner's facile dispatching of the status-based ascriptive models of citizenship then and now. But such inconsistencies between practice and principle provide the cultural leverage on which reform movements depend.

4 See, for example, Chief Justice Marshall's comments in *Ogden v. Saunders*: "If, on tracing the right to contract, and the obligations created by contract, to their source, we find them to exist anterior to, and independent of society, we may reasonably conclude that those original and pre-existing principles are, like many other natural rights brought with man into society; and, although they may be controlled, are not given by human legislation." 12 Wheat. 25 U.S. 213, 345, 6 L.Ed. 606 (1827).

5 It is important to note that the advent of liberty of contract or substantive due process, while one of extraordinary judicial activism, did not result in wholesale invalidations of legislation. More laws survived than perished under the liberty of contract principle, yet courts did substitute their judgment for that of legislatures in many cases, particularly in those dealing with labor and unions. Herbert Hovenkamp, *Enterprise and American Law, 1836–1937* (Cambridge, MA: Harvard University Press, 1991), pp. 171–72, 199–204; Kermit L. Hall, *The Magic Mirror: Law in American History* (New York: Oxford University Press, 1989), pp. 238–45.

6 *Butchers' Union S.H. & L.S. Co. v. Crescent City L.S.L. & S.H. Co.*, 111 U.S. 746, 762 (1883)

7 Chesnutt and Storey shared a mixed attitude toward the free trade concept behind liberty of contract. Both believed in free trade as a matter of theory, but both were also willing to acknowledge that the interests of justice

required that trade be regulated in certain circumstances. See, Chesnutt, "Why I Am a Republican," in *Charles W. Chesnutt: Essays and Speeches*, ed. Joseph R. McElrath, Jr., Robert C. Leitz, III, and Jesse S. Crisler (Stanford, CA: Stanford University Press, 1999), p. 95–96, and William B. Hixson, Jr., *Moorfield Storey and the Abolitionist Tradition* (New York: Oxford University Press, 1972), pp. 154–59.

8 Feminists, such as Stanton, Woodhull, and Anthony, were also aware of the radical social transformations that became possible when one combined the traditional value of free and equal contract with traditional notions of gender and marriage. The former had the capacity, if actually put into practice, to dissolve the latter. Stanley, *Bondage to Contract*, pp. 175–217. Similarly, a Harvard law student, in 1890, recognized the social innovations made possible by the way the judiciary's liberty of contract doctrine yokes contract to the natural rights conceptions of freedom and equality, anticipating that the doctrine, if taken to its logical conclusion, would bar legislative interference with marriage, such as proscriptions on interracial marriage. "The True Meaning of the Term 'Liberty' in those Clauses in the Federal and State Constitutions which Protect 'Life, Liberty, and Property,'" *Harvard Law Review*, 5 (1890): 391.

9 Charles Chesnutt, *Frederick Douglass* (Boston: Small, Maynard, 1899), p. 102; Moorfield Storey and Marcial L. Lichauco, *The Conquest of the Philippines by the United States, 1898–1925* (Freeport, NY: Books for Libraries, 1971), p. v; Moorfield Storey, *Abraham Lincoln: An Address Delivered at the Shawmut Congregational Church in Boston on February 14, 1909* (Boston: Geo. H. Ellis, 1909), p. 6.

10 Chesnutt was the son of free blacks belonging to what was known as the "bright mulatto" class – light-skinned black Americans whose complexion brought with it certain advantages in the color-conscious Fayetteville, North Carolina where Chesnutt grew up. Returning to his birthplace, Cleveland, Ohio, Chesnutt trained for and passed the bar in 1887, but race prejudice confined his professional career to building a very successful court-reporting firm. Chesnutt studied arguments for and against Jim Crow carefully, and, as Frederick Douglass's biographer, he became very familiar with the view of the Constitution Douglass shared with Sumner and Emerson. Eric Sundquist, *To Wake the Nations: Race in the Making of American Literature* (Cambridge, MA: Harvard University Press, 1993), p. 430; Charles Chesnutt, *Frederick Douglass* (Boston: Small, Maynard, 1899). As Sumner's clerk and biographer, Storey obtained considerable experience of the politics of higher law constitutionalism. Storey became one of the nation's preeminent constitutional lawyers, achieving note as an anti-imperialist, mugwump reformer, and ardent supporter of black franchise. As President of the NAACP, Storey framed the constitutional arguments of its early litigation campaign. Hixson, *Moorfield Storey*; Moorfield Storey, *Charles Sumner* (New York: Russell & Russell, 1900).

11 "The Negro's Franchise," May 11, 1901, *Essays and Speeches*, p. 162.

12 Sumner, *The Works of Charles Sumner*, 15 vols. (Boston: Lee and Shepard, 1877), X: 203, 156; XII: 195–96.

13 "Sources of Danger to the Republic," February 7, 1867, in *The Frederick Douglass Papers: Series One: Speeches, Debates, and Interviews*, ed. John Blassingame, 5 vols. (New Haven: Yale University Press, 1985), IV: 158.

14 Douglass, "The American Constitution and the Slave," March 26, 1860, in *Ibid.*, III: 358. The contractualism of Douglass's conception of the Constitution can also be seen in his interpretive approach to the document. Arguing that the "The American constitution is a written instrument, full and complete in itself" and that it is to be interpreted for "intentions expressed in the written instrument itself," Douglass's constitutional hermeneutic parallels the interpretive approach to an integrated contract. *Ibid.*, III: 347; John D. Calamari and Joseph M. Perillo, *The Law of Contracts* (St. Paul, MN: West Publishing, 1977), pp. 99–101. Chesnutt plainly echoes Douglass's notion of rights and duties as contractually correlative, anticipating Wesley Hohfeld's analysis of jural correlatives: "I should say that duties are dependent upon rights, without rights there can be no duties." "Rights and Duties," October 6, 1908, in *Essays and Speeches*, p. 260; Hohfeld, "Some Fundamental Legal Conceptions as Applied in Judicial Reasoning," *Yale Law Journal*, 23 (1916): 16, 30.

15 "WO Liberty," in *The Journals and Miscellaneous Notebooks of Ralph Waldo Emerson*, ed. William H. Gilman *et al.*, 16 vols. (Cambridge, MA: Harvard University Press, 1960–82), XIV: 410.

16 In speeches and essays, Chesnutt expressly pairs Sumner and Douglass as leaders in the effort to reconceive the national charter, and Chesnutt's quotations of the Concord philosopher suggest a kinship between his notions of reform and Emerson's. See, e.g., Chesnutt, *Essays and Speeches*, pp. 25, 102, 45, 88; see also, Storey, *Charles Sumner* (New York: Russell & Russell, 1900), pp. 430–32.

17 Chesnutt, *Douglass*, pp. 1, 44–45, 91, 100. Chesnutt shared his era's Emersonian fascination with "great" men who are capable of shaping history, and Chesnutt considered Douglass to be such a man. Chesnutt, "Self-Made Men," March 10, 1882, in *Essays and Speeches*, pp. 33–39. In the interest of his own self-making, as Richard Brodhead notes, Chesnutt was an inveterate and tireless self-improver, teaching himself Latin, music, history, German, and French. Brodhead, *Cultures of Letters: Scenes of Reading and Writing in Nineteenth-Century America* (Chicago: University of Chicago Press, 1993), p. 182. For Chesnutt's view of a mutable Constitution and the judiciary's retrenchment of the Civil War amendments, see "The Courts and the Negro (1908)," in *Essays and Speeches*, pp. 262–70.

18 Storey, "Emerson and the Civil War," unpublished essay, Concord Free Public Library, pp. 2–3, 29–30.

19 Wai Chee Dimock's *Residues of Justice* offers a provocative comparison between contract doctrine and Kate Chopin's fiction. However, Dimock's literalism and lack of care in moving between law and literature leads to confusion, as when she suggests a correlation between what Morton Horwitz calls the "subjective theory of contracts" and Chopin's emphasis in *The Awakening* on Edna Pontellier's inner feelings and thoughts. In contrast

to Dimock's vague suggestion that the "subjective theory of contract" predominated the nineteenth century, Horwitz describes the theory as a relatively brief stage in the development of contract law. According to Horwitz, "the subjective theory of contract" was replaced in 1855 by an "objective theory of contract" that thereafter dominated American law. Hence, Dimock's implication that *The Awakening* shares an emphasis on "the primacy of the subjective" with contemporaneous American contract law is false even by the account of her sole source on contract doctrine. And Dimock mistakes the phrase "meeting of the minds" as indicating a literal subjectivism in the law of contracts. Whereas Chopin's novel is very much concerned with what Edna "feels like," ever since the 1850s the law of contracts has not primarily been concerned with private feelings but with objective manifestations of mutual assent. The question under this theory of contract formation is not what one has thought or felt but whether one has acted or spoken in a manner so as to induce in a reasonable person the expectation that a deal has been struck. As Oliver Wendell Holmes, Jr., stated a couple of years before the publication of Chopin's novel, "nothing is more certain than that parties may be bound by a contract to things which neither of them intended, and when one does not know of the other's assent." Hence, "the primacy of the subjective in *The Awakening*" was *not* "heralded, amply instantiated," or made "utterly predictable" by the course of nineteenth-century contract law. Dimock, *Residues of Justice: Literature, Law, Philosophy* (Berkeley: University of California Press, 1996), pp. 204–210; Morton Horwitz, *The Transformation of American Law, 1780–1860* (New York: Oxford University Press, 1992), p. 197; Lawrence Friedman, *A History of American Law* (New York: Simon & Schuster, 1985), p. 276; Oliver Wendell Holmes, Jr., "The Path of the Law," *Harvard Law Review*, 10 (1897): 463.

20 Brook Thomas, *American Literary Realism and the Failed Promise of Contract* (Berkeley: University of California Press, 1997), pp. 5, 135, 49.

21 William Hixson's *Moorfield Storey and the Abolitionist Tradition*.

22 One notes, for example, William Andrews's reading of a scene in Chesnutt's novel turning on a distinction between a loyal black retainer of the old school, Mammy Jane, and an example of the new type of Negro who is simply denominated as the "young nurse." Although Andrews observes the basic difference Chesnutt installs between the two characters, he omits the importance of contract to this difference. As we will see, contract is the sign and mechanism of this distinction. William Andrews, *The Literary Career of Charles W. Chesnutt* (Baton Rouge: Louisiana State University Press, 1980), pp. 190–91.

23 For many, law would seem like the last place to look for an alternative to coercion. Under the influence of Michel Foucault's positivism, for instance, one may feel that the notion of a consensual legal mechanism is a contradiction in terms. See, for example, the image of law presented in the famous opening pages of Foucault's *Discipline and Punish: The Birth of the*

Prison (New York: Pantheon, 1977). As Habermas has pointed out, reading Foucault gives one the impression that "the bourgeois constitutional state is a dysfunctional relic from the period of absolutism." Jürgen Habermas, *The Philosophical Discourse of Modernity* (Cambridge, MA: MIT Press, 1987), p. 290. However, despite its reiteration of the totality of power, even Foucault's analysis apparently needs a non-coercive perspective from which to recognize and critique coercive forms of social organization. Foucault locates this perspective in a form of power which is "anti-disciplinarian" and "liberated from the principle of sovereignty." "Two Lectures," in *Power/Knowledge: Selected Interviews and Other Writings, 1972–1977,* ed. Colin Gordon (New York: Pantheon, 1977), p. 108. Despite its rather baroque convolution of his rhetoric of power, Foucault's formulation of "anti-disciplinarian" power puts us back in the presence of the consent/coercion distinction (at least as a matter of practical effect if not of philosophical intent).

24 Following Antonio Gramsci, we may well be suspicious whether what seems to be consent is not the illusion produced by hegemony. Antonio Gramsci, *Selections from the Prison Notebooks of Antonio Gramsci* (New York: International Publishers, 1971), pp. 404, 268.

25 See, Louis Althusser, "Ideology and Ideological State Apparatuses (Notes towards an Investigation)," in *Lenin and Philosophy and Other Essays* (New York: Monthly Review Press, 1971), pp. 156–57, 167–68. Of course, as Terry Eagleton notes, the totality of the individual's enclosure within ideology, described by Althusser, obscures any potential source of political resistance. Eagleton, *Ideology: an Introduction* (New York: Verso, 1991), p. 146. Sacvan Bercovitch, *The Rites of Assent: Transformations in the Symbolic Construction of America* (New York: Routledge, 1993), pp. 45–50.

26 Patricia Williams, *The Alchemy of Race and Rights* (Cambridge, MA: Harvard University Press, 1991), pp. 15, 165; Douglass, "Persecution on Account of Faith, Persecution on Account of Color," January 26, 1851, in *The Douglass Papers,* II: 309, 318–19.

27 Carla Kaplan, "Narrative Contracts and Emancipatory Readers: *Incidents in the Life of a Slave Girl,*" *The Yale Journal of Criticism,* 6 (1993): 93, 115, 117. Kaplan's analysis expressly derives from Carole Pateman's account of how "contract always generates political right in the form of relations of domination and subordination." This claim seems plainly hyperbolic. As Charles Mills points out in *The Racial Contract,* putting contract to positive use requires that the dominations hidden by ostensible contracts be ferreted out, but there is nothing about contract as a mechanism of consensual relations that is inherently coercive. Thus, Mills criticizes the historical "racial contract" founded on domination not by deeming contractarian ideals inherently problematic but by demonstrating, as Douglass and Chesnutt had before him, how the contractual ideal has been betrayed by white contractarians. Pateman, *The Sexual Contract* (Stanford, CA: Stanford University Press, 1988), p. 8; Mills, *The Racial Contract* (Ithaca, NY: Cornell University Press, 1997), pp. 136–37, 129.

28 Gerrit Smith responds to Douglass's charge that to vote and acknowledge the Constitution as law is to abide sin: "A man takes my harrow, and instead of loosening up my ground, roots up my growing corn, should I destroy the harrow? No. So with the Government. You may have the wisest and purest Constitution, and have it perverted." *The Douglass Papers*, II: 231.

29 Kaplan, "Narrative Contracts and Emancipatory Readers," p. 96. Consider, for example, a hypothetical partnership contract between two female carpenters – one white, one black, and both living in the same neighborhood in Berkeley, California. Their average annual income is roughly equivalent, and each has ample employment opportunities. Imagine further that they enter what each deems to be a mutually beneficial contract to share 50/50 all risks, costs, labor, and profits in building a residence in nearby Oakland. The building is built, and each is happy with the result, as is their customer. Where is the domination? In our hypothetical case, there is not even the collateral domination created by partnerships between those in power at the expense of economic opportunities for women or people of color. Any mutually beneficial contract between equals illustrates that there is nothing in the contractual process necessarily tending to create or foster domination. To a skeptic doubting the real-world applicability of this hypothetical case, I would simply ask whether he/she has never paid for a book or a meal worth the payment, obtained medical care worth the cost, or entered into an agreement with a friend or romantic partner that each felt was just.

This hypothetical contract illuminates, by contrast, that the evil we object to in such contracts as the harsh tenement leases described in Jacob Riis's *How the Other Half Lives* (1890) is not created by the contract itself but by the inequalities of power between the parties to the contract. Indeed, the more one party uses its superior bargaining power to force unappealing and harsh terms on the weaker party, the less like a contract the deal becomes because the defining element of consent is increasingly absent. The law of contract expresses this distinction in the unconscionability section of the Uniform Commercial Code (§2–302) and the reluctance of courts to enforce, without qualification or modification, the terms of adhesion contracts, which the average consumer has no ability to negotiate (e.g., insurance contracts).

To avoid confusion, I should say that the mutuality of benefit in my hypothetical contract merely illustrates that oppression is not the necessary and inevitable concomitant of contract. I do not agree with Michael Sandel that justice requires that a contract achieve mutuality of benefit in addition to mutuality of consent. Sandel, *Liberalism and the Limits of Justice* (Cambridge: Cambridge University Press, 1982), pp. 106–08. Mutuality of benefit is, at best, an evidentiary test of the genuineness of the consent of the parties. Though deals with serious disparities in results often betoken a coercive relation between the parties that the contract would disguise, it seems to me one can and does make contracts that prove neither beneficial nor unjust (e.g., an agreement to pay for a service one receives but, as it turns out, one does not need). The lack of any tangible benefit received does not, by itself, make paying for the service one voluntarily engaged unjust. Hence, the justice of any agreement derives from its voluntary nature alone, not from a mutuality of benefit.

30 To condemn consensual devices, such as contract or democratic government, as inherently unjust implies some alternative vision of justice (how else could one discern the injustice one decries?). Accordingly, the absence of a clearly stated alternative to consent as a mode of just human relations would seem to evidence the hyperbolic and hollow nature of the condemnation. Absent an espousal of some form of determinism rendering consent and moral agency illusory, claims that democracy *is* racism, contract *is* domination, consent *is* coercion amount to gross overstatements of the more prosaic (and supportable) observation that in practice democracy, contract, and consent have often been corrupted by their opposites.

31 As Amy Dru Stanley points out, Francis Harper and Harriet Jacobs explicitly drew on contract, as did labor activists and other reformers, to condemn racial and gender oppression. Contrary to Kaplan's reading, Jacobs, as Stanley notes, idealized "relations of voluntary exchange." *Bondage to Contract*, pp. 30–35, 31.

32 Alan Trachtenberg, *The Incorporation of America: Culture and Society in the Gilded Age* (New York: Hill and Wang, 1982); Morton Horwitz, *The Transformation of American Law: 1870–1960* (New York: Oxford University Press, 1992), pp. 65–66; Joel Williamson, *The Crucible of Race: Black–White Relations in the American South since Emancipation* (New York: Oxford University Press, 1984), pp. 109–39; C. Vann Woodward, *The Strange Career of Jim Crow* (New York: Oxford University Press, 1974), pp. 67–109; James Herget, *American Jurisprudence: 1870–1970* (Houston, TX: Rice University Press, 1990), pp. 25–30.

33 Gerard Henderson, *The Position of Foreign Corporations in American Constitutional Law* (Cambridge, MA: Harvard University Press, 1918), pp. 165–66, 174, 242.

34 *United States v. E.C. Knight Co.*, 156 U.S. 1 (1895); *Pollock v. Farmer's Loan and Trust Co.*, 157 U.S. 429, 158 U.S. 601 (1895). While the Court could see no interstate commerce in the Sugar Trust, it was quick to find that the nation's interest in the free flow of interstate commerce justified President Cleveland's action in using military force to end the Pullman strike of 1894, in *In Re Debs*, 158 U.S. 564 (1895). Coming only one week after the Income Tax Cases, *Debs* was seen as further evidence of the Court's prejudice in favor of capital and against labor and the laboring classes. Opposition to the Income Tax Cases resulted in the adoption of the Sixteenth Amendment in 1913. Charles Warren, *The Supreme Court in United States History*, 3 vols. (Boston: Little, Brown & Company, 1922), III: 424, 422.

35 *Adair v. United States*, 208 U.S. 161, 175 (1908); *Hammer v. Dagenhart*, 247 U.S. 375 (1918).

36 Roscoe Pound, "Liberty of Contract," Yale Law Journal, 18 (1909): 454, 479–82.

37 Sylvester Pennoyer, "The Income Tax Decision and the Power of the Supreme Court to Nullify Acts of Congress," *American Law Review*, 29 (1895): 550, 558. Assuming that the Court's apparent conservatism was warranted by the Constitution, one editorial writer argued that "the Constitution was made for a period when there were no railroads, no giant monopolies, no billionaires," suggesting that the Constitution did not anticipate the peculiar economic circumstances of late nineteenth-century America and was gravely flawed as a result (*Public Opinion*, 18 [May 2, 1895]).

38 Gustavus Myers, *History of the Supreme Court of the United States* (Chicago: Charles H. Herr & Co., 1918), p. 8.

39 Charles A. Beard, *An Economic Interpretation of the Constitution of the United States* (New York: The Macmillan Company, 1956), pp. 7–8.

40 Pound, "Liberty of Contract," pp. 454, 457.

41 David Graham Phillips, *The Fashionable Adventures of Joshua Craig* (New York: Grosset & Dunlap, 1909); I.K. Friedman, *The Radical* (New York: Appleton, 1907); Henry O. Morris, *Waiting for the Signal* (Chicago: Schulte Publishing Co., 1897); Frederick Upham Adams, *President John Smith: The Story of a Peaceful Revolution* (Chicago: Charles H. Kerr & Company, 1897); Robert Herrick, *A Life for a Life* (New York: The Macmillan Company, 1910).

42 *The Radical*'s hero, Bruce McAllister, represents the common people, "those who did the work of the world and stood by with hungry eyes while the mighty reaped the profits therefrom." The novel's plot traces McAllister's ill-fated dream of authoring a law restricting child labor. In Congress, McAllister eventually vanquishes the hydra-headed force of capital and commerce personified by Sir Anthony Wycoff (Friedman's version of John D. Rockefeller), who opposes McAllister's bill. But McAllister obtains passage of his anti-child labor bill only to have it nullified by Supreme Court Justices who were inevitably "swayed by the prejudgments and the class consciousness of those to whom they owe birth, education and power." Friedman, *The Radical*, pp. 14, 337.

The legal narrative of Friedman's novel anticipates the course of actual events in the cases of *Hammer v. Dagenhart*, 247 U.S. 375 (1918) and *Baily v. Drexel Furniture Company*, 259 U.S. 20 (1922). In *Hammer*, the Court struck down a statute prohibiting the interstate transportation of goods produced by child labor, and, in *Baily*, the Court invalidated Congress's subsequent attempt at regulating child labor by imposing a tax on goods produced by child labor. In both instances, the Court ruled that the national government was arrogating to itself powers reserved to the states. One notes, however, that the Court generally sustained the child labor regulations enacted by state legislatures. See e.g., *Sturges & Burns Manufacturing Co. v. Beauchamp*, 231 U.S. 325 (1913).

43 Phillips, *Joshua Craig*, p. 21.

44 Herrick, *A Life*, pp. 220–21.

45 Adams, *President John Smith*, pp. 289, 9, 8.

46 *Ibid.*, pp. 114, 42.

47 Friedman, *The Radical*, pp. 336.

48 Hixson notes, as others have, that "the final abandonment of the Negro by his Northern supporters and the appearance of systematic racial proscription in the South did not occur in the supposedly callous and corrupt 1880s; rather, they accompanied the rising tide of reform in the 1890s, and they reached their highest point at the zenith of progressivism during the administration of Woodrow Wilson." Hixson, *Moorfield Storey*, p. 98.

49 In selling the common law model, the legal profession was motivated to some extent by self-interest. If the law is simply the language of political power, the special, autonomous aura of law vanishes and with it the legal profession's claim to be its exclusive interlocutor and expositor. Horwitz, *The Transformation of American Law: 1780–1860*, p. 257 While *Pollock* – the Federal Income Tax Case – was before the Supreme Court, Judge John F. Dillon, an influential jurist, ardently defended private property in a speech before the New York State Bar Association. Dillon accepted "reasonable" taxes imposed, "as a means of raising revenue, but when taxes are imposed as a means of distributing the rich man's property among the rest of the community – this is class legislation of the most pronounced and vicious type; is, in [a] word, confiscation and not taxation. Such schemes of pillage [are] violative of the constitutional rights of the property owner, subversive of the existing social polity, and essentially revolutionary." Dillon, "Property – Its Rights and Duties in Our Legal and Social Systems," *American Law Review*, 29 (1895): 161, 172–73.

50 James Coolidge Carter, *Law: Its Origin, Growth and Function* (New York: G.P. Putnam's Sons, 1907), p. 127.

51 *Ibid.*, p. 138–39, 214–71; Chesnutt, *The House Behind the Cedars* (Boston: Houghton Mifflin & Co., 1900), pp. 34–35.

52 *Plessy v. Ferguson*, 163 U.S. 537, 550–51, 544 (1896).

53 Richard Hofstader, *Social Darwinism in American Thought* (New York: Beacon Press, 1955), p. 60; Sumner, "The Absurd Effort to Make the World Over," in *Essays of William Graham Sumner* ed. Albert Galloway Keller and Maurice R. Davie, 2 vols. (New Haven: Yale University Press, 1934), I: 105, 106. Andrew Carnegie and John D. Rockefeller both celebrated the social Darwinist universe of force. Carnegie blithely asserted that: "while the law [survival of the fittest] may sometimes be hard for the individual, it is best for the race, because it insures the survival of the fittest in every department. We accept and welcome, therefore . . . great inequality of environment." Quoted in *The Columbia Literary History of the United States*, ed. Emory Elliot (New York: Columbia University Press, 1990), p. 528. And in a Sunday School address, Rockefeller divined the hand of God behind unregulated competition:

The growth of a large business is merely a survival of the fittest . . . The American Beauty rose can be produced in the splendor and fragrance which bring cheer to its beholder only by sacrificing the early buds which grow up around it. This is not an evil tendency in business. It is merely the working-out of a law of nature and a law of God. (Quoted in Hofstadter, *Social Darwinism*, p. 45.)

54 Hofstader, *Social Darwinism*, p. 60. Responding to a similar argument made by Justice Lemuel Shaw in *Roberts v. City of Boston*, 59 Mass. 198 (1849), Thoreau stated that "the law will never make men free. [I]t is men who have got to make the law free." Thoreau's injunction mandates both a challenge to the law and to the custom that the law expresses. "Slavery in Massachusetts," in *Miscellanies* (Boston: Houghton Mifflin & Co., 1893), p. 181. Sumner, *Folkways: A Study of the Sociological Importance of Usages, Manners, Customs, Mores, and Morals* (Boston: Ginn, 1906); *Plessy*, 163 U.S., p. 551.

55 In a journal entry, Chesnutt foresaw that literature would "pen the way" for black Americans' "social recognition and equality" by "accustom[ing] the public mind to the idea; and while amusing them to lead them imperceptibly unconsciously step by step to the desired state of feelings." As quoted in Williamson, *Crucible of Race*, p. 65.

56 Sundquist, *To Wake the Nations*, pp. 410–15; Williamson, *Crucible of Race*, pp. 197–201.

57 Williamson, *Crucible of Race*, pp. 183–220, 225–47.

58 As William Andrews points out, many of the novel's major figures are based on actual participants in the Wilmington Race Riot of 1898. Major Carteret appears to be patterned on Josephus Daniels, editor of the Raleigh *News and Observer*, conducting an anti-Negro press campaign during the election year of 1898, and General Belmont would seem to be based on one Alfred Moore Wadell, the leader of the racist *coup*. Andrews, *Charles Chesnutt*, p. 180.

59 Chesnutt, *The Marrow of Tradition* (Ann Arbor: University of Michigan Press, 1969), pp. 33–34. In contrast to the seigneurial society envisioned by men like Carteret and George Fitzhugh, racists like McBane advocated a political system that would be democratic and egalitarian for whites but tyrannical for subordinate classes. George M. Fredrickson, *The Black Image in the White Mind: The Debate on Afro-American Character and Destiny, 1817–1914* (Hanover, NH: Wesleyan University Press, 1987), p. 61.

60 Chesnutt, *Marrow*, pp. 81, 34, 82.

61 We should note in passing that Chesnutt's use of liberty of contract as a basis for political and social association also stands as an alternative to the nationalism of Sutton Griggs's *Imperium in Imperio* (1889, reprinted Miami: Mnemosyne Reprinting, 1969). Griggs's novel, a descendant of Martin Delany's *Blake* (1859), subscribes to the notion that the possession of majority political power is central to the protection of one's fundamental rights. Hence, the necessity of a black republic, which Griggs imagines being carved out of the U.S. in Texas. See Wilson Moses, *The Golden Age of Black Nationalism* (New York: Oxford University Press, 1978), pp. 170–93.

62 Thomas, *American Literary Realism and the Failed Promise of Contract*, pp. 161–62.

63 Chesnutt's fiction is replete with suggestions of the shift from status to contract. For instance, the first short story in *The Conjure Woman*, "The

Goophered Grapevine," begins and ends in the establishment of a new contractual relation between John, the Ohio businessman transplanted to North Carolina, and Uncle Julius, the narrator of the dialect tales. Chesnutt, *Collected Stories of Charles W. Chesnutt* (New York: Mentor, 1992), pp. 1–13.

64 Sumner, *What the Social Classes*, p. 16.

65 Chesnutt, *Marrow*, p. 42.

66 Horace Kallen, "Democracy Versus the Melting Pot," *Nation*, 100 (February 18–25, 1915): 190–94, 217–20.

67 Sumner, *What the Social Classes*, pp. 15–16.

68 Chesnutt, *Marrow*, pp. 306–07. An analogous inconsistency was oft noted by opponents to slavery and later Jim Crow that if the black race were truly inferior there would be no need for laws to keep them down. See, e.g., Storey, *Abraham Lincoln*, p. 16.

69 Griggs, *Imperium in Imperio*, p. 62.

70 Chesnutt, *Marrow*, pp. 26, 206–09, 222–25.

71 *Ibid.*, p. 329 (emphasis added).

72 *Ibid.*, p. 85 (emphasis added).

73 The only version of Manly's editorial I have been able to locate is a verbatim republication of the editorial in *The Wilimington Messenger*, October 20, 1898, p. 3.

74 Woodward, *Strange Career*, pp. 73, 93–94; Williamson, *Crucible of Race*, pp. 116–19.

75 *The Wilimington Messenger*, October 20, 1898, p. 3; Sundquist, *To Wake the Nations*, pp. 410–14; Williamson, *Crucible of Race*, pp. 197–201.

76 Walter Benn Michaels, "Local Colors," *MLN*, 113 (1998): 755–56. One may also observe the presence of property as well as contract in Chesnutt's manipulation of the Manly editorial. In a manner similar to Albion Tourgee's argument in *Plessy* that separate but equal discrimination deprived Homer Plessy, an octaroon, of a property interest in his reputation as a white man, Chesnutt's use of liberty of contract cannily invests interracial relations with the value of property that is destroyed by anti-miscegenation laws.

77 Walter Benn Michaels, *Our America: Nativism, Modernism, and Pluralism* (Durham, NC: Duke University Press, 1995), pp. 1–2, 139–140.

78 Chesnutt, *Paul Marchand, F.M.C.* (Princeton: Princeton University Press, 1999), p. 132.

79 Chesnutt viewed *Plessy* "as epoch making as the Dred Scott decision." "The Courts and the Negro," in *Essays and Speeches*, p. 267.

80 *Plessy*, 163 U.S. 537, 551. As Morton Horwitz points out, in the nineteenth century legal formalism (what Horwitz calls classical legal thought) was deemed to be inherently neutral and impartial because it did not take into account the particular circumstances facing litigants (as though taking into account the factual particularities of a case would inevitably result in a biased judicial outcome). It was assumed that evenhandedness would be assured in such a system by the abstract nature of judicial reasoning that

was not swayed by any personal reaction to the potentially inflammatory details of the case. Horwitz, *The Transformation of American Law: 1870–1960*, pp. 19–20.

81 Lydia Maria Child, *A Romance of the Republic* (Lexington: University of Kentucky Press, 1997), p. 387; Gertrude Dorsey Brown, "A Case of Measure for Measure," *The Colored American Magazine*, 10 (1906): 253–58, 301–04, 11 (1906): 25–28, 97–100, 167–72, 281–84; Chesnutt, "Mars Jeems's Nightmare," *Collected Stories*, pp. 25–39.

82 Chesnutt, *Marrow*, pp. 56, 57–58.

83 *Plessy*, 163 U.S. 537, 551, 544.

84 Chesnutt, *Marrow*, pp. 49, 72, 54. Chesnutt's Dr. Burns hails from Philadelphia. A 1909 article on the topic of Jim Crow laws used a Philadelphia case to illustrate the typical justification for such laws. In *W. Ches. and Phila. Ry. Co. v. Mills*, 55 Pa. S. 209 (1867), the Court declared that Jim Crow laws simply follow the "law of the races, established by the Creator himself, not to compel them to intermix contrary to their instincts." As quoted in Gilbert Thomas Stephenson, "The Separation of the Races in Public Conveyances," *The American Political Science Review*, 3 (1909): 180, 203–04. Charles Lofgren, in *The Plessy Case*, and Leon Litwack, in *North of Slavery*, describe the national prevalence of legal segregation in the nineteenth century. See Lofgren, *The Plessy Case: A Legal–Historical Interpretation* (New York: Oxford University Press, 1987), pp. 7–27; Litwack, *North of Slavery: The Negro in the Free States, 1790–1860* (Chicago: University of Chicago Press, 1961), pp. 113–52.

85 Alexander Hamilton, James Madison, and John Jay, *The Federalist Papers* (New York: New American Library, 1961), p. 77.

86 Francis Lieber, *On Civil Liberty and Self-Government* (Philadelphia: J.B. Lippincott, 1901), p. 31. More recently, Stuart Hampshire has sounded a similar theme. For Hampshire, the value of a democratic constitution lies not in its expression of the popular will, but rather "in the defense of minorities, not of majorities. One needs to ensure, for the sake of justice, that the minorities are properly heard, and that they play their necessary part in the process," which properly includes a right of veto over certain kinds of governmental or private intrusion. Hampshire, *Justice is Conflict* (Princeton: Princeton University Press, 2000), p. 47.

87 Storey challenged the blithe acceptance of majoritarianism with the example of such discrete minorities as Jews and blacks: "Can their rights safely be left to be dealt with as pleases a majority of their fellow-citizens in many states? To ask the question is to answer it." Storey, "The Recall of Decisions," *The Annals of the American Academy of Political and Social Science*, (Philadelphia, March 1914): 21

88 H.N. Hirsch, *A Theory of Liberty: The Constitution and Minorities* (New York: Routledge, 1992), p. 5.

89 The importance of basic norms of proper deportment for black nationalists, such as Sutton Griggs, suggests a general acceptance among late nineteenth-century African Americans that conventions of social

interaction are an indispensable part of creating any polity, whether separatist or integrationist. See, Moses, *Black Nationalism*, pp. 178–81.

90 Carter, *Law*, p. 65.

91 Hazel V. Carby, "Introduction" to Frances E. W. Harper, *Iola Leroy, or Shadows Uplifted* (Boston: Beacon Press, 1987), pp. xii–xiii; see also, Claudia Tate, *Domestic Allegories of Political Desire: The Black Heroine's Text at the Turn of the Century* (New York: Oxford University Press, 1992), pp. 78–83.

92 Henry Louis Gates, *The Signifying Monkey: A Theory of African-American Literary Criticism* (New York: Oxford University Press, 1988), p. 117.

93 Brodhead, *Cultures*, pp. 189, 194–95.

94 Tate, *Domestic Allegories*, p. 120.

95 John H. Van Evrie, *Negroes and Negro "Slavery": The First an Inferior Race: The Latter Its Natural Condition* (Baltimore: J.D. Toy, 1853), p. 30, as quoted in George M. Fredrickson, *The Black Image in the White Mind: The Debate on Afro-American Character and Destiny, 1817–1914* (Hanover, NH: Wesleyan University Press, 1987), p. 63. Because she sees her narrative as a part of the cultural litigation wherein the propriety of slavery is going to be decided by the ultimate tribunal of public opinion, Jacobs characterizes her critique of the moral corruption of the slave system as testimony: "I can testify, from my own experience and observation, that slavery is a curse to the whites as well as the blacks." Harriet Jacobs, *Incidents in the Life of a Slave Girl*, in *The Classic Slave Narratives*, ed. Henry Louis Gates, Jr. (New York: New American Library, 1987), p. 383.

96 Jacobs, *Incidents*, p. 384, 386. As Amy Dru Stanley notes, Jacobs "defended her desperate resort to illicit sexual relations" with Sands "as a matter of free contract." *Bondage to Contract*, p. 31.

97 Hazel v. Carby, *Reconstructing Womanhood: The Emergence of the Afro-American Woman Novelist* (New York: Oxford University Press, 1987), p. 58.

98 Karen Halttunen has convincingly described the desire of mid nineteenth-century Americans to find ways to derive an individual's inner character from her manner and appearance. Faced with the rootlessness and increasing mobility of a rapidly changing society that made Americans strangers to each other, many found a means to interpret the outward appearances of individuals as revelatory of inner character in the typology of conduct prescribed by their sentimental value system. Halttunen, *Confidence Men and Painted Women: A Study of Middle-Class Culture in America, 1830–1870* (New Haven: Yale University Press, 1982), pp. 34–55.

99 Jacobs, *Incidents*, p. 497.

100 Harper, *Iola Leroy*, p. 114.

101 Kwame Anthony Appiah, *My Father's House: Africa in the Philosophy of Culture* (New York: Oxford University Press, 1992), pp. 13, 52–53.

102 Harper, *Iola Leroy*, pp. 199, 84, 218.

103 Chesnutt, *Marrow*, p. 60. Chesnutt apparently drew upon his own experience and ambivalent racial feelings in describing Dr. Miller's experience in the Jim Crow car. Recounting a train trip to Washington, D.C., in

his journal, Chesnutt describes a revealing interruption to an enjoyable conversation with a white "gentleman":

> It was pleasant enough till we took on about fifty darkies who were going to Norfolk to work on a truck farm. They filled the seats and standing room, and sat in each others' laps for want of seats. As the day was warm and the people rather dirty, the odor may be better imagined than described. Although it was nothing to me, I could sympathize with my fellow traveller, who stuck his head out of the window, and swore he would never be caught in such a scrape again.

Although he also appreciates the energy and song of the "merry crowd," this description reflects the genteel tastes and conceptions of proper decorum of a man who was, as Eric Sundquist has put it, resolutely middle class. Williamson, *Crucible of Race*, pp. 62–63; Sundquist, *To Wake the Nations*, p. 298.

104 Chesnutt, *Marrow*, pp. 60–61.
105 Chesnutt, "Etiquette (Good Manners)," in *Essays and Speeches*, p. 1; Chesnutt, "Rights and Duties," in *Essays and Speeches*, p. 260.
106 Michaels, *Our America*, p. 54.
107 W.E.B. DuBois, "The Conservation of Races," in *The American Negro Academy, Occasional Papers* (Washington, D.C.: The American Negro Academy, 1897), p. 9, 10. See, Samuel Fleischacker, *The Ethics of Culture* (Ithaca, NY: Cornell University Press, 1994), pp. 115–25, 209–16.
108 Stuart Hampshire argues that universal justice is found in the procedural norms of conflict resolution, not in substantive values which can and do vary among individuals and groups. One problem with Hampshire's separation of procedural and substantive justice is that the concern for fair play in procedure is substantive. A "well-recognized need for procedures of conflict resolution, which can replace brute force and domination and tyranny" represents a substantive consensus about justice. Hampshire's conception of fair procedure is based on an ethical commitment not to resolve conflicts by brute force but by consent. Procedure and the rule of law are not separate from that substantive commitment but the most dependably universal expression of it. It is particularly odd that Hampshire avers that "There is no end to conflict within and around the civil order" except when it comes to norms of procedural fairness without acknowledging the reciprocal influence such procedural agreement may have on the substantive values of the adversaries. Our agreement to agree may, it would seem at least possible if not probable in all cases, lead us closer to consensus about other substantive values, often without even realizing it. Hampshire, *Justice is Conflict*, pp. xi, 5, 39.
109 DuBois, "The Conservation of Races," pp. 11–12.
110 Storey, "The Recall of Decisions," in *The Annals of the American Academy of Political and Social Science*, (Philadelphia, March 1914): 21; Hixson, *Moorfield Storey*, pp. 101, 117–22; Storey, *Abraham Lincoln*, p. 16. Of course, Storey was not alone in this comparison. Charles Sumner, Oswald Garrison Villard, and

others made it as well. See, e.g., Sumner, *Works*, II: 342; Villard, *Segregation in Baltimore and Washington* (New York: NAACP, 1913), pp. 1–4, 12, 14–15.

111 DuBois, "The Conservation of Races," p. 13.

112 *Buchanan V. Warley*, 245 U.S. 60 (1917).

113 Hixson, *Moorfield Storey*, p. 134; See also Foreword by Arthur Spingarn to the NAACP's publication of the Court's unanimous opinion, *The Decision of the U.S. Supreme Court in the Louisville Segregation Case* (New York: NAACP, 1926).

114 Lydia Maria Child was one of those who most valued Sumner because she saw him as above the claims of mere party politics. She was proud that her Senator was "the politician who has *never* compromised a principle, either for fear or favor." David Donald, *Charles Sumner and the Rights of Man* (New York: Knopf, 1970), p. 67.

115 Letter from James Weldon Johnson to Storey dated November 2, 1921 and letter from Mary White Ovington to Storey dated October 24, 1921 in Library of Congress, Manuscript Division, Storey Collection.

116 Hixson, *Moorfield Storey*, pp. 32, 35.

117 Storey, *Charles Sumner*, p. 432.

118 For his *Roberts* argument, see Sumner, *Works*, II: 327–76. See also, Leonard W. Levy and Harlan B. Phillips: "The *Roberts* Case: Source of the 'Separate but Equal Doctrine," *American Historical Review*, 56 (1956): 510–18.

119 *Negro Suffrage is not a Failure: An Address before the New England Suffrage Conference March 30, 1903* (Boston: Geo. H. Ellis, 1903), p. 3.

120 Hixson, *Moorfield Storey*, p. 43.

121 Storey, *Politics as a Duty and as a Career* (New York: G.P. Putnam's Sons, 1889), p. 3.

122 Storey, *Abraham Lincoln*, pp. 6, 12, 17, 16, 19.

123 Hannah Arendt, "Reflections on Little Rock," *Dissent*, 6 (1956): 45–56.

124 *Buchanan vs. Warley*, 245 U.S. 60, 82, 72–73, 81.

125 *Berea College v. Kentucky*, 211 U.S. 45 (1908).

126 *Landmark Briefs and Arguments of the Supreme Court of the United States: Constitutional Law*, 18, eds. Philip B. Kurland, Gerhard Casper (Arlington, VA: University Publications of America, Inc., 1975), pp. 31–32.

127 Illustrating how the other side, like Chesnutt and Storey, gets the import of the liberty of contract argument – the logical thrust of a natural rights argument accenting the right of free contractual association would plainly extend to marriage – Storey's opponents state that:

> In a large majority of States in the Union *intermarriage* between the whites and negroes is not only forbidden, but in most of these States is made an infamous crime. Certainly the right to choose a mate is as fundamental as the right to choose a home; and yet the State steps in and annuls a contract of association of this sort, although both parties thereto are entirely willing to enter upon the relation, and apparently no one is concerned but the parties themselves; yet for the good of society it is recognized as a valid exercise of the police power to prohibit such relations. (*Ibid.*, XVIII: 130)

128 *Ibid.*, XVIII: 36, 563. The defense cites and quotes DuBois as support for their argument that the NAACP's challenge of the Louisville ordinance threatens integrity of the races:

> The following quotation from an editorial in *The Survey* (New York) of March 28, 1914, has a special significance in this connection, particularly when it is remembered that Dr. du Bois is the Director of Publicity and Research for the [NAACP]: "On December 27th, *The Survey* published a symposium of New Year's resolutions...We asked W. E. Burghardt du Bois to contribute to this symposium...Dr. du Bois replied with a program of Work for Black Folk in 1914 – a stirring presentment of political, economic and social reforms put forward in the name of justice and fair dealing to his people. Paragraph 6 of his contribution reads as follows: 'Sixth. – Finally, in 1914 the Negro must demand his social rights: his right to be treated as a gentleman when he acts like one, *to marry any sane grown person who wants to marry him*, and to meet and eat with his friends without being accused of undue assumption or unworthy ambition.' Dr. du Bois closed with this paragraph: 'This is the black man's program for 1914, and the more difficult it looks the more need for following it courageously and unswervingly. It is not a radical program – it is conservative and reasonable.'" (*Ibid.*, XVIII: 564–65.)

129 *Ibid.*, XVIII: 14–15, 21–22, 19, 27–28, 37.
130 *Ibid.*, XVIII: 102–05, 138–39. Support for Jim Crow law came in part from such sociologists as Franklin Henry Giddings, whose emphasis on "consciousness in kind" began to appear in his published work in 1896. Woodward, *Strange Career*, p. 103.
131 *Plessy*, 163 U.S. 537, 553–54; Chesnutt, *Essays and Speeches*, p. 312.
132 *Landmark Briefs*, XVIII: 127–28, 145.

Index

293